UNDERSTANDING MUSIC

UNDERSTANDING MUSIC

James Glennon

M

Knowledge of a thing engenders love of it;

the more exact the knowledge, the more

fervent the love

Leonardo da Vinci

© James Glennon
This paperback edition published 1980.
First published 1980 by Macmillan London Ltd
4 Little Essex Street, London WC2R 3LF
and Basingstoke, Associated companies in Delhi, Dublin,
Hong Kong, Johannesburg, Lagos, Melbourne, New
York, Singapore and Tokyo.

ISBN 0 333 270487

Printed in Hong Kong

CONTENTS

ILLUSTRATIONS

THE PURPOSE OF MUSIC

1

IF we were asked to explain the purpose of music, our immediate reply might be "to give pleasure." That would not be far from the truth, but there are other considerations. We would need to define such terms as pleasure, enjoyment, tolerance, understanding, for all these are bound up in our search for the true meaning of music.

We might also define music as "expression in sound," or "the expression of thought and feeling in an aesthetic form," and still not arrive at an understanding of its true purpose. We do know, however, even if we are not fully conscious of it, that music is a part of living, that it has the power to awaken in us sensations and emotions of a spiritual kind.

This leads us to the question—how necessary is music? Can we get along without it? The answer is, yes, we *can* get along without it. We can lead healthy, pleasant lives in a physical sense, have comfortable homes, and lack nothing in worldly comfort without ever consciously listening to a note of music. But what a pity to ignore this source of infinite enjoyment!

When the word "music" is used in the following pages it will refer to *serious* music (too often grouped under the misleading term "classical") as distinct from the lighter kinds, such as dance music, musical comedy, popular tunes of the day, all of which have their place.

Then, what can music do for us? It can do many things, and have many desirable results. It can stimulate or soothe the mind, help towards a wider education, or, at least, a wider mental perspective. It can gently plough the mind so that it will be more receptive to the seeds of learning; it can find a response in disciplined physical action. Music can comfort the lonely and the sick, awake pleasant memories in the old, delight the young, and lull a child to sleep.

Throughout the ages poets and philosophers have attempted definitions of music, usually with more imagery than accuracy, Perhaps one of its most fascinating attributes is that it eludes precise definition.

The German reformer, Martin Luther, who was an accomplished musician, placed great value on music and emphasised its importance in education and living. "Music drives away the devil and makes people happy," he wrote. "It induces one to forget all wrath, unchastity, arrogance and other vices. After theology, I accord music the highest place and the greatest honour."

We can go back much farther and find numerous references to the significance of music. Ancient mythology frequently mentions its charm and power, as symbolised by Orpheus. The Bible tells us that Saul's sadness was dispelled by David's playing on the harp; that Elisha experienced a state of ecstasy at the sound of a minstrel's playing.

In ancient Greece much importance was placed on the curative properties of music, also its effect on human behaviour. Plato, in his *Republic*, stresses the value of music in the building of character:

> The beginning is of the greatest importance, especially when we have to do with a young and tender creature. What the child hears when it is young generally becomes fixed fast and indelibly in his mind.

It must of course be remembered that, as much poetry was sung or accompanied, the word "music" meant literature as well as music in our sense of the word. There is, however, sufficient proof in Plato's writings that he regarded true melody as inducive to right thinking, even though in his time music was purely monodic, a simple but subtle art, in which melody was unsupported by harmonic devices.

Aristotle agreed with Plato's theory that each musical mode had its own particular effect upon people's behaviour. Plutarch declared that:

> Musical education in one's youth forms and regulates inclinations to applaud and embrace the noble and the generous; to observe decorum, temperance, and regularity.

Pythagoras firmly believed in music's power to relieve depression.

Galen, the Greek physician (c. 130-c. 200 B.C.) prescribed music as a cure for snakebite. Just how effective this treatment was is not quite clear. Galen's theory

The Guitarist, by Manet. Spain is the home of guitar music, and as a folk art it is very old. It has two distinct types: flamenco, which is largely improvisation, and classical guitar as played by such masters as Andre Segovia, John Williams, and Julian Bream.

had something in common with the fiction associated with the tarantella, an Italian fast dance in 6/8 time.

During the fifteenth, sixteenth, and seventeenth centuries a disease known as *tarantism* prevailed in southern Italy. The inhabitants of Taranto, in the old province of Apulia, believed that by dancing the tarantella at an increasing speed until they dropped through sheer exhaustion, they would rid the body of the poisonous effect of a bite from a tarantula. Although there was no medical evidence to suggest that the kind of spider found in that part of Italy was dangerously poisonous, the superstition persisted for a long time.

The myths and legends of all countries contain numerous references to the influence of music; not only are these a part of poetic imagery, they confirm early man's belief in its effect on living organisms. Much of this may be fantastic and incredible, but it does prove the awareness and cognition of music's power. Several Greek myths refer to the power of the flute, that it was capable of stirring armies into decisive action, also to the harp's ability to subdue anger. The examples are many.

There is a point in history where myth merges into fact; as far back as the beginning of the Christian era we read of physicians prescribing music as a therapeutic aid. With tribes in regions as far apart as Africa, North America, and Australia, musicians, primitive though they might have been, were expected to accompany the doctor on his visits to the sick.

Much of the importance placed on this aspect of music by primitive people was no doubt based on superstition, but we cannot discard the fact that it played a big part in their thinking, and in attempted cures of the physically and mentally sick. In more recent times physicians have been aware of the influence of music on the cerebral centres, through the nervous system to other portions of the body. Today many psychiatric hospitals include on their staffs music therapists who hold positive proof of the efficacy of music. Some years ago Sidney Licht, a Fellow of the New York Academy of Medicine, who contributed a great deal to the results of research into music therapy, wrote:

> I am convinced that listeners are physiologically and psychically affected by such musical characteristics as mood, intensity, pitch, and rhythmical outline. It seems to me that the right music should provoke remembrance and association of thoughts and associations more easily in a mental patient than methods using factual persuasion.

Merely playing records, or the piano, to patients in a hospital cannot rightly be called music therapy; it is providing entertainment, which is a good thing so far as it goes. Music therapy is a great deal more; it depends on an exact knowledge of the musical elements—rhythm, melody, harmony, tone-colour, dynamics—and their effect on patients of all kinds. For the music therapist to prescribe the wrong

4

Performance of the opera *Il Pomo d'Oro*, at the Court Theatre, Vienna, in the eighteenth century. This engraving by Lodovico Burnacini shows the pomp and ceremony of court life at that time.

music where delicately balanced emotions are involved could be as dangerous as the prescribing of a wrong medicine.

In the Renaissance era music was often interwoven with science, philosophy and literature. As far back as history goes music was used in some form or other to promote a devotional response in religious ritual. At the other end of the scale, film-producers have long since realised the emotional effect of background music, and experts have been engaged to compose sounds, from the sentimental and humorous to the dramatic and the grotesque to induce the desired reaction from the audience.

The way is open for all of us to find pleasure and satisfaction in music. To achieve a greater degree of enjoyment we need to know something about the structure of music. But it must be remembered that *music belongs to everyone*. Unfortunately, far too much is said and written in flowery, meaningless terms, or in clinical language as if it were an esoteric cult to be understood by the few. Whether we realise it or not, music is an essential part of good living, and its power and beauty lie within reach of everyone. But we must learn to listen; learn how to listen.

LISTENING TO MUSIC

An English dictionary will probably define listening as "to give ear; to hearken," or in some such terms. We *hear* music every day of our lives, but how often do we really *listen*, that is, listen with our ears and minds?

Music can be a pleasant (sometimes an irritating) background to dining. We can let the sound of a symphony flow over us without making any attempt to listen. Listening consciously and attentively brings its reward; besides, it is the least courtesy we can extend to the artists who are performing.

The performance of music should be a shared experience between the performer and the listener. It calls for participation. A musical work is recreated every time a musician brings it to life. Just as *Hamlet* will lie coldly in print between the covers of a book until spoken or read, so does a piece of music remain a mere collection of symbols until an interpreter breathes life into it.

The performance of music should be a shared experience. If we attend a coldly practical rehearsal of, say, a symphony we may find our attention wandering, but if we attend a performance before an audience on the following night, we will be conscious of a difference. What was at the rehearsal mere pleasant sound is now transfigured by the emotional bond, the *rapport*, between the musicians giving out and the listeners taking in, also between us and the other receptive members of the audience. The symphony has achieved a re-birth.

This is not to say that we cannot derive pleasure and satisfaction from listening *alone* to a record in our own room, but, again, the degree of that pleasure and satisfaction will depend on how far we are prepared to listen attentively, to participate. By listening intelligently and with full attention we become in some intangible way a part of the performance.

Not everyone can be a performer, but everyone can become a listener; in fact, it could be argued that the world has sufficient practising musicians, but far too few active listeners, active being the operative word.

Listening to music can be an emotional experience or an intellectual exercise. If we succeed in blending the two, without excess in either case, we are on the road to gaining the ultimate pleasure from music. Having mastered the gift of listening to, say, a Haydn symphony, the ear and mind should be ready to admit Mozart, then to absorb Beethoven, then Brahms. After that, the pathway to the works of later composers will be found to be less bramble-strewn than we at first imagined.

In the case of music of less familiar patterns, for instance a work by a modern composer, repetition is important, for what may at first sound obscure will gradually gain in appeal and convey its meaning if we hear repeated performances. This is where the record plays a vital part in the development of music appreciation.

If we learn to appreciate the *structure* of music, then our listening pleasure should become even greater. But to study the FORM of music only, and to disregard its emotional impact, is rather like studying the ground plan of a noble cathedral and not bothering to go inside. We can find aesthetic satisfaction in viewing a landscape, or a painting without a knowledge of perspective, colour, and design, but if we take the trouble to acquaint ourselves with the basic principles of artistic design our enjoyment in a worthy work of art will become that much deeper.

This is equally true in the appreciation of music, and that is the subject of this book; to place before the music-lover some basic concepts of music structure so that he may gain a true *understanding* of music.

We must of course decide whether we are concerned with the emotional absorption of sound only, with the structure of the work, or with a combination of both which leads to imaginative listening.

The trained musician and the uninitiated listener may hear music differently. The musician has the training and the awareness that permits him not only to hear the music, but to penetrate to the structure and the meaning of it. The untrained listener hears what his emotions want him to hear and this will vary widely with the individual. After his ear, his listening perception, has been trained, he will be able to distinguish the more subtle shades of tone-colour, for instance, the different sound between a flute and an oboe, a clarinet and an English horn. This will provide a good starting point for a fuller appreciation.

Watching a play, or reading a story, the memory will carry forward the sequence of action. In music the memory must play its part; it must store up the melody line, the harmonic and rhythmic structures, so that it is aware of the logical development of the composition. This is one of the interesting aspects of listening.

In the foregoing we have met the word "listening" many times because it is at the base of the understanding and the complete enjoyment of music. If this is what we wish to attain, then we must learn to listen—with our ears and our minds.

The final scene from the opera buffa *L'Incontro Improviso*, by Haydn, under the direction of the composer at Esterhaz, Austria, in 1775.

Joseph Haydn directing a performance of his oratorio *Creation* in the main hall of the old University, Vienna, 27 March 1808. This was Haydn's last public appearance.

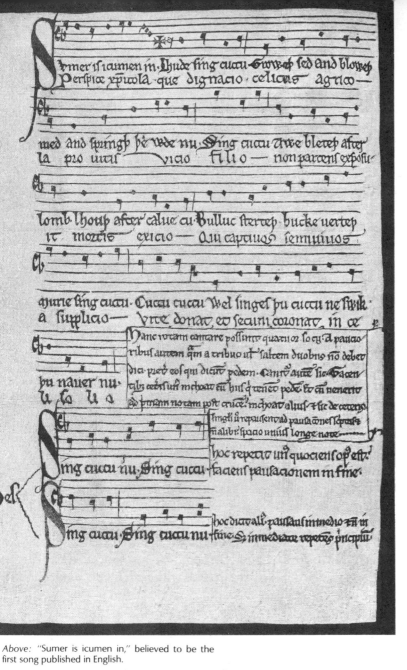

Above and below: English spinets, 1660-1700.

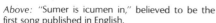

Above: "Sumer is icumen in," believed to be the first song published in English.

English clavichord, 1715.

Octave virginal, 1610.

Modern German harpsichord.

THE BEGINNING OF MUSIC

It may not be too fanciful to say that Nature ordained the first music; that in the first pulsating hours of Creation there was sound. We can imagine that insects hummed and birds sang; that the wind sighed from trees and ferns, and the rain made gentle music as it fell upon rocks and thirsting leaves; that there was happy sound as water trickled down mountain creeks, and waves gurgled and splashed on beaches of pebbles and sand. There was also drama in sound as the thunder boomed across the sky.

We can suppose that primitive man listened with pleasure to these sounds and made attempts to imitate them.

To say when and how *ordered* sounds came into use must of course be pure conjecture. We can assume, however, that when primitive man wished to pass his meaning to others he made use of sounds that came from his throat. Gradually, he learned to make up words, and so speech began. When he had to speak to a group of people in the open air, he found that he could get his message over more effectively if he altered the pitch of his voice. In this way, speaking may have developed into a kind of crude singing.

As time went on, he discovered that he could make agreeable sounds besides those which came from his voice. Perhaps, and this word must be stressed when dealing with a far-off age of which we have no written records, he invented what we might call a drum by stretching the skin of an animal across a hollow log or gourd. (It must be remembered that man's rhythmic sense is stronger than his melodic. Today, as always, the beating of a drum can stimulate action, even thought.)

Perhaps, too, early man discovered that by twanging tightly-stretched strips of skin, he could imitate those sounds that came from the vibrations when the wind played through reeds at the water's edge. Later, perhaps, he learned to make varied sounds by blowing through a pipe pierced at intervals with holes. This would develop into the flute.

Something that began as a means of communication, or self-expression, gradually developed into a form of entertainment in which others could share, and so we have a crude basis for what, centuries later, was to become vocal and instrumental music.

Two primitive forms of musical expression were song and dance, the first melodic, the other rhythmic.

Some 2,500 years ago the ringing of a blacksmith's anvil caused the Greek philosopher, Pythagoras, to investigate the principles of sound. He did not, however, answer the question, "What is Music?" Ever since that time scholars have been trying to arrive at a complete and convincing definition of the word.

As time went on, other instruments, as well as the crude drum and flute, were invented; later the ancient Egyptians and Babylonians found that they could blend

This ceremonial dance by priests of the Yakut tribe of Central Asia in the nineteenth century typifies the primitive songs and dances which developed out of the very beginnings of music.

several instruments together with pleasing effect, which pointed the way to the beginning of orchestras.

The Greeks were somewhat slower in this regard, for they placed greater importance on literature, usually preferring to listen to the words of eminent writers. The Romans, however, found that they could liven up their banquets and festivals by employing musical instruments, some of which they invented.

In the foregoing we began with conjecture. We can now pay more attention to fact.

Musical history does not divide itself snugly into sections, for it will be found that sections overlap one another, but for convenience historians have divided it into periods.

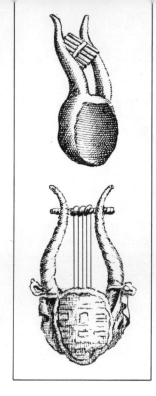

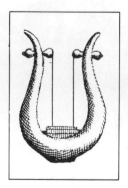

Various types of the Greek lyre, one of the
earliest of the stringed instruments.

The history of music could be briefly, and widely, summed up in this way:

Ancient and Oriental Music
Early Medieval Music (up to 1300)
*Ars Nova and Renaissance (14th to 16th centuries)
The Age of Humanism (c. 1540-1630)
Period of perfection in Choral style, in the time of
    Palestrina (late 16th century)
Opera (from 1600)
Growth of Instrumental Music (17th century)
Beginning of a more modern outlook, with Purcell,
    Bach, Handel, etc. (late 17th to middle 18th centuries)
The development of the Sonata and Symphony with
    Haydn, Mozart and Beethoven (middle 18th to
    early 19th centuries)
Romanticism (19th century)
Modern Music (from about 1890 to present day)

*Ars Nova (Latin New Art) A term indicating a style current in music, particularly in France and Italy, in the 14th century, as distinct from Ars Antiqua (Latin Old Art).

We have come to look upon the three main Periods in music as: CLASSICAL, music written between the sixteenth and eighteenth centuries; ROMANTIC, that written from the early part of the nineteenth century up to about 1900; MODERN, that written during the twentieth century.

THE
STRUCTURE
OF
MUSIC

2

AS certain terms and symbols will be used throughout this book, it may be appropriate at this stage to explain some of these in case they may be unfamiliar to the reader. Other terms will be explained, either in the Glossary, or within the sections devoted to the various types and forms of music. Diagrams will also be given.

We will first take Notation, the system of symbols by which musical ideas can be expressed. The musical notation familiar to the musician today is the result of a long process of evolution; numerous systems of symbols in music have been used over many centuries, but the one that has survived, and is in general use today, is the method of Staff (or Stave) Notation.

In earliest times the method of transferring a melody created by the composer to the performer was purely aural; it had to be conveyed through the ear only. As music-building in Western Europe progressed, it became necessary to invent a musical language which would indicate not only the tune, but how it should be expressed. By the seventh century A.D. a system had developed which gave the outline of a melody, but without indicating the actual pitch. About two hundred years later the Staff appeared, this being a framework of horizontal lines and spaces.

STAFF: Usually associated with the staff is the name Guido d'Arezzo (c. 990-c. 1050), an Italian monk, musical theorist, and teacher. Whether he actually invented the staff, or merely widened its use, is not quite clear; we do know, however, that in his time it consisted of only four lines, the traditional staff of Gregorian Chant. The five-line staff did not come into universal use until some hundreds of years later. When it is necessary to include notes of a higher or lower pitch than can be shown on the five-line staff, short lines, called Ledger (or Leger) Lines are added.

CLEF: The word Clef is from the Latin *clavis*. This sign, placed at the beginning (extreme left) of every line of music determines the position of the note on the staff, and therefore its exact pitch.

The best known clefs are the G (treble) and F (bass), as used in piano music (see diagram). If middle C, which lies on the ledger line between these two clefs, is added to them, the resulting eleven lines constitute the Great Staff, or Stave, which is large enough to cover the bulk of music.

Selections of five lines from the Great Staff can be made for convenience to suit the range of various solo instruments, e.g. viola, alto clef C, and the tenor clef C (see below), sometimes used for cello, bassoon and tenor trombone. In these C clefs the line passing through the gap in the clef is always Middle C and the remainder can be deduced from this.

Alto clef   Tenor clef

NOTES: These can be named for:
  (1) pitch, using the first seven notes of the alphabet, A - G
  (2) length (crotchets, quavers, etc.) (See diagram)
  (3) position in the scale (tonic, supertonic, etc.)

○ = semibreve   𝅗𝅥 = minim   ♩ = crotchet
♪ = quaver   𝅘𝅥𝅯 = semiquaver   𝅘𝅥𝅰 = demisemiquaver
𝅘𝅥𝅱 = semidemisemiquaver

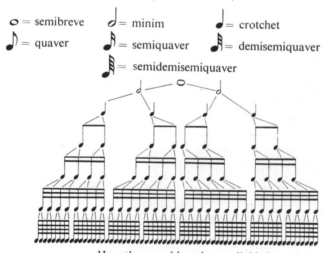

How the sound lengths are divided

14

RESTS: These, representing silence, are named as in (2) for length, corresponding to the table of notes. (See diagram)

NOTES and corresponding RESTS, each twice as long as the next below:

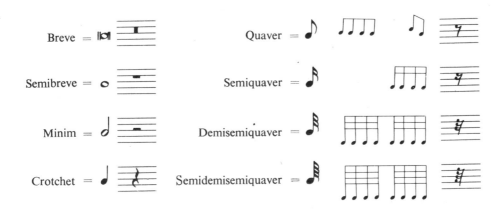

NOTE GROUPS: To assist the eye, notes with tails are often grouped together, usually to clarify the beats.

Piano Staffs

G or treble clef

F or bass clef

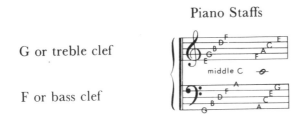

If there is room rests are usually printed in the third space from the bottom:

| treble | bass | breve | semibreve | minim | crotchet | quaver | semiquaver | demisemiquaver | semidemi- semiquaver |

TIME, TIME-SIGNATURES, AND ACCENTS

Time in music means the grouping of sounds into regular sets by means of a strong *accent* on the first of the set.

The *strong accent* defining the *time* of the set is indicated by an upright *bar-line* in front of it across the staff.

The *bar* is the music between two bar-lines. It is divided into equal *beats*, which are themselves sub-divisible.

The *time* of a piece is defined by the *number* and *length* of the beats in a bar expressed in figures,

viz: 2 crotchet beats (duple time) $\frac{2}{4}$

3 crotchet beats (triple time) $\frac{3}{4}$

4 crotchet beats (quadruple time) $\frac{4}{4}$

The figures are called the *time signature*, the upper showing the number and the lower the quality of the beats.

e.g. $\frac{2}{2} = 2$ minims, $\frac{2}{4} = 2$ crotchets, $\frac{3}{8} = 3$ quavers, etc.

(n.b. $16 = $ ♪ $7, 32 = $ ♪ 8)

The beat can equal a dotted note: $\frac{6}{8}$

in which case it is divisible into three instead of two and is called *compound time* instead of *simple time* and the time signature indicates the number of sub-divisions of the beat instead of the number of beats.

Sometimes, in folk music and music of some advanced twentieth century composers, more complicated time-signatures are employed: for instance, Stravinsky's score, *Le Sacre du Printemps* includes such unusual combinations as $\frac{1}{8}, \frac{5}{6},$ and $\frac{11}{4}$.

DYNAMICS AND RELATED MUSICAL TERMS

In music the word *dynamics* applies to the graduations of intensity of sounds, these depending on the amplitude of vibrations of string or tube; therefore, the relative softness or loudness of a note produced. Examples:

ppp	(molto pianissimo)	extremely soft
pp	(pianissimo)	very soft
p	(piano)	soft
mp	(mezzo piano)	moderately soft
mf	(mezzo forte)	moderately loud
f	(forte)	loud
ff	(fortissimo)	very loud
fff	(molto fortissimo)	extremely loud

Most of these and other musical terms meant to denote degrees of tone, pace, style, etc., were expressed in Italian when Italy was the centre of the musical world. This custom has come down through the centuries, although in some cases English and German words are used. For instance, a movement of a Beethoven symphony

This performer in the Red Army choir combines music and dancing in exactly the same way as the most primitive musicians.

will be marked *Allegro*, meaning lively, while a Schumann movement might be shown as *lebhaft*, which also means lively.

The sign $<$ means gradually increase the tone; the sign $>$ (or dim.) gradually decrease the tone.

Words used to denote Pace and Style

Pace

Grave	very slow
Adagio	slow, broad, leisurely
Largo	slow, solemn
Larghetto	rather less slow than Largo
Lento	slow
Allegro	lively, brisk
Allegretto	less lively than Allegro
Andante	going easily, steadily moving
Andantino	diminutive of Andante, but sometimes used to mean a little quicker than Andante
Moderato	moderate
Presto	fast
Prestissimo	very fast

Alteration of Pace

Accelerando, or accel.	increase the pace
Ad libitum, or ad lib.	at pleasure, at liberty
A tempo	return to original pace
Rallentando, or rall.	gradually decrease the pace

Style

Agitato	agitated
Animato	animated
Appassionato	impassioned
Assai	enough or very
Cantabile	in a singing style
Con	with
Con brio	with spirit
Con espressione	with expression
Con spirito	with lively spirit
Dolce	sweetly
Dolente	sadly
Espressivo	in an expressive manner
Fuoco	fire, ardour
Giocoso	humorous, playful
Legato	smoothly

Leggiero	lightly
Maestoso	majestically
Meno	less
Molto	much, very
Non	not
Pesante	heavily
Piu	more
Poco	a little
Sforzando	forced
Smorendo or morendo	dying away
Smorzando	gradually dying away; smothering the tone
Sostenuto	sustained
Staccato	detached, short; notes separated from each other
Troppo	too much (ma non troppo means: but not too much)
Vivace	lively, sprightly

Other musical terms and their meanings will be found in the Glossary towards the end of this book.

ORNAMENTS

The practice of embellishing a melody with ornaments is as old as music itself. It seems certain that in early times those without any musical training whatever instinctively decorated their folk-songs by adding extra notes to the tune itself. With the growth of music this became a convention.

In the case of early keyboard instruments, apart from the organ, the duration of sound from the struck note was short and, until the invention of the pianoforte, with its sustaining pedal, there was no way of prolonging the sound. When the melody moved at a slow pace, silences occurred between the notes. To avoid this, we might say to fill in the blanks, composers of keyboard music decorated slow-moving melodies with various ornaments; trills, turns, runs, and the like. Often, the performer would introduce some of his own.

The custom spread to singers who embellished the music set down for them, according to their technical skill. We can easily imagine how this practice must have been abused by conceited singers!

In the nineteenth century some composers of the Romantic school took full advantage of this device. Liszt tacked on to his melodies and themes elaborate figurations, no doubt for the purpose of displaying his virtuosity. In published form these sometimes amount to little more than skirmishes up and down the keyboard, with more blatancy than musical meaning. Paganini, too, adopted this florid kind of decoration, no doubt because the public paid to hear him perform feats of dexterity that were beyond the ability of other violinists of his time.

When introduced by the composer of artistic discretion, ornaments can enliven the melody, give the music a distinct personality, and please the critical listener. Chopin was a master in the use of appropriate ornamentation which, more than mere adornment, became an integral part of the composition.

Some of the most frequently met musical ornaments are shown below:

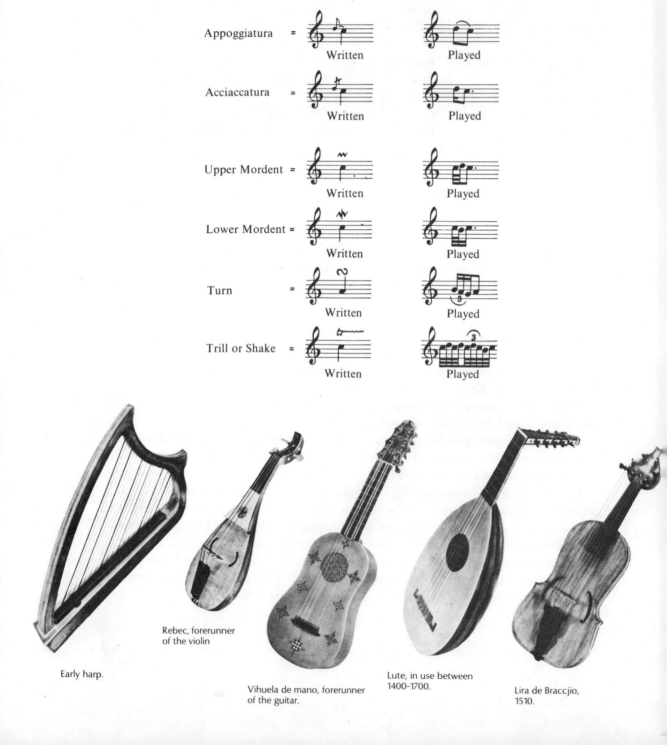

Early harp.

Rebec, forerunner of the violin

Vihuela de mano, forerunner of the guitar.

Lute, in use between 1400-1700.

Lira de Braccjio, 1510.

THE STRUCTURE OF MUSIC

The basic elements in the structure of music are RHYTHM, MELODY, and HARMONY. To these we could add DYNAMICS.

Broadly speaking, these elements in music might be related to form in literature: melody, the story or theme of a literary work; harmony, the choice of words; rhythm, the metre or pulse; dynamics, the degree of intensity of expression. These elements, of course, are subject to subdivisions.

RHYTHM: In music rhythm is not easy to define precisely. We know that the Universe moves to a rhythmic pattern, the stars, the tides, the seasons, growth. Our hearts beat rhythmically. We may suppose that primitive man of remote times was conscious of rhythm and employed it to his advantage.

Dictionaries describe rhythm in such terms as "the recurrence of stresses of long and short sounds"; "the distribution of metre"; "a strongly defined accentuation"; "the distribution of notes in time and their accentuation." None of these gives a precise definition.

One point we must remember is that Time and Pulse are not synonymous with Rhythm. The ticking of a clock is regular, but it is not strictly rhythmical, because it has no defined divisions of accents, no definite shape.

After a composer has devised a tune, he gives it a character by indicating where stresses should occur. It is to a great extent the rhythm that gives any piece of music its specific character, e.g. a sturdy march, a Spanish dance, or an Irish jig. Change the rhythm and the music will have lost that essential character. Let us take a simple example. Pick out the notes of the melody line of Dvořák's *Humoresque*, giving every note the same duration. Immediately the tune has lost shape, its contours have been flattened. We may play a waltz in two ways; first, at a fast pace, and then slowly. The rhythm has not changed, only the pace. The accent in both cases will have fallen on the first beat of each bar.

Tchaikovsky has written a particularly haunting melody for the *Pas de deux* (No. 14) in Act Two of *The Nutcracker*. If we were to strip this of its rhythmic shape by making every note of the same duration, we would get, not a romantic melody, but merely a descending scale.

If successive sounds are organised in some systematic order the ear will at once be conscious of that order.

The fundamental basis of all music, therefore, is rhythm. The hypnotic stimulus of much "pop" music of today depends on the insistence of its rhythmic beat, the words in most cases being of little value. Rhythmic flexibility has increased to a very great extent over the last hundred years or so; one need only compare a work from the classical or romantic periods with music of the advanced modern schools to prove this. For instance, at one time a musical score for a ballet was cast in regular time-patterns, with the time-signature indicating, say, 2/4 or 3/4. As we have mentioned elsewhere, Stravinsky, in his *Le Sacre du Printemps* employed such unusual time-signatures as 1/8, 5/6, and 11/4 with striking effect.

TEMPO: Tempo is the pace at which the rhythmical units progress, varying from slow to quick. Such terms as Lento, Andante, Allegro, and Presto denote the tempo. (The full range of these musical terms, together with their meanings, is given in the section, DYNAMICS AND RELATED MUSICAL TERMS.)

MELODY: Melody is a term that eludes exact definition, but is sometimes described as a related succession of sounds. A scale is just that, a succession of single sounds, but a scale is not a defined melody. A melody must always be *going somewhere*, with an appeal to the senses by its arrangement, its balance and contrast, *saying something*. It must have a clear-cut form arrangement, with some notes higher or lower than the others, some of them longer or shorter than their companions.

Just as every literary work is based on the letters of the alphabet, every melody, be it a simple folk-tune or a symphony, is founded on the notes of the scale. It is the shape and tensions that bring it to life.

Some melodies complete themselves within a few notes, while others may stretch over several bars. We can catch the melody of *Rule, Britannia* from the first few notes; in the case of, say, Wagner, the melody may need several bars before it is complete.

Drink to me only with thine eyes consists of only two lines of melody. The melody set to the words, "Drink to me only with thine eyes, and I will pledge with mine" is the main theme. This is repeated in the second and the fourth line. Only the third line is different. Each successive verse is laid out on the same plan.

A confirmed concertgoer may at once recognise a theme from a Brahms symphony, or a Beethoven quartet, but fail to detect any melody whatever in a composition of Bartók or Hindemith. But melody is there, though less obvious, sometimes obscure. He can come to recognise it by adjusting the ear and the mind to accept new patterns and sound-relationships.

A melody may thread its way through a musical work, from it springing other melodies, usually related in some way, but providing contrast. These we could call tributary melodies. To form a graphic picture of this, we could relate it to a map that indicates a river following a defined course, while receiving or linking other branches, that is, tributaries.

Many works, sometimes great ones, have been built on simple themes. Beethoven composed a series of thirty-three variations on a trivial waltz tune by Diabelli. Beethoven's *Symphony No. 5 in C minor* begins with a two-bar (four notes) phrase which figures dramatically throughout the whole movement. *The Symphony No. 7 in C major* by Sibelius begins with a simple scale passage. This becomes a dominant force, and from it evolve themes which, although seemingly independent, remain part of the constellation of ideas on which the symphony is magnificently built. The germ of the *Symphony No. 2 in D major* by Brahms is contained in the first three notes. On the other hand, Haydn and other composers of his time began their symphonies with a slow and stately introduction before announcing the main theme of the first movement.

The melodic structure of a musical work has several components, some of which may be briefly explained:

Motif (Motive), or *Figure*: A short theme, or leading idea, which must consist of at least two notes to give it meaning and to promote a rhythmic pattern.

Phrase: This can contain one or two motifs; a note-pattern that not only completes itself, but leads logically to that which follows it.

Sentence: There are many kinds of musical sentences, many of eight bars in length, often divided into two parts of four bars each, the first questioning or unanswered, the second completing the statement. The sentence is marked by a perfect cadence, which is explained under *Harmony*.

Harmony: In general terms we can define harmony as the simultaneous and agreeable combination of two or more sounds of different pitch. Harmony is a vertical aspect of music, whereas melody is horizontally constructed. It is also the basic science of chords, their interrelation, and their logical progression, differing from *counterpoint*, which is a combination of two or more melodies. Harmonies themselves are determined by a key system.

In early times people sang the same notes in unison, but by the end of the ninth century it was discovered that variety and additional colour could be gained if other notes were combined with those making up the melody line. This led to a medieval form of part-writing, based on a plainsong which was "harmonised" by additional parts, the technique of doubling a melody at a perfect fourth or fifth being called *Organum*, or *Diaphony*.

Out of this developed *Tonality*, or key-system, which dictated the tonal system of a composition by the observance of a single key. *Tonality* was therefore the result of the process of relating a series of notes to a focal point, in other words, the tonal centre of the key. (In the twentieth century the term *polytonality* is applied to music which employs the simultaneous use of several keys, while *atonality* denotes the absence of key.) The diatonic scale, used as the basis of harmony, had been generally adopted by the seventeenth century, after a process of evolution.

We have already said that harmony is the simultaneous sounding of two or more notes of different pitch. A note and its octave can be sounded together, thus:

 How much more pleasing to the ear if two other notes in relationship are added, thus:

What had been a note and its octave sounded together now becomes a chord.

For chords, or melodies, to allow of agreeable combination, it is necessary that those which are to sound simultaneously should possess certain relationships. These are classified as *consonances* (*concords*) and *dissonances* (*discords*), the *dissonance* requiring a resolution to another chord that will be more agreeable to the ear.

The "parent" note of the harmonic series is called the *fundamental*. Other notes, called *overtones*, or *partials*, sound over the basic one, but the intensity of these *partials* is considerably less than that of the parent note or fundamental.

Every sound is caused by vibration, and the pitch of a note depends on the *frequency* of its vibration. The intensity of the note depends on the *amplitude* of the vibration.

We refer to the quality of a sound, e.g., that of a note produced by this or that instrument, or sung by different voices, as the colour, or tone-colour, or in French, *timbre*.

Cadence: The word Cadence means a succession of chords closing a musical period, section, or composition. The Perfect Cadence in C major is a progression of the dominant (on G) to the tonic chord (on C), which has the effect of bringing a sentence to a full close, performing a similar function as the full stop in a written sentence. The Imperfect Cadence is the progression of the tonic (or other chord) to the dominant, its function being that of a punctuation like the comma. The Interrupted Cadence is from the dominant (on G) to the sub-mediant (on A), giving the effect of an inconclusive punctuation, a substitution for the expected tonic chord. The Plagal Cadence is a progression from the sub-dominant (on F) to the tonic, a kind of delayed cadence, sometimes called the "Amen" Cadence.

For harmonic purposes the names of the Scale notes are: 1 tonic, 2 supertonic, 3 mediant, 4 sub-dominant, 5 dominant, 6 sub-mediant, 7 leading note.

Counterpoint: The word Counterpoint literally means point against point (before the invention of notes, sounds were expressed on paper by points), or the art of combining notes against one another to form individual melodies of equal importance within strict limits. (The adjective is contrapuntal.) A person might sing "seconds" to a melody ("seconds" being an old-fashioned term meaning the singing of an additional vocal line to harmonise with the melody without introducing another melody), but that would not be counterpoint. When we combine two or more melodic lines of distinct character in harmonic unity into a coherent whole, then we do have counterpoint. Bach was one of the greatest contrapuntalists of his time.

Modulation: In order to avoid monotony or sameness in a musical composition, and to give it variety of tonal colour, composers use various devices, one of these being modulation.

Modulation is the changing of one tonal centre to another, e.g., a change of key C to G. So that the change will take place smoothly, the relationship between keys is observed. Modulation is usually indicated by the presence of *accidentals*, the word meaning sharps, flats, or naturals which do not belong to the original key-signature.

The first page of a music score.

MUSICAL FORM

When we speak of Form in music we mean the term to relate to the melodic and rhythmical shape of musical ideas. It is, of course, something more than that. Pitch, melody, harmony, and rhythm play their parts in forming the structure of a musical composition, but unless the work has a definite shape, that is form, it may fail to establish its true identity, The form of a composition is the system of relationship existing between its consecutive parts, and true musical form contains variety within the bounds of unity. This applies equally to any work of art by a composer, a painter, a sculptor, an architect. A musical work, from a simple song to an extended symphony, needs to be *built*, and anything built without the observance of form is shapeless.

In the chapter Structure in Music we have mentioned such terms as *motif, phrase*, and *sentence*, all of which contribute something to the desired form. We can now briefly consider certain other components and aspects of form.

Scales: Even the untrained ear can generally recognise a scale, a sound associated with music students. As it plays an important part in both the theoretical and practical study of music it should be allotted a little space at this stage.

We know that an INTERVAL is the distance, or the difference in pitch, between two notes; that an OCTAVE is the interval of eight notes, counting both the bottom and the top notes. A SCALE is a progressive series of notes moving upwards or downwards from any note to its octave. The word scale comes from the Latin *scala*, meaning ladder.

The Western European scale system dates from about the early part of the seventeenth century, when it began to replace the *modal*, system. In ancient times the Greeks named their scales, or modes, after their tribes, the four principal modes being the Dorian Mode, which proceeded from D to the octave D; the Phrygian (E to E); Lydian (F to F); and the Mixolydian (G to G). To these were added subordinate modes, for instance the Aeolian, which moved from A (below the stave) to A, and the Ionian, C (below the stave) to C.

By the end of the seventeenth century the modal system had generally been supplanted by the major and minor scale system. Modes, however, survived in plainsong, and to some extent in folk-song, and some twentieth century composers, including Vaughan Williams, have used the ancient modes to achieve an archaic effect.

The scales in use today are the Diatonic, Chromatic, Pentatonic, and Whole-tone.

The Diatonic (meaning through the tones), has five tones and two semitones and can be in either the major or the minor key, according to its 3rd and 6th note. The Chromatic Scale consists of twelve consecutive semitones, starting from any note, ascending or descending, accidentals marking the notes which do not belong to the scale of the key in which the passage occurs. The Pentatonic Scale (from *penta*, meaning five) consists of only five notes, e.g., the five black keys of the piano, beginning on F-sharp. This ancient scale, sometimes called the "Scotch" Scale, is supposed to have been used by the ancient Egyptians, Assyrians, Chinese, and others, and is widely used in the folk-music of many countries. The Whole-tone Scale, as its name suggests, is made up entirely of whole tones.

Some examples of form are Binary, Ternary, Rondo, Fugue, Variation, and Sonata-form.

Binary Form: This is usually represented by the letters A B, or A A B. As the word might suggest, binary consists of two divisions, or it can be a movement founded on two themes or principal subjects. Songs, or other pieces, set in binary form comprise two sections which are in some way related to each other, without being actually alike. These sections can be repeated without affecting the form.

The binary form in melody resembles a question and an answer in speech. As we have explained in another chapter, the song *Drink to me only with thine eyes* is made up of two musical phrases, A and B. The structure of each verse of this song is this: the first line is A; the second (the same as the first) A; the third (taking on another melodic curve) B; the fourth (the return of the first line) A. Each verse of this song contains only two phrases, but monotony is avoided by the introduction of a contrasting phrase in the third line.

Ternary Form: Meaning three sections, this is symbolised by the letters A B A, or A A B A. The ternary differs from the binary form in that B is in complete contrast to A, although in some way relevant. An example of the ternary form is a minuet by Haydn or Mozart, the *Trio* section being in contrast to the minuet proper. Many of Schubert's *Impromptus* are ternary in form.

Rondo: The French spelling of this term is *Rondeau*. This form has one principal subject which, having established itself at the start of the composition, recurs intermittently, its reappearances being separated by a contrasted subject. There are two rondo forms: (a) A B A C A, simple or short rondo form; (b) A B A C A B A, compound or sonata rondo form. A represents the principal subject, B and C the episodes.

Each recurrence of the principal subject is in the tonic key. This may be repeated in its original form, or it may be embellished by simple ornaments to give it variety.

Fugue: The word Fugue (from the Latin *fuga*) literally means flight. This type of composition, whether vocal or instrumental, is written for a number of "voices," each voice entering with the same subject, or tune, in imitation of the other. The fugue commonly consists of three sections: the exposition, the middle section, and the final section.

Fugues vary widely in pattern, but the following may be given as an example: The exposition contains successive statements of the principal theme by each voice in turn. The theme, or subject, usually of defined character, is stated alone by the

Various types of early stringed instruments of the
seventeenth and eighteenth centuries.

top voice in the tonic key. This is answered by another voice in the dominant key.
The counter-subject enters simultaneously with the "answer" in free counterpoint
"against" the tonic voice. The final section begins at the point where the main
subject returns to the tonic key, this leading to the final rounding-off. When the
principal subject has been heard for the last time, a Coda (from the Latin *cauda*,
"tail") brings the work to an end with a convincing flourish.

When a short linking passage is introduced between the subject and the answer,
this is called a *Codetta*.

Bach carried the fugue to a point higher than any other composer had before him.
To realise this one need only study the masterly manner in which he treated it in
many of his compositions. His *Die Kunst der Fuge* (*The Art of Fugue*), a series of canons
and fugues, all in the same key and all deriving from a single theme, was his last
work and remained unfinished at the time of his death in 1750. It stands as a monument to his amazing genius.

28

A
Song

OF THE

WOMEN OF THE MENERO TRIBE,

Near the

Australian Alps.

ARRANGED

with the assistance of several Musical Gentlemen

for the

Voice and Pianoforte,

most humbly inscribed, as the first specimen of

Australian Music.

TO

Her Most Gracious Majesty

ADELAIDE,

Queen of Great Britain & Hanover.

By Dr. J. Lhotsky, Colonist N S Wales.

Sydney.
Sold by John Innes, Pitt St

London
By commission, at R. Ackerman's Repository of Arts, Strand.

J. G. Austin, Lith. Sydney N.S.W.

THE PIECE OF MUSIC FIRST COMPOSED AND PRINTED IN AUSTRALIA.

(From the original in possession of Miss Rose Scott.)

SONG OF THE WOMEN OF THE MENERO TRIBE.

The words may be translated:

Unprotected race of people
Unprotected are we

And our children shrink so fastly
Unprotected why are we?

SONATA FORM (or FIRST-MOVEMENT FORM): This term refers to the structure of the opening movement of a sonata, a symphony, a quartet, an overture; also, to some extent, to a concerto. As a defined form, this developed in the time of C. P. E. Bach, about the middle of the eighteenth century. This ternary or three-part form (not to be confused with the simpler ternary form) possesses three basic divisions: Exposition, Development (or "Free Fantasia"), and Recapitulation. The three divisions may briefly be described in this way:

Exposition: The principal subject, which is clearly stated with strong emphasis, is set in the tonic key. The second subject is usually *in the dominant key*, and the exposition ends with a codetta in this key. We could, with some licence, liken the subjects of this plan to the two main characters in a play, the first being strong, or "masculine," the second lyrical, or "feminine." In this way contrast is achieved.

Development: The music heard in the exposition is now given free treatment by various means: e.g., greater variety of key (from major to minor or minor to major), changes of harmony, the extension of a rhythmical figure, melodic decoration, or the introduction of new material to give greater contrast. Normally the section closes with a return to the tonic key.

Recapitulation: This brings a re-statement of the whole exposition, with both main subjects in the tonic key, the listener being reminded of what has gone before. Key relationships play an important part in this. The movement ends with a Coda to convey a sense of finality.

The above is a general plan, but exceptions are to be found in many works, including those of Mozart, Beethoven, Brahms and other composers.

VARIATION: As we may deduce from the term, Variation in music means the repeated presentation of a theme, each appearance of it, after the initial statement of the theme itself, being treated to melodic, harmonic, and rhythmical changes. The use of this device goes back many centuries, but is still employed by composers of today.

(A fuller discussion of this subject will be found in the section VARIATIONS.)

Related to the variation form are the *Chaconne* and the *Passacaglia*. The chaconne was originally a slow dance. It is usually in 3/4 time (although Couperin wrote one in 2/4 time) in which a theme is repeated over and over in the bass, with variations above it. Purcell, Bach, Handel, and other composers of their time adopted the *chaconne*, often repeating the theme as many as twenty times.

In the *Passacaglia*, also originally a dance tune in triple time, a theme is continuously repeated, not necessarily in the bass, and sometimes more elaborately embroidered. Like the *Chaconne*, the *Passacaglia* was adopted by composers of the seventeenth and eighteenth centuries, and even those of later times. The fourth movement of the *Symphony No. 4 in E minor* by Brahms is a vast *passacaglia*, in which eight slow chords undergo thirty variations.

31

PITCH, TONE and TONE COLOUR

Pitch refers to the height or depth of a note in relation to another and is determined by the number of its vibrations per second, in other words the *frequency* of the vibrations. The more rapid the vibrations of a sound, the higher the pitch; the slower the frequency, the lower the pitch. The *intensity* of the sound depends on the amplitude of the vibrations.

TONE is the *quality* of the sound. "Good intonation" means the accurate pitching of the notes.

TONE-COLOUR (in French *timbre*) gives a sound its individual character and enables us to distinguish the tone of one instrument from another (e.g., a trumpet or violin), or one voice from another. Each note possesses overtones, called *partials*, or *harmonics*, which sound simultaneously over the basic note, but with less intensity, giving the note extra quality or brilliance.

Colour in a painting registers immediately through the eye; a dozen people may see the colours in a picture in varying degrees of intensity, but the primary colours and their combinations are usually recognisable to a person without art training, unless that person is "colour-blind." Likewise, unless a person is "tone-deaf," he will be able to recognise (the degree varying with his training or his aural perception), even without seeing the instrument, the tone-colour of a note played on a flute, a saxophone, or a violin.

When a composer plans a composition for orchestra, he inwardly hears the desired tone-colour for each section of the work. He achieves this by the grouping of instruments. This work will take on a different tone-colour if performed by a brass band. A song, with the melody written for voice, will have a different sound if played as an instrumental solo.

If we listen to the familiar melody *The Swan* played by a solo cello (as Saint-Saëns conceived it), and then hear it played as an oboe solo we at once note the wide difference in the tone-colour of the solo part, although the piano accompaniment may be the same in both cases.

Let us consider two other examples of changing the tone-colour of compositions from that intended by the composers. In his Legend for Orchestra, *The Swan of Tuonela*, Sibelius gives the haunting melody that threads its way through the whole work to the English Horn. If this solo were given to another instrument, the lonely, melancholy character of the work would be changed and much of the poignancy lost.

Debussy composed his *Clair de Lune* for piano, and that is where it belongs. It has been transcribed for orchestras, large and small. The orchestral versions are of luscious tone-quality, but they suggest coloured floodlights, rather than cold, chaste moonlight.

The subject of transcriptions and arrangements is covered in some detail under that heading.

OPUS NUMBERS AND THE LIKE

Such signs as Op., K.V., and BWV, as seen in concert programmes and on record labels, will be familiar to music-lovers, but a few words of explanation may be helpful to anyone meeting these for the first time; they were devised as methods of numbering musical compositions, supposedly in the order of their composition.

Opus, or *Op*: A composer may have written two or more works in the same form (symphonies, concertos, or sonatas) and in the same key. To avoid confusion he added another label to the title — Opus, often printed as Op. For instance Beethoven wrote two symphonies in the key of F major; one is Op. 68, the other Op. 93.

Opus is the Latin word for *work*, meaning in this case a musical composition, and though it made occasional appearances in the seventeenth century, it did not come into general use until about Beethoven's time. An Opus number came to serve the same purpose as an index number for the works of a composer.

In some cases several works of the same kind may be included in one Opus number; e.g., Beethoven's violin-piano sonatas, Op. 12, Nos 1, 2, and 3, and Beethoven's set of six string quartets, which are grouped as Opus 18.

K., or *K.V.*: These letters apply only to Mozart's work. This composer wrote so many works (more than six hundred) that something had to be done about indexing them for easy reference. (In those times descriptive, or identifying titles were seldom used.) A musician-botanist named Köchel took up the task and, starting from Mozart's earliest composition, he classified them all and gave each a number.

When we see the letter "K" applied to a Mozart work, such as K.315, we know that it means Number 315 in the Köchel list. Sometimes this is written "K.V.", standing for *Köchel Verzeichnis*, meaning Köchel List.

BWV: These initials stand for *Bach Werke Verzeichnis*, meaning Index to Bach's works.

D (Deutsch): In 1951 Otto Erich Deutsch, an Austrian musicologist, published a complete thematic catalogue of Schubert's works. In has now become the practice to refer to these by their "D" numbers.

Titles

Such titles as *Moonlight Sonata* and *Jupiter Symphony* are much easier to remember than *Sonata No. 14 in C sharp minor, Op. 27, No. 2*, or *Symphony No. 41 in C major, K.V. 551*. These titles, however, were not bestowed by the composers. Beethoven did not call his sonata "Moonlight"; the title is thought to have come from a fanciful idea of the German critic, Heinrich Rellstab, to whom the first movement suggested moonlight on Lake Lucerne. Just why Mozart's last symphony should have become known as the "Jupiter" is not clear, but it is thought likely that the title was first used by the London Philharmonic Society.

Titles applied to works written before the Romantic period were in most cases given by publishers, often without the composer's consent or after his death, with the idea that a name rather than a number would attract more attention to it.

Even the purist who frowns on the adoption of nicknames for musical works must admit that they do help in certain cases, for instance the Haydn symphonies. Twenty-nine of Haydn's 104 symphonies have been given titles. Music shops and record dealers will probably tell you that the Haydn symphonies most called for are those with nicknames, e.g., *Surprise, Farewell, Military, Clock, Drum-roll.*

Lady with two children at a harpsichord.
Painting by Jan Miense Molenaar.

PERIODS IN MUSIC

3

ALTHOUGH there is no sharply defined dividing line between periods in music, since they are inclined to overlap and merge into one another, we generally place composers and their music into three broad categories, Classical, Romantic, and Modern. However, we come across such terms as Renaissance and Baroque, so first let us deal briefly with these.

RENAISSANCE: Renaissance meant a rebirth, that is, a rebirth of the arts and literature, and customs; a transition from the Middle Ages to the modern world. It was a period of humanism and scholarship. This began in Italy about the fourteenth century, and includes such great names as Dante, Petrarch, Boccaccio, Michelangelo, and Leonardo da Vinci; an era that witnessed the gushing of new humanised intellectual, artistic, spiritual, and social currents. Before long the ideals of the Renaissance, and the increased desire for learning, dominated French, Spanish, and English culture, and gradually spread to other countries.

By that time music had thrown off the limitations of the Middle Ages and was entering a stage of tonal and formal revolution, one innovation being (choral) *polyphony*, a word meaning the harmonious combination of two or more harmonies, as distinct from *homophony* which, vertical in structure, confined the interest to a single line of melody, any other sounds acting as accompaniment.

Wolfgang Amadeus Mozart (1756-1791). One of the greatest classical composers, he wrote in all forms, including forty-one symphonies and many outstanding operas.

The crowning peak of the polyphonic style was exemplified in the writing of such fifteenth and sixteenth composers as Palestrina, Victoria (or Vittoria), Lassus (or Lasso), Okeghem, Obrecht, Dufay, Binchois, Josquin des Prés (also known as Després and Deprés), Byrd, and Dunstable.

By the year 1600 choral music had reached a high watermark, with instrumental music developing more slowly.

During the Renaissance many composers had their training in cathedrals and the larger churches, often at first having obtained salaried positions as singers, and later securing the patronage of influential families. In the cities groups of instrumental musicians were maintained to provide entertainment at civic functions, even though the scope of the instruments and the music was limited; in country districts composers used folk-song as the basis of vocal and instrumental works.

So it came about that the Renaissance, honouring the arts as an indispensable part of living, developed cultural activities to a point higher than ever before.

BAROQUE: Although *baroque* connotes a certain kind of music, the word eludes precise definition. Rightly, *baroque* is an architectural term, dictionaries describing it variously as "twisting," "misshapen," "antiquated," "elaborate," "bizarre," none of which definitions are completely suited to the elegance of the music.

36

Johann Sebastian Bach (1685-1750). A towering genius. His vast output includes five *Passions*, 200 cantatas, plus many important oratorios, concertos, motets, and chamber music.

Baroque might more correctly be reserved for an artistic style that existed throughout Europe until the emergence of the *rococo*, a style of decoration current in Louis XV's time, and marked by decorations in which shells and wave-like designs predominated, without relation to the basic pattern.

Today, we associate the *baroque* in music with compositions written during the seventeenth and the first half of the eighteenth centuries, e.g., the music of such composers as Corelli, Marcello, Vivaldi, Quantz, and the earlier works of Handel and J. S. Bach.

In the seventeenth century Italian composers placed great importance on contrast, and a realistic form of expression, and like other Italian innovations, it gradually filtered through to other countries.

CLASSICAL: This is one of the most frequently mis-used terms in music, often applied to music of any period that is not "popular." In music it has much the same meaning that it has in literature.

We can apply the word to (a) music written in a "classical" idiom; (b) works written in forms existing from about the end of the sixteenth century to the end of the eighteenth century; (c) music conforming strictly to formal patterns, as distinct from the emotional and descriptive styles that came into use with the birth of

37

George Frederick Handel (1685-1759). His numerous oratorios, including *Messiah*, and operas won him great success. He was prolific in most musical forms of his day.

Romanticism. For example, the music of Haydn and Mozart belongs to the *classical* period, whereas that of Schumann and Liszt belongs to the *romantic* period.

Although Beethoven is usually placed in the *classical* period, his later works showed romantic tendencies, just as Schubert is sometimes referred to as the last of the Viennese classical composers. Brahms, born sixty-three years after Beethoven, and thirty-six years later than Schubert, stood as a link between the *classical* and the *romantic* periods. At heart he was a romantic, but he kept a tight rein on emotion, always respecting the highest principles of classical form and artistic reticence. He has been called both a "romantic classicist" and "a classical romanticist." Mendelssohn, who was born about the same time as Schumann, Liszt, and Chopin, coloured classical workmanship with romantic ardour.

The classical period in music saw the moulding of the sonata-form, or first-movement-form, from which developed the true symphony, concerto and string quartet, advanced progressively by Haydn, Mozart, and Beethoven. This resulted in a broader use of instruments and a widening of sonorities, a greater flexibility in vocal forms, all based on unified standards. The forms and standards established in the classical period have survived up to the present time.

We could perhaps sum up the classical style of the seventeenth and eighteenth centuries as a style that placed more emphasis on a universal objectivity, rather than on the specific or personal, a style that aimed at mastery of form and emotional restraint.

38

Guitars and mandolins of various periods. *Top row, from left:* Dobbro steel guitar;
flat backed guitar; two mandolas. *Bottom row:* Angel guitar; belly-back mandolins.

German guitar

Hawaiian guitar

Two-armed guitar: tenor and bass

Concertinas

C, F, & G button accordion

French tenor banjo

Mandolin harp

Greek bouzouki

Jean-Baptiste Lully (1632-1687). Regarded as the founder of French opera, he collaborated with Molière in such works as *Le Bourgeois Gentilhomme* and *Monsieur de Pourceaugnac*.

ROMANTIC: Romanticism in music was the result of a reaction against stereotyped conventions, and a desire for expression of more human, more personal emotions. In this brief survey we could perhaps do no better than begin with Robert Schumann (1810-1856), often called the Founder of the Romantic Period in Music.

Schumann's arrival on the musical scene came at a time most suited to his imagination and temperament. It was a period when romanticism was releasing literature and art from the tyranny of the pseudo-classical; when music was calling for composers to replace platitudinous formalism with more flexible concepts.

The romantic trends in literature, particularly in Germany, were to have a decided effect on music. The poems of Goethe, Schiller, Heine, Schlegel, and Eichendorff were to inspire musical settings by Schubert, Schumann and Wolf. The *Faust* legend has been traced back to the early sixteenth century, but it is Goethe's dramatic version which has been treated to more than thirty musical settings.

As a boy Schumann had found absorbing interest in the literary works of Jean Paul Richter and E. T. A. Hoffmann, a stimulus that was to bear fruit in his own literary work and in his songs.

The romantic era was responsible for a close interrelationship between the composer and the literary artist. Berlioz, Liszt, Mendelssohn, and Wagner possessed keen literary appreciation, even if at times their judgement showed signs of faltering.

John Bull (1563-1628). His compositions for virginals, viols, and organ have historic interest. He travelled through Europe, and became cathedral organist in Antwerp.

On the other hand, Chopin, although he moved in literary circles in Paris, gave no evidence of a significant discrimination in that direction. Perhaps he left that to the authoress, "George Sand" (Aurore Dudevant) with whom he lived for seven years.

New types of melody and harmonic structure came with the flowering of romanticism. Compositions bore titles, instead of mere key signatures. In 1850 Liszt invented the Symphonic Poem (or Tone Poem) and during the next ten years composed twelve of these, eight being orchestral illustrations of literary works.

The colourful light of romanticism fell on opera, urging composers to turn to romantic subjects, rather than those dealing with ancient history and classical mythology.

The technical demands made by romanticism led to greater tonal scope and virtuosity, e.g., in piano music with Liszt and Chopin; in orchestral music with Berlioz and Wagner. New sonorities and more flexible combinations were added to music. Romantic elements continued to lend colour and fragrance to music composition up to the end of the nineteenth century. With the arrival of a new century many composers felt that the time had come to curb excessive emotionalism, and to bring musical thinking down to earth.

MODERN: To dismiss all modern music as meaningless is like saying "I don't like fruit" because bananas give us indigestion. The person who makes such rash statements — that the present century has produced no worthwhile music, literature, or art is really flaunting his conceit in backing his own limited knowledge and ill-informed judgement against the expert knowledge and experienced judgement of critics who have assessed these things with balanced understanding.

What do we mean by "modern" music? Do we mean contemporary music; a work written in the modern style by a composer dead some fifty years; a work written in a traditional style by a contemporary composer? Do we mean music written in the whole-tone system; atonality, polytonality, serialism, electronic music? Or do we mean music that is beyond the periphery of our own limited appreciation?

It could be argued that, if we took the word "modern" to mean "new," or "of the age," then the thirteenth century composition *Sumer is Icumen in*, or the eighteenth century *Rule, Britannia* were examples of modern music in their time.

Many genuine music-lovers, content to "like what they know," withdraw into a conservative armour at the mention of music by modern composers; some, in fact, have not yet caught up with Brahms and Debussy. The conservative music-lover feels *safe* with "the old masters," doubly secure in the knowledge that Time has canonised such names as Bach, Mozart, and Beethoven.

This kind of conservative attitude makes it difficult for the modern composer to reach an audience beyond a circle of open-minded listeners who are prepared to give their earnest attention to musical works outside the range of the familiar. Even then, if such works are presented in the concert hall, they will perhaps hear them only the once. Fortunately for the modern composer, the mass-communication media of the radio and the record make it possible for such works to be heard on more than one occasion. It is through repetition that music written in a less familiar idiom is allowed to make itself better known.

If the reader finds some of the foregoing arguments inconclusive, even false, it may pay him to ponder over the rashly false judgements mentioned in the section of this book marked MUSIC CRITICISM.

It is safe to say that not all music written during the present century will stand up to the test of time; one wonders how many musical works written in former times, some perhaps by highly respected composers, have failed to survive, because they lacked that intangible quality of durability.

But it is time for us to consider modern music in more specific detail, and if we give more space to musical composition of our own time it is because it is less understood than that of previous periods.

Over the centuries Western music has continually created new values. It is a comforting thought that art in all its forms refuses to remain static; that composers, writers and artists of all ages have felt the urge to express the spirit of their times.

Towards the end of the nineteenth century the cult of an over-romanticised Wagnerism, and effusions of excessive emotionalism reached a breaking-point. Then, about the turn of the century, a reaction followed, finding composers ready to explore other territories and to create music that was restrained. This switch from stock patterns of sentimentality and turgid romanticism spread to other forms of creative effort; to novels, plays, ballet, painting, and the plastic arts.

One of the most frequently mentioned of "modern" composers is the Austrian-born Arnold Schoenberg. At the age of twenty-five his creative impulses were still throbbing under the influence of post-Wagnerian romanticism. It was at that time (1899) that he composed his tone-poem *Verklärte Nacht* (*Transfigured Night*), first as a string sextet (thereby carrying the plan of the tone-poem into the realm of chamber music), obviously strongly influenced by Wagner's *Tristan and Isolde*. A wide gulf exists between this flagrantly sentimental (though haunting) work and the later music of Schoenberg, whose excursions into atonality and his adoption of the twelve-note method at first brought abuse about his head. He was later to have a widespread influence on musical thinking.

By that time twentieth century music had already taken on new dimensions, new harmonic textures, greater rhythmic flexibility, and, to those brought up on formal harmonies, new sounds. Many self-appointed critics complained that it "wasn't music" (whatever that means), just as people complained that a picture "wasn't art" because it diverted from long-established formulae, or was different from the styles of Rembrandt or Reynolds, or the picture on the Christmas calendar.

Criticism of modern music often finds its loudest clamour where knowledge and experience of it is least to be found. Just as a person whose literary appreciation has extended no further than Enid Blyton would find even a novel by one of the lighter authors "hard going," so a person, brought up on formal, hymn-tune harmonies and melodies of the Rubinstein *Melodie in F* kind would be inclined to protest against elasticity of melodic, harmonic, and rhythmic patterns that are outside his limited perspective.

Modern music is not entirely new; it is an extension of the past, for all periods in music overlap. Every composer, no matter in what age, has derived something from what has gone before; even when striking out on his own in some form of advanced technique, he acknowledges allegiance to some branch of musical heritage. In any age the advanced of today may become the commonplace of tomorrow. No doubt it is true that in music, as in painting, there are some experimenters who express themselves in violent and illogical terms without saying anything new, but Time has a habit of rejecting the spurious and retaining the genuine.

During this century composers have explored the once-suspect regions of dissonance, that is, harmonies that had been considered dissonant, but over the years the listener's ear has come to accept these without flinching. By their use of dissonance, giving greater variety and new *sound* to their compositions, such composers as Schoenberg, Hindemith, and Bartók, to name only three, have established tonalities that are no longer rejected by the attentive and trained ear.

As far back as 1913 Igor Stravinsky broke through the barrier of long established

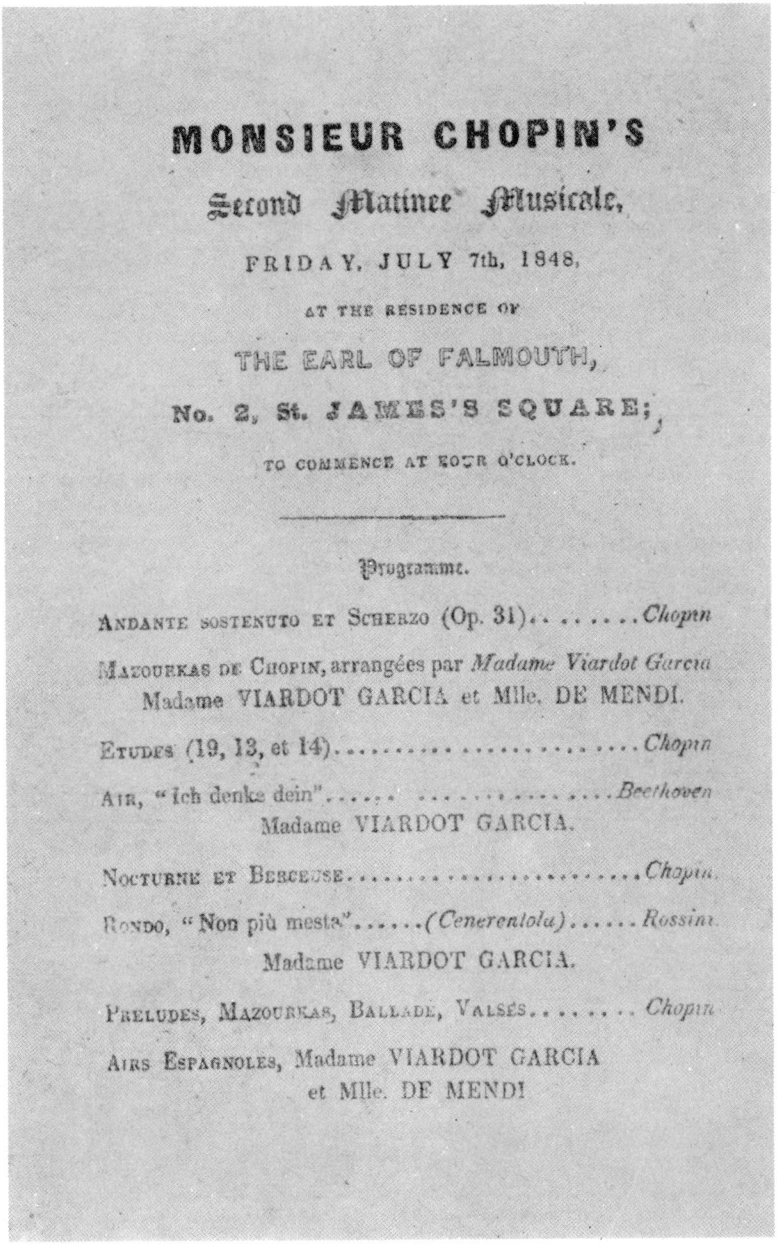

MONSIEUR CHOPIN'S

Second Matinée Musicale,

FRIDAY, JULY 7th, 1848,

AT THE RESIDENCE OF

THE EARL OF FALMOUTH,

No. 2, St. JAMES'S SQUARE;

TO COMMENCE AT FOUR O'CLOCK.

Programme.

ANDANTE SOSTENUTO ET SCHERZO (Op. 31).........Chopin

MAZOURKAS DE CHOPIN, arrangées par *Madame Viardot Garcia*
Madame VIARDOT GARCIA et Mlle. DE MENDI.

ETUDES (19, 13, et 14)...................Chopin

AIR, "ich denke dein"...............Beethoven
Madame VIARDOT GARCIA.

NOCTURNE ET BERCEUSE.................Chopin.

RONDO, "Non più mesta"......(*Cenerentola*)......Rossini
Madame VIARDOT GARCIA.

PRELUDES, MAZOURKAS, BALLADE, VALSES........Chopin

AIRS ESPAGNOLES, Madame VIARDOT GARCIA
et Mlle. DE MENDI

Programme of one of Chopin's first recitals in London.

Frédéric François Chopin (1810-1849). Perhaps the world's greatest composer of piano music. His compositions revealed new horizons of brilliance and subtlety.

44

regular metrical accentuation in his music for the ballet *Le Sacre du Printemps* (*The Rite of Spring*), employing such unusual time signatures as 1/8, 5/6, and 11/4 with a definite purpose. The first performance in Paris ended in near-riot. Today recording companies find a steady demand for this work.

Not long ago the author was present at a concert when an *avant garde* composer spoke to the audience about his latest work which that night was being performed for the first time. It had been designed on ultra modern lines. Fortunately, the composer was lucid in his remarks, and the performance began in an atmosphere of somewhat enlightened expectancy. Following the closing bars of the work there was a spontaneous and prolonged ovation. The audience apparently had appreciated, perhaps enjoyed, the experience. I wondered if the reception would have been less enthusiastic if the audience had no previous idea of its structure beyond the few lines in the printed programme, which no doubt only some of the audience had read. In any case, it will be growing familiarity with the music by repeated performances that will decide whether or not it will become a favourite.

Musical composition has explored a great deal of new territory during the last fifty years or so. Some of the more adventurous excursions may have resulted in cerebral works, the appeal of which is denied to the conventional minded listener. Some of it may be worthless, or impermanent, but no matter how revolutionary, the composer and his work are entitled to consideration. Conductors and performers are prepared to study these works and risk the inclusion of the best in their programmes, and record companies are willing to issue these to the general public, even if the financial gain is uncertain. Time, no doubt, will give permanence to the worthy, and the meretricious will meet the doom of ephemera.

It is only natural that some modern music, by imaginative and impressionable composers, should reflect the restless, revolutionary, and violent age in which they have lived. How could they convincingly build musical works on out-moded themes and conventions out of step with the times? The vogue of the offensively sentimental has given way to the headlong rush of realism.

One need only reflect on the changes in pictures and books. The "pretty" pictures that graced the parlour in the first years of the twentieth century have been replaced by abstract designs, not intended to convey any emotional message beyond a stimulus exerted by an arrangement of colour and design. The sentimentalised novels of the nineteen-twenties have retreated before the flood of stories more closely reflecting true-to-life realism; the contrived "happily ever after" ending replaced by a more logical culmination; cardboard types replaced by people. Well-fed music publishers began to feel the demand easing for such *morceaux célèbres* as *The Robin's Return* and songs of *The Rosary* type, and the once venerated cottage piano was being exchanged for a radio set.

Fashions in music, art, and literature were vigorously changing. As the Russian composer Shostakovich has said:

An art rich in content is always closely linked with the discovery of "new" things in life and the indispensable and inevitable search for the means of recording and fixing these new observations and sensations.

There are also cases where modern composers, turning their backs on emotionalism, have gone back not only to older forms (e.g. the *concerto grosso*), but to a lineal style based on economy and purity of line, even though the harmonic treatment may immediately suggest the "contemporary," rather than the "classical." Stravinsky, Prokofiev, Poulenc are three such composers who come readily to mind. In a series of works under the general title *Bachianas Brasileiras*, the South American composer Villa-Lobos attempted to fuse the Brasilian idiom with that of Bach.

The mechanics of music has a scientific foundation; for instance, harmony and dissonance belong to the science of acoustics, the physical basis of sound, on which the art of music rests. To these principles the composer adds his own technique, imagination, and personality. The disciplined composer follows a set of rules, but he may bend or break these in order to create new sounds and structures.

Music has never remained static; it has always undergone gradual, but continuous, change. Groups of notes at one time considered ugly discords are now accepted as concords, the ear having become accustomed to new sounds.

Even in the twentieth century some composers have found the long established musical vocabulary sufficient for the expression of their ideas. On the other hand, composers of a more advanced, more adventurous, school have extended the musical vocabulary, sometimes to a point where the average listener may have difficulty in keeping up with them. This is another case where *conscious listening* must be fully brought into play, with the mind, as well as the ear, willing to come to grips with new harmonies, new melodic lines, and new rhythmic complexities.

There may be, of course, some truth in the charge that some modern music has become intellectualised to the extent that it is meaningless to all but the composer and his intimate circle.

To keep in step with developments in modern musical composition the mind must be kept alert in order to assimilate a new vocabulary and a new syntax. A person whose musical taste has not extended beyond Rubinstein's *Melodie in F* is not likely to find interest in a Brahms sonata. Nor will a person who has advanced no farther than Brahms find attraction in a work by Prokofiev.

MODERN MUSICAL TERMS: In these modern times musicians have brought into use various terms, such as Twelve-Note, Atonality, and Serialism. We will briefly examine some of these.

Atonality: One feature of musical innovation that has made a definite impact on musical thinking in the twentieth century has been the rejection of *tonality* (the observance of a single key) in favour of *atonality* which, in broad terms, means that

46

the music is not cast in any particular key. It also negates the traditional division of harmonic combinations into consonances and dissonances.

Although other composers (e.g., the American Charles Ives) experimented with this system, it was Schoenberg who went farther than any musician of his time to establish atonality, his atonal melodies being based on a system of relationships existing between the twelve notes of the chromatic scale. Schoenberg's use of the Twelve-Note method paved the way for further experiments in sound-combinations.

Twelve-Note: This term refers to a system of composition in which all twelve notes within the octave are treated as equal, as distinct from the major-minor key system with its fixed Tonic.

The Austrian theorist and composer, Josef Matthias Hauer (1883-1959) has been credited with having "invented" the twelve-note system, arriving at his conclusions independently from Schoenberg, with whose name, and those of his pupils, Berg and Webern, the system has been associated.

Polytonality: This means the simultaneous employment of different tonalities in a single harmonic structure. Where only two keys are thus involved, the correct term is *bitonality*.

Serial Technique: Originated by Schoenberg, this technique is to distribute the twelve tones in a series. Once the series has been established, a note cannot be repeated until the other eleven have been played. In other words, no note appears twice consecutively in the series.

Mathematical Music: A technique using computers to calculate the elements of a musical composition.

Musique Concrète (Concrete Music): A technique of "organised" sound, originated in Paris in the late nineteen-forties by Pierre Schaeffer, and carried on by his collaborator, Pierre Henry, and others. By this technique sound could be recorded, electronically mixed, and if desired distorted, then assembled into a time-structure. These sounds were directly recorded from those occurring in everyday life, but subjected to varying degrees of distortion.

Electronic Music: Someone once referred to this as music *by* engineers *for* engineers. Will this in time completely take over traditional music, or will there be a co-existence between the two?

The process of Electronic Music differs from that of Concrete Music in that it begins with laboratory sound, not sounds from outside sources.

One of the most important cultivators of Electronic Music is Karlheinz Stockhausen, a German composer, born in 1928, a pupil of Frank Martin and Olivier Messiaen. He became interested in the concrete music experiments of Pierre Schaeffer and Pierre Henry, but soon found the urge to carry these techniques farther. In 1953 he founded an electronic music studio, one of his principles being that the individual sound be replaced by collective sound. "I wanted," he said, "to transmit sounds from the cosmos, and to do this I had to make them myself."

In 1956 Stockhausen became the first composer to have an electronic diagram (the equivalent of the traditional score) published. He introduced a new style of concert, with such mathematical-like titles as *Mikrophonie 1, Contacts, Squares for Four Orchestras and Choirs, Counterpoint No. 1, Short Waves, Telemusik, Mixtur,* and *Moments for Soprano.*

The first recital of electronic music was given in Cologne in 1954, with works by Herbert Eimert of Germany, Stockhausen, the Belgian Henri Pousseur, the Dutch Henk Badings and the French Pierre Boulez.

In 1970 Stockhausen performed at the World Fair in Japan, and visited other countries, including Australia.

There have been fashions, cults, schools, and systems in modern music — evolutionary, revolutionary, reactionary. Will future audiences look towards a mass of complicated electronic equipment where once an orchestra sat? Will a single unit, by the switching of a knob, emit new sounds to assail or bewitch the ear and mind, where, back in the nineteen-seventies a world-famous soprano, with an accompanist at heel, sang for the thousandth time a song by a composer named Schubert about a trout?

Will musicians have to sell their instruments in order to pay for tuition as engineers? Who at this date can say? We do know that music cannot stay still. Whatever the changes and developments, we can be sure that Radio, itself a modern scientific means of communication, will bring the new sounds into our homes.

NATIONALISM AND MUSIC OF DIFFERENT COUNTRIES

4

BY the middle of the nineteenth century, as another phase of the Romantic movement, composers were finding more and more inspiration in their racial heritage. The time had come to emancipate the music of their countries from the domination of "foreign" concepts and conventions. The moving force behind the "nationalism" of this period was the urgent desire for independence, a condition that in some cases stemmed from political causes.

One of the first countries to raise the banner of nationalism was Russia, which had two rich sources of material as bases of an independent musical repertory, Russian folk-song and the music of the old Russian Church. The composer to champion this cause was Glinka (1804-1857), the "Prophet-Patriot" of Russian music, who submerged Western-European influences by establishing a new national school. Before Glinka, the only secular Russian music had been folk-song. His aim, he said, was to compose music that would make his people "feel at home."

Glinka's first opera, *A Life for a Tsar*, based on incidents of seventeenth century Russian history, was first performed in St Petersburg in 1836. (For political reasons the title has been changed to *Ivan Sussanin*.) His second opera, *Russlan and Ludmilla*, was first performed in 1842.

Glinka's immediate successor was Dargomizhsky (1813-1869), who adopted "nationalist" ideas. The next important link in the chain was Balakirev (1837-1910). His own creative output was comparatively small; he is best remembered as the

Michail Glinka (1804-1857). Acclaimed as the "Father of Russian Music," he united the vigour of Russian folk music with the European classical tradition.

driving force in establishing *Kuchka* (The Five), a group which included Borodin, Cui, Moussorgsky, and Rimsky-Korsakov, all aiming at a Russian nationalist school.

The use of folk-song by "The Five" varied considerably, but the idiom was so deeply ingrained in their musical make-up that it influenced the rhythms and the melodic outlines of almost everything they wrote. Rimsky-Korsakov borrowed more liberally than did his colleagues from actual folk-songs, as well as inventing pseudo folk-melodies.

Tchaikovsky (1840-1893), less ardent in his nationalist patriotism, worked independently and was the first Russian composer to win widespread international recognition. In his music strong Russian influences blend with his individual temperament. Rachmaninov (1873-1943), who had been brought up to regard Tchaikovsky as the greatest of Russian composers, found living under the Soviet regime intolerable, and settled in the United States of America. His style of composition continued to combine the grand and the sorrowful and so his music found universal approval.

Stravinsky, born forty-two years after Tchaikovsky and seventy-eight years after Glinka, and a pupil in his younger days of Rimsky-Korsakov, adopted a definite Russian idiom in his early works, but as something of a cosmopolitan he has frequently changed with the times, his music going through various stages of transition from the romantic and the adventurous to neo-classicism.

50

Bedrich Smetana (1824-1884). One of the greatest Czech composers. His folk opera *The Bartered Bride* and the symphonic cycle *My Fatherland* inspired Czech nationalism.

"Soviet music," says the author Lyudmila Polyakova, "is sometimes spoken of as 'Russian music.' This is not correct, because Soviet Art is the Art of nearly forty nationalities, to say nothing of the smaller national groups."

Glière and Vasilenko were followed by several professional composers who helped to further new national cultures, among these, Vladimir Vlasov, Yevgeny Brusilovsky, and Vladimir Fere. Among the many Armenian and Georgian composers who adopted new trends were, Alexander Spendiarov, Zakhary Paliashvili, Smitri Arakishvili, Armen Tigranyan, and Meliton Balanchivadze.

Prominent in the nineteen-forties and nineteen-fifties were, Herman Galynin, Nikolai Peiko, Kara Karayev, Yury Sviridov, Nazib Zhiganov, Otar Taktakishvili, Alexei Machavariani, and Mikhail Gnesin.

The most universally acknowledged Soviet composers are of course Prokofiev, Shostakovich, Kabalevsky, and Khachaturian.

Other composers who have contributed to the various forms of Russian and Soviet music are: Vissarion Shebalin, Yury Shaporin, Lev Knipper, Ivan Dzerzhinsky, Tikhon Khrennikov, Georgii Sviridov, Boris Asafiev, Grigori Kiladze (Georgian), Moissei Vainberg, Galina Ustvolskaya, Marian Koval, Boris Chaikovsky, and Valery Zhelobinsky.

CZECHOSLOVAKIA: Prague, the capital of the historic kingdom of Bohemia (now Czechoslovakia) can boast a musical history that goes back to the tenth century. During the late Baroque era it was an important centre for church and organ music.

51

Roger Sessions (b. 1896). Contemporary American
composer of four symphonies, concertos, orchestral
and chamber music, and the operas *Montezuma* and
The Trial of Lucullis.

While the influence of its own composers, including Stamitz and Dussek, spread to other parts, Bohemia was ready to extend a welcome to musical performers and composers from other countries. Mozart was a favourite there.

For centuries, however, the Czechs were dominated by Teutonic cultural influences. In 1848 a nationalist rising was crushed by the Austrians, but, like all oppressed people, the Czechs guarded with intense pride their own customs, language, and cultures.

What Glinka had done for Russian music, Smetana (1824-1884) did for the music of his country, becoming the founder of the National School of Modern Czech Music. During his career he became conductor of the Prague National Theatre and established a national school of opera. His most famous work, the opera *The Bartered Bride* was first performed in 1866.

An ardent patriot, Smetana set out to glorify his homeland in a cycle of six symphonic poems under the generic title *Ma Vlast* (*My Fatherland*). These he dedicated to Prague.

Smetana was followed by Dvořák (1841-1904), whose musical interest had been awakened as a boy when he heard the folk-songs of his country played by travelling musicians. A set of thirteen songs for soprano and alto, the *Moravian Duets*, played an important part in his early career. He later wrote in many forms, his music having a

52

Gustav Mahler (1860-1911). A great Czech-Austrian
musician. His symphonies were composed on a vast
scale, but they also contain passages of touching
simplicity.

Schubertian melodic flow, his tunes carrying a rhythmic spontaneity that is always
fascinating.

The pattern of Czech music having been firmly established by Smetana and
Dvořák, it was adopted by other composers, including Zdeněk Fibich (1850-1900),
Leoš Janáček (1854-1928), Josef Foerster (1859-1951), Vítézslav Novák (1870-
(1949), a pupil of Dvořák, Josef Suk (1874-1935), a pupil and son-in-law of Dvořák,
Otakar Ostrčil (1879-1935), Jaroslav Kvapil (b. 1892), Otakar Jeremiaš (b. 1892),
a pupil of Novák, and Bohuslav Martinů (1890-1959), a pupil of Suk. For some years
resident in France and the United States, Martinů struck out on an idiomatic path
of his own.

Some of the more noteworthy Czech composers born during the twentieth century
include: Isa Krejčí, Emil Burian, Jan Novak, Pavel Bořkovec, Jaroslav Rídký,
Václav Trojan, Jan Kapr, Jan Hanuš, Jří Pauer, Jaroslav Doubrava, Zdeněk
Blazek, Miloslav Kabeláč, Jan Rychlík, Vladimir Sommer.

HUNGARY: During the nineteenth century Franz Liszt was generally looked
upon as Hungary's most important musician; he was the greatest pianist of his age
and a prolific composer in many forms and styles. His *Hungarian Rhapsodies* became
world-famous. Every virtuoso who followed him played them; every piano student
aspired to.

Edvard Grieg (1843-1902). His delicate scene painting vividly expresses the spirit of Norway, and strongly influenced the impressionist composers such as Delius.

For many years these *Rhapsodies* were thought to have derived from Magyar origins and from the tunes of Hungarian gipsies. After Bartók and Kodály had exhaustively studied the traditional music of their country, it was discovered that Liszt had been influenced by obscure composers and by gipsy versions of melodies belonging to other countries.

About the year 1905 the Hungarian composer Zoltán Kodály (1882-1967) began collecting genuine folk-songs of Hungary, and some time later he was joined in the search by Béla Bartók (1881-1945), the partnership resulting in their collection of almost 4,000 folk melodies which they classified in detail. Much of the other music of these composers was strongly influenced by the Hungarian native idiom.

Among the contemporaries of Bartók and Kodály and later Hungarian composers, the following must be mentioned: Sándor Veress, Mátyás Sieber, Géza Frid, Carl Goldmark, Leo Eeiner, László Lajtha, Ernst von Dohnányi. Those born in the twentieth century include: Lajos Bárdos, Zsolt Durko, Ferenc Szabó, Jenö Kenesey, János Viski, Reysö Kókai, György Ligeti, Tibor Sárai, András Mihály, Pál Járdányi.

NORWAY: Before the nineteenth century the great writers of Norway were better known to the outer world than its composers. Richard Nordraak, who lived for only twenty-four years (1842-1866) exerted a great influence on Edvard Grieg (1843-1907) in the direction of a Norwegian national style of music. It was Grieg who brought to the attention of the world the wealth of Norwegian folk-song, an idiom that he combined with his own melodic invention.

54

Franz Liszt (1811-1886). Considered the greatest pianist of his time, he was also a composer of great importance. He "invented" the symphonic poem to express in music literary themes.

Above: The town band of Salem, Massachusetts, dresses up in eighteenth-century costume during each Christmas season and parades through the town, playing Christmas carols through the streets.

Below: This fine example of one of the earliest Broadwood pianos, now in the possession of the Art Gallery of South Australia, shows the transitory period from the spinet and harpsichord to the grand piano of today.

Johann Halvorsen, whose works were strongly influenced by Grieg, married Grieg's niece.

Grieg's contemporary, Johan Svendsen, studied in Leipzig and was for a time associated with Liszt and Wagner, but left works of distinct Norwegian flavour. Among Norway's composers born towards the end of the nineteenth century and in the twentieth century are: Fartein Valen, Harald Saeverud, Klauss Egge, Ludvig Jensen, Sparre Olsen, Arne Nordheim, Knut Nystedt.

SWEDEN: Like most countries, Sweden has imbibed influences from neighbouring parts, while preserving its own musical culture. Festivals, radio, and the record have made known the work of such Swedish composers as Karl-Birger Blomdahl, Hilding Rosenberg, Sven-Erik Bäck, Hugo Alfvén, Ingvar Lidholm, Lars Erik Larsson, Bengt Hambraeus, Emil Sjögren, Ture Rangström, Bo Nilsson, Jan Carlstedt, Hans Edlund, Maurice Karkoff and Vilhelm Stenhammer.

DENMARK: One of the most widely known Danish composers of his time was Niels Gade (1817-1890) who composed music flavoured by the cadences of Scandinavian folk-song, although some of his writing contained more of "Mendelssohnianism" (as Grieg called it), than true national characteristics. Denmark was to find its greatest composer in Carl Nielsen (1865-1931) who wrote with outstanding purpose and skill in almost every musical form.

Early in his career, Nielsen was encouraged in his musical studies by Gade. He was to exert a powerful influence upon the musical thinking of his time and upon composers who came afterwards.

With Nielsen as the point of departure from traditional "moderation," other Danish composers continued to bring credit to their country; to name some of these, Poul Schierbeck, Knud Jeppesen, Knudåge Riisager, Jørgen Bentzon, Vagn Holmboe, Finn Høffding, Herman Koppel, Svend Erik Tarp, Rued Langgaard, Poul Rovsing Olsen, Svend Schultz, Ebbe Hamerik, Kjell Roikjer, Erik Jorgensen. Tage Nielsen, Per Norgaard, Ib Nørholm, Flemming Weis, Bernhard Lewkovitch, Leif Kayser, Niels Viggo Bentzon, Jorgen Jersild, Jan Maegaard, Axel Borup-Jorgensen, Pelle Gudmundsen-Holmgreen, Gunnar Berg, Else Marie Pade, Jorgen Plaetner, and Leif Thybo.

FINLAND: Sibelius (1865-1957), a national figure, refused to be gripped by the tentacles of "schools" and "coteries." He adapted to his use whatever technical devices he considered appropriate to express his ideas, and while there are elements in his writing in common with the folk-music of Finland, he at no time used a tune not of his own creation. His national pride found outlet in his affinity with the legends of his country, and so we find in his orchestral tone poems repeated references to the *Kalevala*, the epic of Finnish mythology. An American writer once said, "Sibelius has translated the *Kalevala* into the universal of music."

Sibelius composed little during his later years. By the time of his death, younger Finnish composers had forged ahead on individual lines; among them Tauno

Jean Sibelius (1865-1957). One of the world's greatest symphonists. His compositions, highly personal in style, breathe with the cold harsh beauty of Finland.

Pylkkänen, Ahti Sonninen, Nils-Eric Fougstedt, Einojuhani Rautavaara, and Aulis Sallinin. Selim Palmgren (1878-1951) has left some charming works, many of nationalist significance.

POLAND: The most important musical figure of nineteenth century Poland was Moniuszko (1820-1872), who composed a great deal of church music, as well as other works, including operas, in a Romantic style regarded as "national."

Poland's most universally recognised composer is, of course, Chopin (1810-1849) who, although a Polish patriot at heart, spent much of his life in Paris. While his music is indebted to the Polish idiom, his own unmistakable style is evident in everything that he wrote. Even to the two Polish dance forms, the mazurka and the polonaise, he added his own blend of spirit and colour.

Today Poland owes a considerable debt to Karol Szymanowski (1882-1937). After studying in Berlin he was for a time influenced by Richard Strauss and Debussy, then developed a style that at times carried overtones of Polish folk-music, but a style that bridged the gap between the works of Karlowicz, Rózycki and their contemporaries and those of more forward-thinking composers.

Some of the most prominent Polish composers of the twentieth century are: Józef Koffler, Roman Palester, Artur Malawski, Andrzej Panufnik, Grazyna Bacewicz, Witold Rudzinski, Michal Spisak, Witold Lutoslawski, Boguslaw Schaffer, Witold Szalonek, Wojciech Kilar, Henryk Górecki, Krzysztof Penderecki, Tadeusz Kassern, Karol Rathaus (b. 1895), Stanislaw Wiechowicz (b. 1893), and Zygmunt Mycielski.

56

NETHERLANDS: In the early fifteenth century the Netherlands played an important part in the development of European music. Three of the outstanding composers of that time were Guillaume Dufay, Johannes Ockeghem, and Jacob Obrecht. Prominent in the first part of the sixteenth century were Josquin des Préz (Després), Nicolas Gombert, and Adriaan Willaert.

As the sixteenth century moved on, dances and secular songs took their place alongside church music by Dutch composers. A Dutch composer who was to make a lasting impact was Jan Pieterszoon Sweelinck. He was followed during the next two hundred years or so by such worthy creative musicians as Quirinus Gerbrandt van Blanckenburg, Carel Rosier, Antonio Mahaut, Pieter Hellendaal, Albertus Groneman, Hendrik Anders, Anton Berlijn, Richard Hol, Bernard Zweers, Alphons Diepenbrock, Johan Wagenaar, Cornelius Dopper, Jan van Gilse, Bernhard van den Sigtenhorst, Henri Zagwijn, Matthias Vermeulen, Daniël Ruyneman, Sem Dresden, Hendrik Andriessen, and Willem Pijper (1894-1947), who influenced many of the younger Dutch musicians of his day.

After the first World War there emerged in Holland several composers of the "modern" school who combined in forming the *Society for Modern Creative Music*. Among the leaders of this movement were Henri Zagwijn, Matthias Vermeulen, Daniël Ruyneham, and Sam Dresden.

Dutch composers born in the generation before 1900 included several women: Dina Appledoorn, Henriëtte van Keukelom-van den Brandeler, Bertha Frensel Wegener-Koopman, Johanna Bordewijk-Roepman, Henriëtte Bosmans.

Prominent Dutch composers born since 1902 include: Karel Mengelberg, Piet Ketting, Guillaume Landré, Bertus van Lier, Kees van Baaren, Henk Badings, Saar Bessem, Rudolf Escher, Hans Henkemans, Willem van Otterloo, Jan Felderhof, Cor de Groot, Herman Strategier, Albert de Klerk, Léon Orthel, Robert de Roos, Koos van de Griend, Hans Osieck, Marius Flothuis.

The following are the names of some of the Netherlands composers born later than 1922: Jaap Geraedts, Jurriaan Andriessen, Ton de Leeuw, Hans Kox, Otto Ketting.

BELGIUM: According to Jean-Marie Andrieu, the earliest musical document still in existence dates back to A.D. 814. This, the *Planctus Karoli*, a plaintive ballad, is thought to have been composed by Columban, the Abbot of Sint-Truiden on the death of Charlemagne.

Other music, chiefly liturgical and Gregorian chants, were known before that, particularly in the Liége region. Further developments were advanced by Léonin and Pérotin, and between the end of the fourteenth century and the middle of the fifteenth century, Belgian musicians carried their new theories to Italy.

Before the seventeenth century the only music written was for liturgical use; after that songs and dances were written for aristocratic courts, also for various festivals. The artistic revival of the fifteenth century—the first era of the Burgundian Period—was localised in that area now covered by northern France, the southern

Netherlands, Belgium, and the Grand Duchy of Luxemburg. It was the age of such great musicians as Binchois, Dufay, Ockeghem, Obrecht, Josquin des Prés, who were to be followed in the sixteenth century by Willaert, Lassus, and Monte. The time had come for polyphony to replace monody.

Music continued to develop via the works of such composers as Henry Dumont (1610-1684), François-Joseph Gossec (1734-1829), André Grétry (1741-1813) and others up to the time of César Franck (1822-1890), who, although born at Liége, settled in Paris in 1844. As mentioned in the section under France, César Franck's influence extended to many important French composers, also to the Belgian, Guillaume Lekeu.

The list of other notable Belgian-born composers includes: Peter Benoit (1834-1901), Jan Blockx (1851-1912), Lodewijk Mortelmans (1868-1952), Charles-Auguste de Bériot (1802-1870), Paul Gilson (1865-1942), Samuel Holeman (1863-1942), and Désiré Paque (1867-1939). Equally notable among the Flemish and Walloon composers of the late nineteenth and the twentieth centuries are: Flor Alpaerts (1876-1954), Arthur Meulemans (b. 1884), Robert Herberigs (b. 1886), Michel Brusselmans (1886-1960), Henri Sarly (1885-1947), Alex de Taye (1898-1953), Georges Monier (b. 1892), André Collin (b. 1898), Joseph Jongen (1873-1953), Theo de Joncker (b. 1894), Charles Hens (b. 1898), Raymond Moulaert (1875-1962), François Basse (1873-1954), Armand Marsick (1877-1959), Francis de Bourguignon (1890-1961).

Among the Belgian composers born in the late nineteenth century and the twentieth century, some of whom have ventured into polytonality, atonality, and other advanced techniques, may be mentioned: Gaston Brenta (b. 1902), Jean Absil (b. 1893), Fernand Quinet (b. 1898), Auguste Baeyens (1895), Gérard Bertouille (b. 1898), Jacques Stehman (b. 1912), Marcel Poot (b. 1901), Raymond Chevreuille (b. 1901), Victor Legley (b. 1915), Jean Louël (b. 1914), Louis de Meester (b. 1908), Jef van Durme (b. 1907), Karel Goeyvaerts (b. 1923), Henri Pousseur (b. 1929), and Camille Schmit (b. 1908).

SWITZERLAND: The stream of Swiss music has moved in several directions, according to the variety of regions of that country. Despite the relatively small size of many Swiss cities and towns, but because of their economic security, time and money have been found for the encouragement of music.

Choral singing is a rich tradition in Switzerland; in fact, the first musical organisation in that country was in this association, this being the Schweizerische Musikgesellschaft, founded in 1808 by Hans Georg Nägeli, publisher and composer, born at Zürich, who published some of Beethoven's works.

In the early part of this century the musical world became aware of the far-reaching influence of such composers as Arthur Honegger, Frank Martin, and Othmar Schoeck. Other names became known: Albert Moeschinger, Walther Geiser, Wladimir Vogel, Paul Müller, Walter Müller von Kulm, Hans Haug,

Samuel Barber (b. 1910). American composer of
symphonies, operas, and orchestral works. The
Adagio for Strings, taken from a string quartet, is his
most famous composition.

Conrad Beck, Adolf Brunner, Volkmar Andreae, Robert Oboussier, Willy·
Burkhardt.

Composers of the French area include Heinrich Sutermeister, Rolf Liebermann,
Robert Suter, Klaus Huber, Rudolf Kelterborn, and Heinz Holliger.

FRANCE: With a long musical heritage, France had less need than many other
countries to liberate her music from foreign influences. She had always shown an
individualistic approach to art. What did happen, however, was a renaissance in
the nineteenth century that had national ideals as its basis, after these had been for
some time submerged in a flood of "popular" works for the stage.

The formation of the *Société Nationale de Musique* (National Music Society) was
"to aid the production and popularization of serious music by French composers."
Prominent in the rebirth of French music were Saint-Saëns, and César Franck, the
latter a Belgian by birth but a naturalised citizen from 1873. Also taking part in this
revival were Berlioz, Lalo, Fauré, and Massenet. Franck's teaching spread to his
devoted pupils, d'Indy, Chausson, Pierné, Duparc, and Lekeu. Debussy and Ravel
were to map out paths for themselves.

Since the end of the second World War French composers have revealed to a
steadily growing audience their musical independence. Prominent in this way are
Pierre Boulez and Olivier Messiaen who have exerted a particularly wide influence.
Others upholding modern French ideals include: Michel Fano, Jean-Louis

Martinet, Serge Nigg, André Hodeir, Jean Barraqué (pupils of Messiaen); Henri Barraud, Robert Casadesus, André Casanova, Jean-Michel Damase, Henri Dutilleux, Antoine Duhamel, Maurice Le Roux, Maurice Ohana, Jean Françaix, Tony Aubin, Georges Migot, Manual Rosenthal, Jean Rivier, Henri Tomasi, André Jolivet, also *The Six* comprising Georges Auric, Louis Durey, Arthur Honegger, Darius Milhaud, Francis Poulenc, and Germaine Tailleferre.

SPAIN: Felipe Pedrell (1841-1922) musicologist and composer, holds a significant place in the history of Spanish music. His folk-lore studies led him to a true assessment of Spain's musical heritage and through his stimulus a national school came into being.

Pedrell's followers were Isaac Albéniz (1860-1909), Enrique Granados (1867-1916), Manuel de Falla (1876-1946), Joaquín Nin (1879-1949), and Joaquín Turina (1882-1949).

The year 1958 saw the formation of the *Grupo Nueva Música*. The aims of this group —to rid Spanish music of superficial elements and to examine the best of contemporary music in other countries—were strengthened by its director, Fernando Ruiz Coca, who had studied modern musical trends in Central Europe.

Since 1958, therefore, the younger generation of Spanish composers have received practical encouragement; to mention some of these: Cristobel Halffter, Luis de Pablo, Gerardo Gombau, Ramón Barce, Manuel Carra, Enrique Franco, José Maria Mestres, Juan Hidalgo, José Cercós, Xavier Benguerel, Carmelo Bernaola and Miguel Coria.

Federico Moreno Torroba (b. 1891) has made valuable additions to the classical guitar repertoire.

PORTUGAL: During the last fifty years Portuguese music has emerged from the restriction of Italian, French, and German influences. Very little had been borrowed from Spain. Today the Portuguese Government provides considerable encouragement to native composers.

The late José Viana da Mota, who was born in 1868, has been called the father of modern Portuguese music. He was worthily followed by Luis de Freitas Branco (1890-1955). Other composers of this country born at the end of the nineteenth century or early in the twentieth are: Claudio Carneyro, Ruy Coelho, Ivo Cruz (born in Brazil), Frederico de Freitas, Fernando Lopes Graça, Armando Fernandes, Jorge Croner de Vasconcelos, Joly Santos, Filipe Pires, and Fernando Oliveira.

ITALY: As we have noted in another chapter of this book, Italy was the cradle of opera. Folk-song, too, played its part in earlier Italian music; thus the music of the provinces took on a character of its own. Over the centuries, Italy, while giving so much to the musical world, has absorbed outside influences and has adopted styles of composition of various "schools."

While not forgetting her Bellinis, Vivaldis, and Verdis, Italy saw fit to encourage such of her composers as Ottorino Respighi, a pupil of the Russian Rimsky-Korsakov,

Béla Bartók (1881-1945). One of the most original twentieth century composers, he explored new dimensions of music and has greatly influenced modern composers.

Alfredo Casella, a pupil of the French Fauré, Ildebrando Pizzetti, Luciano Chailly, and others of the twentieth century.

Among the Italian twelve-tone practitioners we find: Luigi Dallapiccola, Luigi Nono, Riccardo Nielsen, Luciano Berio, a pupil of Dallapiccola, Bruno Maderna, Franco Donatoni, Antonio Veretti, Niccoló Castiglioni. Camillo Togni, a pupil of Casella, is said to have composed the first serial score in Italy.

AMERICA: If we take "nationalism" to mean a composer's use of his nation's folk-idiom, we might hesitate to place the music of the United States in a "school"; not only is that country's history shorter than that of many others, but a larger geographical area has given it a wider variety of cultural aims.

The words of Edward MacDowell (1861-1908) are worth quoting:

> What we must arrive at is the youthful optimistic vitality and the undaunted tenacity of spirit that characterises the American man. That is what I hope to see echoed in American music.

Though less than two centuries old, American-composed music *is* vital, and rich in invention and variety. It is therefore surprising that, considering the widespread and constant flow of America's products, including its literature, films, Broadway musical shows, "pop" music, its speech patterns, customs, cars, and so on, comparatively little of its serious music reaches other English speaking countries.

61

Aaron Copland (b. 1900). Distinguished American composer. His compositions such as *Appalachian Spring* and *Rodeo* abound with rhythmic vitality and orchestral colour.

Mainly through sporadic records from the more adventurous record distributors is it heard outside the region of its origin.

Since the late nineteen-thirties, and with the extension of mass media communication; e.g., radio, records, films, television, composers have found both a new stimulus and a wider audience within the United States.

The best known of the eighteenth century American composers was Francis Hopkinson (1737-1791). He was an amateur musician, a lawyer, a writer, a statesman, a signatory to the Declaration of Independence, and one of the framers of the Constitution. His song *My Days Have Been So Wondrous Fair* is said to have been the first published composition by a native-born American.

Another link in the development of American music was William Billings (1746-1800), a tanner by trade, who gained most of his musical knowledge from the hymn books of his day. Billings is known especially for his "fuguing pieces," in which he treated hymn tunes contrapuntally.

After the Civil War there was renewed musical activity, though most of the composers had studied in Germany, returning to the United States to write in the style of Mendelssohn or Schumann.

It was the Czech composer Dvořák who, while director of the National Conservatorium in New York from 1892 to 1895, urged the students to "Stop trying to compose like Europeans. Learn to stand on your own feet."

As composer, administrator, lecturer, and conductor, Aaron Copland (b. 1900)

62

Virgil Thompson (b. 1896). The "Elder Statesman" of American music, he has composed in all forms, including operas, symphonies, ballets, concertos, and film scores.

holds a position of honour in American music; it has been his chief aim to find the "American voice" in music.

Among Copland's contemporaries we can first mention: Roy Harris, William Schuman, Virgil Thompson, Walter Piston, Roger Sessions, Howard Hanson, Carl Ruggles, Bernard Rogers, Douglas Moore, Wallingford Riegger, Henry Cowell.

Following close on the heels of these came: Samuel Barber, William Bergsma, Peter Mennin, Elliott Carter, John Cage, Marc Blitzstein, Hugo Weisgall, Leonard Bernstein, Harold Shapiro, Leon Kirchner, Norman Dello Joio, Ben Weber, Paul Frederick Bowles, Lukas Foss, David Diamond, Herbert Haufreucht, Gail Kubik, Robert Moevs, Vincent Persichetti, Paul Creston, Roger Goeb, Lou Harrison, Robert Palmer, Robert Ward, Christian Wolff, Marton Feldman, Earle Brown, Ross Finney, Roger Reynolds, and the Italian born Gian-Carlo Menotti.

In Charles Ives (1874-1954) we find one of the most interesting, if unconventional, figures in American music. He invented his own rules and, to some extent, anticipated methods adopted by Schoenberg and other later composers.

Many of the American composers mentioned above studied in Europe. The style and range of their compositions move over a wide area, from the traditional to the *avant-garde*. Many are based on home-grown subjects, even if the allegiance to straight-out "nationalism" may not always be obvious.

The basing of operas on the folk-idiom, and on the American way of life, is found

63

César Franck (1822-18Su). Great Belgian composer, organist, and teacher. His works include the inspiring cantata *The Redemption, Symphonic Variations,* and symphony in D minor.

in such works as Kurt Weill's *Down in the Valley,* in which folk-songs mingle with "composed" songs in the same style. American legend and history supplied the basis for *The Ballad of Baby Doe* and *The Devil and Daniel Webster* by Douglas Moore. In his *Porgy and Bess,* sometimes with a certain licence called a folk-opera, George Gershwin made no direct use of Negro folk-songs, although a style borrowed from Negro spirituals and jazz coloured much of the music.

Perhaps the most universally known American composer is Stephen Foster. He composed songs; simple songs, yes, but they made millions of people aware of the musical voice of America before that country's most important composers were born.

ENGLAND: The word Nationalism if applied to British music would not mean quite the same thing as it would in association with, say, Russian or Czech music.

Though national characteristics have stamped themselves on the music of composers of most countries, there is a borderland between the indigenous and the applied. A composer of one country may write in the style of another without succeeding completely in the use of the basic elements. Cross-pollination, too, has played its part in varying degrees in the creation of musical works.

England has a rich musical heritage. The Tudor period, for example, was particularly fortunate in its composers, e.g., Fayrfax, Tye, Whyte, Tallis, Byrd, Morley, Gibbons, Wilbye, to name only some of these.

After the death of Henry Purcell in 1695 the glory of English music faded. The renaissance came with Sir Edward Elgar (1857-1934) who carried on classic traditions and spurred others into producing works of lasting importance. Ralph Vaughan Williams (1872-1958) awakened a continuing interest in British folk-song. Elgar, on the other hand, though he did write marches of circumstantial pomp belonging to a blatantly patriotic era, made little use, if any, of folk-tunes. Yet his music is considered essentially English, even if some musicologists have found a Teutonic sturdiness in his symphonies. With such composers as Bax and Ireland an idiom evolved from spirit of place.

The list of British composers of the twentieth century is a long one. The following names are drawn from this imposing list: Benjamin Britten, Sir William Walton, Michael Tippett, Lennox Berkeley, Alan Rawsthorne, Edmund Rubbra, Richard Rodney Bennett, Peter Racine Fricker, Malcolm Arnold, Peter Maxwell Davies, Nicholas Maw, Julius Harrison (b. 1885), Sir Arthur Bliss (b. 1891), Harrison Birtwistle, John Ireland (b. 1879), Sir Arnold Bax (b. 1883), Stanley Bate, Brian Easdale, Granville Bantock (b. 1868), Christopher Edmunds (b. 1899), Richard Hall, Hugh Wood, Ralph Walter Wood, Thomas Wood (b. 1892), Haydn Wood (b. 1882), William Alwyn, Michael Head, Elizabeth Maconchy, Elizabeth Lutyens, Pamela Harrison, Richard Arnell, Francis Burt, Alan Bush, Gerald Finzi, Geoffrey Bush, Easthope Martin, Alexander Goehr, Gustav Holst (b. 1874), Wilfred Mellers, Humphrey Searle, Arthur Oldham, Roger Smalley, Thea Musgrave (born Scotland), Iain Hamilton (born Scotland), Robert Crawford (born Scotland), Anthony Miler, Robert Simpson, Anthony Hopkins, Richard Arnell, Constant Lambert, Peter Warlock (Philip Heseltine), Frank Bridge (b. 1879), Cyril Scott (1879-1971), Havergal Brian (b. 1876), James Stevens, and Gordon Crosse.

CANADA: Records show that musical interest in Canada dates back to that country's discovery and its colonisation by the French. Among the early compositions preserved is a seventeenth century setting in plain chant of *Sainte-Famille*, written about 1670 by Abbé Charles-Amador Martin.

Little information exists concerning music written in the eighteenth century, but by the middle of the nineteenth century there were healthy signs of musical life, with the growth of cultural organisations, the spread of concerts, and the increase of teachers and instrument makers.

From then, Canadian music went through phases of European imitation, French impressionism, modernistic tendencies, also the production of works inspired by Canadian history and its modern life.

Since the nineteen-forties creative music in Canada has taken a vital upward surge with the older composers creating new works, and many younger musicians making an impact by having their compositions performed, not only locally, but in other parts of the world. It is also interesting to note that many women's names have prominence in the lists of composers writing large-scale works.

Listed here are some of the notable Canadian composers born during the twentieth century: Murray Adaskin, Louis Applebaum, Violet Archer, Roy Alexander Angus, John Beckwith, Maurice Blackburn, Alexander Brott, Robert Barclay, Louis Bédard, Felix R. Bertrand, Lorne M. Betts, Maurice Boivin, Lydia Boucher, Adrian Butler, Marius Benoist (b. 1896), Claude Champagne (b. 1891), Jean Coulthard, Hugh Davidson, Maurice Dela, Marvin Duchow, Robert Farnon, Gordon Fleming, Harry Freedman, John Fenwick, Robert Fleming, Serge Garant, Phyllis Gummer, Lewis Hill, Kelsey Jones, Morris Kates, Lucienne Lafleur, Roger Matton, Pierre Morel, William McCauley, Fraser Macdonald, Paul McCaughan, Bernard Naylor, Barbara Pentland, Jean Papineau-Couture, Clermont Pépin, Michel Perrault, Maurice Rosseau, Eldon Rathburn, Godfrey Ridout, Joseph Roff, Georges Savaria, Harry Somers, Norman Symonds, Robert Turner, Arnold Walter, John Weinzweig, Healey Willan, Charles Wilson.

SOUTH AFRICA: It is known that interest in serious music in South Africa goes back for more than three centuries; that its folk-dance music is as varied as the peoples of that wide country. The creative aspect did not come into full flower until the twentieth century. Gradually composers mapped out clear-cut lines on which to base their works. Symphony orchestras expanded and universities established faculties of music.

Many South African composers, after initial training in local music organisations, went for further study to England, France, Austria, Holland, and the United States of America, notably Priaulx Rainier, John Joubert, Stefans Grové, Arnold van Wyk, and Hubert du Plessis.

Other well-known composers of South Africa are: William Henry Bell, Reuben Tholakele Caluza, Dawid Engela, Gideon Fagan, Blanche Gerstman, Rosa Nepgen, Percival R. Kirby, Peter Klatzow, Michael Moerane, Joshua Polumo Mohapeloa, Graham Newcater, Stephen O'Reilly, Benjamin Peter Tyamzashe, Cromwell Everson, Stanley Glasser and Carl van Wyk.

These are finding recognition for their works.

AUSTRALIA: Compared with other countries mentioned, Australia is a young nation, and while its music has had less time to develop a distinctive personality, great strides have been taken in the creative arts during the last half-century. In that period it has absorbed the best of European and Asian traditions, at the same time forming an individual style in musical expression, even to the point where its most adventurous composers have adopted daring *avant-garde* techniques.

The names of some of the many Australian composers whose works have reached widespread audiences are mentioned in this book in the sections on opera, symphony, and other kinds of music.

During recent years much research has been carried out in the study of Australian Aboriginal music. This has resulted in historical facts, and musical chants and songs associated with various ceremonies and activities being brought to light by anthropologists and ethno-musicologists.

66

Arnold van Wyk (b. 1916). A South African composer who studied in London, he has written symphonies, a *Christmas Cantata*, and the song-cycle *Of Love and Forsakeness*.

NEW ZEALAND: In the first half of the nineteenth century New Zealand's colonists brought with them from Britain musical concepts and patterns. In time, teachers and practising musicians from Britain and Europe joined with New Zealand-trained musicians in nourishing the growth of home-grown musical projects.

Many became more acutely aware of the heritage of Maori music, and in recent years successful attempts have been made to establish archives of Maori and Pacific Islands music.

Today New Zealand is rich in creative musicians and many of their works have gained recognition from performances overseas. Among such composers may be mentioned: Douglas Lilburn, David Farquhar, Ronald Tremain, Jenny McLeod, Larry Pruden, John Ritchie, Edwin Carr, Ashley Heenan, Dorothea Franchi, Vernon Griffiths, Richard Hoffmann, Robert Burch, Robin Maconie, and Gillian Whitehead.

OTHER COUNTRIES: In this chapter we have spoken briefly on Nationalism and music in various countries. Throughout the whole world there is today, perhaps more than ever, widespread musical activity.

In other sections of this book much has been said in relation to *German* music over the centuries. In addition to the historic names, we can add: Boris Blacher, Hugo Distler, Werner Egk, Wolfgang Fortner, Harold Genzmer, Karl Amadeus Hartmann, Hermann Reuter, Hans Werner Henze, Joseph Haas, Joseph Ahrens, Hermann Schroeder, Max Baumann, Helmut Bornefeld, Günther Raphael,

67

Giselher Klebe, Karlheinz Stockhausen, Carl Orff, Rudolf Wagner-Régeny, Paul Dessau, Hanns Eisler, Ottmar Gerster, Günter Bialas, Ernst Pepping, Johann David, Siegfried Borris, Karl Höller, Kurt Hassenberg, Johannes Driessler, Jürg Bauer, Reinhold Finkbeiner, Friedrich Voss, Heinz Werner Zimmermann, Winifred Zillig, Fritz Büchtger, Bernd Alois Zimmermann, and Rudolf Kelterborn.

From the eighteenth century, that is from the time of Haydn and Mozart, *Austria* has upheld its musical traditions. We have only to think of Arnold Schoenberg, Alban Berg, Anton Webern, and the Bohemian-born Austrian composer Gustav Mahler, who gave musical expression new meaning.

Between the two World Wars German romanticism was kept in mind by Erich Korngold, Wilhelm, Julius Bittner and others, while Austrian Romanticism had one of its last adherents in Franz Schmidt. Franz Schreker kept near to the traditional, while his pupil Ernst Krenek ventured into the twelve-tone system and electronic music.

Among the many Austrian-born composers active during this century, some of whom have settled in other countries, are Egon Wellesz, Hans Erich Apostel, Ernst Toch, Joseph Polnauer, Heinz Füssl, Michael Gielen, Friedrich Cerha, Kurt Schwertsik, György Ligeti, Josef Hauer, Anton Heiller, Paul Angerer, Gottfried von Einem, Theodor Berger, Wohann David, Michael Rubin, Fritz Streicher, Karl Schiske, Alfred Prinz, Alfred Peschek, Fritz Leitermeyer, Robert Stolz.

One of the best-remembered composers of *Rumania* is Georges Enesco (1881-1955), whose influence has continued up to the present time. Some of the more prominent composers who have contributed towards Rumanian music are: Alfred Mendelson, Tiberiu Brediceanu, Constantin Brailoiu, Theodor Rogalski, Alexander Boscovich, Martian Negrea, Alfred Alessandrescu, Mihail Andricu, Mihail Jora, Zeno Vancea, Sigismund Toduta, Tudor Ciortea, Sabin Dragoi, Paul Constantinescu, Ion and Gheorghe Dumitrescu, Laurentiu Profeta, Anatol Vieru, and Tiberiu Olah.

The music of *Yugoslavia* is as varied as its peoples. Among the more recent composers of Yugoslavia and its environs are: Stjepan Sulek, Mihajlo Vukdragović, Matija Bravničar, Milan Ristic, the Slovenian Danilo Svara, the Croatian Milo Cipra, and Yugoslavia's leading woman composer, Ljubica Marić.

Among the composers of modern *Greece* are: Mikis Theodorakis, Yorgo Sicilianos, Georges Poniridis, Petro Petridis, Nikos Skalkottas, Jani Christou, Antiochos Evanghelatos, Yannis Ioannidis, Stephanos Gazouleas, Arghyris Kounadis, Theodor Antoniou, Manos Hadzidakis, and Ianis Xenakis. Some of these have studied and have settled elsewhere.

Modern Israel has its composers, too. Many who arrived there from Central Europe prior to the second World War could at first speak no Hebrew. Today the list of Israeli musicians is growing, the list of composers carrying such names as: Oedoen Partos, Mordecai Seter, Yitzhak Sadai, Ben-Zion Orgad, and Habib

Touma. Joseph Tal, born in Poland in 1910 is regarded as Israel's foremost electronic composer.

The first *South American* composer to become world-famous was the Brazilian Heitor Villa-Lobos. He was born about 1887 and died in 1959. He wrote in many forms, but at one time became so deeply interested in folk-lore that he ventured into the farthest reaches of the Amazon to study at first-hand Indian and other folk-music. From that time much of his writing derived inspiration from two widely-spaced sources—Brazil and Bach. This gave the general title *Bachianas Brazileiras* to a set of works for various instrumental groups, sometimes with voices, these intended to fuse the Brazilian idiom with that of Johann Sebastian Bach.

SUMMARY: In honouring, rightly, the composers of the past, we sometimes pay insufficient attention to those of more recent times, and perhaps even less to those of today. We like to play safe, admiring a composer who has been dead long enough for time to have canonised his name and his music.

While placing laurel wreaths on the graves of the dead, surely we can spare a few petals for the living!

In the foregoing comments we have mentioned composers of various countries who, inspired by their racial heritage, have produced music of national, or near-national, character. Modern composers, having seen tradition honoured, have looked towards the future, adopting new techniques of expression. Much of the music being written today belongs to the present, a space-age, de-romanticised present, owing little to localised national characteristics, even if ideologies and political and social protest have had their effects on creative thinking.

Listening to a musical work that is unknown to us, we might say that it sounds Russian, or Spanish, Scottish, or Oriental. It may be more difficult to recognise at once the idiom of other places, but every country has its own musical idiom, its own accents, as in spoken language, although in some cases recognition may not be immediate. To become familiar with music from different parts of the world can be an infinite source of enjoyment.

THE DANCE
AND
DANCE FORMS

5

MUSIC and the dance are closely linked, but while the performance of a dance would lose much of its meaning without a musical accompaniment, dance music often possesses an independent character. To emphasise this point, one need only mention the Ländler of Schubert, the Hungarian Dances of Brahms, the Slavonic Dances of Dvořák, or the Viennese Waltzes of Johann Strauss.

Precise details of the dance before the fourteenth century are obscure, but it is certain that from earliest times man has expressed his emotions—his joys, sadness, fears, and hopes—in rhythmic movement, and his beliefs in some kind of ritual. We can also assume that primitive man indulged in some kind of calculated motion to suit his daily activities.

From Egyptian carvings, fashioned more than 6,000 years ago, and from the classic sculpture of early Greece and Rome, we learn that dancing played an important part in ritual and special occasions. Over the centuries rhythmic movement developed into a more orderly arrangement of steps and body movements, and in time miming was introduced to make the meaning clearer. Later, dancing grew into an art as well as a social pastime.

Until the coming of the Sonata and the Symphony, instrumental works often consisted of Suites, the Suite in the seventeenth and eighteenth centuries consisting of a set of pieces in dance style which, although in contrast with each other in tempo and character, lacked a unified form.

The fandango, one of the dances improvised to a guitar accompaniment by Spanish peasants and gypsies.

The Suite in those times had no fixed number of movements, but the usual arrangement was the *Allemande, Courante, Sarabande*, and the *Gigue* (or *Jig*), with the optional addition of *Passepied, Loure, Bourée, Gavotte*, and *Rigaudon*, and certain others according to the composer and the country.

These dances, also others which the music-lover is likely to meet, can be briefly described as follows:

Allemande: Thought to be of German origin, this is in 2/4 or 4/4 time of moderate tempo. It consists of two parts, and usually begins with a short note before the bar-line.

Bourée: French, this is in sprightly 4/4 time, beginning on the up-beat.

Courante: A French dance, the name derived from *courir*, to run, is in 3/2 time. This, too, begins with a short note at the end of a bar. The Italian *courante* is livelier, and is usually in 3/4 or 3/8 time.

Fandango: A lively Spanish dance in triple time, with strong emphasis on the second beat of each bar. Usually accompanied by castanets or guitar.

The Royal Winnipeg Ballet has gained an international reputation and has toured widely.

Farandole: A dance peculiar to Provence, in 6/8 time. Normally a chain-dance; a long line of young men and women hold hands, handkerchiefs or ribbons.

Furiant: A Czech dance of fiery character, often in changing rhythms. Dvořák used this in several of his works.

Galliard: A lively dance, usually, but not always, in 3/2 time; this was popular in England in Elizabethan times, and often followed the *Pavan*, thereby providing contrast.

Gavotte: Probably came from the *pays de Gap* in France, where the people were called Gavots. It is in 4/4 time and starts on the half-bar. Like the *minuet*, it was introduced into the Court of Louis XIV.

Gigue (*Jig*): An old Italian dance, having derived its name from the *Giga*, an early fiddle. It is written in a variety of times.

Habanera: Although for a long time popular in Spain, this is understood to have come from Cuba. Singing often accompanies the dancing of it.

Halling: A characteristic dance from Norway, deriving its name from Hallingdal; generally in 2/4 time. The form was used by Grieg and other Norwegian composers.

Hornpipe: In its original form this triple-time dance was popular in England during the sixteenth and seventeenth centuries. Examples are to be found in the music of Purcell and Handel.

Jota: A Spanish dance in quick triple time, traditionally with castanets. The name is said to have derived from a Moor named Aben Jot.

Loure: A slow French dance, the term thought to have come from a rustic type of bagpipe, or *musette*. Usually in 6/4 time.

Mazurka: A traditional dance of Poland, in triple time, with the accent on the second beat of each bar. Chopin composed fifty-eight *mazurkas* for piano, refining them with his own elegant style.

Minuet: Supposedly of French origin, a stately dance in 3/4 time. During the seventeenth and eighteenth centuries, Purcell, Bach, Handel and other composers included a *minuet* in some of their suites. Later, Haydn and Mozart included a *minuet* in some of their symphonies, adding a *trio* as a central section. Beethoven also used it in this way, later replacing it in his symphonies with a *scherzo*.

Passepied: A jig-like French dance in 3/4, 3/8, or 6/8 time, starting on the third beat.

Pavan (Eng.); *Pavane* (Fr.); *Pavana* (It.): A slow and solemn dance in common time, popular in the sixteenth century in England. Some references state that it originated in Spain, others in Italy, the name having derived from the Italian *padovana*.

Polka: Thought to be of Bohemian origin, becoming widely popular in the nineteenth century. In 2/4 time.

Polonaise: A stately Polish dance in 3/4 time. Chopin wrote thirteen for piano, adding spirit, colour and rhapsodic style to its original rigid form.

Reel: A quick dance, usually for two or more couples. Found chiefly in Scotland and Ireland.

A scene from Brian Macdonald's *Aimez-vous Bach*,
performed by the Royal Winnipeg Ballet.

Rigaudon (Eng. *Rigadoon*): It is not quite certain whether this originated in Provence, or in England. In 2/4 or 4/4 time, its nature is brisk.

Salterello (*Saltarella*): A famous couple-dance of central Italy. A vigorous dance, incorporating jumps. Mendelssohn introduced this dance form in the final movement of his *Italian* symphony.

Sarabande: A slow and stately dance of early origin, thought to have originated in Spain, although this is sometimes disputed. It is set in 3/4 and 3/2 time.

Sardana: A national dance of Catalonia, traditionally danced to pipe-and-drum accompaniment.

Seguidilla: A fairly quick Spanish dance in triple time, often accompanied by castanets. Its origin is uncertain, but it is said to have existed in La Mancha at the time of Cervantes (1547-1616), famous for his *Don Quixote*.

Sicilienne: A dance in slow 6/8 time, probably from Sicily, often of a pastoral character.

Strathspey: A lively Scottish dance in common time, closely related to the *reel*. Derives its name from the strath, or valley, of the Spey, in the north of Scotland, where it was first danced.

Tarantella: A lively Italian dance in 6/8 time.

Waltz: This became universally popular in the nineteenth century and numerous composers have used it in various types of composition. Its characteristic is a three-in-a-bar lilt, with only one chord (the first) to each bar. This is another dance form taken up by Chopin, who refined it for the *salon*.

Josef Lanner and Johann Strauss II have shared the credit for having created the *Viennese Waltz*, which owed something to the Austrian *Ländler*. Strauss in his later waltzes extended both the introduction and the *coda* sections.

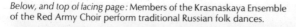

Below, and top of facing page: Members of the Krasnaskaya Ensemble of the Red Army Choir perform traditional Russian folk dances.

The mazurka is a traditional Polish dance. Here it is performed as a
ballet by members of a Polish company.

The folk dances of Eastern Europe are performed to a very rapid tempo and call for great vigour and agility on the part of the dancers.

BALLET AND BALLET MUSIC

Ballet is a glamorous page in the long history of dancing. While developing side-by-side with opera, it has preserved its own character. The word ballet derives from the Italian *ballare* (to dance).

Although every nation throughout the centuries has translated into dance forms its histories, legends, and rites, ballet as we know it today may be said to have begun at the Court of France.

Towards the end of the sixteenth century Catherine de Medici installed the Florentine pattern of ballet in her own court in France, chiefly for the amusement of her sons. In 1581 she commissioned the Italian violinist, Baldasarino da Belgiojoso (who became known in France as Balthasar de Beaujoyeulx) to take charge of the festivities associated with the betrothal of Marguerite de Lorraine to the Duc de Joyeuse. The dances were performed by the ladies and gentlemen of the court.

Under the influence of Catherine de Medici, Paris attracted dancing masters and musicians from Italy and other countries, and Court Ballet took on a new importance. Once it was firmly established in France, ballet became even more lavish in presentation under Louis XIV, who in 1661 established the *Académie Royale de la Danse*, the first institution of its kind in the world. Eleven years later he extended its scope and renamed it *Académie Royale de la Musique et de la Danse*.

In time ballet became a definite part of theatre entertainment. Marie Camargo, soon after her début in 1726, improved the technique of movement and expression, which raised the art to a professional level.

Another important figure in the development of ballet was Jean Georges Noverre (1727-1810), the son of an *aide-de-camp* to Charles XII. Noverre, whom David Garrick named "the Shakespeare of the Dance," was the first of the great ballet masters. He set about advancing the technique of his dancers, restoring the art of mime, reforming stage costumes, strengthening the story-lines of the ballets, and creating a new unity of related arts instead of routine, disconnected *divertissements*.

Further progress in ballet was stemmed by the French Revolution but, meanwhile, in Italy, where interest in dancing had revived, there were new ideas and developments. Linked with this Italian renaissance was Salvatore Vignano (1769-1821), who made his debut as ballet master in Venice, and his pupil, Carlo Blasis (1803-1878), often referred to as "the father of classical ballet."

Famous ballerinas added lustre to the ballet of their time: Marie Taglioni (1803-1844), Fanny Elssler (1810-1884), Fanny Cerrito (1821-1899), and Carlotta Grisi (1821-1899), to mention the most prominent. While these stars continued to shine with increasing brilliance in the ballet firmament, public interest in the presentation itself—choreography, décor, music, and story—waned. The audience paid their money to applaud the star. For them that was sufficient.

The revival of ballet as a serious art came from Russia. From early time dancing there had been a popular form of entertainment. After passing through an era of extravaganzas, in which taste and interpretation were subordinated to acrobatics and vivid stage effects of little artistic value, Russian ballet took on a new artistic stature, attracting such composers as Tchaikovsky, Glazunov, Rimsky-Korsakov, and Tcherepnine, and producing great dancers, choreographers, and scenic artists. The results were great ballets with great music.

A significant date was 1735, when the Russian Imperial Ballet School was founded in St Petersburg. French and Italian ballet masters, among them C. L. Didelot (1767-1837), Marius Petipa (1822-1910), and Enrico Cecchetti (1856-1925), were called in to direct the work of European choreographers.

Another vital force in Russian ballet was Serge Diaghilev (1872-1929). Although not a dancer himself, he promoted the fullest understanding and co-operation between choreographer, décor-artist, composer, and dancer, gathering into his company outstanding people in all branches of art. In 1909 he took to Paris his Les Ballets Russes de Serge Diaghliev, a company that caused a theatrical sensation and again fixed Paris as the world capital of the dance. It was an achievement that continued to grow in importance and one that was repeated in other capitals; and it marked a renaissance in which Anna Pavlova was to play an important part.

Diaghilev's supremacy continued for twenty years, during which period great

Scene from *Swan Lake*, performed by the Bolshoi Ballet.

ballets were created; dancers, artists, and composers finding a new stimulus to their art. Among the many dancers associated with his company were Nijinsky, Karsavina, Ninette de Valois, Lopokova, Markova, Nikitina, Lifar, Massine, Woizikovsky, Pavlova, Fokine, Dolin, and Sokolova.

The Pavlova Ballet Company, founded in 1910, travelled extensively, its public appeal depending chiefly on the artistic perfection of Pavlova herself.

After the death of Diaghilev, the Russian Ballet tradition was sustained by Colonel de Basil's Ballets Russes.

In England a new vitality and excellent achievement in ballet were evident from about 1910, qualities which have been nobly maintained. In the 1930s a wave of newly awakened interest swept through the United States of America, and other countries, including Australia and New Zealand; companies were formed dedicated to the highest ideals in classical, romantic, and modern ballet.

Ballet Music

As record collectors will have discovered, music of the ballet provides numerous works of tuneful and colourful interest, many written by great composers.

Following is a list of some titles of ballet music, of which performances are normally listed in the record catalogues, with new recorded performances periodically being issued.

Members of Maurice Béjart's 20th Century Ballet.

The reader who is only beginning to establish a friendship with this attractive branch of music may be advised to begin with titles marked *. Others may need more frequent hearing before their true value and appeal are fully appreciated.

Après-Midi d'un Faune, L' (Debussy)
* Aurora's Wedding (Tchaikovsky) (See The Sleeping Princess)
Baiser de la fée, Le (The Fairy's Kiss) (Stravinsky)
* Ballet Egyptien (Luigini)
* Beau Danube, Le (J. Strauss)
Les Biches (Poulenc)
Bolero (Ravel)
* Boutique Fantasque, La (Rossini-Respighi)
* Carnaval (Schumann; arranged by various composers)
Chout (Prokofiev)
* Cid, Le (Massenet)
* Coppelia (Delibes)
Coq d'Or, Le (Rimsky-Korsakov)
Corroboree (Antill)
Cotillon (Chabrier)
* Dance of the Hours (Ponchielli)
Daphnis and Chloë (Ravel)
* Deux Pigeons, Les (Messager)
Façade (Walton)
* Faust (Gounod)
Fille mal gardée, La (Hérold)
Firebird (L'Oiseau de Feu) (Stravinsky)
Francesca da Rimini (Tchaikovsky)
* Gaieté Parisiénne (Offenbach)
Gayne (Gayaneh) (Khachaturian)
* Giselle (Adam)
* Gods Go A-begging, The (Handel-Beecham)
* Good-humoured Ladies, The (Scarlatti-Tomasini)
* Graduation Ball (J. Strauss-Dorati)
* Jeux d'Enfants (Bizet)
* Nutcracker (Casse-Noisette) (Tchaikovsky)
* Patineurs, Les (Meyerbeer-Lambert)
Petrouchka (Stravinsky)
* Pineapple Poll (Sullivan-Mackerras)
Pulcinella (Stravinsky)
* Raymonda (Glazunov)
Rite of Spring (Le Sacre du Printemps) (Stravinsky)
Romeo and Juliet (Prokofiev)

* Scheherazade (Rimsky-Korsakov)

* Seasons, The (Glazunov)

* Sleeping Princess (or Beauty) (Tchaikovsky) (Aurora's Wedding is a one-act ballet, from the three-act Sleeping Princess)

* Spectre de la Rose, Le (Weber)

Sun Music (Sculpthorpe)

* Swan Lake (Tchaikovsky)

* Sylphides, Les (Chopin-various)

* Sylvia (Delibes)

Three-Cornered Hat, The (Falla)

* William Tell (Rossini)

Wise Virgins (Bach-Walton)

This scene of dancers in Maurice Béjart's 20th Century Ballet Company is typical of modern ballet, in which lighting and decor play a far greater part than in ballets of the nineteenth century.

Ekaterina Maximova dances the part of Odile in Tchaikovsky's *Swan Lake*, in a new version choreographed for the Bolshoi Ballet by Yuri Grigorovich.

INSTRUMENTS AND THE ORCHESTRA

6

THE word "orchestra" comes from the Greek, meaning "a dancing place," i.e., that part of the early Greek theatre situated between the semi-circular rows of seats of the auditorium and the area occupied by the actors. In this space the "chorus" sang and danced and, at a later time, played ancient instruments, many of which had been introduced into Greece from other countries. Even then, instrumental music in Greece was subordinate to the spoken word.

The Romans were less conservative than the Greeks in their attitude towards instrumental music, and sustained, successful efforts were made to improve the instruments themselves, in particular those of the woodwind and brass kinds.

The progress of the orchestra was slow, and it is a far cry from those instrumental groups that went under that name three or four hundred years ago and the symphony orchestra of today.

One of the most significant factors in the development of the orchestra was provided by Italy when violin making became a highly specialised art. The violin, which had replaced the viol, reached its stage of perfection in Cremona during the sixteenth, seventeenth, and early eighteenth centuries, when the Amati, the Stradivari, and the Guarneri families practised their craft. (Stradivarius and Guarnerius are the Latinised form of those names.) Some of their violins and other instruments of the string family are still in use today. The best of the French, German, and English violin makers came on the scene somewhat later.

In France orchestral music for its own sake, rather than as a mere instrumental accompaniment to operas, masques, and ballets, did not become firmly established until the early part of the eighteenth century. In England there had always been an active interest in music, and in the sixteenth century instrumental groups, generally referred to as "bands," were maintained at the courts of Henry VIII and Queen Elizabeth I, but these consisted chiefly of brass instruments for use on ceremonial occasions.

Since pre-Roman times, the stirring music of drum and trumpet has been the signal
for battle. Until Napoleonic times, brass bands actually led troops into action. Now,
they are used only on ceremonial occasions as in this scene of the Grenadier Guards
marching past Buckingham Palace.

Side by side with continued improvement in musical instruments, capable of
producing a wider range of tonal qualities, came a greater variety of instrumental
compositions, resulting in the Suite, and later the Symphony.

As we have mentioned in the section Symphony, Haydn at first wrote for orchestras
of between twelve and fifteen players, this number increasing towards the end of the
eighteenth century to thirty-five or forty. Mozart, in carrying on the development of
the symphony, added the clarinet to the orchestra, and extended the capacity of
certain instruments within their families. Beethoven in his orchestration called for
a larger orchestra than that used by Mozart and, in addition to increasing the total
number of musicians, extended the bass range of the woodwind and the brass.

Until about 1840 orchestras in the most musical cities, and under the direction of
famous conductors, consisted of something like half the number of players of the
"virtuoso" orchestras of today.

Berlioz, as well as writing for a larger orchestra, greatly extended the scope of
the instruments themselves, and Wagner scored for about 100 players. Richard
Strauss and other later composers have used similar numbers.

Today most cities of the world have permanently-established orchestras, sometimes more than one, employing up to 110 and 120 members. If America lagged

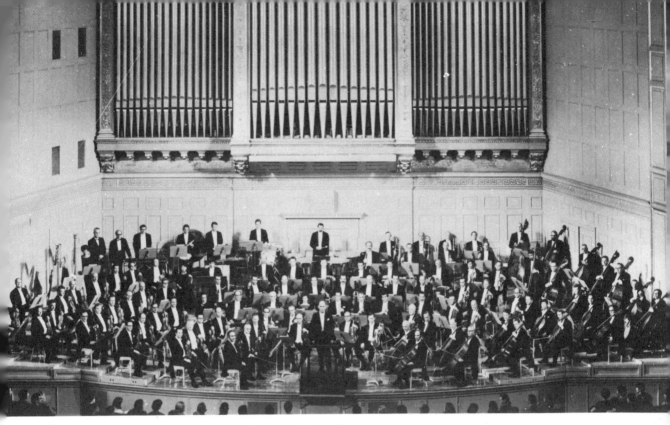

A full symphony orchestra contains over a hundred musicians. The symphony orchestra as we know it today developed from small groups of musicians and reached its present formation during the nineteenth century. The photograph is of one of the world's best known orchestras: The Boston Symphony Orchestra. Founded in 1881, it has 106 members.

a little behind certain other countries in establishing orchestras of equivalent size, she can now boast some of the largest, and the most skilfully trained, in the world.

The term *Symphony orchestra* generally refers to the fully-equipped orchestras that are capable of performing symphonies. *Philharmonic* is not actually a *type* of orchestra, but a term used as part of the title. *Chamber orchestra* originally applied to small ensembles of woodwind and strings formed for the performance of music suitable for a room or a small hall. The term still applies today.

MUSICAL INSTRUMENTS

In early times composers were concerned chiefly with providing music for the church and it was not until late in the fifteenth century that they gave serious attention to compositions for independent performance by musical instruments. As the range of religious and secular music widened, so did the scope of musical instruments expand.

Before dealing with the instruments of the modern orchestra, we can mention briefly some of the instruments in use in an earlier age.

85

Fretted Instruments

LUTE: Of all the instruments still played today, and then only rarely by the dedicated few, the lute is the most ancient. It was introduced into Europe and elsewhere by musicians from Arabia towards the end of the thirteenth century, and is looked upon as the forerunner of all instruments whose strings were plucked with the fingers, or plectrum; in other words, not played with a bow as in the case of the violin family. Its body is pear-shaped. The lute was much in demand from about 1400 to 1700 as an accompanying instrument for songs, for solos, and as a member of small instrumental groups. J. S. Bach composed several pieces for it, and even as late as 1723 he included it in his orchestration of the *St John Passion*.

VIHUELA: The Spanish equivalent of the lute, this was either plucked by a plectrum or with the fingers (*Vihuela da mano*). By 1700 it had become superseded by the guitar.

GUITAR: There are, and there have been, many kinds of guitar, the best known being the Spanish Guitar, an expressive plucked-string instrument that in recent times has enjoyed a great deal of popularity in many parts of the world. Credit for much of this revived interest has been given to Andrés Segovia, who brought to light many interesting guitar works. Normally there are six strings.

It is worth mentioning that the nineteenth century Italian violinist Paganini in the early stages of his dazzling career laid aside his violin for some time to devote his full attention to the guitar.

SITAR: Amir Khusrau, a statesman-musician of the thirteenth century is credited with having invented the sitar, the most widely known stringed instrument of India. The fingerboard is about three feet long, sometimes longer, this length giving the neck a giraffe-like appearance. There are from sixteen to twenty-two movable frets made from brass or silver.

Originally the sitar had only three strings (the name derived from the Persian *seh-tar*, meaning three strings), but the modern instruments have six or seven strings, with sympathetic strings (*tarab*) which run almost parallel to the main strings under the fret. These are secured to small pegs fixed to the side of the finger-board.

The sitar is played with a wire plectrum (*mizrab*) worn on the forefinger of the right hand.

MANDOLIN (MANDOLINE): A plucked-string instrument of Italian origin, usually played with a plectrum. Derived from a small-type lute, *mandora*, or *mandola*. Among composers who wrote for this instrument were Vivaldi, Handel, Mozart, and Beethoven.

Early Stringed Instruments

VIOL: The ancestor of the violin, therefore an instrument played with a bow, the viol was invented in the fifteenth century, but ceased to be in general use soon after 1700. Unlike the violin, the viol originally had a fretted finger-board, and a different style of bowing was used. The three principal kinds were the *treble viol*, the *tenor viol*, and the *bass viol* (or *viola da gamba*, i.e. *leg-viol*) which was held between the legs.

In the sixteenth and seventeenth centuries it was the fashion for families to form groups consisting of a "Chest" of viols. Usually these were six in number, the instruments when not in use kept in a special wooden box, often lined with a baize material: hence the term, Chest of Viols.

VIOLA D'AMORE (LOVE-VIOL): Related to the viol family, this stringed instrument was played with a bow, but the finger-board had no frets. Usually it had seven strings over which the bow moved, and seven (or more) "sympathetic" strings underneath.

Wind

RECORDER: This reedless instrument was popular from the sixteenth to the eighteenth centuries, after which it stepped aside in favour of the flute. It is blown from the end and held downward instead of crosswise (as in the case of the flute), and is equipped with a fipple, or "whistle." During the seventeenth century four sizes were in use, but later the number had increased to nine. Of recent years a widespread revival of interest has been evident, particularly in schools, it being inexpensive and comparatively easy to learn. Five sizes are generally in use today, the most popular being the "descant."

There are still available many fine compositions written by such composers as Bach and Handel; also several modern composers have written for it.

FLAGEOLET: Invented in the sixteenth century, this primitive flute, related to the recorder, is now almost obsolete. It had six finger-holes and was blown from the end. It is mentioned in *Pepys's Diary* in 1667; Handel and Gluck were two of the early composers who wrote for it.

Keyboard Forerunners of the Pianoforte

HARPSICHORD: The word Harpsichord is the English form of the Italian *arpicordo*. The earliest surviving reference to it goes back to the early part of the fifteenth century. During the sixteenth, seventeenth and eighteenth centuries this keyboard instrument held a position similar to that held by the piano today. For about 150 years from the beginning of the seventeenth century it was used in the orchestra as an accompanying instrument for solo voices, especially in recitative passages, and of course as a solo instrument.

Whereas the strings of the piano are struck by hammers, those of the harpsichord are plucked by quills or hard leathers. This is done by a mechanical agent which connects the keyboard and a wooden upright, or "jack." Each key has its own jack which actually plucks the corresponding string. The degree of tone depends directly upon the amount of force used in striking the key, but it is a tone of short duration, there being no way of prolonging it.

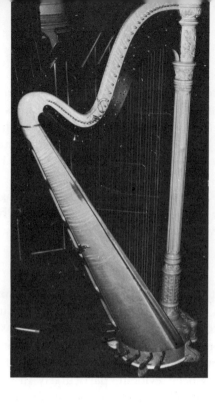

The harp is a descendant of the earliest types of plucked instruments. It is an instrument adopted by many women, though some of the best-known harpists have been men. A number of concertos have been written for the harp, notably Mozart's *Concerto for Flute and Harp* and Boieldieu's *Harp Concerto*.

From time to time the harpsichord has seen a number of improvements, e.g., pedals being added to control the mechanism by which it is possible to vary the number of strings used for each note, so varying the quality of tone.

Harpsichords have from one to three keyboards; in the case of the larger instrument, these are placed one above the other in a similar manner to the manuals of an organ.

CLAVICHORD: This keyboard instrument, the strings of which are struck by metal "tangents", was in favour from the sixteenth to the eighteenth centuries. Its tone, being softer than that of the harpsichord, made it more suitable as a domestic instrument, rather than one used for concertos played in company with other instruments.

The earliest records of the tangent clavichord go back to early in the sixteenth century. Its use continued until the beginning of the nineteenth century. It is said that J. S. Bach preferred it to the harpsichord.

VIRGINAL: The virginal, or virginals, is a plucked-string instrument, smaller than the harpsichord, and of oblong shape, its single keyboard being placed along the longer side of the soundboard, and operated by one set of jacks. This, like the clavichord and the spinet, was a domestic instrument, and particularly popular in Elizabethan England.

The origin of the name is uncertain. At one time it was said to be so-called because it was a favourite instrument of Queen Elizabeth I (the "Virgin Queen") but the name, however, was in use before her time. Another theory was that the name was invented because the playing of the virginal was considered part of the cultural education of well-brought-up maidens, a theory that probably owes its origin to a lexicographer named Blount who, in 1656, wrote:

> *Virginal (virginals), maidenly, virginlike, hence the name of that musical instrument called virginals, because maids and virgins do most commonly play upon them.*

A more likely, if less romantic, explanation is that the name derived from the Latin word *Virga*, meaning a rod or jack.

SPINET: This wing-shaped keyboard instrument was of the harpsichord type, but smaller. In use from the sixteenth to the eighteenth centuries, this was described by the eighteenth century historian Burney as "a small harpsichord or virginal with one string to each note."

All the keyboard instruments mentioned above have been revived during the present century.

CLAVIER: The term clavier was first used in France to denote any keyboard instrument, including the organ. It was later adopted in Germany (Klavier) for stringed keyboard instruments, harpsichord, clavichord, pianoforte, etc.

The *Well-tempered Clavier* was the title given by J. S. Bach to his Twenty-four Preludes and Fugues, which in these days are usually played on the piano.

PIANO: "Piano" is the commonly used term for Pianoforte, which comes from two Italian words: *piano* (soft) and *forte* (loud). The instrument itself evolved from the harpsichord and the clavichord and first came into general use in the early part of the eighteenth century.

The invention of the piano is attributed to Bartolommeo Cristofori (1665-1731), a harpsichord-maker and the custodian of musical instruments to Prince Ferdinand dei Medici of Florence. He produced his first model of the piano soon after 1700. Among other craftsmen who followed Cristofori were his assistant, Giovanni Ferrini, and notably Gottfried Silbermann (1683-1753), and later instrument-makers of other countries, including the English house of John Broadwood and Sons.

The invention and the development of the piano is an outstanding example of advancing musical expression seeking and finding an instrument capable of making such expression possible.

The piano's superiority over instruments of the harpsichord type was achieved in two main features: (1) whereas the strings of the harpsichord and its related instruments were plucked, those of the piano were struck by hammers, this producing louder and fuller tone; (2) when foot pedals were added, the left, or "soft," pedal reduced the volume by allowing for few strings to be struck, the right, or "sustaining" pedal not only adding to the tonal richness, but permitting the "partial" tones (harmonics) to vibrate. (Some pianos have a third pedal for allowing certain notes to sustain an independent resonance.) With such improvements the piano was

The number of instruments used in the percussion section of a symphony orchestra has grown considerably during this century. Modern composers write parts for instruments which were not previously used in orchestral music. Illustrated are 1: Gong 2: Bass drum 3: Clash cymbals 4: Chimes 5: Roto-toms 6: Marimba 7: Xylophone 8: Jazz kit 9: Suspended cymbal 10: Triangle 11: Snare drum 12: Timpani 13: Effects (tambourine, castanets, wood block, etc.) 14: Glockenspiel 15: Vibraphone.

Instruments of the brass section of a symphony orchestra:
From left: Tuba, Bass Trombone, Tenor Trombone, Trumpet,
French Horn. More than one of each of these instruments are
used in the full orchestra.

elevated from a percussive instrument to one that "sings," i.e., that produces round,
sonorous tones that carry a sustained resonance.

Broadwood produced his first iron-framed grand piano in 1781. Today pianos
of this type usually have eighty-eight notes, sometimes more in larger concert grands.
the tone range covering seven octaves and over. The strings number about 200,
because many of the notes employ two or three strings in unison for more power.

By the year 1880 the "upright" piano came into general use in small rooms.

Beethoven, Schumann, Liszt, Chopin, Debussy, and Ravel were some of the more
adventurous composers who strove for greater range of tone-colour, more powerful
sound, and more subtlety of expression in their compositions for piano, and instrument-makers were encouraged to meet these demands. Early keyboard music will
sound agreeable on modern pianos, but to play the music of such composers as
mentioned in this paragraph on a harpsichord or a clavichord would deprive it of its
true character.

ORGAN: The history of the organ reaches so far back into antiquity, and its
modern structure is so complicated, that it can be only briefly touched on in these
pages.

Instruments of the woodwind section of a symphony orchestra. *From left:* French Horn (which is classified under woodwind as well as under brass), Piccolo, Clarinet, Flute, Bass Clarinet, Oboe, Bassoon, English Horn, Double Bassoon. There are usually two Flutes, Oboes, Clarinets, and Bassoons in a symphony orchestra. The Piccolo, English Horn, Bass Clarinet, and Double Bassoon are added if required by the score.

Legend would have us believe that the organ owes its origin to the pipes of the Arcadian god Pan, who cut reeds that grew by the water's edge and fashioned a crude instrument of five pipes from them, on which he played his simple tunes. Classical mythology refers to such a primitive instrument as "Pan's pipes," or "Syrinx," which survived in certain countries for many centuries. Mozart revived pan-pipes in his opera *The Magic Flute*.

It is recorded that Greek shepherds of ancient times made pan-pipes with seven or eight reeds fastened together with wax or tied with thongs.

An early reference to the organ is found in the Old Testament (Genesis IV, 21), where Jubal is called the "father of all such as handle harp and organ." The word "organ," as used in the Psalms and elsewhere in the Old Testament may not have specifically meant the organ as such, as Greek usage was inclined to apply the word to any musical instrument.

The Cheng, which had been used in China as far back as 5,000 years, bore some resemblance to the features of the primitive organ.

About the year 265 B.C. an engineer named Ctesibius, who lived in Alexandria, is credited with having improved the water-organ, or Hydraulus. This, after

Instruments of the string section of a symphony orchestra. *From left:* Violin, Viola, Cello, Double Bass. The number of players in the string section varies with the total number of the orchestra.

undergoing various additions and improvements, came into general use. Nero is said to have been a capable performer on it.

The organ developed considerably with the early Greeks and Romans; with the collapse of the Roman Empire, organ-building for a time was confined to the Middle East, later returning to Europe when the instrument was used as an aid to Christian worship.

By the fifteenth century the organ had developed into an instrument with two or more manuals, pedals, separate stops; also flues and reed pipes to produce a greater variety of tone-colours.

During the eighteenth century, the historian Burney stated that large organs seemed to be a natural growth in Germany, that from the twelfth century there were many large instruments in that country.

As a specific art form, organ music dates from about the second half of the fifteenth century. From about that time organ-building, in developing stages, was carried out in several countries, including Germany, France, Spain, Italy, the Netherlands, England, and in Scandinavian countries. Between the years 1650 and 1720 (the so-called "High-Baroque" period) the organ attained its greatest popularity and artistic importance.

Richard Strauss (1864-1949). A German romantic composer and conductor, he was influenced by Wagner but soon evolved his own passionate style.

Whatever its origin, and whatever its changes and development in the course of evolution, the organ became not only a part of religious ritual but one for which some of the greatest composers, notably J. S. Bach, wrote enduring works.

In the nineteenth century some composers found the organ alien to the current Romantic style of expression; yet that period did yield much fine organ music from such composers as Liszt, Mendelssohn, Franck, Reubke, and some late-romantics, including Reger and Elgar. Among the many modern composers who have written works for organ are Hindemith, Schoenberg, and Messiaen.

INSTRUMENTS OF THE MODERN SYMPHONY ORCHESTRA

Strings

VIOLIN: The violin, which is the smallest instrument of the string family, is held under the chin. Each of its four strings (G.D.A.E.) has a different tone-colour, the notes being formed by the fingers of the left hand, and the sound produced by drawing the bow across the strings with the right hand, this action causing the strings to vibrate.

The vibrations activated on the strings are communicated to the wooden body of

Ludwig van Beethoven (1770-1827). Acclaimed as one of the world's greatest composers, he changed the course of music and gave it new freedom of emotional expression.

the instrument by a bridge over which the strings are tightly stretched, the body acting as a resonator. The player alters the pitch of the sounds thus produced by pressing the strings towards the fingerboard.

The violinist, who reads from the treble clef, can play two melodies together by fingering and bowing on two strings at the same time. Four-note chords may be played by sweeping the bow across the four strings.

When the strings are plucked by the finger, this is called *pizzicato*. Sometimes, particularly in solo music, a violinist will attach a mute to the bridge of the violin to produce a soft, veiled tone.

The word Vibrato (from the Italian *vibrare*, "to vibrate") can mean two things. Although it need not concern us at this point, the first can mean a "wobble" in a singer's uncontrolled vocal line. (We refer here to singers of serious music; "Pop" singers go to no end of trouble to produce this jelly-like effect, probably to suggest an emotion which the words and music might lack.) The second, more legitimate, kind of *vibrato* is a device, or art, by which string-players (some other instrumentalists, too) obtain a throbbing effect on sustained notes by the rapid oscillating motion— from the wrist—of the finger stopping the note. When overdone it causes a tasteless wavering of pitch; when completely controlled, it produces a tone-quality that is pleasing to both the listener and the performer. Almost all strings players today feel that their tone becomes lifeless without the use of *vibrato*.

The violin section of the orchestra is divided into First Violins and Second Violins.

Johannes Brahms (1833-1897). Great German composer, often called a "classical romantic." His compositions are deeply emotional, yet are set in a rigidly classical form.

The instruments, of course, are the same, but the Second Violins play a different part of the orchestral score, much in the same way as second tenors sing "seconds" in a choir. The old-fashioned term "seconds" refers to a line that harmonises with the main melodic line.

The Bow which violinists use today was invented by François Tourte (1747-1835). The stick is curved inward towards the strands of horsehair stretched from the tip (*point*) to the other end (*nut*). An earlier type of bow, the stick of which curved outward, was more suitable for the early type of bridge.

As we have mentioned elsewhere, violin-making reached its peak of craftsmanship in the Italian city of Cremona. This dynasty began with the Amati family. The first member was Andrea Amati (c. 1520-1580), he being succeeded by his sons, Antonio and Girolamo, but it was Nicolo Amati (1596-1684), a son of Girolamo, who produced the finest models.

In Italy the art of violin-making was carried to its highest point by Nicolo Amati's pupils, Antonio Stradivari (c. 1645-1737), and Guiseppe Antonio Guarneri (1687-1745), who became known as "Guiseppe Guarneri del Gesù" to distinguish him from the son of Andrea. (Stradivarius and Guarnerius are the latinised forms of these names.)

96

Meanwhile, other violin-makers continued to arrive at improvements in their models, not only in Italy, but in other parts of the world. In Germany the Austrian-born Jacob Stainer (1621-1683) developed an individual model, and his contemporary (perhaps his pupil), Egidi Klotz, laid the foundation of a line of violin-makers. In France members of the Vuillaume family were eminently successful in making copies of the Cremonese violins, and built up a successful business.

In England the first violin-maker of note was Jacob Rayman, who came from the Tyrol to settle in London in 1620. From that time others produced copies of the best Cremonese models, notably Benjamin Banks of Salisbury (1727-1795), and later the famous Hill family.

Since then many fine violins have been made in other countries, including Belgium, the Netherlands, Russia, America, and Australia.

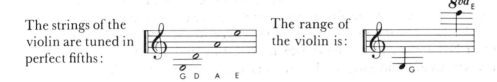

The strings of the violin are tuned in perfect fifths: G D A E

The range of the violin is: 8va E   G

VIOLA: The Viola, as used in the modern orchestra, the string quartet, and as a solo instrument, is of similar shape to the violin, but slightly larger. It has four strings tuned in perfect fifths, five notes lower than those of the violin, is held under the chin and is played with a bow. Its tone is warm and mellow, but less brilliant than that of its companion instrument.

The viola player reads for the most part from the alto clef, because that clef is the most suitable for the compass of the instrument.

Middle C in the alto clef is placed thus: middle C

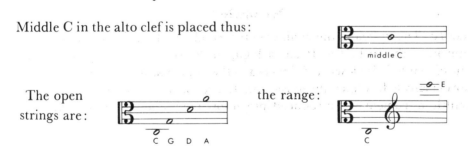

The open strings are: C G D A

the range: E   C

VIOLONCELLO: Generally called the Cello, this string instrument is much larger than the viola and therefore is held between the knees, a spike raising it from the floor. The cello is tuned in fifths, one octave below the viola, the player reading from the bass clef. The upper notes, however, are written in the tenor clef, and in the highest passages the treble clef. The rich, sonorous tone reaches over a wide range. While its glowing voice adds considerable beauty to the combined sound of an orchestra or a string quartet, it is often used in solo works that have been specially written for it over a period of about three centuries.

The strings of the cello are tuned to: the range:

DOUBLE-BASS: Also known as bass-viol, contrabass, string-bass or bass, this is the fourth and largest member of the string family. Its shape is slightly different from that of its companions, the top sloping towards the neck. It has four strings (sometimes five), which are tuned in fourths. The player stands, or half-sits on a stool.

In order to avoid the use of many ledger (leger) lines, (i.e., short lines written above or below the staff for notes which exceed its limits), music for the bass is usually written an octave higher than it sounds. The bass clef is used.

The strings are tuned to: ; its range:

Woodwind

PICCOLO: The Piccolo is the smallest of the woodwind family; in fact, the smallest instrument of the orchestra. It has a high, shrill voice that can penetrate a full volume of sound. It is blown and fingered in the same manner as the flute. To avoid the use of many ledger lines, the music is written an octave lower than it sounds. This perky little instrument was introduced into the orchestra about the time of Beethoven.

Its range is:

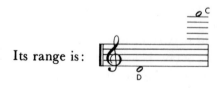

FLUTE: The history of the flute is as old as history itself, but the modern flute and the method of holding it horizontally and blowing through a side opening dates from the early part of the eighteenth century. It was the first woodwind instrument to appear regularly as a member of the orchestral family. Until about the end of the nineteenth century flutes were made of wood, but today they are mostly of metal, usually silver.

The design of the cylinder flute as we know it today is generally attributed to Theobold Boehm, a German flautist and composer, who lived from 1793 or 1794 to 1881. Certain writers, however, hold the view that Boehm may have been indebted to others.

The flute is an agile instrument, its tone clear, warm in the lower register and brilliantly expressive in the upper.

Its range is:

OBOE: Unlike the flute, the oboe is blown from the top of a conical tube and is played with a double reed consisting of two thin canes with a small opening through which air is blown into the instrument. Its tone has a distinct, expressive quality that is equally attractive in solo work as in the full orchestra. It is also used in chamber music and in military bands.

The oboe gives the pitch (A) for the whole orchestra to tune from.

Its range is:

ENGLISH HORN (COR ANGLAIS): This is a somewhat longer type of oboe with a short metal tube to which a double reed is attached. It is a fifth lower in pitch than the oboe, its notes written a fifth higher than they actually sound.

The tone has a haunting beauty. To realise this, one needs only to listen to the long role assigned to it by Sibelius in his *The Swan of Tuonela*, and the solos parts written for it in the second movement of the *Symphony in D minor* by César Franck and the Largo movement of Dvořák's Symphony *From the New World*.

Its range:

CLARINET: In shape the clarinet resembles the oboe, but it is blown through a *single* reed which vibrates in a slot in the mouthpiece of the instrument. Its tone range is wider than that of the oboe. While some writers have other opinions, the clarinet is generally thought to have been the invention of the Leipzig-born Johann Christoph Denner. In 1843 Hyacinth Klosé reorganised the fingering, based on a system called after Boehm, which also applied to the flute, oboe, and bassoon.

Although some composers wrote for the clarinet somewhat earlier, its general use in the orchestra dates from the 1770s when Mozart included it in his scores. Haydn wrote sparingly for it until he went to London towards the end of the eighteenth century, where he found skilful clarinettists plentiful.

Its clear, mellow tone is particularly suitable for solo works, Mozart, Weber and Brahms being only three of the great composers who wrote concertos and chamber works for it.

Owing to a peculiar break in the middle of its voice, two kinds of clarinets are used, one for music set in flat keys, another for music in sharp keys. The clarinet in A sounds a tone and a half lower than the music written for it, the other, in B-flat, sounds one tone lower.

Its range is: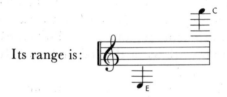

BASS CLARINET: The sound of this deep-voiced instrument is an octave lower than the ordinary clarinet. Also, it is much longer, its tube being bent at both ends and the bell rising in an upward tilt.

Its range:

BASSOON: The English word *bassoon* derives from its pitch, or in other words, its place as the natural bass to the oboe and similar reed instruments. The German name, *Fagott* and the Italian *fagotto* probably came about from the instrument's resemblance to a bundle of sticks, or faggots.

Like the oboe, the bassoon is a double-reed instrument, but because of its length, it is doubled on itself to allow the player to hold it more comfortably. It is often called

100

"the buffoon of the orchestra" because of the tone quality of its low notes; these are often called on to suggest the grotesque or the broadly humorous. The top notes are clear, though rather melancholy. The bassoonist plays the actual notes written on the stave, using the bass, tenor, and sometimes treble, clefs.

Its range:

DOUBLE BASSOON: Because of its great length, the tube of this ponderous instrument is twice doubled and has a compass an octave lower than that of the ordinary bassoon. As orchestral scores call for its use only occasionally, it is usually played by the third bassoonist. The music is written an octave above the actual sound.

Its range:  roughly an octave below the bassoon.

SAXOPHONE: Though not normally a member of the orchestra, the saxophone is sometimes brought in to play a solo part specially written for it. Saint-Saëns, Liszt, d'Indy, Ravel, Debussy, Bizet, and Strauss are some of the composers who have paid respect to it in this way.

The saxophone is named after a Belgian instrument-maker, Adolphe Sax, who invented it in 1840. Five years later it was officially introduced into French army bands. Later, its inclusion in jazz and dance music made it universally popular. Its various sizes and kinds are usually classified as woodwind instruments, though made of metal. They are usually in E flat and B flat.

HORN (FRENCH HORN): In its primitive form the Horn was probably the most ancient of all wind instruments. In its present form and tone-colour it stands as a link between the woodwind section and the rest of the brass section, its tone blending effectively with both, also with strings. It became firmly established in the orchestra during the second half of the eighteenth century.

The horn has a brass conical tube, coiled up and widening at the end into a large bell. It was formerly called the Hand Horn, for up until the eighteenth century the player inserted his hand into the bell and altered the pitch by "stopping" the sound. This method is still used but the addition of valves in about 1850 gave the instrument a chromatic range of notes.

This is probably the most difficult of all wind instruments to master, but in the hands of a skilful player it produces a range of sounds of unmistakable and beautiful quality. Composers from Mozart to Strauss to those of this century have written important works for it. Horn parts sound a fifth lower than written.

Its range:

HARP: This stately instrument has a long history; in fact, one might say that it had its origin in the stretched string of a primitive bow. Egypt, Babylonia, Persia, Assyria and other parts of the world have yielded evidence that instruments that might conceivably be called harps existed many centuries ago. The oldest specimen is the Sumerian harp, the design of which can be seen on a vase fashioned about 3,000 B.C.

Time brought many changes to its shape and character, and with the advance of instrumental music, the harp, in common with other instruments, has undergone many adjustments and improvements. A Parisian, Sébastien Erard (1752-1831), opened a workshop in London and took out English patents for mechanical improvements towards the end of the eighteenth century. This led to the introduction of the pedal harp.

In the year 1894 the piano manufacturing firm of Pleyel and Sons in Paris brought out an instrument that replaced the harp's pedal mechanism with a separate string for each semitone. To popularise this innovation, Debussy was commissioned to write a work for it. This resulted in his *Danse Sacré et Danse Profane*. The chromatic harp was not the success the makers hoped it would be, but Debussy's piece for solo harp and orchestra is still in the repertoire.

The strings of the harp are plucked by the player's fingers, his feet operating the pedals (usually seven) fixed to the base of the instrument. By the operation of these pedals, which raise the strings a semi-tone or a whole tone, it is possible to play in any key. To assist the player's eye, the C strings are coloured red, and the F strings blue.

The harp is admirably suited to the playing of chords and arpeggios, and is particularly effective in the *glissando*, when the fingers are swept across the strings.

Its compass is: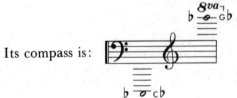

The Sun Music Ballet, one of the most spectacular of modern ballet performances.

Guiseppe Verdi (1830-1901). Composer of some of the most popular operas in musical history. His operas such as *La Traviata* and *Aida* are full of colour and beautiful melodies. He composed his master-pece, *Falstaff*, when he was eighty years old.

Brass

TRUMPET: The modern Trumpet, which in the course of time evolved from related instruments that go back to the hunter's horn, has a cylindrical tube, in which the air column is set in vibration by the vibrations of the player's lips placed in a cup-shaped mouthpiece. The tube is half the length of that of the horn in the same key, and therefore sounds an octave higher than the horn; in fact, it is the highest-pitched, or "soprano" of the brass instruments.

In former times the trumpet had no keys, but keys were added early in the nineteenth century, and valves soon after. The narrow bore of the tube gives it a brilliant tone. Trumpets in B flat and in A are the most commonly used.

Its range:

CORNET: The cornet is not normally to be seen in the modern symphony orchestra, but it is an important member of military and brass bands, and can be very pleasing in solo work. The cornet today is a valved instrument and, like the trumpet, is constructed in B flat or in A.

Its range:

TROMBONE: This, the tenor instrument of the brass family, was in the Middle Ages known as the Sackbut. Like the trumpet, it has a cup-shaped mouthpiece. The Slide-Trombone is so-called, because instead of valves and keys it has a slide which the player pushes in and out, thus lengthening or shortening the tube.

The tenor trombone is built in the key of B flat and reproduces the actual notes written, usually in the tenor clef.

Gluck and Mozart are two of the composers who used the trombone in opera scores, but it was not used in the orchestra until Beethoven wrote a part for it in the finale of his *Symphony No. 5 in C minor*, first performed in 1808. It now plays an important part in compositions, sections of which call for majestic, ominous and dramatic sounds.

Range:

The range of the Bass Trombone is one and a half tones lower than that of the tenor instrument. The bass clef is used.

TUBA: The Tuba is the lowest-voiced, or bass, instrument of the brass family, playing a similar part as the double bass in the string section and the double bassoon in the woodwind section. It has a wide-bore tube which opens out into a broad funnel, which gives it a pompous power and sonority. Though its tone may lack the smoothness of the trombone, it can produce mellow notes.

The tuba has four or five valves which enable it to produce a complete harmonic scale. The most generally used is the bass tuba.

Range:

Percussion

Percussion is the collective name for instruments the tone of which is produced by their surfaces being struck by some kind of stick, or by the hand.

TIMPANI: Also known as "kettle-drums," these are generally used in pairs. The tension of the stretched skin over the bowl, which is supported by legs, is varied by turning a set of thumbscrews set around the rim. The degree of tension applied raises or lowers the pitch. Often the desired notes on the drums need to be altered to fit in with a change of key, which means that the timpanist is required to retune his instrument while the rest of the orchestra is playing.

The timpanist usually has beside him several pairs of drum-sticks of different weights and textures, the heads of which are covered with felt, leather, or other material, ranging from soft to hard. The tone of the timpani can be muted by the placing of a piece of felt or cloth on to the vibrating surface. A "roll" can be produced by two sticks being used alternately and at a rapid speed.

The timpanist is the leader of the percussion family, he and his assistants being called upon to play any of the instruments of his group as required. Range:

SIDE DRUM: This smaller drum, which normally rests at an angle of forty-five degrees, has a crisp tone produced by tapering hardwood sticks striking the surface of the skin, or vellum, which is stretched at both ends of a shallow cylinder. The lower skin can be brought into contact with gut strings or wires, called "snares," to produce various effects.

BASS DRUM: The orchestral bass drum is supported on a low cradle and is covered with thick skin. It differs from the timpani in not producing definite notes and, as its name suggests, gives out a deep sound. When used in dance bands, the drum-stick is often operated by pedals.

104

Effects

CYMBALS: Two circular metal plates are brought together to produce a clashing effect, or by rubbing their edges together, or by striking them with a timpani stick.

GONG: Probably of oriental origin, this hangs from a frame, and when struck by a single hammer produces tones that range from the startling to the solemn. It has no definite note.

TRIANGLE: This triangle-shaped steel bar, with one end open, can be seen in various instrumental groups, from the school band to the symphony orchestra. It is suspended from a stand and can produce rolling or tinkling sounds. It has no definite pitch.

CASTANETS: Of Spanish origin, the "clappers" consist of two round, hollowed pieces of wood or ivory, a pair held by the fingers of each hand. Their clicking sound is frequently heard in Spanish music. They have no definite notes.

TAMBOURINE: This instrument is probably of Arabian origin, but has been known in Europe since about the year 1300. It has a parchment stretched across a wooden hoop, can be struck by the knuckles, rubbed with the thumb, or shaken. To this are affixed little metal plates which produce jingling sounds.

XYLOPHONE: The xylophone, in some form or other and by other names, has existed for many centuries. The modern instrument consists of a series of tuned wooden bars laid out in the form of a table. Metal tubes placed at right angles underneath the bars act as resonators. The bars are struck with wooden sticks, or beaters. It has a compass of from three to four octaves. While the upper notes are dry and "woody," the lower notes yield a more resonant sound. The players can produce arpeggios, consecutive intervals such as thirds and sixths, and also obtain effective *glissandi*, by sliding the stick quickly along on the bars.

In his symphonic poem, *Danse Macabre*, Saint-Saëns achieved a vivid effect by having the xylophone impersonate skeletons rattling their bones against tombstones.

GLOCKENSPIEL: The literal translation of this German word is "play of bells." According to some writers, the glockenspiel originated as a toy imitation of the Flemish carillon. This percussion instrument, which gives out small, bell-like sounds, consists of two rows of steel bars, arranged somewhat in the manner of the piano keyboard. The bars are struck by two metallic hammers, one held in each hand. Formerly, the glockenspiel stood upright in the shape of a lyre, but now rests horizontally on a four-legged table.

TUBULAR BELLS (CHIMES): These are large metal tubes of graded lengths, suspended from a wooden frame and struck at the top with a wooden or raw-hide hammer. They are capable of sounding like church bells and are particularly suited to music of solemn character.

The range,
including semi-tones, is:

CELESTA: This word sometimes appears as "celeste." A keyboard instrument, which has the appearance of a small piano or harmonium, was invented in 1866 by Auguste Mustel of Paris. It has a single keyboard of four octaves, has an action similar to that of the piano, but only one pedal. Its soft, gentle sound was first introduced into the orchestra when Tchaikovsky assigned to it the *Dance of the Sugar-Plum Fairy* in his *Nutcracker* ballet music.

Its range:

Some scores require the use of extra effects; for example: slight-bells, wind machine, wood block, and an anvil. In regard to these *written* compasses, authorities sometimes differ; an extra note or two are often possible.

Having considered the instruments of the string, woodwind, and brass families in some detail, let us see how their tonal ranges compare with those of the human voice.

First, however, a word about Pitch and Quality.

Suppose one player sounds a note (say, Middle C) on a violin, and then a player on a trombone, and another on a clarinet sound the same note. The *Pitch* is the same in all cases, but they sound different, because they have different sound qualities; that is, *Timbre*, or *Tone-colour*.

A woman singing Middle C uses a voice an octave higher than a man singing Middle C. So there is a difference in pitch as well as tone-colour between women's and men's voices.

Within the range of women's and men's voices there are further divisions: high, medium, and low ranges. A woman's voice can be soprano, mezzo-soprano, or contralto; a man's tenor, baritone, or bass.

106

The relationship between the range of musical instruments and the human voice is more or less this:

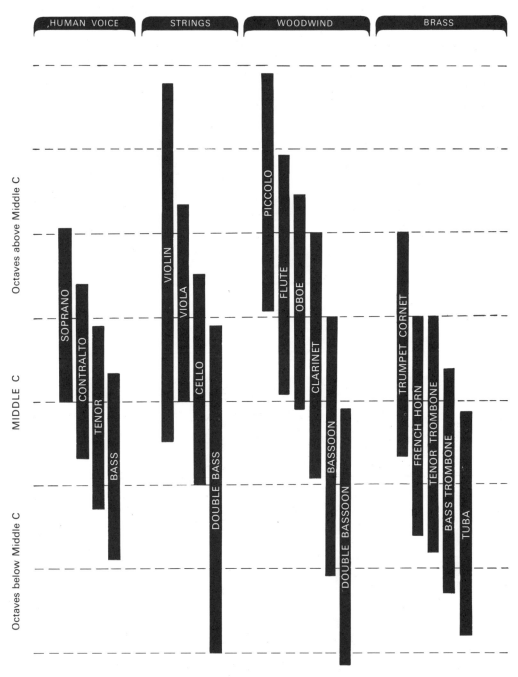

There is nothing new about "pop" music. Spaniards of the eighteenth and nineteenth century improvised music on guitars, tambourines, and castanets just as young people nowadays play variations and improvisations of popular songs in their guitar and rhythm groups.

Modern pop groups are responsible for introducing Indian instruments, especially the sitar, into western-style music. Indian and other Asian music, however, has a very different tonal range from that provided by instruments of European origin. Illustrated above are Northern Indian instruments. *From left*: Two Sitars, one long Tamboura, Sarod (lying down), one Tamboura, two Sitars. In the foreground are two sets of Tabla (small drums and round drums).

Left: Drums, originating from hollowed gourds or logs, were the earliest instruments used by many primitive peoples. The example is from the Congo.

109

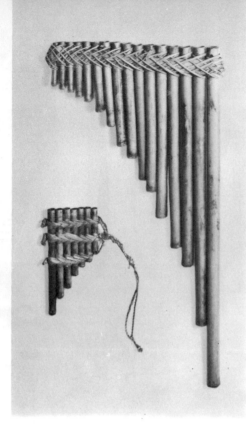

Primitive instruments. At top are reed pipes of the type used throughout Southern Europe and the Middle East for centuries. The "Pan pipes," or syrinx were of this type. At right are didgeridoos, which are amongst the very few musical instruments used by the Australian Aborigines. The didgeridoo is a drone pipe of bamboo or hollowed out sapling, usually about five feet long but for some ceremonial occasions they are as much as fifteen feet long and ornately decorated.

Top: Turkish instruments of the eighteenth century. At left is a trumpet; at right a bugle. Simple instruments of this type did not have reeds. The sound was created by the players lip and breath movements and magnified by the bell. Beneath them are ceremonial drums of the type widely used throughout the South Pacific. Often these smaller drums were carried by dancers and beaten to give tempo for the dance. These specimens came from Papua.

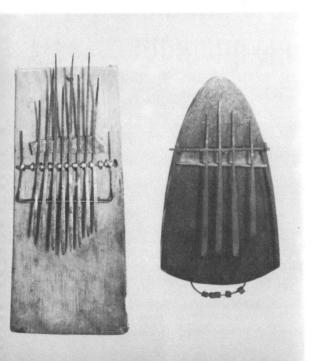

Left: Among the instruments used by people of the Middle East were these simple "twanging" instruments, which were sounded by plucking the vibrating strips of metal. They might be regarded as very early forerunners of the piano.

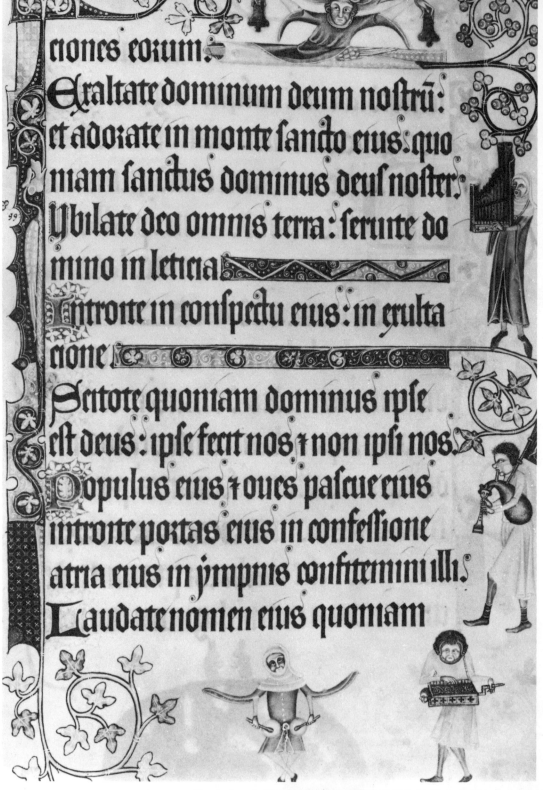

ciones eorum.

Exaltate dominum deum nostru:
et adorate in monte sancto eius: quo
niam sanctus dominus deus noster.

Iubilate deo omnis terra: seruite do
mino in leticia.

Introite in conspectu eius: in exulta
cione.

Scitote quoniam dominus ipse
est deus: ipse fecit nos, t non ipsi nos.
Populus eius t oues pascue eius
introite portas eius in confessione
atria eius in ympnis confitemini illi.
Laudate nomen eius quoniam

The mediaeval artist who illuminated the Luttrell Psalter illustrated this page with
musicians of his period. From the top down, musicians play the bells, the mouth
organ, the bagpipes, hand organ, and drums.

THE
CONDUCTOR 7

BROADLY speaking, the function of a conductor directing a symphony orchestra, a choir, or a small group of instrumentalists, is similar in principle to that of a play producer. Both the conductor and the stage producer bring to life what the composer, or the playwright, has intended should be heard. The medium of communication is through the performing musicians, or the actors.

Good actors may be inadequate as producers. First-rate musicians may fail as conductors. Conversely, a musician who possesses no more than adequate skill as a performer, may succeed as a conductor because of his knowledge, his personality, and the magnetism necessary for inspiring his players (or choristers) to give reality to his directions.

There are, of course, some "virtuoso" conductors of the "prima donna" kind who, lacking solid musical penetration and a full respect for musical truth, will aim to impress by certain extravagances, in the hope that their audience will think that, since their interpretation is "different," they have been gifted by some inner interpretative light. Only the least-critical of their listeners will fall for that bogus attitude; most audiences *know* when a performance is *right*, or at least when something seems wrong with it.

Hans von Bülow, the late-nineteenth century pianist-conductor (who for a time was married to Liszt's daughter) used to say: "A score should be in the conductor's head, not the conductor's head in the score." Gustav Mahler, another dynamic conductor, went so far as to say, "There are no bad orchestras, only bad conducting."

Otto Klemperer (1885-1973). Great German-born conductor, he was expelled from his homeland by the Nazis and became an American citizen. He has composed a Mass and other works.

For as long as group-performance has existed there has been some form of direction from the musician in charge, this at first achieved by hand signals, but in early times the conductor's function was little more than that of a time-beater. Even until the time of Handel, Haydn, and Mozart, the direction was in the hands of either the musician at the keyboard, or the first violinist.

The need for a conductor who could not only set the tempo and beat time, but guide his performers through a more complicated score, came about when the number of players in an orchestra increased and the music developed in complexity. Towards the middle of the nineteenth century orchestral composers with a larger body of players and a greater scope in the instruments to write for, employed more subtle tempi and a wider range of dynamics, and introduced more romantic and colourful elements in their works. It therefore became necessary for the conductor not only to set the ruling tempo at the beginning of the performance, but to remain in firm control throughout.

Although certain references tell us that some conductors in the latter part of the eighteenth century, including Anselm Weber and Johann Reichardt, may have directed with some object held in the hand, it was Louis Spohr who introduced the baton to London. The occasion was a Philharmonic Society Concert, given on 10 April 1820. Spohr in his autobiography tells us that at first the Philharmonic directors protested at this innovation, but it was not long before the word "conductor" replaced the term "at the pianoforte." Mendelssohn also used the baton when he directed a series of London Philharmonic Concerts some little time later. This became the usual practice.

114

Sir Adrian Boult (b. 1889). English conductor, he formed
the B.B.C. Symphony Orchestra in 1930, and later
became chief conductor of the London Philharmonic
Orchestra.

While it is true that in this present century conducting has become a highly
specialised art, over-emphasis is sometimes placed on the conductor at the expense
of the music he is interpreting. Without detracting from his importance, which is
indeed considerable, it is a fact that in these days of lavish publicity he has become
surrounded by an aura of glamour that once was reserved for the prima donna. It is
likely that most serious conductors dislike such a form of Hollywoodian puffery,
while others, given to extravagant gestures, might find it agreeable to bask in the
full glare of the spotlight, both on and off the rostrum.

In the case of the latter kind, it could be said that the conductor stands between
the music and his audience.

The vogue of the "virtuoso conductor" probably began with Louis Antoine
Jullien, a nineteenth century French conductor who sported extravagant moustaches,
brightly-clashing clothes, and many rings. The rostrum on which he stood was
usually decked out in gaudy colours. When he directed a work of Beethoven he
would ostentatiously don a pair of gloves, and a menial would then hand him a
jewel-studded baton on a silver tray. Sometimes, in the middle of a performance,
he would take an instrument from one of the orchestral players and caper round the
platform with it. He died insane. . . .

Arturo Toscanini (1867-1957). Considered one of the greatest conductors in the twentieth century, he escaped from fascism and conducted the N.B.C. Symphony Orchestra in America.

Before taking the first rehearsal of a work the conductor needs to be thoroughly familiar not only with the complete musical edifice, but every single stone that has gone into the making of it. It is not sufficient that he be familiar with the characteristics of every instrument in his orchestra; he must be fully aware of the modern composer's more subtle use of each one, both singly and in its association with the other instruments. His knowledge must cover a wider range of musical idiom than ever before. Modern opera, as well as orchestral scores, demands a great deal more detailed attention than was expected in operatic works written on conventional lines.

When a conductor begins rehearsals of a familiar work, he will have pre-knowledge to guide him. With a new composition he will have nothing to go on (unless there is a record of it) but his own sensitivity to the composer's ideas, and the skill to produce a performance from a blue-print.

A composer may apply himself to an orchestral work for a year, perhaps several years, but it will remain unheard and unknown until an orchestra performs it in the concert hall or in the recording studio. To produce a set of parts, with a copy for every player and a full score for the conductor costs a good deal of time and money. Even then, the composer is to a great extent at the mercy of the conductor to interpret

Leonard Bernstein (b. 1918). American composer, conductor, and pianist, he became famous for his mod-opera *West Side Story*, and is conductor of the New York Philharmonic Orchestra.

Sir John Barbirolli (1899-1970; real name Giovanni Battista). English conductor
of Italian and French descent, he succeeded Toscanini as conductor of the
New York Philharmonic, and later conducted the Hallé Orchestra (1943-68).

every bar as he planned it, and of the musicians' ability to carry out faithfully the
conductor's instructions.

In exceptional cases conductors have the ability to commit every detail of a score
to memory. But more important than such a memory is the deep understanding of
the work itself. To conduct from memory may leave greater freedom for the direction
of finer detail, but a score open on the stand must always be an insurance against
lapses of memory.

Sir Thomas Beecham could conduct a full opera without referring to the score.
Toscanini conducted from memory, one reason being that he was extremely short-
sighted.

Where professional orchestras or choirs are concerned, and of course opera
companies, rehearsal time costs money; therefore, the time must be given to intense
concentration. All concerned must place themselves at the service of the music.

This painting by T. Hill, entitled "Garton Orme at the Spinet," gives a clear picture of the spinet as used in the late seventeenth and early eighteenth centuries as well as showing that an ability to play on such an instrument was regarded as a natural accomplishment for a young gentleman.

An ability to play a musical instrument or at least to sing with reasonable facility was regarded as one of the "elegant achievements" to be expected from educated men and women in Britain and Europe during the eighteenth and nineteenth centuries. This painting is of the Morse family by J. Zoffany.

Sir Eugene Goossens (1893-1962). English conductor and composer, in 1947 he became conductor of the Sydney Symphony Orchestra and Director of the N.S.W. Conservatorium.

A conductor's personality plays a vital part in his control of a group of performers. Some conductors by the magnetism of their personalities supporting the effective word or phrase, can make known to the least-receptive of his players what he requires from them. It is equally true that others, usually in amateur groups, while knowing what they want, are unable to make their meaning clear, and are therefore unable to coax from the performers under their direction the utmost in phrasing, colour, dynamics, and all the subtle points that bridge the gap between the dull, uninspired performance and the memorable one that comes vitally alive.

It goes without saying, of course, that the alert conductor can detect any departures from perfect intonation on the part of any instrument in the orchestra, or from any singer in the choir.

Accompanying a soloist in a concerto demands from the conductor a high degree of sensitivity. He must quickly assess the soloist's musical personality, respect his views concerning the interpretation of the solo part, and should there be a difference of opinion regarding a point of tempo or phrasing, discuss it quietly and tactfully with the artist, on whom the main attention of the audience will be directed at the performance.

When a choir and an orchestra are combined both units should be prepared separately by the chorus-master and the orchestral conductor, so that rehearsal time will not be wasted.

Sir Bernard Heinze (b. 1894). Distinguished Australian conductor, he has received many honours for his services to Australian music. In 1956-66 he was Director of the N.S.W. Conservatorium.

It has been said that the ideal conductor should achieve the maximum effect with the minimum physical effort. This applies at the performance. Gestures should be economical, but expressive. The conductor can explain his wishes in detail verbally at rehearsal, but he must depend solely on gestures during the performance.

Should the reader be unfamiliar with the conductor's method of beating time, the following notes may help:

Simple Duple Time   = 2 beats = down-up
Simple Triple Time   = 3 beats = down-right-up
Simple Quadruple Time   = 4 beats = down-left-right-up.

In the matter of accents, these fall as under:

2 beats in a bar (Simple Duple Time) Strong-weak
3 beats in a bar (Simple Triple Time) Strong-weak-weak
4 beats in a bar (Simple Quadruple Time) Strong-weak-medium-weak.

There are of course many variations in time-beating, for instance waltz time. Instead of beating one-two-three for every bar, which can be tiring for the conductor and sometimes confusing for the orchestra, the conductor may beat only the *first of every bar*.

120

Above: Yehudi Menuhin (b. 1916). American violinist whose wide sympathies have been of great service to music. Since 1959 he has been director of the Bath Festival chamber orchestra.

Below: Herbert von Karajan (b. 1908). Famous Austrian conductor, renowned for his imaginative, impassioned style. He was musical director of the Vienna State Opera and now conducts the Berlin Philharmonic Orchestra.

Lukas Foss (b. 1922). German-born composer who settled in U.S.A. in 1937. His compositions range from a symphony to *Recordare*, inspired by Gandhi's assassination.

From a mere time-beater, the baton has assumed a more subtle role, being used almost as an extension of the conductor's hand, shaping the musical phrases and indicating the character of the music.

The left hand is kept in reserve for sudden accents, an extra intensity or reduction of tone, or as a warning signal. All gestures should be clearly seen by all the players; therefore they should be made at a level no lower than the waist. When a gesture is to reach an unusually large body of performers, e.g., combined choirs or orchestras, or in the case of community singing, it should be appropriately higher and wider and the baton, or hand, raised so that it can be clearly visible to those in the farthest rows.

Not only should the down beat be definite; the preparatory beat is almost equally important. This gesture precedes the action and makes for a clean entry by the performers concerned. In recent years some conductors have preferred to direct a performance without a baton. The above rules apply equally.

Famous conductors come and go. Among those of the nineteenth century whose names we still meet in connection with historic orchestras and performances are: Hans von Bülow, Camille Chevillard, Éduard Colonne, Charles Lamoureux, Hermann Levi, Gustav Mahler, Felix Mottl, Artur Nikisch, Jules-Etienne Pasdeloup, Hans Richter, Vassily Safonoff, Anton Seidl.

Sir Malcolm Sargent (1895-1967). A major British musician, he conducted the Royal Choral Society, Liverpool Philharmonic Orchestra, and B.B.C. Symphony Orchestra.

As we have indicated earlier, first-rate musicians and composers do not always make outstanding conductors. Among the more recent composers well equipped to direct performances of their own works, as well as works by other composers, were Gustav Mahler, Sergei Rachmaninov, Sir Edward Elgar, Jean Sibelius, Richard Strauss, Igor Stravinsky, Ralph Vaughan Williams, Sir William Walton, Benjamin Britten, and Dmitri Shostakovich.

Two conductors whose names are household words are Arturo Toscanini, short in stature and, as we have said, extremely short-sighted, but a martinet, and Sir Thomas Beecham, a champion of Delius and Sibelius, also opera in England, and noted for his sharp wit.

The record has introduced many new and fine conductors to the public.

KINDS OF MUSIC (Vocal)   8

VOCAL music is perhaps the most basic of all musical forms, because music can be created by the voice alone and unaccompanied. In the Highlands of Scotland there is even a form of singing known as "mouth music," in which the singers do not use words but make music by humming and chanting. Composers have used the range and scope of the human voice to create many types of music, from the hymns and anthems of the church to the complex patterns of opera.

Opera

The term Opera means a drama, whether serious or comic, set to music, with acting and scenery, and sung throughout by soloists and chorus, supported by orchestra. Although the date of the first produced opera is usually placed at the year 1600, the word itself, which is an abbreviation of the Italian *opera in musica* ("a musical work") did not come into general use until about the middle of the seventeenth century.

The meanings of related terms, e.g., Opéra Bouffe, Opéra Comique, are given at the end of this chapter.

The Florentine composer Jacopo Peri (1561-1633), known to his contemporaries by the nickname *Il Zazzerino* because of his long hair, is credited with having written the first opera. Peri sought to restore the kind of declamation associated with Hellenic tragedy and thereby set a plan for what we know as *recitative*. The result was a music-drama called *Dafne*, for which the poet Ottavio Rinuccini supplied the libretto. This was privately performed at the Palazzo Corsi in Florence in 1597 and created such a deep impression that it was repeated several times. The music, however, has been lost.

The success of *Dafne* encouraged Peri to experiment further and in 1600 he was invited to provide another music-drama for the festivities associated with the marriage of King Henry IV of France with Maria de' Medici. With a text supplied by Rinuccini, Peri's *Euridice* was produced; this is generally referred to as the first opera.

ITALY: We can therefore look upon Italy as the cradle of opera, this form of sung drama encouraged by a group known as the *Camerata* who thought in terms of a return to the classic Greek play wedded to music. An important member of this group was Vincenzo Galilei, father of the astronomer Galileo Galilei. He and certain others of the *Camerata* advocated the replacement of polyphony with a simple vocal line, and a stylised type of declamation for a single voice with only a strictly economical accompaniment.

Other Italian composers were soon lured to this interesting form, notably Giulio Caccini (c. 1558-1618) who, it is said, had some of his own compositions included in Peri's productions.

At first operas were performed privately, or within a select circle at the courts, but in 1637 the first "commercial" operatic venture took place when a public opera house was opened in Venice. Later, public opera migrated to Paris, Vienna, London, and other cities.

The next important figure in opera was Claudio Monteverdi (1567-1643), a native of Cremona, who put new theories into practice. Whereas Peri and Caccini had placed rather more emphasis on the action and words, Monteverdi developed a finer balance between the words and the music. A new era in operatic convention began when Monteverdi's *Orfeo* (*Orpheus*), with libretto by Alessandro Striggio, was produced in 1607 at Mantua. This work possessed so much vitality and appeal that it was repeated elsewhere; indeed, it has often been revived in modern times.

Monteverdi not only brought a new dignity and unity to opera, he increased the value of the orchestra to the extent of adding a greater variety of instruments.

Before the end of the seventeenth century Italy had many opera houses, Venice alone about ten, and gradually more spectacular staging and scenic effects were introduced.

With such approval extended by the public to opera in its new form, many composers turned to it, the greatest about that time being Alessandro Scarlatti (c. 1659-1725), who is understood to have been born at Palermo, Sicily. Scarlatti, whose numerous works included more than 100 operas, cultivated a type of Italian opera that swept through Europe in the eighteenth century. His first-known opera, bearing the impressive title, *L'errore innocente ovvero gli equivoci nel sembiante*, was produced in Rome in 1679. He was also responsible for popularising the three-movement operatic overture.

Claudio Monteverdi (1567-1643). He increased the range of operatic expression by introducing richer harmonies and more dramatic orchestration. His operas include *Orfeo* and *The Return of Ulysses*.

During the seventeenth and eighteenth centuries some of the principal singers in continental opera, and in churches, were *castrati*, this being the Italian word for castrated. These eunuchs retained their high-pitched voices, although the vocal quality was not necessarily the same as that of a boy. Many leading roles in Handel's operas were written for *castrati*. This practice was later discontinued when women were more generally included in the opera cast.

The long list of Italian composers who contributed much to opera includes: Cavalli (1602-1676), Pergolesi (1710-1736), Piccinni (1728-1800), Paisello (1741-1816), Cimarosa (1749-1801), Rossini (1792-1868), Donizetti (1797-1848), Bellini (1801-1835), up to Verdi (1813-1901), today the best-known of these if we consider the proportion of his works still in the standard repertoire.

A musical heir of Donizetti and Rossini, Verdi first achieved fame by writing operas of popular appeal, in which melodramatic, sometimes tawdry, subjects became vehicles for melodic decoration. But he took care that his principal characters always had something ear-catching to sing. After completing *Aida* in 1871 he retired from the operatic scene, to emerge again sixteen years later, at the age of seventy-four, as the composer of *Otello*. Six years later he completed *Falstaff*, which proved that an octogenarian could adapt himself to a totally new form of operatic expression. This marked him as a musical phenomenon.

Gioacchino Rossini (1792-1868). A prolific operatic
composer. His works abound with melodic richness,
colourful orchestration, and exciting crescendos.
He was celebrated in his own lifetime.

From the time of Verdi, indeed, from that of Peri, Italy has faithfully preserved its
love of opera. Prominent towards the end of the nineteenth century was Puccini
(1858-1924) who composed little else but operas. His unerring dramatic instinct
and his sense of "theatre" led to the choice of plots convincingly suited to operatic
treatment, stories set in different countries: a bohemian Paris (*La Bohème*), Japan
(*Madam Butterfly*), Peking (*Turandot*), Rome (*Tosca*), a mining town in California
(*Girl of the Golden West*).

Throughout his career his creative urge hovered between Italianate romanticism
and stark realism; in the latter he followed a trend known as *Verismo* (truth-like
realism) that was based on the violent and the sordid. This was a distinct breakaway
from the unconvincing conventions of earlier works.

Two early examples of this realistic approach were Leoncavallo's *I Pagliacci*,
a swiftly moving melodrama based on an actual incident involving jealousy and a
fatal stabbing, and Mascagni's *Cavalleria Rusticana*, a passionate tragedy of unfaith-
fulness and violent death.

Puccini's one-act opera, *Il Tabarro* (The Cloak), first played in 1918, with a river
barge as the setting, ends in grim realism when the jealous husband, offering to give
his wife shelter under a cloak, discloses her lover's corpse and savagely throws her
on to it.

Giacomo Puccini (1858-1924). One of the world's most successful operatic composers. His operas are characterised by expressive melodies and a vivid sense of theatre.

Modern opera, whether from Italy or from other countries, usually revolves around real people in real situations; people have replaced conventionalised types.

Space permits mention of only some of the Italian opera composers of the late-nineteenth and the twentieth centuries: Boito, Busoni, Alfano, Respighi, Montemezzi, Pizzetti, Cilèa, Giordano, Ponchielli, Wolf-Ferrari, Malipiero, Dallapiccola, Zandonai, Lualdi. Gian-Carlo Menotti, a composer of "realistic" operas for which he wrote his own libretti, was born in Italy, but moved to the United States of America at the age of seventeen.

FRANCE: Having flourished in Italy, opera spread throughout Europe and other parts of the world. In France it was at first associated with the court ballet, the most favoured French kind of entertainment, new works being commissioned by noble families.

Having touched on this aspect, we might mention that the linking of ballet and opera continued to a greater or lesser degree until recent times. In 1834 Berlioz stated that French opera would find an excuse for the inclusion of ballet, "even as a representation of the Last Judgment!" When Weber's *Der Freischütz* was revived in Paris some years after his death, Berlioz was asked to orchestrate Weber's piano piece, *Invitation to the Dance*, this being interpolated within the action of the opera.

A scene from Act II of *La Bohème*, by Puccini,
performed by the Australian Opera.

Conforming to the French tradition that an opera must include an elaborate ballet, Gounod introduced into Act V of Faust (while the ill-starred Marguerite is asleep in a prison cell) a scene, in which Faust meets the most famous beauties of history—Laïs, Cleopatra, Helen of Troy, Phryne. There are, of course, numerous other examples.

To return to our historical outline. If we disregard dramas with music played by the Trouvères, in the thirteenth century, and early attempts at opéra comique, we arrive at the year 1646, when *Akebar, roi de Mogul*, written and composed by the Abbé Mailly, was performed at Carpentras. This is generally referred to as the first real French opera. In 1659 Robert Cambert, who was born in Paris in 1628 and died in London in 1677, collaborated with the librettist Pierre Perrin in several works, the most successful being *Pomone* (1671), the first French opera to be publicly staged in Paris.

Then came Lully, who was to exert a powerful influence on French opera. Originally known as Giovanni Battista Lulli, this composer was born near Florence in 1632, went to Paris at an early age, became a naturalised French citizen and lived for the rest of his life in that country.

In 1664 Lully began a collaboration with Molière in a series of comedy-ballets, which eventually evolved into a vital form of French opera. He developed the unaccompanied *recitative* designed to suit the French language and declaimed in a manner modelled on the best actors of his time. He also created the "French" or "Lully" type of overture. Beginning with a slow, sometimes a pompous, section, this style of overture was soon copied by other composers. Among his most successful operas were *Alceste, Amadis de Gaule, Armide et Renaud, Cadmus et Hermione,* and *Persée.*

Jean Philippe Rameau (1683-1764) is another prominent figure in the progress of French opera. A skilful performer on the harpsichord, organ and violin, he taught himself to compose and in 1726 published his *Traité de l'harmonie,* a treatise that advanced revolutionary theories in relation to harmonies and chord progressions that had a powerful effect on other composers.

Rameau had reached the age of fifty before his first opera appeared. This was *Hippolyte et Aricie,* founded on Racine's *Phèdre,* produced at the Académie de Musique in 1733. This production and those that followed, which came in for lavish praise and harsh abuse, did much to spark off a series of conflicts concerned with the writing and presenting of opera.

Although the subject-matter of Rameau's operas often followed in treatment the Italian conventions, the music contained significant innovations, and stereotyped accompaniments were replaced by orchestrations that ventured into bolder harmonies and more ingenious rhythms. He also used the orchestra to striking effect for descriptive purposes, for example the suggestion of storms and angry seas.

Speaking of operatic reforms, we naturally think of Gluck. Like most reformers, he met a great deal of bitter opposition.

Christoph Willibald von Gluck (1714-1787) was born in Bavaria, studied in Prague, visited London in 1745, lived in Paris between 1773 and 1779, then settled in Vienna, where he died. Rebelling against the stereotyped alternation of arias and *recitatives* and the lack of unity in the operas of his day, he sought to link one aria logically with the next, and carry on the action more convincingly by fitting *recitatives* with unobtrusive accompaniments. His aim, as he explained, was "to restrict music to the true office of serving poetry by means of expression, and following the story without interrupting the action or stifling it with a useless superfluity of ornaments."

Gluck succeeded in obtaining the patronage of Marie Antoinette, who had been his pupil in Vienna, through whose support he presented his *Iphigénie en Aulide* in Paris in 1774. French versions of his *Orphée, Alceste,* and *Armide* followed during the next three years.

Christoph Willibald Gluck (1714-1787). An important operatic reformer, he insisted that music and dramatic action should be combined to create an effective unity.

Then in Paris a war waged between the supporters of Gluck and those of Italian composers, chiefly Nicola Piccinni (Piccini), an Italian composer of more than 100 operas, who spent most of his life in Paris, where he died.

Gluck's influence on other composers, if indirect, was significant. In his striving for dramatic truth, he encouraged his librettists to write with classical simplicity; his arias evolved naturally from the text; his *recitatives* were alive with declamatory realism, and vain singers found no outlet for a display of vocal acrobatics.

Another important figure in opera was Giacomo Meyerbeer (1791-1864), the eldest son of a wealthy Berlin banker. During a visit to Italy in 1815 he came under the influence of Rossini and other Italian composers. In 1826 he took up residence in Paris, went back to Germany in 1842 to become musical director to the King of Prussia, but returned to Paris some years later and died there.

Meyerbeer's first operas were in German, some later ones in the Italian style, but from 1826 he became immersed in the study of French opera to which he brought fresh ideas. He introduced to the Paris stage spectacular effects that to some extent anticipated those of Wagner. Among his most successful operas were *L'Africaine*, *Dinorah*, *Robert le Diable*, *Les Huguenots*, and *Le Prophète*.

On this foundation French opera developed its own personality and during the nineteenth century became adorned by the works of such composers as Halévy, Hérold, Auber, Boïeldieu, Adam, Berlioz, Gounod, Méhul, David, the Italian-born

Cherubini, Chabrier, Delibes, Lalo, Thomas, Belgian-born Grétry, Bizet, Saint-Saëns, Dukas, Massenet, Roussel, and Charpentier.

In line with those of other countries French operas became more flexible in their subjects and treatment; a closer association with literature lent it a greater degree of lyricism, and the tragic became more credible. The music, too, assumed greater freedom and logic. Also, opera production, with the aid of developing stage mechanics, became more spectacular.

In 1902 Debussy adopted a new approach when he transferred to the operatic stage Maeterlincks' play *Pelléas et Mélisande*. In this, Debussy insisted on a sensuous unity of poetry and music, intensity being achieved by the power of suggestion. During rehearsals he instructed the cast to avoid conventions of acting and singing, in fact, to forget they were singers. He asked that the dialogue be spoken with subtle intonation and that every word should be enunciated with the utmost clarity.

Debussy's contemporary, Ravel, is more closely identified with piano and orchestral compositions and songs than with opera, but with *L'Heure Espagnole* (1911) and *L'Enfant et Les Sortilèges* (1925) he added two delightful works to the French repertoire. These short operas, the first set in a Spanish clockmaker's shop, the second the tale of a naughty child in a setting in which pieces of furniture come to life, reveal Ravel's original mind and artistic restraint.

French composers of opera continued to experiment and venture beyond the periphery of operatic convention. Milhaud's *Christophe Colomb* (1930) demanded vast staging, including a cinema screen on which scenes were flashed between the acted scenes. Poulenc, a brilliantly witty composer, completed his first opera in 1944. His *Les Dialogues des Carmélites* had for its subject the guillotining of nuns in 1794; *Les Mamelles de Tiresias* is described as an opera-burlesque. Jolivet, who with Baudrier, Lesur, and Messiaen formed in 1934 a group called *La Jeune France*, stretched the modern operatic formula still farther.

GERMANY: According to most music historians the first German opera appears to have been *Dafne* by Heinrich Schütz, first performed at Torgau in 1627 on the occasion of festivities associated with the marriage of George II, Landgraf of Hesse, with the sister of the Elector of Saxony. Rinuccini's libretto, which had served the Florentine Peri in 1597, was used in a German translation by Martin Opitz. The music has been lost.

For a while Italian operas continued to be imported, then German opera took a more definite step forward when Johann Theile's *Adam and Eva* was produced in Hamburg in 1678; this was the first *Singspiel* ever publicly performed in the German language.

Hamburg then became the chief centre of opera in Germany, where Reinhard Keiser (1673-1739), the director of the Hamburg Theatre reigned supreme. His operas, totalling more than 100, mixed German and Italian words. Among the other composers who wrote operas for that theatre were: Nikolaus Strungk, Johann

Franck, Johann Förtsch, Johann Conradi, and Johann Mattheson. In the early years of the eighteenth century Handel brought out some of his operas in Hamburg.

Of equal, and perhaps of greater popularity, were the light comic operas of Johann Adam Hiller (1728-1804). These included the interpolation of songs and spoken dialogue, the works known as *Singspiel* (*song-plays*), of which Hiller is credited to have been the real originator.

In the history of opera, Wolfgang Amadeus Mozart carved for himself a special niche. He was born in Salzburg, Austria, in 1756 and as well as elevating every musical form that he touched, he composed some of the greatest operas of their kind.

Mozart wrote nineteen stage works, the first a *Singspiel*, entitled *Die Schuldigkeit des ersten Gebotes*, completed at the age of eleven, the last *Die Zauberflöte*, written three months before his death at the age of thirty-five. His *Bastien et Bastienne*, written at the age of twelve, and his *Il Seraglio* (*Die Entführung aus dem Serail*) fourteen years later can be placed in the *Singspiel* class, having dialogue instead of *recitative*, but the music is more unified with the drama than in the case of earlier composers writing in that style.

To a great extent Mozart's operatic sympathies were with the Italian school, but in his case the arias and concerted vocal items were conceived to suit the situation and to invest every character with a definite identity. While accepting many conventions of opera, he made the best possible use of them, infusing a new vitality and a new dimension into the mould.

German opera stands greatly in debt to Carl Maria von Weber (1786-1826), often referred to as the founder of German Romantic Opera. A member of an aristocratic family, he had the benefit of excellent musical training with Michael Haydn, the brother of Joseph Haydn, in Salzburg, with Kalcher in Munich, and with the Abbé Vogler in Vienna. (A relation, Constanze Weber, married Mozart in 1782.)

Part of his training was with theatre companies and, after gaining valuable experience as Director of Music at a Breslau theatre, he became court musician to the Prince Eugene of Württenburg at Carlsruhe, travelled through Germany, and in 1813 was engaged to reorganise and direct the Prague Opera Company.

Weber was a practical man of the theatre and became the pioneer of romanticism in German opera, his *Der Freischütz* standing as a landmark in the history of German operatic music. He foreshadowed Wagner in the treatment of the supernatural and anticipated him in the use of the *leitmotif*.

Among his best-known operas are *Der Freischütz*, *Oberon*, *Euryanthe*, *Abu Hassan*, and *Peter Schmoll und seine Nachbarn*.

Ludwig van Beethoven (1770-1827), who enriched every form of music that claimed his attention, wrote only one opera, *Fidelio*, but it stands as another land-mark in the history of opera. Whereas many composers had been content with trivial stories on which to base their works, and with flimsy libretti, Beethoven held to the

Hugo Wolf (1860-1903). Great Austrian composer of songs. His music is deeply expressive, the beauty of his settings revealing the true marriage between poem and music.

conviction that in opera the dramatic treatment and the music were equally important.

When at last he came across a text by Josef Sonnleithner, based on *Léonore ou L'Amour Conjugale* by Jean Nicholas Bouilly, he knew at once that in this story of liberty's struggle against oppression, and of a woman's unswerving devotion, he had found the right material. He set himself the task of composing music that, rather than becoming a vehicle for vain singers, would glorify the ideals expressed in the story. So carefully did he plan the score over the next two years that he made eighteen versions of Florestan's aria *In des Lebens Frühlingstagen*, ten of *Wer ein holdes Weib*, while one sketch-book alone contained three hundred and forty-six pages of notation, with sixteen staves to a page. The opera completed, he wrote four overtures for it.

Towards the middle of the nineteenth century a great innovator entered the arena of German opera, and the musical world became aware of a man called Richard Wagner.

In his penetrating study, *Wagner as Man and Artist*, the English author and critic Ernest Newman said of him, "He was one of those dynamically charged personalities after whose passing the world can never be the same as it was before he came."

Wagner was born at Leipzig in 1813 and at a time when Romanticism was ready to burst into full flower in literature, art, and music. His life story divides itself into

134

Carl Maria von Weber (1786-1826). Founder of German romantic opera. His operas such as *Der Freischütz* and *Oberon* are notable for their poignant melodies and stirring orchestration.

three main periods: poverty and struggle; frustration of his aims; ultimate fulfilment and a place of honour in the musical world.

In time, Wagner was to take up opera where Weber had left off, but as a reformer he developed slowly. His first two operas, *Die Feen* and *Liebesverbot* gave no indication whatever that this was the composer who would one day create massive music-dramas. He had his first success in 1842 with *Rienzi*, a kind of imitation-Meyerbeer, based on Bulwer-Lytton's novel about that fourteenth century Roman patriot.

Wagner's next operas were *Der Fliegende Holländer* (*The Flying Dutchman*) (1843), *Tannhäuser* (1845), and *Lohengrin* (1850). Having advanced this far, he became convinced that the old forms must be cast aside and a new one created. He reached his ultimate goal with his massive music-dramas, in which words and music were wedded in dramatic unity; when the orchestra, rather than providing an accompaniment for the singers, became an integral part in building up emotional moods and directing the attention to detail in the action. He employed as no other composer before him the *leitmotif*, or guiding theme, that associated itself with the main characters and ideas.

After scaling new peaks with the cycle, *The Ring of the Nibelung* (*Das Rheingold*, *Die Walküre*, *Siegfried*, and *Götterdämmerung*), he sustained his greatness with *Tristan und Isolde* and *Parsifal*.

While it is true that he combined music and action dynamically, there are some orchestral excerpts from his operas and music-dramas that have achieved independence in the concert hall.

In 1873 the foundations of a "Wagner Theatre," designed by the composer himself, were laid at Bayreuth and three years later this opened with the first complete performance of the "Ring" series, *Der Nibelungenring*, and from that time until the present, with advice from Wagner's heirs, this Festival City has perpetuated the composer's genius, in productions that kept strictly to tradition.

Wagner had his imitators, many of whom during this century have languished in the shadows. The next German composer to make a dramatic, even startling, impact on opera was Richard Strauss (1864-1949) who, in no way related to the Viennese family, was born in Munich. After conducting orchestras in many parts of Germany, he was invited by Wagner's widow to direct the first Bayreuth performance of *Tannhäuser*.

Strauss grew up in a Germany throbbing with the ideologies of her poets, philosophers, artists, and musicians. He conceived his symphonic poems in terms of tonal splendour, applying new sonorities to the orchestral opulence introduced by Wagner. His first work for the stage was *Guntram*, produced in 1894, his first real success in the theatre the comic opera *Feuersnot*, presented in Dresden in 1901.

Gradually he broke away from Wagnerian influences and developed his own style of emotional projection, creating a musical language of his own. Most of his later operas are dominated by female characters whom he placed under a psychological microscope, while he examined their innermost feelings with uncanny insight. His orchestra he treated with amazing virtuosity.

In 1905 Strauss created something of a scandal by his stage treatment of Oscar Wilde's play, *Salomé*. While some people found it "hideous" and "revolting," it helped to make his name as a great composer of opera. His next opera, *Elektra*, which followed four years later shocked the squeamish even more. A change in style began with the lighter, romantic *Der Rosenkavalier*, still an operatic favourite in many parts of the world.

For his opera *Ariadne auf Naxos* (1916) Strauss adopted another new approach and used an orchestra of only thirty-five players, thus pointing the way for other "chamber" operas. Although the story is complicated and not likely to be understood fully by audiences unless they study it beforehand, this opera contains some of Strauss's most appealing melodies. It was said that the *coloratura* part written for one of the sopranos, Zerbinetta, was the most difficult of its kind written up to that time.

Unlike many opera composers, Strauss was fortunate in his choice of librettists, for most of his operatic music is written to libretti of true literary quality. His greatest collaborations were with Hugo von Hofmannsthal, a dramatist and at that time one of Austria's foremost poets.

During and since the time of Richard Strauss German opera, despite wars, political upheavals, and *avant garde* intrusions, has remained in a reasonably healthy

Morag Beaton in the title rôle of Puccini's *Turandot*, in a
production by the Australian Opera which premiered in
1967 and was re-staged in 1971.

state, mixing the experimental with the conventional. We can mention briefly some of the composers who have attempted to keep the flame alight.

Otto Nicolai (1810-1849), choosing an English subject, achieved a distinct success with his tuneful *Die lustigen Weiber von Windsor* (*The Merry Wives of Windsor*), while Friedrich von Flotow (1812-1883) wrote operas in his native German, also in French and Italian. *Marta* and *Alessandro Stradella* were the most successful. Peter Cornelius (1824-1874), originally an actor and critic, and a pupil of Liszt con- tributed several stage works, notably *Der Barbier von Bagdad*.

Engelbert Humperdinck (1854-1921), an assistant to Wagner, may not be numbered among the greatest of post-Wagner composers, but in *Hänsel und Gretel*, based on a Brothers Grimm tale, and using German nursery tunes and original melodies, he created a charming work that is still periodically revived.

Hans Pfitzner (1869-1949) who clung to a romantic formula that owed something to Schumann and Humperdinck, had a brief fame with his *Palestrina* and other operas. Franz Schreker (1878-1934), Austrian born but for some years resident in Berlin, brought an impressionistic approach to his *Der ferne Klang* (*The Distant Sound*), produced in 1912, and eight other operas. Max von Schillings, born in 1868, a chorusmaster at Bayreuth, enjoyed a good deal of popularity at the beginning of this century, his *Mona Lisa*, showing Wagnerian influences, meeting a fair measure of success after being staged in 1915. Kurt Weill (1900-1950), a pupil of Humperdinck and Busoni, had an early success with *Die Dreigroschenoper* (*The Threepenny Opera*), a modern adaptation of *The Beggar's Opera*, slanted towards social problems of the day.

With Schoenberg, Berg, and Hindemith, we group three composers of more imposing stature. Arnold Schoenberg (1874-1951) was born in Austria but lived and worked in Berlin until driven from Germany by the Nazis who condemned him as a composer of "decadent" music. *Moses und Aron*, of which only two of its three acts were completed, is thought to contain some of his best opera music.

A distinct contribution was made to European opera when the Austrian-born Alban Berg (1885-1935) presented his *Wozzek* in Berlin in 1925. The composer wrote his own libretto, basing it on a play by Georg Büchner. Despite its "advanced" technique, *Wozzeck* reached a wide and appreciative audience.

Opera became one of the many interests of Paul Hindemith (1895-1963), who was born in Germany but settled in the United States in 1939. His best-known opera is *Mathis der Maler* (*Mathis the Painter*), based on the life of the artist Grünewald. This he also arranged as a symphony.

The prolific German composer, Paul Graener (1872-1944), wrote several operas, his most successful being *Don Juan's Last Adventure*, first produced in Leipzig in 1914. German opera composers born in the early years of the twentieth century include Boris Blacher, who followed an individual path in his *Romeo and Juliet* and *Prussian Fairy Tale*; Werner Egk, who chose subjects from various sources, for

Richard Wagner (1813-1883). One of the greatest innovators of all time, he had tremendous influence on the course of music. His "music dramas" culminated in the magnificent *Ring* cycle.

example *Peer Gynt* from Ibsen, *Irish Legend*, after Yeats, and *The Government Inspector*, after Gogol. Wolfgang Fortner, a composer drawn to the twelve-note method, based his *Blood Wedding* on Lorca's play, while Karl Amadeus Hartman, a pupil of Webern, wrote a "pacifist" opera, entitled *Simplicius Simplicissimus*.

Eugène d'Albert, a brilliant pianist, who was born in Scotland of French-English parents, settled in Germany. He composed twenty operas, written for and produced in Germany, although his most famous, *Tiefland* was first produced in Prague.

One of the early names in Austrian opera is Johann Joseph Fux (1660-1741) who wrote eighteen. Since then Austrian composers of opera have kept in step with those of Germany; indeed, many of their works have become part of the German repertoire. These include Ignaz Brüll (1846-1907), Wilhelm Kienzl (1857-1941), Julius Bittner (1874-1939), Egon Wellesz (b. 1885) who settled in England in 1939, and Ernst Krenek (b. 1900).

It is of some historic interest that the Austrian-born Hugo Wolf (1860-1903), one of the greatest composers of German *lieder*, wrote one opera. Entitled *Der Corregidor*, this was produced at Mannheim in 1896—for one night only. It was not performed again during his lifetime.

ENGLAND: Until the end of the sixteenth century in England, music, on any extended scale, belonged to the church. The forerunner of English opera was the Masque, a form of entertainment chiefly cultivated in the seventeenth century that

Grand opera makes particular demands upon the performers because they have to combine singing with dramatic acting, as shown in this photograph of Waldimiro Ganzarolli.

combined poetry, vocal and instrumental music, and spectacle. Among the earliest masques of real significance were *Comus*, with Milton's words set to music by Henry Lawes (c. 1595-1662), and *Cupid and Death*, a setting of words by James Shirley, composed by Matthew Locke, performed in 1653, and revived in 1659, with additional music by Christopher Gibbons. This form continued into the eighteenth century, T. A. Arne's *Alfred* (which contains the famous *Rule, Britannia*) being brought out as late as 1740.

Most music historians place the first real English opera at 1656, when *The Siege of Rhodes* was produced in London. The libretto was by W. d'Avenant, the music written by Locke, Lawes, and other composers. The music was lost.

Opera in London in those times had its setbacks. Among the reasons for this were the Puritans' attitude towards public theatres, the Civil War, the Great Plague of 1665, and the Great Fire of London in 1666.

A high watermark in English opera was reached about 1689 (the actual date is uncertain), when *Dido and Aeneas*, an opera by Henry Purcell, with text by Nahum Tate, was first performed. This was written for a School for Young Gentlewomen kept by Josias Priest at Chelsea. The duration of this work is little more than an hour, but its emotional range gives the impression of being a work of considerably greater length. It is certainly a masterpiece of early English opera. It is most likely that *Dido and Aeneas* was played only once at the school, but it has had many revivals, even up to the present day.

After the early death of Purcell in 1695, English opera languished until George Frederick Handel came on the scene. Just what course opera and oratorio in England would have taken had not the German-born Handel taken up residence there is a matter for interesting conjecture. As a tribute to his greatness, and his service to England, he was buried in Westminster Abbey.

Handel was twenty-five years of age when he paid his first visit to England, then under the influence of Italian opera. When his first London opera *Rinaldo* (completed within two weeks) was presented with success during the following year, he decided to make England his permanent home. Other operas by him quickly followed but, despite his unrivalled reputation, he subsequently reached a stage of near-bankruptcy after losing heavily on elaborate productions of his stage works. It was his oratorio, *Messiah*, written within twenty-four days and produced in Dublin in 1742, when his fortunes were at their lowest ebb, that turned poverty into riches.

Handel's music embraced a wide range of expression. He introduced greater variety into his orchestras; he completely understood the human voice and wrote with unerring skill for it. His operas still offer a challenge to the vocal flexibility of singers.

Ballad Opera

A new style of English ballad opera came with the production of *The Beggar's Opera* in 1728, with words by John Gay and music arranged from various kinds of popular tunes—English, French, and Italian—by Dr Christopher Pepusch. It was first produced by John Rich at a theatre in Lincoln's Inn Fields. John Gay's text introduced characters of questionable behaviour, but the public reacted to the work with relish.

Gay and Pepusch collaborated on a sequel, entitled *Polly*. Although published in 1729, the censors considered it subversive of authority and banned its public performance. It was not produced until 1777. *The Beggar's Opera*, however, was kept alive by frequent performances, and has remained before the public by new arrangements by various librettists and composers. In a modernised version it was produced in Berlin in 1928, two hundred years after its initial presentation, with libretto by Bert Brecht, and music by Kurt Weill. It was given under the German title *Die Dreigroschenoper*. Benjamin Britten has adapted the original for the modern stage.

In the early eighteenth century the popularity of *The Beggar's Opera* gave impetus to a stream of ballad-operas, a form that mixed spoken dialogue with existing music, often tunes of the day, set to new words.

The romantic elements of the English novel spread to the theatre and, in addition to the home-grown product, romantic operas from Italy, France, and Germany were staged in England. In 1824 the German composer Weber was offered £1,000 to direct his *Der Freischütz* and *Preciosa* in London. He was then commissioned to compose a new opera for Covent Garden, which resulted in *Oberon* being first performed there in April, 1826, a few weeks before his death.

Operatic romance flourished in England and a succession of light operas appeared, written by Barnett, Benedict, Balfe, Wallace, Macfarren, Bishop, Goring Thomas, Cowen, Mackenzie, Stanford and other British composers who had brief successes.

Between 1871 and 1896 London was to find great delight in the operas of Gilbert and Sullivan who created a style all their own. Sullivan, whose real ambition was to write grand operas, achieved something of that ambition in 1891 when his *Ivanhoe* was produced in London. This was to run for 160 nights, after which it had but few performances.

The list of operas by English composers produced during the twentieth century is a long one. In 1909 Sir Thomas Beecham conducted *The Wreckers* by Dame Ethel Smyth at His Majesty's Theatre and repeated the success at Covent Garden in the following year. This opera had had its first production in Leipzig in 1906.

Due largely to Beecham's unflagging interest, Frederick Delius became more widely known, and in 1910 Covent Garden staged his *A Village Romeo and Juliet* (Beecham conducting), which had first been produced in Berlin in 1907. Other operas by Delius, *Irmelin*, *Koanga*, *The Magic Fountain* and *Fennimore and Gerda* were staged in later years.

The 1914-1918 War seriously affected large-scale opera seasons in London, although some were produced in other parts of England. In 1919 Covent Garden became active again, and from that year world *premières* of operas by British composers have been presented there, also in other theatres throughout England.

Some of the operas by British composers given world *première* performances at Covent Garden during the fifty years from 1919 have been: *David Garrick* (Somerville), *Judith* (Goossens), *Pickwick* (Coates), *Julia* (Quilter), *Don Juan de Mañara* (Goossens), *The Serf* (Lloyd), *The Olympians* (Bliss), *Troilus and Cressida* (Walton), *The Midsummer Marriage* (Tippett).

One of the most prolific English composers of opera during recent times has been Benjamin Britten, whose first opera, *Peter Grimes* appeared in 1945. Among other Britten operas are: *The Rape of Lucretia, Albert Herring, Billy Budd, The Turn of the Screw, Gloriana, A Midsummer Night's Dream, Let's Make an Opera* ("an entertainment for young people") and three "Church Parables for Church Performance," *Curlew River, The Burning Fiery Furnace,* and *The Prodigal Son.*

Other notable additions to twentieth century opera by British composers are: *The Immortal Hour* (Boughton); *Hugh the Drover, Riders to the Sea, Pilgrim's Progress, Sir John in Love* (Vaughan Williams); *King Priam* (Tippett); *Savitri, At the Boar's Head, The Perfect Fool* (Holst); *The Lodger* (Phyllis Tate); *The Olympians* (Bliss); *Nelson, A Dinner Engagement* (Berkeley). *A Tale of Two Cities*, and two comic operas, *The Devil Take Her* and *Prima Donna* were composed by the Australian composer, who took up residence in London, Arthur Benjamin. Malcolm Williamson, another Australian composer now living in London, has written a number of operas, including *English Eccentrics, Our Man in Havana, The Violin of Saint Jacques, Dunstan and the Devil*, and *Lucky Peter's Journey*.

Humphrey Searle's opera *Hamlet* was commissioned by the Hamburg State Opera and first performed there in March 1868, exactly one hundred years to the month after an opera of the same name, by Ambroise Thomas had its first production in Paris. Searle's opera had its British *première* at Covent Garden in April 1969. In April 1970 the world *première* of an opera commissioned by The Friends of Covent Garden took place, this entitled *Victory*, based on the novel by Joseph Conrad, with score by Richard Rodney Bennett.

RUSSIA: Until the early part of the nineteenth century Russian opera was little known outside its geographical borders. No doubt there was little of it, the people being content with Italian forms. In 1836 Michail Glinka (1804-1857), described by Liszt as the "prophet patriarch of Russian music," brought out his *A Life for a Tsar (Ivan Sussanin)*, thereby earning the distinction of being called the "Father of Russian Opera." His *Russlan and Ludmilla* followed in 1842.

With these works a Russian national school of opera began, and Glinka was to have a profound influence on the composers of his country who followed him. Russian history and orientalism were to play important parts in the development of

The partnership of W. S. Gilbert and Sir Arthur Sullivan produced a
series of light operas which have known constant popularity throughout the English-speaking world for over a hundred years. Above is a
scene from *Iolanthe*.

locally conceived opera, with folk-songs and writers of the stature of Pushkin and
Tolstoi providing further stimulus.

Glinka was followed by Alexander Dargomijsky (1813-1869), a "nationalist"
composer who strove even more vigorously to rid his country's music of Italian
influences. His *Russalka* (after Pushkin) was produced in St Petersburg in 1856.
His finest work, *Kamennyi Gost* (*The Stone Guest*) was not quite finished at the time of
his death. Completed by Cesar Cui and orchestrated by Rimsky-Korsakov, it was
produced in 1872.

Another important link in the development of Russian opera was Alexander
Borodin (1833-1887), who became one of the "nationalist" group of composers
known as *Kuchka* ("The Five"), or in an English translation of a term used by
Stassov, "The Mighty Handful." The other members were Balakirev, Cui,
Moussorgsky, and Rimsky-Korsakov.

144

At the age of twenty-eight Borodin became a professor of chemistry at the Academy of Medicine in St Petersburg. His busy academic life left him little time for composition. As he once said, "I can compose only when I am too unwell to give lectures." He did, however, contribute a significant work to Russian opera with his *Prince Igor*, completed by Rimsky-Korsakov and Glazunov.

Rimsky-Korsakov (1844-1908) enriched Russian opera with *Sadko*, *The Golden Cockerel* (which is also known as a ballet), *The Snow Maiden*, *Ivan the Terrible* (sometimes given the title *The Maid of Pskov*), *May Night*, *The Tsar's Bride*, *The Tale of Tsar Saltan*, *Mozart and Salieri*, and *The Tale of the Invisible City of Kitezh*.

Undoubtedly the greatest Russian opera of that period was *Boris Godunov*. Modest Moussorgsky (1839-1881) completed this about 1869, a lavish spectacle based on Pushkin's drama concerned with a famous sixteenth century Tsar. It was first produced in St Petersburg in 1874, in Moscow two years later, and afterwards became known outside Russia in a revised version by Rimsky-Korsakov, who went so far as to conventionalise Moussorgsky's individual idiom, and to "correct" the harmonic realism. In this version much of the power and dramatic truth were lost. Some more "traditional" producers prefer the original.

Moussorgsky left *Khovantschina*, and *Sorotchinsky Fair* unfinished, his way of life, i.e., living in squalid quarters in deep depression and drinking to excess, sapping his capacity for serious work.

Never a member of the "nationalist" group, Tchaikovsky (1840-1893) held a lifelong interest in opera; between the years 1868 and 1891 he composed ten. Even when advised by sincere friends that his talents lay in other directions, he replied, "To refrain from writing operas is the act of a hero. The stage, for all its tawdry glitter, attracts me irresistibly."

Today, Tchaikovsky's best-known operas are *The Queen of Spades* and *Eugen Onegin*. With the latter work, based on Pushkin's poem, the composer, realising its lack of theatrical development, preferred to call it a series of "Lyrical Scenes" rather than an opera. For all that, it is a work of great charm and melodic interest.

Among those composers born towards the end of the nineteenth century who attempted to continue the Russian nationalist tradition were Ippolitov-Ivanov, Vassilenko, and Glière. Ippolitov-Ivanov composed six operas and completed Moussorgsky's unfinished opera *The Marriage*. Vassilenko, a pupil of Ippolitov-Ivanov, remodelled his cantata, *The Legend of the City of Kitszh* as an opera and, after absorbing French and Asian influences, brought out his opera *The Snow Storm*. Glière, also a pupil of Ippolitov-Ivanov, and best known for his music for ballet, composed *Shah-Senem* and other operas.

Gnessin, Krein, and Asafiev adopted a more modern approach, and Julia Weisberg, a prominent woman composer of the Soviet Union wrote *Gulnara*, an opera based on the Scheherazade stories.

Rachmaninov (1873-1943) wrote three operas, *Aleko*, *The Miserly Knight*, and

Francesca da Rimini, which have never quite rivalled the popularity of his other works.

Stravinsky (b. 1882) has always shown a rare gift for writing convincingly in any medium he chose. His ballet scores, *L'Oiseau de Feu*, *Petrouchka*, and *Le Sacre du Printemps*, written in 1910, 1911, and 1913, broke new ground in ballet music. His opera *Le Rossignol* (*The Nightingale*), begun in 1910 but interrupted by the three Diaghilev commissions mentioned above, was completed in 1914.

Stravinsky's later works for the stage fall into the categories of either opera or opera-oratorio. His one-act *Mavra* is in the style of *opera buffa*, his *Oedipus Rex*, with libretto by Jean Cocteau, after Sophocles, in the nature of opera-oratorio. His most important full-length opera is *The Rake's Progress* (1951), which to a great extent followed established conventions.

Soviet Opera

Operas by Soviet composers began to make their appearance in the nineteen-twenties, but at first there was only a limited relationship between the revolutionary subjects in the texts and the musical idiom that merely imitated older traditions. It therefore became obvious that the new Soviet operatic form could not progress with such passive imitation. Creative reforms were called for.

In the late twenties such operas as Deshevov's *Ice and Steel*, Knipper's *The Northern Wine*, set a style with new sounds expressing the text, rather than the musical plan falling back on melodious arias, ensembles, and choruses.

The Georgian composer, Zakhary Paliashvili, a pupil of Taniev, and the author of *Abesalom and Eteri* (1919) and *Daisi* (1923) has been called the "father of professional music" in his Republic.

Ivan Dzerzhinsky's *And Quiet Flows the Don* presented realistic features. This, first produced in Leningrad in 1935, helped to determine the pattern of Soviet opera.

Other operas written and produced about the same time included *The Kamarinsky Peasant* (1933), *Namesday* (1935), and *Mother* (1939) by Valery Zhelobinsky, and *Battleship Potemkin* (1939) by Oles Chishko.

Although Sergei Prokofiev (1891-1953) wrote in a number of large-scale forms, he retained a lifelong interest in opera. He composed his first, *The Giant*, to his own libretto, at the age of nine, and *Feast During the Plague*, after Pushkin, at twelve. His first mature opera, *The Gambler*, based on Dostoevsky's novel, was written in 1917, *The Love of Three Oranges*, the most successful opera of his early years, following in 1919. *The Flaming Angel*, dealing with witchcraft and obsession, occupied his attention from 1922 to 1925.

Prokofiev's later operas are *Semyon Kotko* (1939), *Betrothal in a Nunnery*, after. Sheridan's play *The Duenna* (1940), and *Story of a Real Man* (1948). In 1952, a few months before his death, the final version of *War and Peace*, based on Tolstoi's novel, saw completion.

146

A valuable contribution to Soviet opera was made by Dmitri Kabalevsky with his *Colas Breugnon* (1937), *In Flames* (1942), *The Taras Family* (1947), and *Nikita Vershinin* (1955).

In 1953 *The Decembrists*, a Soviet opera of the post-war period, by Yury Shaporin, had considerable success. Other notable operas were added to the Soviet repertoire by such composers as Kasyanov, Spadavecchia, Molchanov, Rubin, and Shantyr.

Shostakovich (b. 1906), a dominating figure in Soviet music, has always shown power and striking originality in his writing, even if bureaucratic control interfered with his artistic conscience in the earlier stages of his career. His opera *The Nose*, after Gogol, was written in 1929. From 1930 to 1932 he was occupied with *Lady Macbeth of Mtsensk*, this stressing certain unsatisfactory aspects of the old regime. Although this opera was enthusiastically received by the public, it was condemned for its "faults" by Soviet officials; *Pravda*, the official organ of the Communist Party, criticised it severely on the score that it "tickled the perverted tastes of the bourgeois audience by its jittery, noisy and neurotic music."

SPAIN: In Spain operatic history owes much to the *Zarzuela*, a national lyrico-dramatic form of entertainment combining singing and spoken dialogue. The term *zarzuela* is said to have derived from the name of the Spanish royal residence near Madrid where these entertainments were first performed. The chief forms are the *zarzuela chico* in one act, usually comic, and *zarzuela grande* in two or more acts, and usually of a more serious nature. The music is generally of definite Spanish character.

The *zarzuela* has gone through many transformations since the seventeenth century, since when numerous composers have adopted the form, the music in some respects being comparable with that of Offenbach and Lecocq.

Among the early composers of full-scale Spanish opera were Tomas Bretón (1850-1923), whose *La Dolores* (1895) had a conspicuous success, and Felipe Pedrell (1841-1922), the teacher of Falla and Granados, who worked towards a Spanish nationalist school of composition. Attempts to follow this lead were made by Albéniz (1860-1909) with his *Pepita Jimeniz* (1896), and Granados with *Goyescas* (1916), and Falla (1876-1946), whose *La Vida Breve* became known in many countries. Falla, who aimed to free the music of Spain from outside influences, particularly those of France and Italy, seldom used folk-tunes, but he invested his music with characteristic Spanish colour and feeling.

Under Falla's stimulus, Esplá wrote *La bella durmiente*, and Halffter, *La Mort de Carmen*.

Many other modern Spanish composers, while not contributing to opera, have greatly enriched song. Some of these are mentioned in the chapter on Song.

OTHER COUNTRIES: Although recording companies have extended their interest to operatic works by other European composers, many of their works have remained unheard outside their own countries. Some, however, deserve our attention.

In Czechoslovakia, Smetana, the founder of the National School of modern

Czech music, wrote a number of operas, including *Dalibor*, *The Kiss*, *The Devil's Wall*, *The Secret*, *Libusa*, and the universally acknowledged *The Bartered Bride*. Dvořák followed with *Armida*, *Russalka*, *The Jacobin*, *Dimitrij*, and others; Fibich with *Sarka* and *The Tempest* (after Shakespeare); Weinberger with *Schwanda the Bagpiper*; Nivak with *The Imp of Zvikov*, *A Night at Karlstein* and *Lucerna*. Janáček composed eleven operas, including *Jenůfa*, *The Cunning Little Vixen*, *The Whirlpool*, and *The Makropulos Affair*.

In Finland Melartin, Palmgren, Kuula, and Merikanto have given some attention to opera, although their orchestral work and songs are of greater importance.

Switzerland produced Sutermeister, Klose, Schoeck, Liebermann, Honegger, Einem; Holland, Dopper, Brandt-Buys; Hungary, Erkel, Dohnanyi, Bartok, Kodaly; Poland, Moniuszko, Szymanowski; Denmark, Klenau, Paterson-Berger; Sweden, Atterburg, and Blomdahl, whose prophetic opera *Aniara* has for its setting a space-ship in the year 2038.

Australian opera composers include John Antill, Arthur Benjamin, Colin Brumby, Clive Douglas, Eric Grose, Raymond Hanson, Alfred Hill, Duncan McKie, James Penberthy, Larry Sitsky, Margaret Sutherland, Peter Tahourdin, Felix Werder, and Malcolm Williamson, who is referred to under England.

The operas of these and other Australian composers vary in character, from operetta type to tragic grand opera, in duration from thirty to one hundred and fifty minutes.

AMERICAN OPERA: Locally written opera in the United States of America has not had a long history, but during the last hundred years or so her composers have attempted vigorously to make up for lost time.

One of the first American grand operas was *Leonora*, based on Bulwer-Lytton's play, *The Lady of Lyons*, with music by William Henry Fox, produced in 1845. Ten years later George Frederick Bristow composed *Rip Van Winkle* to a text arranged from Washington Irving's tale. *The Pipes of Desire* by Frederick Shepherd Converse was written in 1906, this, later, to be the first opera by an American composer to be staged at the Metropolitan Opera, New York. Converse followed this in 1911 with *The Sacrifice*, for which he wrote his own libretto.

Victor Herbert, Irish-born cellist, composer and conductor, settled in New York in 1886. He wrote such successful operettas as *Naughty Marietta* and *Babes in Toyland*, then a full-scale opera, *Natoma*, based on a story of early California. This was first staged in Philadelphia, with such stars as Mary Garden, Huberdeau, McCormack and Sammarco in the cast. Herbert's second opera was *Madeleine*.

Horatio Parker included two operas among his works, his opera *Mona* winning a prize of ten thousand dollars.

Walter Damrosch's first opera was *The Scarlet Letter*, based on the novel by his father-in-law, Nathaniel Hawthorne. His next opera was *Cyrano*, after Rostand's *Cyrano de Bergerac*, produced at the Metropolitan in 1913. *The Man Without a Country* was another of his stage works. Charles Wakefield Cadman, a composer of ballads, wrote an American opera, entitled *Shanewis*, the story of a white man's infatuation with an American Indian girl.

Other American operas produced about this time were: *The Temple Dancer* by John Adam Hugo, *The Legend* by Joseph Breil, *The Canterbury Pilgrims* and *Robin Hood* by Reginald de Koven, *Azora, Daughter of Montezuma* and *Cleopatra's Night* by Henry Hadley. When Hamilton Forest took Dumas' *La Dame aux Camelias* as the basis for his *Camille* he could not have been aware that it would be compared with Verdi's setting, *La Traviata*.

Writer and radio commentator Deems Taylor composed two operas that remained in the Metropolitan repertoire for some years, *The King's Henchman*, a variation of the *Tristan and Isolde* legend, and *Peter Ibbetson*. His third opera was *Ramuntcho*.

Louis Gruenberg, born in Russia but brought up in the United States from the age of two, contributed several operas to the American stage, *Emperor Jones*, based on Eugene O'Neill's play being the best-known. Howard Hanson scored a success in 1934 with *The Merry Mount*, in which Lawrence Tibbett starred. Dutch-born American song writer, Richard Hageman added *Capon Sacchi* to the growing list.

Variety was introduced into American opera in 1937 when Fritz Reiner in Philadelphia conducted an opera-buffa by the twenty-six years old Gian-Carlo Menotti, *Amelia Goes to the Ball*. Menotti was born in Italy but took up residence in the United States of America in 1928. He was to follow this with *The Island God* (1942), *The Medium* (1946), *The Telephone* (1947), *The Consul* (1950), *The Saint of Bleecker Street* (1954), *Maria Golovin* (1958), and the ballad-opera, *The Unicorn, The Gorgon and the Manticore*. Menotti's *Amahl and the Night Visitors* was commissioned for television in 1951, *The Old Maid and the Thief* for radio some years before that.

It was Menotti who supplied the libretto for *Vanessa*, an opera by Samuel Barber, who also wrote *A Hand at Bridge*. For his operas *Four Saints in Three Acts* and *The Mother of Us All*, Virgil Thompson chose texts adapted from Gertrude Stein.

Aaron Copland (b. 1900) is usually referred to as one of America's most important composers. In 1937 Orson Welles produced his first opera *The Second Hurricane* ("to be sung by young people") and his next operatic venture was *The Tender Land*, commissioned by Richard Rodgers and Oscar Hammerstein II in recognition of the thirtieth anniversary of the League of Composers. The story was concerned with family life in the Midwest in the early nineteen-thirties.

A wide diversity of theme and musical style exists between operas written by three pupils of Bloch: *The Warrior* (Bernard Rogers), *Solomon and Balkis* (Randall Thompson), and *The Trial of Lucullus* (Roger Sessions). William Schuman gave his opera *The Mighty Casey* a baseball background. Operas by Marc Blitzstein, a pupil of Schoenberg, include *The Cradle Will Rock* and *No for an Answer*. Leonard Bernstein, one of the most versatile American musicians of his generation, has written works for the stage, including *Trouble in Tahiti* and *West Side Story*.

When first presented (Boston) in 1935, George Gershwin's *Porgy and Bess* was billed as "An American Folk Opera." The question whether it is just that, a folk opera, has often been debated. Call it what you will, it is a definite landmark in American opera, a work expertly written for a Negro cast, a score packed with haunting tunes of original character. *Porgy and Bess* is based on a vivid story by Du Bose Heyward, who collaborated with George Gershwin's brother, Ira, in writing the libretto.

Among the younger American composers who have made use of American folk melodies are Carlisle Floyd in *Susannah* (1955) and Douglas Moore in *The Ballad of Baby Doe*.

Kurt Weill's *Down in the Valley* (originally for students) makes use of five American folk songs, the others composed in a similar style.

TYPES OF OPERA

OPERA:
: The parent term covering stage works which are sung.

GRAND OPERA:
: Operas in which every word is sung. There are some exceptions, when some lines are spoken. A useful term to distinguish "serious" opera from the lighter forms, e.g., operetta.

OPERA BOUFFE:
: A French term referring to a light opera or operetta.

OPERA BUFFA:
: An Italian term referring to a form of comic opera, particularly the eighteenth century kind.

OPERA COMIQUE:
: A French term, meaning literally comic opera of a type which received a vital stimulus from such composers as the eighteenth century Philidor and Monsigny. In the nineteenth century the term was applied to an opera, whether comic or serious, which contained spoken dialogue.

OPERA SERIA:
: An Italian term signifying serious opera, in contrast to *opera buffa*.

OPERA-BALLET:
: Stage works in which opera and ballet shared equally, e.g., those of Lully and Rameau.

OPERA-ORATORIO:
: A blend of the two forms, generally using soloists, chorus, and orchestra, but with the action curtailed, which can be as effectively presented on the concert platform as on the stage. Stravinsky's *Oedipus Rex* is an example.

BALLAD OPERA:	A type of state entertainment with spoken dialogue popular in England during the eighteenth century, its character more closely related to comic opera than to grand opera. The success of *The Beggar's Opera* stimulated a long succession of such works in these times.
CHAMBER OPERA: (German *Kammeroper*)	An intimate form of opera, employing a limited number of soloists, a small chorus and orchestra, suitable for the smaller type of theatre or hall.
COMIC OPERA:	A type similar to the *opera buffa* in which the spoken lines share equal importance with the music; in other words, dialogue is interspersed with songs, duets, trios, and choruses. This term has been applied to the stage works of Gilbert and Sullivan, these are also called operettas, and Savoy Operas, eight of them having been produced at the Savoy Theatre, London.
MUSIC DRAMA:	A term usually referring to large-scale stage works conceived on a broader pattern than the usual opera. The post-*Lohengrin* productions of Wagner fit into this category.
OPERETTA:	An Italian term, meaning "little opera"; in French *opérette*. The word came into general use first in France when the composer Hervé so called his short stage works of light character. In English-speaking countries the word has been applied, often loosely, to works not of the *grand opera* type.
MUSICAL COMEDY:	Another broad term, referring to popular stage entertainments containing dialogue and singing, the music often less unified, and much lighter, than in the true *operetta*.

Some Thoughts on Opera

Someone once described opera as a bigamous marriage between three arts—music, acting, and décor. The union, however, be it illicit or otherwise, has been condoned for a long time; opera has existed for several centuries, and it still attracts large audiences. Composers in every country are still writing operas.

The purist playgoer may criticise opera on the grounds that if the plot is a sound one it is interfered with by the intrusion of music. He may argue that *Othello*, *Faust*, and *Salomé* are self-sufficient in the form Shakespeare, Goethe, and Wilde wrote them, that the adding of music could not improve them. It could be argued the other way, that a composer in turning an established stage work into an opera is not adding to it; he is presenting it in another art form. An artist, in painting a landscape does not aim to improve on nature, but *re*-present it in art. Just as the landscape continues to retain its identity, so does the status of the original literary work remain unaffected.

Opera is often censured for being unreal, artificial. So is a man speaking in verse, or indulging in long monologues; so is ballet. People do not ordinarily speak in the manner of a character in *The Tempest* or *Lysistrata*, or move in the manner of Giselle or Daphnis.

An audience at an opera is unconcerned because the people on the stage are not behaving as people in ordinary contemporary life. As in classic drama or ballet, they accept operatic conventions which suggest an illusion of reality. If the music fits the action, then these are accepted more readily. The opera house becomes a place for, to use an overworked phrase, "the suspension of belief." It is the beauty, or expressiveness, of the music that holds the attention.

It is true that we seldom meet convincing acting in opera. Good singers are not always good actors. After all, it cannot be easy for an operatic singer to concentrate on the words, the music, and the action at the same time, even supposing he has been thoroughly trained in acting. But matters are improving in that regard.

Up to the nineteen-thirties opera singers were automata; they had two gestures, a sweep of the right arm, a sweep of the left. A corpulent Rodolfo found the physical task of embracing a stout Mimi somewhat less than successful. (Leading tenors and *prima donnas* diet and exercise these days.) But the public came to *hear*; music is what they wanted: it mattered little if Faust, in his love-duet with Marguerite, left the poor lady stranded while he came down-stage to address his closing impassioned phrases direct to the audience. And the audience applauded, which is just what the company, and the composer, wanted.

The author can remember an incident (by no means rare) in the pre-television era during the Tomb Scene of *Lucia di Lammermoor*, when the ill-fated Edgardo, having delivered his last aria, stabbed himself, and gave a convincing exhibition of dying. Then, in response to the applause, he got up, repeated the aria with even greater emotion and, after searching on the floor for the dagger, met a histrionic death for the second time.

The production of opera has come nearer to reality since that time, that is, as near as conventions allow. As we have already noted, *verismo* had taken a grip on opera plots with such works as *Cavalleria Rusticana* and *I Pagliacci*, and other operas followed in which stark realism was played up by librettists and composers. Producers aimed at *verisimilitude*. Acting became more realistic, if not always completely natural. Although extravagant movements were curtailed, gestures, like the story, were still larger than life. But no one minded. The music was still the main inducement to attend opera.

Something could, of course, be said about the social cult of "going to the opera," especially fashionable first nights, but that need not concern us here.

Donald Smith (tenor) as Don Alvaro with Robert Allman (baritone)
as Don Carlo in Verdi's *The Force of Destiny*.

The once prevailing fashion, introduced by vain and selfish singers, of repeating arias in response to applause, and thereby holding up the action, has generally disappeared. The producer and the conductor have louder voices in the production of opera these days.

At one time opera stars dictated to both management and conductor; to the composer if he were still alive. When Bizet's *Carmen* went into rehearsal in 1875, the leading lady objected to the aria written for her first appearance on stage. Bizet wrote thirteen others, and when none of these met with the *prima donna*'s approval, he brought into use an old Spanish air which he adapted as the now famous *Habanera*. Campanini, when taking over the role of Don Jose in *Carmen* in 1878, strongly protested because he had to sing in what was the nearest thing to a love duet, not with the leading lady in the title role, but with Micaela, a less important character.

Numerous interferences from principal singers could be quoted. Opera singers still have their temperamental moments, and still indulge in outbursts of jealous indignation, many no doubt being exaggerated either by gossip reporters or publicity writers. Producers and conductors of opera no doubt are still sorely tried, but conditions generally have improved a great deal.

Libretti

When Puccini appeared on the Italian opera scene towards the end of the nineteenth century, the stage met a composer with an unerring dramatic instinct that led him to stories suited to convincing operatic treatment. He would wait until he had found the right plot, searching vigorously all the time. He called himself a "hunter of wild-fowl and opera libretti." No Italian composer had ever gone to greater lengths to obtain the best librettists, nor to ensure a faithful carrying out of his own ideas.

It was not uncommon for Italian composers before Puccini to show poor taste in choosing subjects for their operas; moreover, many were ill-served by their librettists. Verdi was one of these. Until well on in his career his music had to rise above flimsy plots and poor libretti. With his two greatest operas, *Othello* and *Falstaff*, written late in life, he was fortunate in having as librettist Arrigo Boito, who was a successful composer as well as a fine poet.

Richard Strauss, in planning his operas, sometimes took over established plays and almost all his operatic music is wedded to texts of high literary quality. Also, he was singularly fortunate in securing as librettist for certain of his stage works Hugo von Hoffmannsthal, one of Austria's foremost poets and dramatists.

Quite a number of composers have written their own libretti, with varying degrees of success.

Performances

During the last hundred years more and more attention has been given to the actual *production* of opera, some of the best men in their profession being called into service. According to dependable writers, performances during the first half of the nineteenth century left much to be desired. The productions were inadequately and inexpertly rehearsed, the supporting orchestras were of insufficient numbers and of low musical quality, and self-opinionated principals, with a total disregard for "team-work," paid as little attention to artistic standards as they did to the conductors.

Nor were the audiences any more disciplined. At Milan, Berlioz found "the theatre full of people talking at the top of their voices, with their backs to the stage." Today, the behaviour of thoughtless people still causes irritation by their noisy arrival after the overture has begun, and their audible chatter during the performance. It has often been mentioned that Sir Thomas Beecham once found it necessary to silence a loquacious Covent Garden audience with a "shut up!" delivered in loud and clear tones from the rostrum. Audiences generally have improved in the matter of manners over the last twenty years, but there is still room for further improvement.

Which Language?

A knowledge of the text, at least of the story-line of an opera, helps towards the understanding and enjoyment of the work.

A point often debated is whether opera should be sung in the language in which it was originally written, or in the language of the country where it is being performed. The answer remains a matter of personal opinion. If, for instance, we attend a performance of a Verdi opera, we can sit back and enjoy the melodies that pour from the throats of the principal singers. If the libretto has been translated into English, we are often too painfully aware of the inequality between the text and the music.

Throughout the world, particularly in cities without permanent opera companies, operatic works have been kept alive by the record which has brought the greatest music, and the finest singers and orchestras, into the home. During the twentieth century the vast music-dramas of Wagner have reached widespread converts when recording companies engaged the best artists to record, first excerpts, and later complete versions. Then followed complete recordings of performances from Bayreuth, an immense technical undertaking. This is only one instance of the public arriving at an appreciation of opera through the record.

Despite the predictions of pessimists, it seems that opera is here to stay.

Oratorio

Oratorio is a dramatic poem, usually of sacred character, written for solo voices and chorus to the accompaniment of an orchestra. Unlike opera, it is performed without action, scenery or costumes.

Dramatic-choral representations of religious subjects, e.g., incidents from the

Old and New Testaments, have been traced back to the twelfth century, so we can regard oratorio as the outcome of the medieval Mystery and Miracle plays.

The term Oratorio came into use when a Florentine priest, St Filippo Neri organised a congregation of Oratorians and presented a series of sermons in the oratory of his Church of San Girolamo della Carità in Rome. To make his sermons more attractive, and to illustrate more clearly their meanings, Neri introduced the *lauda spirituale*, a type of religious song set for several voices which had its origin in Florence in the year 1310.

The success of this innovation went towards developing the Oratorio, or, as it was called, *Rappresentazione per il oratorio*. Originally, these choruses had little thematic unity in relation to the sermons, but gradually they became more appropriate to the subject and assumed a more compact continuity.

This type of performance, holding its popularity, continued after the death of Neri in 1595, and was further developed by Emilio del Cavalieri, an Italian composer who spent most of his life in the service of the Medici family. Cavalieri's *La Rappresentazione dell' Anima e del Corpo* (*The Story of the Body and the Soul*), produced in Rome in 1600 is generally considered the first noteworthy oratorio. This, an allegorical piece, written for soloists, chorus and orchestra, was of elaborate structure.

Following this landmark numerous oratorios were written by Italian composers, including Giacomo Carissimi (1605-1674) and his pupil Alessandro Scarlatti (1660-1725). Scarlatti broadened the scope of the oratorio by giving the aria a more definite status, and melodies a more impassioned sweep. Others of that time who were writing in that form were Caldara, Colonna, and Stradella, but none of their oratorios surpassed those of Scarlatti. Such composers as Lotti, Marcello, Leo, and Jomelli produced oratorios in the early part of the eighteenth century; after this those of Italy paid more attention to their new love, opera.

Sometimes the operatic and the oratorio patterns overlapped and we find Rossini's *Mosè in Egitto* (*Moses in Egypt*) referred to as an opera and as an oratorio, it having been performed both on the stage and on the concert platform.

Oratorio in Italy by the turn of the twentieth century had receded into something of a backwater until it was revived by Lorenzo Perosi who composed about twenty-five New Testament oratorios for the Vatican.

Before we pass on to Germany we must of course mention Palestrina, who included works in the oratorio form among his church compositions, which total several hundred, also Giovanni Gabrieli, the teacher of Heinrich Schütz during the latter's stay in Venice. We might, therefore, regard Schütz as a link between Italian and German oratorio, the latter an outcome of the *Geistiges Schauspiel*, a type of presentation illustrating a religious subject in musical terms, which had become popular early in the fourteenth century. On his return to Germany Schütz introduced Italian styles into his music, including his six oratorios. He also adopted a type of *recitative* which had an affinity with the old plainsong.

The arrival of Johann Sebastian Bach on the scene came at a time when musical thinking in Germany was changing, when, in the case of the oratorio, more emphasis was being placed on the contemplative than on the Italian-style drama. This point is borne out if we consider Bach's Passions and his use of the *chorale-prelude*.

The Passion, a musical setting of the biblical story of Christ's death became in Bach's hands a noble expression of religious faith. Sir Hubert Parry has described the *St Matthew Passion* (more correctly, *The Passion According to St Matthew*) as "the richest and noblest example of devotional music in existence."

Only part of Bach's total output has come down to us. (We must remember that it was Mendelssohn who rescued from obscurity the *St Matthew Passion* and other works of Bach after they had remained in manuscript, and forgotten, for over a century.) Certain authorities claim that Bach wrote five Passions. Those according to *St Matthew* and *St John* are still frequently performed. In 1939 German musicologists set about reconstructing the available parts of the *St Mark Passion*.

It could be mentioned in passing that in 1946 the Swiss-born composer, Frank Martin, completed his oratorio *Golgotha*, inspired by Rembrandt's etching *The Three Crosses*, which some critics at that time hailed as "the finest *Passion* since J. S. Bach." To quote the composer himself:

> My aim in this oratorio is quite different from that of J. S. Bach. His work being church music written for his church, it seems that his *Passions* express primarily the emotions of the faithful towards the crucifixion . . . these directed to professing Christians whose faith and feelings they express. But my *Golgotha* tries to present the event itself—and allow the listener to learn his own lesson. It is indeed an oratorio to be played in a church, but it is not church music.

A more recent work in this style is the *Passion*, to give its full title *Passion and Death of our Lord Jesus Christ*, by the Polish composer (b. 1933) Krzystof Penderecki.

The oratorio style has been used in various countries and in various ways, according to the message intended to be conveyed. The first Soviet oratorio, for instance, was written in 1927 by a group of eight student composers to mark the anniversary of the October Revolution.

Bach's *Christmas Oratorio* is the collective title for six cantatas, each intended for performance on six days from the First Day of the Festival of Christmas to the Feast of Epiphany. His *Easter Oratorio* differs from his setting of the Christmas story in that it has no Evangelist to recite the narrative, it contains no quotations from the Gospels, and there are no chorales.

Unlike Bach, Handel did not have to cope with amateurs in the performance of his large choral works; his choirs were composed of professional singers, all male, the soprano parts being sung by boys and the alto parts by men. His choirs, however, contained no more than twenty-five or thirty members, this number being increased in the case of special performances of the festival kind.

Another scene from Verdi's *The Force of Destiny*, with Donald Smith
as Don Alvaro and Franca Como (soprano) as Leonora.

It must also be remembered that Handel's oratorios were presented in theatres
or halls, not in churches. His *Messiah* was first performed in the Music Hall,
Fishamble Street, Dublin. His long list of oratorios begins in 1704 with the *German
Passion according to St John* and ends with *Jephtha* in 1751.

The pattern of oratorio set by Handel was used by Haydn and many other composers, and with the increasing popularity of large-scale choral works, composers
in Europe, England, and America found the oratorio a rewarding form of musical
expression. Among those in Germany were Keiser, Mattheson and Telemann, all
contemporaries of Bach and Handel. Somewhat later were Graun, Hasse, J. C.
Bach, Hiller, and Dittersdorf. C. P. E. Bach, another son of Johann Sebastian,
made some outstanding contributions to an advanced style in oratorio.

Of the late eighteenth century Viennese composers of oratorio, Haydn was one
of the most successful. His *The Creation* and *The Seasons* still hold honoured places in
the choral repertoire, his earliest, *Il ritorno di Tobia,* first performed in Vienna in
1775 is less known.

Mozart composed a considerable number of choral works, but his oratorios are not considered the most significant, while Beethoven's reputation in this form rests on *Christ on the Mount of Olives*.

Almost a quarter of Mendelssohn's works are in some form of choral writing. Of particular importance are his oratorios, *St Paul*, first presented at Dusseldorf in 1836, and *Elijah*, the first performance of which was given at Birmingham under the composer's direction. The German text had been translated into English by William Bartholomew.

"No work of mine," Mendelssohn wrote in a letter to his brother, "ever went so admirably the first time of execution, or was received with such enthusiasm."

Mendelssohn's contemporary, Liszt, wrote two oratorios that enjoyed considerable success in their time, *The Legend of St Elizabeth* (1865) and *Christus* (1873).

In the nineteenth century France was not a strong competitor with other countries in the field of oratorio, although Gounod's *The Redemption* enjoyed a fair measure of success in his time. Berlioz added a bright page to the history of French choral music with his sensitively conceived *l'Enfance du Christ* (*The Childhood of Christ*) set to his own text. *Les Béatitudes* was a notable achievement by the Belgian-born César Franck. *Samson et Dalila*, composed by Saint-Saëns as a biblical opera, has at times been performed in concert form, then referred to as an oratorio.

There are numerous borderline cases where a choral work stands either between the conventional oratorio and cantata, or with a foot in each territory. In *La Légende de Saint-Christophe*, composed by César Franck's pupil, Vincent d'Indy, there is a combination of oratorio and music-drama. Brahms's *Ein Deutsches Requiem* (*A German Requiem*), written to texts from Luther's translation of the bible, is non-liturgical and differs from the Roman Catholic Requiem, its theme being the living, rather than the dead. Written on a large scale for soloists, chorus and orchestra, this is sometimes referred to as an oratorio.

England became more fully aware of composers of other countries through their choral music. We need mention only two at this point. In 1845 the German Mendelssohn was invited by England to "provide a new oratorio," which resulted in his *Elijah* having its first performance in Birmingham. The Czech Dvořák found a wider appreciation of his value as a composer when his *Stabat Mater* was presented in London in 1882, and his cantata *The Spectre's Bride* in Birmingham five years later.

Handel was born at Halle, Saxony, but was naturalised in his adopted country. He was of German birth, but is buried in Westminster Abbey. So completely did he dominate the musical scene in London that he is looked upon as having set a standard in English oratorio that served for succeeding generations.

Oratorio, of both inspired quality and academic rectitude, continued to flourish vigorously in England during the nineteenth century. Of particular importance during the latter part of the century were the choral works of Parry and Stanford. Perhaps we could look upon them as the musical descendants of such composers as Thomas Arne, whose *Judith* was originally produced at Drury Lane, London in 1761. When this was presented at Covent Garden in 1773 it marked the first occasion in London when women were permitted as members of the chorus; even then they sang only the soprano parts.

Judith also was taken as the subject for an oratorio by Parry, about whom Delius remarked, "Had he lived long enough he would have set the whole Bible to music." (Perhaps Delius was paraphrasing Schumann's flattering comment on Schubert as a song-writer in relation to German poetry.)

Two of Stanford's best-known oratorios are *The Three Holy Children* and *Eden*. His two hundred published works include choral works in almost every form.

Among the many British composers who added works to the oratorio repertoire at about the same time as Parry and Stanford were Cowen, Macfarren, Mackenzie, Bridge, Stainer, Coleridge Taylor, Sullivan, and Elgar.

Sir Arthur Sullivan is best remembered as the musical member of the historic partnership of Gilbert and Sullivan. His real ambition was to compose grand operas and other serious works. When his oratorio *The Light of the World* was presented at the Birmingham Music Festival in 1873, the music critic of the *Standard* went so far as to declare that Sullivan had successfully "entered the lists against those giants, Handel, Bach and Mendelssohn."

Elgar, born in 1857, and in his time called the greatest English composer since Purcell, wrote several large-scale choral works, including *The Black Knight*, *The Light of Life*, *The Kingdom*, *The Apostles*, *King Olaf*, *The Banner of St George* and *Caractacus*. While these enjoyed a good deal of success between the years 1893 and 1898, they were overshadowed by *The Dream of Gerontius*, which is still looked upon as one of the most important oratorios of the early twentieth century. Set to an abridged version of Cardinal Newman's poem, this had its first performance at a Birmingham Festival in 1900.

With the success of this great work of Elgar's as an inspiration, English composers continued to produce a steady stream of large-scale choral works, if sometimes the word "oratorio" was liberally interpreted. Vaughan Williams' *Sancta Civitas*, first performed in 1926, broke away from nineteenth century patterns, but more especially did William Walton's *Belshazzar's Feast* (1931), a landmark in twentieth century writing, challenge the conventional concept of oratorio.

Arising directly out of a war-torn period, Michael Tippett's oratorio, *A Child of Our Time* burst on the English scene in 1944. An impassioned protest against oppression, in particular against Nazi persecution, the text (by the composer) was based on an actual event, the shooting of a German diplomat in Paris by a young Jewish refugee.

Also speaking of the cruel folly of war, Benjamin Britten's *War Requiem* (1962) was hailed as a masterpiece of contemporary choral writing.

American composers have maintained an imposing output in works of oratorical expression, and works of related choral style. These have shown a wide diversity of form. Building on a choral repertoire established in the late nineteenth century by Horatio Parker, George W. Chadwick, Dudley Buck, Arthur W. Foote, Frederick G. Gleason and others, many American composers of the present century have carried on the tradition. Among such are: Charles Ives, Howard Hanson, Roger Sessions, Roy Harris, Aaron Copland, Randall Thompson, Virgil Thomson, Walter Piston, Henry Cowell, Leo Sowerby, Leonard Bernstein, Wallingford Riegger, William Schuman, Norman Dello Joio, Samuel Barber, Paul Creston, Elie Siegmeister, Lukas Foss, Alan Hovhaness, Elliott Carter, Henry Brant, Lou Harrison, Ned Rorem, Marvin Levy, Peter Menin, Robert Ward, Ernst Bacon, William Bergsma.

Cantata

The term "Cantata" was originally used to distinguish a musical work to be sung (*cantare*) from one to be sounded (*sonare*). In the early part of the seventeenth century it applied to vocal works, consisting of *arias* and *recitatives*, for a single voice, accompanied by a lute, a cello, or a harpsichord. Such works were usually of a dramatic or a narrative character.

Giacomo Carissimi (1605-1674) was perhaps the first of the Italian composers to adopt this form for church subjects, *cantata da chiesa*, as distinct from the *cantata camera*, to be followed by many others, including Astorga, Rossi, Marcello, Gasparini.

In time the accompaniments became more elaborate, and at the beginning of the eighteenth century Alessandro Scarlatti broadened the scope still further in some of his 600 cantatas, which consisted of two contrasted subjects, introduced by an instrumental *ritornello* and accompanied by a string orchestra. Pergolesi followed his example.

Among French composers of that time who wrote in much the same manner were Couperin, Campra, Bernier, and Morin.

In Germany secular cantatas were written as part of public celebrations, festivals, weddings, and funerals. The church cantata became a more extended form and this was brought to perfection by J. S. Bach, who composed 295 in five cycles of fifty-nine each. He also composed some secular cantatas which bear such titles as *Coffee*, *Peasant*, and *Hunting*.

Among other German composers of church cantatas were: Mattheson, Keiser, Buxtehude, Telemann, Handel, Krieger, Kuhnau, and Schütz.

In form the cantata gradually became more elastic and we find Haydn, Mozart, Beethoven, and Schubert applying the word to some of their works.

If we take a cross-section of nineteenth century cantata composers, there are: Mendelssohn, Weber, Spohr, Hiller, Liszt, Schumann, Brahms, Wolf, Berlioz, Saint-Saëns, d'Indy, Gade, Stainer, Bennett, Bridge, Stanford, Parry, Cowen,

Sullivan. In the twentieth century we have Bantock, Vaughan Williams, Boughton, Scott.

The term cantata is generally applied in these times to choral works of substantial size, and of sacred character, but less pretentious than oratorio, or to those based on secular themes.

In 1952 Stravinsky composed a work called *Cantata* for two solo singers, a female chorus, and five instrumentalists; in 1930 Bartok wrote a *Cantata Profana* for two soloists, chorus, and orchestra.

In this present century cantatas have been written by composers of most countries and on a variety of themes and in various styles. In 1900 the English Coleridge-Taylor took as the subject for his Trilogy, Longfellow's narrative poem, *Hiawatha*. In 1937 the German composer Carl Orff based his *Carmina Burana* on texts going back to the thirteenth century, these dealing in broad terms with love and liquor. Orff designated this, "Profane songs for singers and vocal chorus with instruments and magical tableaux." Six years later he produced *Catulli Carmina*, "a scenic cantata," telling the story of a poet's passion for the promiscuous Clodia, or "Lesbia," as she is called in the poems by the Roman poet Gaius Valerius Catullus, who lived between 87 and 54 B.C. Both works are strikingly rhythmic and often startlingly percussive.

In 1954, when in his eighty-second year, Vaughan Williams completed his *Hodie* (*This Day*), described as a Christmas Cantata.

Among Benjamin Britten's numerous works for combined voices are the *Cantata Academica*, commissioned by and dedicated to the University of Basle for the celebration of its 500th anniversary in 1960. The Latin words were taken from the charter of the University and from older orations in praise of Basle. His *Cantata Misericordium* was composed for the Commemoration Day of the Centenary of the Red Cross, Geneva in 1963. The Latin text by Patrick Wilkinson is a dramatised version of the parable of the Good Samaritan.

Among the many present-day British composers who have written cantatas are: Michael Tippett, Alexander Goehr, Gordon Crosse, Harold Darke, Arthur Benjamin, David Cox, Cedric Thorpe Davie, John Gardiner, Patrick Hadley, Alun Hoddinott, Imogen Holst, Gordon Jacob, Robin Milford, Robin Orr, Alan Rawsthorne, Peter Maxwell Davies.

Many of the younger American composers of cantatas, and choral works generally, have been mentioned in the section on *Oratorio*.

Soviet composers have used the cantata form, as well as the oratorio form, to project historical, heroic, philosophical, and revolutionary subjects. In the late nineteen-forties, a steady flow of such patriotic cantatas included: Yury Shaporin's *On the Field of Kulikovo* (1938), Sergei Prokofiev's *Alexander Nevsky* (1939), *Kirov Is With Us* (1941-42) by Miaskovsky, *Cantata About Motherland* (1948-49) by the Armenian composer Arutyunyan, and *The Heart of Kartli* (1952) by Chimakadze.

162

Mass

The word Mass (Lat. *Missa*; Ital. *Messa*; Ger. *Messe*) refers to the principal service of the Roman Catholic Church, which usually consists of the *Kyrie, Gloria, Credo, Sanctus, Benedictus,* and *Agnus Dei.*

As a form of choral music it has attracted composers of many countries from early times to the present day and it is of interest that one of the greatest works in this form, the *Mass in B minor* of Bach, was written by a composer not of the Catholic faith.

After counterpoint had become established, composers used the Gregorian melodies in polyphonic masses for two, four, six, or eight voices, this leading to the Golden Age of Polyphonic Catholic Music, which culminated with Palestrina in the sixteenth century.

Among the early names associated with the liturgical mass are: Machaut (c. 1300-1377), Dufay (b. before 1400-c.1474), Ockeghem (c. 1430-c. 1495), Josquin des Prés (c. 1450-1521), Obrecht (1452-1505), Willaert (c. 1490-1562), Morales (c. 1500-1553), Lassus (1530-1594), Victoria, or Vittoria (c. 1548-1611).

Shortly after the middle of the sixteenth century Pope Pius IV took steps to end the abuse that had gradually crept into ecclesiastical music, and sought to replace the "lascivious or impure" with music of appropriate dignity.

Palestrina (c. 1525-1594), who spent his musical life in the service of the Church and was summoned to the Vatican by the Pope, did more than any composer of his time to reform the music of the church. He composed more than 100 masses, some having been given titles, for instance "Pope Marcellus Mass."

Among the numerous examples of later choral music associated with the Mass, written both for the church and the concert hall, are Beethoven's *Missa Solemnis*, and those of Jomelli, Haydn, Mozart, Schubert, Cherubini, Gounod, Rossini, Bruckner, Kodaly, Verdi, and Vaughan Williams.

Many other composers came near to the Mass proper by writing Requiems, among these Berlioz, Dvořák, Brahms, who called his work *A German Requiem* (as opposed to the Latin), Pizzetti, and Delius whose *Requiem* was adapted to a "pagan" text, compiled by the composer from the writings of Nietzsche, and *A Mass of Life,* also based on Nietzsche.

During recent times we find the Mass included among the works of such composers as Stravinsky, Rubbra, Berkeley, Milner, Walton, Jolivet, Gardner, Leighton, and Smalley.

Keeping in step with the times, others have written masses and near-masses in a modern, even a "popular" style. To mention some of these: *A Twentieth Century Folk Mass* (Weinberger), *Folk Mass* (Father Geoffrey Beaumont), *Anglican Folk Mass* (Martin Shaw), *Mass of Five Melodies* (Patrick Appleford). *Misa Criolla* by Ariel Ramirez is a setting of the Catholic Mass based on rhythms and traditions of Latin-American folk-lore.

Song

The word "song" has been given many definitions, some of them confusing, but for the purpose of these notes it will be taken to mean a relatively short composition in which poetry and music are combined. Some songs may be performed as duets, or arranged for full choirs, but it is as a composition for solo voice and instrument that we will consider the song here. As an independent form of musical expression, song goes back to the earliest years of the Christian era, often with its roots in folk-song.

FRANCE: In France, in the tenth century, song was part of the stock-in-trade of the *jongleurs* who wandered about the country providing entertainment that combined singing and instrumental playing (usually on a fiddle) with juggling and acrobatics.

Towards the end of the eleventh century France saw the coming of the *troubadours* who were itinerant poet-musicians from the south of France, and some little time later the *trouvères*, their northern counterparts. Early in the fourteenth century both the *troubadours* and the *trouvères* (both names had almost identical meanings) had disappeared from the scene, but not before their influence had spread to Italy, Spain, and Portugal.

In the first part of the sixteenth century the development of French music, including song, benefited a great deal from the compositions of Claude de Sermisy (c. 1490-1562) who wrote more than 200 *chansons*, Clement Janequin (c. 1475-1560), whose *chansons* were long and dramatic, and Guillaume Machaut (c. 1300-1377), poet-composer and priest, whose contributions to music were of outstanding importance. One of the foremost composers of the *romance* in the latter part of the sixteenth century was Pierre Guédron.

The French Revolution produced many fine songs, probably the most famous being *La Marseillaise* which became the French national anthem. Rouget de Lisle (1760-1836) composed both the words and the tune in 1792.

The burgeoning of Romanticism in the early nineteenth century painting, literature, and music, naturally found a response in the song-writers of France, but much of their output was of passing interest. With Berlioz, French art song was beginning to develop.

Such nineteenth-century French opera composers as Gounod, Thomas, Bizet, Delibes, Saint-Saëns, Reyer and Massenet added some lyric blooms to the song-bouquet, as did d'Indy, Leroux, Chausson, Hahn and others some time later.

Some of the most exquisitely fashioned songs to come out of late-nineteenth century France are by Gabriel Fauré and Claude Debussy. Maurice Ravel also composed songs of originality and charm, some of which reflect the character of other countries. The fame of Henri Duparc (1848-1933) rests almost entirely on his sixteen songs, set to texts by some of the finest French poets. These are of great beauty.

164

Dame Nellie Melba, one of the world's best-known
operatic sopranos, as Gilda in Verdi's *Rigoletto*.

Other song-writers of the late nineteenth and the twentieth centuries are:
Bemberg, Breville, Pierné, Roussel, Chausson, Delannoy, Poulenc, Durey,
Honegger, Auric, Tailleferre, Françaix, Lesur, Dutilleux, Baudrier, Jolivet, de
Severac, Messiaen, Martinet, Nigg, Migot, Barraud, and Cartan.

Franz Schubert (1797-1828). A great romantic composer. His superb songs, piano music, and symphonies are characterised by charm, subtlety, and great emotional range.

GERMANY: In Germany the *Minnesinger* (or *Minnesänger*), who generally were of noble birth, flourished during the twelfth and thirteenth centuries, and took over French song and adapted it to their own use. While their counterparts, the *troubadours* preferred to sing of love and gallantry, the *Minnesinger* sang of the beauties of nature. Two of the most famous of this company were Walther von der Vogelweide and Wolfram von Eschenbach, whom Wagner featured as characters in his opera *Tannhäuser*.

Next in Germany, came the *Meistersinger*, most of them artisans and registered in guilds, the most famous of them being Hans Sachs, the cobbler of Nuremberg (1494-1576), who became the central character in Wagner's *Die Meistersinger von Nürnberg*.

The *Meistersinger* possessed a large store of melodies, to which they set any of the available poems. Many of these melodies bore some affinity with church modes, and in some cases had been transferred from *Volklieder*. They at least helped to spread the love of music throughout the country.

German Lieder

To the average music lover the word *Lieder* will, no doubt, have a special connotation, the names Schubert, Schumann, Brahms and Wolf immediately springing to mind. The word *Lied* means nothing more than *song*, the plural, *Lieder*.

These primitive instruments show that the principle of musical instruments has changed very little down the centuries. The percussion instruments are exemplified by the zebra-skin drum from South Africa, the woodwinds by the elephant-tusk horn from India, and the strings by the instrument from the Pacific islands.

Top left: Before the invention of the gramophone, "recorded" music was provided by a very wide range of musical boxes. Some were very large and complicated and gave the effect of several instruments playing in harmony. The illustration is of one manufactured in 1900.

Top right: This early catalogue page shows three models of the Edison Phonograph.

Left: Scottish dances are among the most widespread of all folk dances, having been carried to many parts of the world by Scottish migrants. These girls are dancing in Adelaide, South Australia.

Among the important composers of vocal music in Germany in the sixteenth century was Hans Leo Hessler, who was born at Nuremberg in 1564. He studied in Venice as a pupil of A. Gabrieli, which probably accounts for the touch of Italianate lightness in his music. He composed many fine songs, including the original tune used by Bach as the "Passion" chorale, *O Sacred Head*.

Johann Adam Hiller (1728-1804), the founder of that type of opera known as *Singspiel*, is thought to have been the first composer of the *Durchkomponiert* (German, through-composed) lied which follows no prescribed form, apart from fitting the words to their various shades of meaning.

Gluck, better-known as a reformer of opera, composed a number of songs, calling most of them odes. Haydn's influence on instrumental music was greater than it was on song, but many of his songs are of considerable interest, some being settings of English texts, others based on Scottish, Irish, and Welsh airs.

Mozart's best-known writing for voice is found in his operas, but he published more than thirty songs, described as arias or lieder. Beethoven's sixty songs and Weber's seventy-eight, apart from his two books of *Volklieder*, Op. 54 and Op. 64, added further status to German lieder.

Another composer who figures prominently in the history of lieder is Johann Carl Gottfried Loewe who was born in Germany in 1796, one year before Schubert. Like Schubert, he was the son of a poor schoolmaster. His greatest songs are ballad settings, these often of highly dramatic, even uncanny character, the best known being *Edward*, *Tom der Reimer*, *Prinz Eugen*, and *Erlkönig*.

Franz Schubert has been called the greatest master of the lied. He wrote more than 600 songs, anticipating and developing every form of song, including the strophic, the declamatory, the lyric miniature, and the extended *scena*. As one of the greatest melodists of all time, his songs express all shades of emotion, without losing direct simplicity. Moreover, they are singable, offering reward for both singer and pianist. His use of harmonic colouring in the accompaniment throws the words in their full meaning into sharp relief.

Apart from his single songs, Schubert created two famous song-cycles, *Die Winterreise* (*The Winter Journey*) and *Die Schöne Müllerin* (*The Fair Maid of the Mill*).

The title *Schwanengesang* (*Swan Song*) was given, not BY Schubert but by a publisher, to a collection of fourteen songs published after the composer's death.

Schubert wrote at great speed, sometimes completing as many as eight to ten songs in a day. A victim of avaricious publishers, he was often compelled in order to pay for a meal to sell some of his immortal songs for a few pence each. His selection of poems was extremely wide, not always reflecting a high literary merit. So prolific was he that Schumann once remarked that, if Schubert had lived longer, he would have in time set the whole of German poetry to music.

"There is not a song of Schubert's," Brahms said, "from which we cannot learn something."

The opera, as a musical form, began in the early seventeenth century and still flourishes. A number of operas have been written in this century, including Stravinsky's *The Rake's Progress* from which the Bedlam Scene is shown above. Robert Gard (tenor) plays Tom Rakewell.

A Schubert song is a duet for voice and piano; it calls for a perfect partnership between the singer and the pianist, a fact often overlooked by insensitive "accompanists." In many of these the introduction, and of course the piano part throughout suggests the character of the song. To give some of the best-known examples: in *Die Forelle* (*The Trout*), the piano should clearly depict the darting movements of the trout in the stream. *Ständchen* (*Serenade*) is introduced and accompanied by a guitar-like musical figure; in *Die Post* (*The Post*) we should hear the gallop of horses as they draw the post-coach.

One of Schubert's most famous (and earliest) songs *Der Erlkönig* (*The Erl King*) describes the frenzied ride of a father carrying his sick child who hears the voice of the Erl King. In this Schubert convincingly suggests the three voices by changes of key, the piano part (a test for the pianist) vividly colouring the dramatic quality of the poem. The climax, with the words, *In seinen Armen das Kind war tot* (*the child in his arms was dead*), is a masterpiece of declamation.

Robert Schumann is generally looked upon as having inherited the tradition of lieder along the lines established by Schubert. Until after his long-delayed marriage with Clara Wieck in 1840 Schumann had written little but piano music, but during their first year of married life he entered what he called his "Song Year," during which he composed more than 130 songs, many of these among the most beautiful examples in the lieder repertoire.

Unlike Schubert, Schumann rarely set words that lacked literary value. It is not surprising that, having written so expressively for piano in the best Romantic style, he should have paid particular attention to the piano part; in fact, in some instances the "accompaniment" is even more important than the vocal line.

Chief among the poets selected by Schumann for his songs are, Goethe, Heine, Rückert, Eichendorff, Chamisso, Mörike and Kerner.

In addition to his independent songs, his song-cycles *Dichterliebe* (*A Poet's Love*), *Frauen Liebe und Leben* (*Woman's Love and Life*) and *Liederkreis* (*Song Cycle*), the latter a collection set to poems by Josef von Eichendorff, reveal his genius for combining voice and piano to form the perfect duet.

Mendelssohn, who by date of birth comes between Schubert and Schumann, really belongs to an earlier school of song-writers. His influence upon the development of the German *lied* was slight. His songs, while they have a sweet charm, show far more emphasis on the melody than on the variety of expression inherent in the poems. Among his best known songs are: *Auf Flügeln des Gesanges* (*On Wings of Song*), *Neue Liebe* (*New Love*), *Venetianisches Gondellied* (*Venetian Gondola Song*), *Frühlingslied* (*Spring Song*) and *Der Mond* (*The Moon*).

Born in 1813, four years after Mendelssohn, Wagner is of course most famous for his operas and music-dramas. His songs are comparatively few, among them the *Five "Wesendonk" Songs* for voice and orchestra, settings of poems by Mathilde Wesendonk, to whom they are dedicated.

Frank Liszt was Hungarian by birth, but some of his songs are often included in collections of lieder. The best of them possess a poetic lyricism. The title, *Liebesträum* was given by Liszt to piano arrangements that he made of three of his songs, originally entitled *Nocturnes*. The third, in its piano-solo form, has survived frequent repetition and ill-treatment by insensitive pianists, to say nothing of lacrymose instrumental arrangements.

Robert Franz, the pen-name of Robert Franz Knauth (1815-1892), was a German composer of more than 250 songs, many of which once enjoyed a fair measure of popularity. Taking German folk-songs, even hymns, as models, he made attractive settings of poems by Heine, Mörike and other worthwhile German poets, without breaking new ground.

The songs of Brahms represent a considerable part of his creative output. His songs for voice and piano total almost 200; in addition he published seven volumes of folk-song arrangements. In most of these he shows himself to be a true Romantic, the range of his vocal writing was wide, some of it possessing the affinity with German folk-song, some of it with Hungarian influences, but all displaying a distinctive melodic gift and perfection of structure.

In his songs Brahms gives more attention to melodic flow than to declamation, treating the accompaniment as an integral part of the song, although he developed the "duet" principle less than did Hugo Wolf who came after him. He used the words of many poets, including Heine, Daumer, Rückert, Holty, Allmers, and Reingold. For his *Vier ernste Gesänge* (*Four Serious Songs*) he adopted Luther's translation of the Bible.

In considering the songs of this composer we must not overlook the two beautiful songs for Voice, Viola, and Piano, *Gestillte Sehnsucht* (*Silent Longing*) and *Geistliches Wiegenlied* (*Sacred Lullaby*), also his *Zigeunerlieder* (*Gipsy Songs*). Among his concerted vocal works are the *Liebeslieder Walzer* (*Love-Song Waltzes*), a set of eighteen waltzes "for piano duet and vocal parts *ad lib.*," and fifteen more called *New Love-Song Waltzes* for four voices and piano duet.

So far as the true unity of words and music is concerned, Hugo Wolf raised the *Lied* to its highest peak. He was born in Austria in 1860 and spent the greater part of his life of forty-three years in poverty, hovering precariously on the brink of mental instability. He had an unshakable belief in his own creative potency; by the year 1890 he had written more than 200 songs. In between extended periods of inactive depression he would take up composing in a frenzy of eagerness, often completing several songs in a day.

Wolf carried on the tradition of German *Lieder*, but more than any other composer, penetrated to the meaning of every *word* of the poems which he selected with unwavering care. His songs are the perfect marriage of poem and music. His literary assessment was incomparable; he was able to suggest atmosphere and mood, and portray every psychological and emotional situation with the strictest economy, yet

One of the best-loved and most often performed operas is Puccini's
La Bohème. This scene shows Anson Austin (tenor) as Rodolfo and
Glenys Fowles (soprano) as Mimi.

A Bayreuth production of *Die Götterdämmerung*, one of the four music-dramas of Richard Wagner which make up *The Ring of the Nibelung*.

with artistic completeness. Not only did he write with uncanny understanding for the voice, but he built the piano part logically, often from a single phrase, that subtly matched the words and the vocal line. The title-pages of many of his volumes carry the description, "Songs for voice and piano."

Wolf's song-collections include those set to poems by Mörike, Eichendorff, and Goethe; forty-six settings of Italian poems (in German translation) in *Italienisches Liederbuch* (*Italian Song-Book*), and forty-four of Spanish poems in *Spanisches Liederbuch* (*Spanish Song-Book*). Twenty-three songs were orchestrated by the composer.

Mahler the symphonist has overshadowed Mahler the song-writer to some extent, yet in his songs we find clues to his symphonies, for both are closely linked. Song strongly influenced him throughout most of his life. He wrote his earlier songs with piano accompaniments, but he later found voice and orchestra to be more in keeping with his musical temperament and imagination.

One of his two unified song-cycles, *Kindertotenlieder* (*Songs on the Death of Children*) contains five settings of poems by Rückert with alternative accompaniments for orchestra or piano. *Lieder eines fahrenden Gesellen* (*Songs of a Wayfarer*) are settings of four songs for voice and orchestra on texts by Mahler himself.

The twelve orchestrated songs of *Des Knaben Wunderhorn* (*The Youth's Magic Horn*) are from the collection of German folk-verse published in an anthology by Achim von Arnim and Clemens Brentano. These songs, like those of his song-cycles, are quoted in some of Mahler's symphonies.

The author-critic, Neville Cardus, once said of Mahler's songs: "Several are as much dramatically, pictorially and psychologically bound to the poem set as anything in Hugo Wolf."

Apart from occasional songs, there is a group of five settings of other Rückert poems, published in 1902.

One of Mahler's greatest works, written in 1908, is *Das Lied von der Erde* (*The Song of the Earth*), a symphony for Tenor, Contralto (or Baritone) and Orchestra, based on six eighth-century Chinese poems by Li-Tai-Po, Chang-Tsi, Mong-Hao Jan, and Wang-Wei, translated into German by Hans Bethge.

In his operas Richard Strauss was fortunate in his choice of librettists, for most of his operatic music is wedded to libretti of true literary quality. His greatest collaborations were with Hugo von Hofmannsthal, a dramatist and one of Austria's foremost poets.

In his songs, however, he was not always so particular in his choice of poems. Although he did at times turn to Goethe, Heine, Eichendorff, and Shakespeare, some of the texts that he used are banal and unworthy of the music that clothes them.

In a letter dated 1903, Strauss wrote:

A poem will strike my eye, and I read it through. If it agrees with the mood I am in, at once the appropriate music is instinctively fitted to it.

173

Inspired by words, when in the right mood, he could write at great speed; he is said to have composed *Traum durch die Dämmerung* (*Dream in the Twilight*), one of his most favoured songs, within a period of twenty minutes—while his wife sat near by waiting for him to accompany her on a walk.

Strauss's songs cover a wide range of subject and mood, from the lyrically poetic to the passionately rhapsodic; from the blatantly sentimental to the starkly dramatic. Sensuous beauty is to be found in many, such as *Die Nacht* (*The Night*), *Zueignung* (*Dedication*), *Morgen* (*Tomorrow*), *Ruhe, mein Seele* (*Rest, my Soul*), *Ständchen* (*Serenade*), and the *Vier letzte Lieder* (*Four Last Songs*), a group of settings of poems by Hesse and Eichendorff: (1) *Beim Schlafengehen* (*Going to Sleep*), (2) *September*, (3) *Frühling* (*Spring*), and (4) *Im Abendrot* (*In the Sunset Glow*).

Prominent among contributions to *Lieder* by post-romantic composers are: *Fifteen Poems from The Book of the Hanging Gardens* and *Pierrot Lunaire* (*Moonstruck Pierrot*), a song-cycle for voice and instruments by Schoenberg; *Five Songs from " The Seventh Ring,"* Op. 3, *Four Songs by Various Poets*, Op. 12, and occasional songs by Webern; songs to poems by Storm, Mombert, and George (after Baudelaire) by Berg; and songs to poems of Trakl and Rilke by Hindemith.

Technically and musically the songs of these latter-day composers demand much from the singer, which may be why they are seldom heard in our concert halls.

Some of the German and Austrian composers, born between 1837 and 1882, who included songs in their creative output were: Adolf Jensen, a pupil of Liszt, Hans Pfitzner, Max Reger, Erik Meyer-Helmund (born Russia), Franz Schreker, and Joseph Marx.

ITALY: More vigorously identified with opera, Italy may have contributed somewhat less to art song than some other countries, but her love for folk-song has lasted through the centuries. As we have already learnt, the influence of the French *jongleurs* and *troubadours* spread to Italy, as it did to Spain and Portugal, about the middle of the thirteenth century.

In cultivating the wedding of music to fine poetry, Italy had its early inspiration in the sonnets and lyrics of Dante and Petrarch. The *ballata* and the *intuonata* were probably the oldest songs written in the vernacular, these being love-songs accompanying a dance.

According to some authorities, Vincenzo Galilei, father of the astronomer Galileo Galilei, was the first composer of his country to write melodies for the single voice.

During the fifteenth century the *frottola*, a street-song, or a song of light character for several voices with the melody on top, and, a little later, the *villanella*, usually a part-song set to rustic words, became popular. Another type of Italian song in vogue about that time was the *canzona*, a graceful air of somewhat elaborate construction.

After absorbing styles from other countries, Italy had advanced in the art of singing by the end of the sixteenth century. An important figure about that time

Enrico Caruso was one of the most famous Italian tenors of the golden age of opera. In this photograph he is shown as Des Grieux in Massenet's *Manon*.

was Guilio Caccini. He pioneered the type of music called *canzoneta* and pointed the way to other song-writers. This led up to Monteverdi, one of the great figures in the history of opera and vocal music in general.

Prominent among the Italian composers who furthered song were Peri, Carissimi, Caldara, Cimarosa, Mercadante, Stradella, Alessandro Scarlatti, Vivaldi, Marcello, Lotti, Gasparini, and Pergolesi. In later times Giordani, Tosti, Denza, Donaudy, Pinsuti, Pizzetti, Respighi, Dallapiccola, also others more closely associated with opera, have added songs and ballads to the concert repertoire.

BELGIUM: The history of song in Belgium is rather nebulous until we come to the nineteenth century, when a group of musicians aimed to give the music of their country a truly national character. The most prominent member of this movement was Pierre Benoît (1834-1901) who, with several dedicated countrymen, formed the Flemish School of Music in Antwerp in 1867, this with Government support.

Benoît wrote some colourful songs, which apparently influenced younger Belgian composers. Then, Edgar Tinel (1854-1912), for four years director of the Brussels Conservatoire, added many fine songs to his output of choral and orchestral works.

Although César Franck concentrated on works of a larger scale, his influence on these composers was of great importance.

Other names associated with songs and ballads are: J. P. Van den Eeden (1842-1917), Hendrick Waelput (1845-1885), Jan Blockx (1851-1912), Paul Gibson (1865-1942), Guillaume Lekeu (1870-1894), and Joseph Jongen (1873-1953).

Among the most prominent of twentieth century Belgian song-writers are Jean Absil and Marcel Poot.

HOLLAND: The first Dutch song-writer of note was Constantijn, who, besides composing music, wrote poems in several languages. The most significant composer of the eighteenth century to give his country's song status was Johannes Verhulst (1816-1891), who spent four years in Leipzig, where he was well received by Mendelssohn.

Among the most typical of Holland's song-writers in the nineteenth and twentieth centuries were Richard Hol, Jan Brandts-Buys, J. Wagenaar, H. van Tussenbrook, G. Mann, J. Röntgen, K. Kuiler, A. Spoel, J. H. Loots, H. Viotta, C. Ossterzee, and Willem Pijper.

Of present-day Dutch composers Henk Badings, a pupil of Pijper, is perhaps the most versatile. The pianist-composer, Hans Henkemans, Marius Flothius, and Lex van Delden have shown a great deal of imagination in writing for the voice.

SWITZERLAND: Until the latter part of the nineteenth century the songs of Switzerland varied in idiom according to the language spoken. Hans Georg Nägeli published fifteen books of songs late in the century, other composers about that time being Louis Niedermeyer, Joachim Raff, Friedrich Hegar, all of whom made worthwhile contributions to song. Rudolph Ganz, who subsequently settled in the United States of America, wrote about 150 songs in an eclectic style, while Gustave Ferrari, in addition to writing songs in a Gounod style, edited Yvette Guilbert's collection of old French chansons during the time he acted as her accompanist.

Led by E. Jaques-Dalcroze (1865-1950), inventor of the *Eurhythmics* system, a group of enthusiastic musicians set out to unify national musical expression. Some of the composers who followed his lead, and who gave attention to songs, were: V. Andrae, O. Barblan, E. Bloch, E. Combe, G. Doret, J. Ehrhart, W. Pahnke, W. Rehberg, and G. Pantillon.

Othmar Schoeck (1874-1951), a pupil of Reger, devoted much of his creative career to song-writing, his style at first favouring that of German *Lieder*, but later reflecting the Swiss character.

Frank Martin is generally considered the most important of modern Swiss composers, but his contribution to song is comparatively slight.

SPAIN: Spanish song has had a long and varied history, some examples known today dating back to the first half of the eleventh century. During the latter part of the eleventh century and until the end of the thirteenth century, the new songs of Spain took on some of the characteristics of those brought into the country by the *troubadours* and other musicians from France and Italy. Somewhat later, an art-song

The Red Army Choir is one of the world's best-known male choirs,
known to many people through records and international tours.

literature began to extend; some of the compositions were founded on folk-songs,
or were transcriptions of madrigals.

In the sixteenth century important collections of songs were published by lutenists
and vihuelists, among them: Luis Milán, Luis de Narváez, Alonzo Mudarra, Diego
Pisador, Miguel de Fuenllana and Esteban Daza.

After this flourishing period, the song for solo performer gave way to some extent
to polyphonic songs for three or four voices. From the seventeenth to the nineteenth
centuries secular music of Spain became more than ever associated with the theatre,
or, more specifically, with the *zarzuela*, a music-drama form of entertainment, the
term deriving from the name of the Spanish royal residence near Madrid where it
was first performed. During the nineteenth century the *zarzuela* developed into the
equivalent of the Viennese operetta and the French opéra comique. By the end of
the century, however, it had been overshadowed by a new and more popular form
of Spanish theatre, known as the *tonadilla*, the term deriving from *tonada*, or song.

The first important composer of *tonadillas* was Luis Misón (Missón), who died in
Madrid in 1766, having written more than eighty works in this form.

During the first half of the nineteenth century Spanish song was considerably influenced by Italian vocal composition, but later composers added to the repertoire of song, in which the Spanish idiom was strong. Among those who brought about this development were: Blancafort, Palau, Nin, Falla, Granados, Mompou, Valverde, Albéniz, Turina, Pedrell, Massana, Nin-culmell, and Montsalvatge.

RUSSIA: The colourful history and the race characteristics of Russia found a wealth of expression in song; in fact, no nation is richer in its folk-song, the basis of a great deal of its vocal art. Fortunately, much attention has been paid to Russian song-literature, musicians of the highest rank being officially engaged to carry on research in various parts of the country.

Peasant life, too, yielded a store of songs of interest and beauty, some sung to the accompaniment of the balalaika. Irregular rhythms often give Russian songs an individual character, and many composers made a study of the tonality and the harmonies of these, notably Glinka (1804-1857), the first Russian composer to win recognition beyond the limits of his own land.

Among the nineteenth-century writers to give status to Russian song was Alabiev, whose *Nightingale* was sung by such famous sopranos as Patti, Viardot, and Sembrich in the singing-lesson of Rossini's *Il Barbiere di Seviglia*, and which continues to find a place in the repertoire of modern singers.

Others who contributed to the form were Varlamov, Kozlovsky, Vertovsky, Vassilev, Dargomïzhsky, Serov, Balakirev, Borodin, Rubinstein, Moussorgsky, Cui, Rimsky-Korsakov, Tchaikovsky, Arensky, Davidov, Glazunov, Liadov, Liapounov, Scriabin, Ippolitov-Ivanov, Medtner, Kalinnikov, Rachmaninov, and Stravinsky.

Among the more recent composers of Russia who have included songs in their compositions are Prokofiev, Shostakovitch, Miaskovsky, and Kabalevsky.

POLAND: In the early centuries the songs of Poland mostly took the form of hymns. One of the earliest known examples, belonging to the tenth century, was St Adalbert's hymn to the Virgin, *Boga Rodziça*. Secular songs were often associated with the dance.

National characteristics were to be found in the songs of Kazynski, Dobrzynski, Zarzycki, and other nineteenth century composers, but these do not appear to have been well known outside their country.

With Moniuszko (who wrote more than 300 songs) and Chopin, Polish music became universally accepted. Later musicians who included songs in their compositions were: Paderewski, Fitelberg, Rózycki, Zelenški, Szymanowski, Karlowicz, and Lutolawski.

CZECHOSLOVAKIA: With the coming of Christianity to Bohemia (later to become known as Czechoslovakia) at the end of the ninth century, the influence of the Church brought about the eclipse of secular songs in favour of hymn-like compositions. But the people liked to sing, as they liked to dance, and gradually a song literature was built up.

Names associated with the cultivation of the Czech art-song were Jiri Benda, Leopold Kožulah, Jakub Jan Ryba, and Václav Tomášek; then Bedřich Smetana (1824-1884) founded a National School of Modern Czech Music, his work being carried on by Dvořák. Czech composers who followed Dvořák, all contributing something to art-song were Fibich, Janáček, Foerster, Novák, and Suk.

HUNGARY: The characteristics of Gypsy music were to be found in the early songs of Hungary. In the sixteenth century they were inspired by the joys and sorrows of the Magyar people, the words echoing a strong national spirit. The name of Tinodi, who died about 1559, figured prominently in Hungarian song-writing. A sharp diversity of rhythms, and the alternation of gaiety and melancholy coloured the songs of this nation.

Among the nineteenth century song-writers were: B. M. Vágvölgyi, K. Huber, E. Szekely, L. Zimay, E. Bartay, V. Langer, Korbay, Goldmark, and F. Liszt. Among those of the twentieth century were: E. Abranyi, P. Dankó, E. Lanyi, B. Bartók, and Z. Kodaly.

SCANDINAVIA and FINLAND: The Scandinavian people, and those of Finland, all in common have an intense love of music. This, allied to a rich store of legends and folklore, has led to the creation of many beautiful songs. A wealth of epic folk-songs has existed for many hundreds of years, but it was not until early in the nineteenth century that songs became imbued with romantic lyricism.

The earliest important song-writer of Norway was Halfdan Kjerulf (1815-1868), who fused folk-song with an art-song style. Following much the same path were Richard Nordraak (1842-1866) and Edvard Grieg (1843-1907), whose songs combined strong national feeling with lyric romanticism. Grieg wrote about 150 songs, many of which have become highly favoured throughout the world.

In Denmark C. E. F. Weyse was prominent in founding a Danish School of Music, his valuable work being carried on by F. Kuhlau, J. Hartmann, his son, J. P. E. Hartmann, Niels Gade, and many others.

In the nineteenth century songs by such Swedish composers as Olof Ahlström and Adolf Lindblad were popular, as were those, a little later, written by Emil Sjogren, whose style bore influences of both Grieg and Schumann. Of the composers of the present century, Dag Wiren and Lars-Erik Larsson merit mention, although their production of songs was less than works in larger forms.

In Finland Sibelius became the first composer of his country to be universally recognised. He is most famous for his orchestral works, but he composed about 100 songs beginning with Op. 1 in 1895 and ending with Op. 90 in 1917.

Selim Palmgren and Armas Järnefelt wrote some appealing songs in addition to instrumental works, but Yrjö Kilpinen, who died in 1959, concentrated on song, the total number, based on Finnish, Swedish, and German poetry of high literary merit, running into several hundreds.

ENGLAND: England merits an honoured place in the history of song. One of the

Michael Tippett's third opera, *The Knot Garden*, was staged at the
Royal Opera House, Covent Garden, in December 1970. Tili Gomez
played Flora, and Robert Tear played Don.

earliest English songs to have survived is *Sumer Is Icumen In*, thought to have been
written about the year 1240 by John Fornsete, a monk of Reading Abbey. It has
been called "The Reading Rota," the term rota being used for round, or "perpetual
canon," in which the voices, entering in turn, all sing the melody at the same pitch,
or in octaves. *Sumer Is Icumen In* is the oldest known canon, also the oldest existing
six-part composition.

In the period between 1480 and 1550 social and political ballads became popular.
During the reign of Queen Elizabeth the people laughed lustily and sobered
mournfully. Exuberance veiled a prevailing melancholy, and this is often detected
in the songs of that period.

180

In Elizabethan England song was greatly cultivated, and music for the people was performed by bards, minstrels, and ballad-mongers, popular tunes often being used for ballad-poems. England was at that time rich in composers for the voice and numerous songs of that time have come down to us today.

William Byrd (1542(3)-1623), although best known for his church music, became an important figure in the development of the madrigal and wrote many secular songs, as did his contemporary, Thomas Tallis, these composers jointly holding from Queen Elizabeth a monopoly for music-printing in England.

One of the greatest song-writers of his time was John Dowland (1563-1626), the English lutenist and composer, whose fame spread so widely that some of his music was published in eight capitals. The year 1597 saw the publication of his *First Booke of Songs and Ayres*, further books coming forward in 1600, 1603, and 1612. Although these songs were "of foure parts with tablature for the Lute," Dowland probably intended them for his own solo performance, the instrumental accompaniment being provided by himself.

Among the numerous composers of that period in England who numbered songs among their compositions were: Thomas Morley, a pupil of Byrd, Thomas Ford, Francis Pilkington, William Lawes, William Cornische, Robert Johnson, Thomas Weelkes, Orlando Gibbons, Giles Farnaby, Philip Rosseter, and John Blow.

Many other English composers of the sixteenth and seventeenth centuries, while engaged in writing church music, instrumental, and other forms of music, found inspiration in song. One of these was Matthew Locke (c. 1630-1677), who predated Purcell in the composition of English stage music. Interest in his songs has been revived in recent years.

English music reached its high-water mark with Henry Purcell (c. 1659-1695), often referred to as "The Flower of English Composers." He was born, he lived and he died in London. He wrote for church, theatre, and ceremonial occasions; his songs alone would have put him among the great.

After the death of Purcell, English music drifted into something of a backwater, although many fine songs continued to be written.

Thomas Arne, who lived between 1710 and 1778, can be considered as a link between Purcell and Elgar. It was unfortunate for him that his first successes came at a time when London was dominated by Handel. The actor, David Garrick, spoke of him as "the greatest musical genius of our country." These, of course, were the words of a man of the theatre; no doubt Garrick had in mind Arne's outstanding flair for setting to charming and appropriate music the poetry of Shakespeare. Fortunately for posterity, this gift was recognised and, when new productions of Shakespearean plays were planned for Covent Garden and Drury Lane, Arne was commissioned to compose the music for these productions.

Many composers, from before the time of Arne and until the present day, have found Shakespeare a rich field of inspiration for their songs. In this way musicians have paid their tribute to a great poet, in whose works there are more than 500 references to music, a subject which he treated with affection and accuracy.

Although music generally flourished less from 1700 to 1800 than it had during the previous two centuries, many fine songs were written. John Eccles and Richard Leveridge added a considerable number to the singer's repertoire, also Henry Carey, a popular song-writer in his time, now best remembered for his *Sally in our Alley*, and Henry Bishop for his enduring *Home, Sweet Home*. James Hook (1748-1827) is credited with more than 2,000 songs.

Song-writing in England has been carried on during the later-nineteenth and the twentieth centuries by many gifted composers, including Frederick Delius, Frank Bridge, George Butterworth, Thomas Dunhill, Benjamin Frankel, Edward Elgar, Hamilton Harty, John Ireland, Gustav Holst, Hubert Parry, C. V. Stanford, Arthur Somervell, Henry Russell, Peter Warlock, Herbert Howells, Michael Head, Vaughan Williams, E. J. Moeran, Arthur Bliss, Lennox Berkeley, Herbert Hughes, Roger Quilter, Granville Bantock, Arnold Bax, Eugene Goossens, Joseph Holbrooke, Landon Ronald, Julius Harrison, Armstrong Gibbs, Constant Lambert, Charles Wilfred Orr, Maude Valérie White, Edgar Bainton, Norman O'Neill, Frederic Clay, Graham Peel, Martin Shaw, Rutland Boughton, William Hurlstone, Mary Plumstead, Edmund Rubbra, Alan Bush, Cyril Scott, Gerald Finzi, Ivor Gurney, Norman Peterkin, Alan Rawsthorne, Phyllis Tate, William Walton, Robin Milford, Richard Walthew, Haydn Wood, Elizabeth Maconchy, Michael Diack, Lord Berners, Harrison Birtwistle, Victor Hely-Hutchinson, Alan Murray, Hugh Roberton, Wilfred Sanderson.

UNITED STATES OF AMERICA: This widely-spaced continent may not have produced a Schubert or a Schumann, but it looks with pride on its copiously varied treasury of folk-songs, ballads, and art-songs.

One of the first to put American song on the map was Francis Hopkinson, who lived in Philadelphia from 1739 to 1791. He was not only a song-writer, but a poet and statesman, and a friend of George Washington. He has been called the first native-born poet-composer of the United States, his first song, *My Days Have Been So Wondrous Fair* bearing the date 1759.

During the nineteenth century German *Lieder* migrated to the United States, finding many imitators. Then native-born composers became active in writing songs closer to the American spirit. These included: G. F. Root, who wrote stirring Northern war songs, J. K. Paine, Dudley Buck, George Whiting, Frederick Gleason, W. W. Gilchrist, and Homer Bartlett.

Meanwhile Stephen Foster, who was born in Pennsylvania in 1826, came on the scene, publishing almost two hundred songs in his own inimitable style. One wonders what greater impact he would have made on American music had he lived for a longer span than thirty-seven years. He was an instinctive song-writer, using simple

Although the bagpipes are now associated almost exclusively with the Scots, they are in fact one of the musical instruments which once were played in many parts of Europe, including England, and in the Middle East. Probably they were introduced into Britain by Roman soldiers. Basically they consist of an airtight leather bag which the performer fills with air. The sound is produced when the air escapes through the "pipes" which the player fingers in similar style to that used on other reed instruments.

Military bands developed from the use of drums, trumpets, or bugles to convey commands during the noise of battle. Then they were assembled for ceremonial parades, and for encouraging troops on their way into action. When troops first began to march in step, during the eighteenth century, the practice developed of using the band, especially the drummers, to beat the march cadence. The modern British military band consists of more than thirty players, and there have been special schools for military bandsmen since 1857. The bandsmen illustrated are of the Band of Central Command, Australian Army.

harmonies to defined melodies that have travelled the world and are still widely popular today. Foster died in poverty in a charity ward of Bellevue Hospital.

Among the numerous composers who aimed to give American song a distinctive status were: Arthur Foote and George Chadwick, both of New England, who each wrote about a hundred songs; also Shelley, de Koven, Nevin, Burleigh, Hadley, Farwell, Mason, Speaks, La Forge, Cadman, Taylor, and, one of the first American composers to win international standing, Edward MacDowell.

Moving nearer to our time were John Alden Carpenter, whose songs were coloured by Debussy influences, Charles Loeffler, and Charles Griffes, who had studied in Germany with Humperdinck. Sidney Homer produced more than a hundred songs, many of excellent quality, between the years 1899 and 1915.

During the twentieth century the busiest American composers working in larger musical forms have not neglected the song, among these being Charles Ives, Ernst Bacon, Paul Nordoff, Theodore Chanler, Virgil Thompson, Walter Piston, Aaron Copland, Samuel Barber, David Diamond, Elliott Carter, William Schuman, Norman Dello Joio, Miriam Gideon, Wallingford Riegger, and Leonard Bernstein.

To check recent catalogues from song-publishers is to find many composers who are writing in this form, and here we find the eclectic, the traditional ballad type, the modern and the *avant garde*.

No country has a wider variety of styles adopted by her song composers. A complete study of American ballads and folk-songs would require space equal to the whole of this book. Among the subjects treated in song were the railroad, chain gangs, whisky, the mountains, songs for children, cowboy songs, the mines, ships and sailors, war and soldiers.

There is, too, the rich heritage of Negro spirituals that combine memorable melodies with deep religious conviction. These, also, would merit specific treatment.

KINDS

OF MUSIC

(Instrumental)

9

THROUGHOUT the centuries, men have created music from such simple instruments as the conch shell of the Pacific islanders and the didgeridoo of the Australian Aborigines. In more sophisticated societies, musicians discovered that it was possible to make many variations on the basic materials of wood, metal, reed, and catgut or wire. As new instruments were developed, the musicians and composers were able to create new types of music, and to blend the music of the different instruments together into orchestras.

Suite

The Suite has a long history. Between the sixteenth and the seventeenth centuries this form flourished widely and vigorously. In those times it denoted a set of instrumental dance tunes, put together without any notable degree of unity, although they were contrasted. (This form developed into the sonata.)

Before the time of Haydn, the suite contained such dance forms as the *allemande, courante, saraband,* and *gigue.* Optional additions were the *minuet, bourrée, gavotte, passepied, loure, rigaudon, pavan,* and *galliard.* (These are explained in some detail in the section THE DANCE and DANCE FORMS.) In more recent times, and up to the present, the term Suite has been used in a much wider sense.

Far too much space would be required to list all the suites that appear in concert programmes and on records, but we can mention some of these at random: the suites of Handel; those of Bach; the *L'Arlésienne* by Bizet made up from his incidental music for a play; Debussy's *Children's Corner,* composed for his five-year-old daughter, his *Suite pour le Piano,* and the *Bergamasque,* which includes the well known *Clair de Lune.*

The *Holberg Suite*, which bears the subtitle *Suite in the Olden Style* was written by Grieg in 1884 to celebrate the 200th year of the birth of Ludwig Holberg, the Norwegian dramatist. This suite for strings is a delightful work, but it has been overshadowed by Grieg's two *Peer Gynt* suites made up from incidental music written for Ibsen's play of that name. In 1910 the impresario Diaghilev commissioned Ravel to write music for the ballet *Daphnis et Chloé* which he hoped to produce in the following year. Due to a series of frustrating delays, the first presentation was not given until 1912, by which time two suites, arranged by the composer, had already been performed in the concert hall. These contain some of Ravel's greatest orchestral writing.

The Planets, a suite for large orchestra, with a wordless women's chorus in the last movement was completed in 1917 by Gustav Holst, these, according to the composer, "suggested by the astrological significance of the planets."

The *Karelia Suite* by Sibelius applies to the province of Karelia in the south of Finland. The two *Façade Suites* are orchestral arrangements of music written by William Walton for "an entertainment, with poems by Edith Sitwell." The *Háry János* Suite was drawn by Kodaly from his opera of the same name.

Respighi's *Fountains of Rome* and *Pines of Rome* are perhaps his best known orchestral works, but he wrote two other suites of considerable charm, *The Birds*, based on seventeenth and eighteenth century pieces by Italian and French composers, also *Ancient Airs for Dances for the Lute* (in two suites), which are discreetly modern orchestral arrangements of dance tunes of a past age.

Some well known suites by twentieth century English composers are *St Paul's Suite* by Holst, written for the orchestra of the St Paul's Girls School at Hammersmith, and his *Brook Green Suite*, written for the junior orchestra of the same school. The *English Folk Song Suite* includes the popular *Seventeen Come Sunday*.

Peter Warlock (the assumed name of Philip Heseltine) composed an attractive *Capriole Suite* based on old French dances, and the conductor Sir John Barbirolli has written a *Suite for Strings*, using music by Henry Purcell, and *An Elizabethan Suite*, which includes such well known tunes as *The Earl of Salisbury's Pavane*.

In the examples mentioned above we have merely scratched the surface. There are, as well, many suites made up from ballet music, e.g., *Nutcracker* and *Swan Lake* which often contain only some of the complete scores.

Sonata

The term Sonata came into use to denote a piece of music to be sounded (on an instrument), as distinct from Cantata, a piece to be sung. Charles Burney, the eighteenth century historian, stated that the earliest example of sonata he was able to find was by Turini, and published in Venice in 1624.

The sonata evolved from the Suite which, in the seventeenth and eighteenth centuries, was made up of unrelated pieces in dance form. (See SUITE and DANCE AND DANCE FORMS.)

Early examples of the sonata were compositions written for solo keyboard, or for keyboard and other instruments, e.g., harpsichord and flute. Domenico Scarlatti (1685-1757) wrote sonatas in one movement based on one theme, but in style his sonatas were the exception to the accepted form. Since the time of Haydn and Mozart (considered the classic era for this type of work), the sonata has usually consisted of three or four movements, usually contrasted by the alternation of fast and slow movements. The sonatas for violin or other solo instruments, accompanied by harpsichord or clavichord, came in with the increased popularity of those keyboard instruments. Some of the sonatas of Corelli (1653-1713) had five movements, while those of Tartini (1692-1770) possessed three.

Haydn and Mozart usually wrote three-movement sonatas and in general this practice has been followed up to recent times. There are other examples called sonatas which departed from the generally accepted form, for instance, Liszt's *Sonata in B minor* (1853), which is a one-movement piano work, containing three distinct divisions.

Haydn put the stamp of his genius on sonata-form and established the first movement as bi-thematic, thereby giving the sonata a new unity and a greater dignity. Mozart followed his lead. Beethoven established the four-movement sonata.

We might mention here the *Sonatina* (French Sonatine), meaning a "little sonata," a work of shorter and lighter character than the sonata.

We must not forget that some of the first clavier sonatas, which broke away from the suite, were written by Joseph Kuhnau (1660-1722) and the Belgian Jean Baptiste Loeillet (1680-1730). Bach and Handel took up from these composers.

With Beethoven the *Minuet*, one of the movements of the sonata, became a *scherzo*, and the *gigue* the *rondo*. The slow movement had evolved from the *aria* of seventeenth opera.

Although influenced by Beethoven, Schubert introduced romantic elements in his twenty-one piano sonatas.

In the early nineteenth century further changes came into the sonata which often became even more romantic in character. Schumann wrote three for piano in a somewhat freer style; Brahms three for piano, two for 'cello, three for violin, and two for clarinet, in which he blended classic and romantic aspects. Chopin's three sonatas for piano, which depart from strict formalism, are expressions of his own daring musical personality. The four sonatas of the American MacDowell are frankly romantic in style. The ten piano sonatas of the Russian composer Scriabin are distinctly modern in style.

Like every other kind of music, the twentieth century sonata has advanced with

Johannes Brahms, one of the great symphonists, in middle life.

the times; in these we find a condensation of material, the rejection of unessential detail, and a reduction of repetition.

Ravel's *Sonatine* for piano (1905) pointed the way to a neo-classic style. Among his French contemporaries who applied their individuality to the sonata are Debussy and Fauré.

Composers of many countries have included sonatas for various instrumental combinations among their works. Among those of the United States may be mentioned Charles Griffes, a pupil of Humperdinck, who led the way for others.

Symphony

In standard modern use, the word Symphony refers to an extended orchestral composition (normally) in sonata form, or a sonata for orchestra. We have noted in an earlier reference that the word Sonata means a "sound piece," that is, a piece of music to be sounded (on an instrument or instruments), as distinct from a piece to be sung, e.g., Cantata.

In passing, it could be mentioned that the words Symphony and Symphonic have in recent times been twisted into other shapes that have little generic relevance. For instance, a popular melody from, say, a Broadway production may re-emerge in an orchestral arrangement, bearing some such grandiose designation as "symphonic realisation," (The word Concerto has come in for similar misuse.)

187

The term Symphony, literally meaning "a sounding together," in early times referred to the instrumental part of a larger composition not wholly instrumental. In other words, it referred to interludes which occurred during a choral or an operatic work, when the voices remained silent while the instruments, briefly released from the accompanying role, were given full prominence. These interludes became known, even as far back as Peri (1600), and Monteverdi a little later, as symphonies. Another is the "Pastoral Symphony" which occurs in Handel's oratorio *Messiah*.

Historically, we find the germ of the symphony in the Italian overture of three movements, fast-slow-fast, directly opposite to the French overture, slow-fast-slow. In time, the influence of Italian music reached Vienna where we find the true genesis of symphonic composition. This influence eventually spread throughout Europe, and became particularly active in Paris, London, and Mannheim, in Germany.

One of the important members of the Viennese group was Georg Matthias Monn, born in 1717, who has been credited with having written the first symphony, although some authorities prefer to name the Bohemian-born Johann Wenzel Stamitz, who was also born in 1717, as the most revolutionary of the early symphonists.

It was Stamitz who founded the Mannheim Orchestra which numbered up to fifty performers, this orchestra and those associated with it giving a new stimulus to both orchestral playing and to the symphonic style of composition. The Mannheim School of orchestral playing cultivated the type of symphony that was the forerunner of the Haydn-Mozart form.

Another composer associated with symphonic development was Franz Adolf Berwald, a Swedish composer.

As we know it today, the symphony is a unified work, that is, the fusion of diverse elements into an organic whole, based on sonata form, that came into its own late in the eighteenth century.

The symphonic form adopted by Mozart and Beethoven, and composers up to the present day, stemmed from the pattern set by Haydn about the middle of the eighteenth century. Haydn has been called "The Father of the Symphony." The form, as we have said, existed before his time, but, in establishing new concepts, he extended its scope and brought a new unity and a new dignity to compositions under that heading which had formerly side-tracked true sonata form and which often had been merely a series of flimsy melodies accompanied by other instruments.

The total number of symphonies generally attributed to Haydn is 104. Some writers have given the total number as 150, but those written prior to the D major, now indexed as No. 1, do not strictly qualify for the title of symphony. These were either of the *Divertimento* type, which did not follow strict sonata form, or were mere elaborations of his chamber works.

Haydn composed the first of his 104 symphonies in 1759 or 1760. At that time he held the position of Musical Director and Chamber Composer to Count Ferdinand Maximilian Morzin, who maintained an orchestra of twelve to fifteen players at his summer castle at Lukavec, near Pilsen, in a part of the country now known as Czechoslovakia. For many years Haydn had to work with, and compose for, orchestras of no more than fifteen musicians, but, while in Prince Nicholas Esterhazy's service at Eisenstadt from 1761 to 1790, the orchestral strength was increased to thirty-five instrumentalists, in addition to an organist and six singers. In London, which he visited in 1791 and 1794, he was able to work with even larger numbers. This is a point to be kept in mind when following the orchestration of his symphonies.

Haydn's Symphonies Nos. 82-87 are known as the *Paris* Symphonies, these written for a series of concerts in Paris. The Symphonies Nos. 93-104 are known as the *Salomon* Symphonies, these having been commissioned by J. P. Salomon in London. Twenty-nine of his symphonies have titles, most of them given not by the composer but by publishers and others.

The next great name in the development of the symphony is Mozart, who was born twenty-four years after Haydn. Musically and historically the early symphonies of Mozart, some of them written when he was a boy of nine, are of comparatively little importance in relation to those written during the full flowering of his genius. Some of these first excursions into the symphonic field were rather in the nature of overtures in three movements and were strongly influenced by J. C. Bach.

Mozart's first symphony of significance was the *No. 25 in G minor*, K. 183, written in 1773, when he was seventeen. From that date he gradually advanced the status of the symphony, which reached its peak in his last three symphonies, completed within six weeks in 1788: *No. 39* on 26 June, *No. 40* on 25 July, and *No. 41* (*Jupiter*) on 10 August. He lived for three years after completing the *Jupiter*, but he wrote no more symphonies. Having reached Olympian heights, he left the symphonic road clear for Beethoven.

Beethoven's nine symphonies represent the most revolutionary, yet the most rational, development in that form. Building on the solid and inspiring foundations laid by Haydn and Mozart, he broke away from restricting conventions and advanced the power and scope of the symphony. In doing so he broadened the scope of instruments and instrumental combinations.

The nine symphonies of Beethoven were first performed between the years 1800 and 1824. Some of these, indeed many of his greatest and most profound works, were composed after deafness had sealed his ears.

Many other composers adopted the symphonic form established by Haydn, Mozart, and Beethoven, among them Schubert, Mendelssohn, Schumann, and Brahms. The greatest of these was Brahms who was born six years after the death of Beethoven.

Brahms's musical career coincided with the Romantic period which burgeoned in the early nineteenth century, bringing a new quality to literature, art, and music.

Robert Schumann (1810-1856). Sometimes called the founder of romanticism in music. His compositions often display a dreamy, romantic quality. He is especially acclaimed for his piano music and songs.

His musical nature having been nourished on a formal classical diet, Brahms stood as a link between the Classical and the Romantic periods in music. At heart he was a romantic, but he kept a tight rein on emotion, always respecting the highest principles of form and artistic reticence. He has been called both "a romantic classicist" and "a classical romanticist." His reverence for Bach and Beethoven remained with him all his life.

He sketched the first movement of his *Symphony No. 1 in C minor* when he was only twenty-three; he had reached his forty-fourth year before he considered himself ready to complete it. Catch-phrases applied to music are often highly exaggerated, but many conductors and musicologists have agreed with the often-stated opinion that it is "the greatest First ever written."

The first performance of this work was given in 1876. Brahms's *Symphony No. 2 in D major* followed in the next year, *No. 3 in F major* in 1883, and the *No. 4 in E minor* in 1885.

Before passing on to later composers, we should fill in some details on three, already mentioned, who came between Beethoven and Brahms.

Schubert wrote his nine symphonies between the years 1813 and 1828, five of them before he had reached the age of twenty. The earlier ones do not reflect a master of the symphonic form, but structural shortcomings are made up for by inventiveness and lyrical charm. The finest are the *No. 8 in B minor (Unfinished)* and *No. 9 in C major*, often called *The Great C major* to distinguish it from *No. 6* in the same key.

Mendelssohn's published symphonies total five. Of these, the *No. 3 (Scotch)* and *No. 4 (Italian)* are best known. The others are: *No. 1 in C minor, No. 2 (Hymn of Praise)*, and *No. 5 in D major (Reformation)*. The *Hymn of Praise* is as much a cantata as a symphony. Classic in form, and containing lyric-romantic elements, these seldom touch profound depths.

Schumann added four works to the symphonic repertoire. Although musicologists have hesitated to place this composer among the great symphonic writers (it is in smaller forms that we find the essential Schumann) these works, for all their defects in orchestration, contain moments of romantic beauty, interesting harmonies, and rhythmic subtlety. They are: *No. 1 in B-flat (Spring), No. 2 in C, No. 3 in E-flat (Rhenish)*, and *No. 4 in D minor*.

The early symphonies of Haydn subscribed to the three-movement form, e.g., *Allegro, Andante, Presto*, later adding a *Menuetto* as a fourth movement, and sometimes beginning with a slow introduction. The Mozart symphonies followed much the same pattern. Beethoven in time substituted a *scherzo* for the *menuetto*, although he returned to *menuetto* in the third movement of his *Symphony No. 8*.

Berlioz adopted a programmatic style in his *Symphonie Fantastique*, which he subtitled *An Episode in the Life of an Artist*, giving the five movements the names: *Dreams, Passions; A Ball; Scene in the Meadows; March to the Scaffold*, and *Dream of a Witches' Sabbath*.

The *Dante* and *Faust* Symphonies of Liszt come nearer to the symphonic poem than to the classical symphonic form.

The *Symphony in D minor* of César Franck was unusual for its time in having only three movements. After its first performance critics protested that the composer had departed too boldly from accepted symphonic form, while the Director of the Paris Conservatoire declared, "This is no symphony. Who ever heard of a symphony employing an English horn?"

Saint-Saëns composed five symphonies, but two, written in 1856 and 1859, remained unpublished. His *Symphony in E-flat major, Op. 2* was published in 1855; the *A minor Op. 55* (numbered the second) remained unpublished until 1878. He had reached the age of fifty-one when his third symphony appeared. This, *Symphony No. 3 in C minor, Op. 78* differs from the usual pattern; it is divided into two parts, instead of into three or four movements, and the score calls for an organ and a piano-duet.

When this symphony first appeared in 1886 it received a warm welcome, for at that time the list of French symphonies was a short one. Bizet was only seventeen when he completed his *Symphony in C major*, a charming work reminiscent of Mozart, Haydn, and Rossini. He wrote no other. Chausson was another one-symphony composer. His contemporary, d'Indy produced his *Symphony on a French Mountain*

Air, which he described as a Symphony for Orchestra and Piano. Respect for classical form is to be found in the symphonies of Roussel.

The Austrian Anton Bruckner, who was born in 1824, wrote nine symphonies between the years of 1866 and 1894, the *No. 9 in D minor* remaining unfinished. In these he followed his own path after throwing off Wagnerian influences. Wagner once described Bruckner as the only real symphonist since Beethoven.

Taking composers chronologically, we come to the Russian, Alexander Borodin (1833-1887), whose first two symphonies add strong contrast to the orchestral repertoire. His Third symphony, left unfinished, received attention from Borodin and Glazunov. Tchaikovsky's six symphonies, particularly the Fourth, Fifth, and Sixth, enjoy enduring popularity with concertgoers and record collectors. In these Tchaikovsky followed his own star. The First is sometimes called *Winter Reveries*, the Second *Little Russian*, the Third *Polish*, the Sixth *Pathétique*.

The Bohemian (Czech) composer Antonin Dvořák, born one year later than Tchaikovsky, enriched music with his nine symphonies. Because Dvořák withdrew two of his earlier works in that form, the remaining nine were renumbered; for instance, the best-known, *From the New World*, formerly No. 5, is now listed as No. 9.

Elgar's *Symphony No. 1 in A-flat major* has received the compliment of being called "the first symphony by an Englishman." In four movements, this has no "programme" beyond the composer's intention to express "a wide experience of life with a great clarity and hope in the future." The score of his *Symphony No. 2 in E-flat major* bore the inscription, "Dedicated to the memory of his Late Majesty, King Edward VII."

The Bohemian-born Austrian composer, Gustav Mahler (1860-1911) completed nine symphonies, the tenth left unfinished. Contemporaries of Mahler have said that he composed four other symphonies in his youth, but it is thought likely that these were destroyed at the composer's wish. The published scores belong to the years from 1885 to 1910.

The names of Bruckner and Mahler have often been coupled; both during their lifetime met with bitter critical antagonism, also hysterical adulation. To some extent, a division of opinion in each case exists today. The *Symphony No. 8 in E-flat major (Symphony of a Thousand)* of Mahler calls for a large orchestra, two mixed choruses, a boys' chorus, eight solo voices, a piano, an organ, and a mandolin.

Das Lied von der Erde (*The Song of the Earth*) followed the *Symphony No. 8* and, although Mahler called it a symphony, he wished it to be known by its title, reserving "No. 9" for a purely instrumental work. This is scored for Tenor, Contralto (or Baritone) and Orchestra, and is a setting of six eighth century Chinese poems.

Carl Nielsen (1865-1931) is considered Denmark's most important composer. He was born during the Romantic era, but one would hesitate to call him a romanticist. Nor was he a nationalist in the sense that Smetana was a nationalist, or Grieg. His symphonies were classical, the best of his works balanced in allegiance to traditional form, to melody, and to Danish folk-music, yet independent. There is a strong sense of organic unity in his six symphonies.

Born in the same year as Nielsen, Jean Sibelius is regarded as one of the greatest symphonists of modern times. Remaining aloof from "schools" and cultural confusion, he created his own idiom, which owed much to romanticism, while being faithful to classical principles. Each new symphony marked an advance in independent thinking, in style, directness of utterance, and symphonic mastery.

Although his *Symphony No. 7 in C major* was completed in 1925, thirty-two years before his death, he wrote no other. Perhaps he considered that, in this, he had expressed his last word in that form.

The *Sinfonia Domestica (Domestic Symphony)* and *Eine Alpensinfonie (An Alpine Symphony)* of Richard Strauss owe much to "programme" music.

The nine symphonies of Vaughan Williams date from 1914 to 1956; this proves that, while he composed large and small works in many forms, the symphonic form attracted him until his last years. After giving such titles as *London*, *Pastoral* and *Sea* to three of his symphonies, the *No. 7* is known as *Sinfonia Antartica* which was the outcome of incidental music which he had written for the film *Scott of the Antarctic*. Even at the age of eighty this composer was still youthfully enthusiastic for experiment.

Sergei Rachmaninov (1873-1943) wrote three symphonies: *No. 1 in D minor*, *No. 2 in E minor*, and *No. 3 in A minor*. Like much of this Russian's music, these reflect the composer's introspective nature. Luscious scoring, melodies of melancholy lyricism, and dynamic climaxes characterise these opulent works.

Charles Ives (1874-1954) was one of the most interesting, if unconventional, figures in American music. He set his mind on fashioning a new musical language, but realising that his music was hardly likely to bring him much financial return, he entered the business world as an insurance broker. Music became a spare-time occupation. In time he became a wealthy man and he had reached the age of fifty-six before he withdrew from commercial life.

Most of Ive's music was composed before 1920, but it was not until twenty or more years later that his country realised his musical importance. He created his own rules of composition and, to some extent, he anticipated methods adopted by Schoenberg and other later composers.

Anyone wishing to become acquainted with Ives the symphonist might be advised to begin with his *Symphony No. 1 in D minor*, which he completed while still a student. Although this does not represent the true Ives, it is a work of strong melodic interest that is likely to capture the average music-lover's attention at first hearing.

Coming next in chronological order is the English composer Sir Arnold Bax. In 1922 his First Symphony exploded on the London musical scene with the impact of a bombshell, and caused one writer to nickname it "Adventures on the Edge of a Precipice."

Of Bax's seven symphonies, the No. 6 is the one most likely to appeal to the average music-lover. Composing it in 1934, Bax was probably influenced by the growing tensions of the time, as well as by the Scottish highlands. Celtic influences are strong in the music of Bax.

Although Prokofiev had his early musical training in the traditional Russian school (Rimsky-Korsakov was one of his teachers), he became something of a sophisticated cosmopolitan. He suffered the scorn of myopic critics in the earlier stages of his career, his "own way of thinking," as he called it, being unrecognised as the expression of an original mind. He reached the peak of his fame with critics still snapping at his heels.

Throughout his life Prokofiev clung to such traditional forms as the sonata, the concerto, and the symphony. While he produced his own brand of orchestral sonorities and based his melodies on a rich vein of melodic expression, he became known as a "classical modernist." His *Symphony No. 1 in D major* ("*Classical*" Symphony) stands apart from the other six. In a mere fifteen minutes the composer says all that needs to be said, and he speaks with wit and charm. The language is of the eighteenth century, but the accent is unmistakably that of Prokofiev.

There is strictly disciplined writing in his symphonies, yet we find the symphonic formalism often competing with programmatic elements. For instance, in the *Symphony No. 7*, completed five months before his death, there are moments when we feel he is expressing himself in balletic terms.

The Soviet composer Shostakovitch has so far produced thirteen symphonies. The first, written in 1925, suggests that he had not quite shaken off the influences of such composers as Tchaikovsky and Richard Strauss. The later ones contain a good deal of striking originality, but one wonders how far bureaucratic control has interfered with his artistic conscience.

The *Symphony No. 13* was first performed in December 1962. By using Yevgeny Yevtushenko's controversial poems—passionate outbursts against Stalinist and other evils—as a basis for the work, Shostakovitch must have been aware that he was lighting a torch too near an explosive political keg. After a third performance in November 1965, the symphony was withdrawn by the powers-that-be and further performances banned. Being completely vocal, with bass soloist and male chorus, with orchestra, this work is nearer to the cantata than to the symphony.

Among other Russian composers who added symphonies to their creative output were Reinhold Glière (1875-1956); his pupil Nikolai Miaskovsky (1881-1950), who wrote twenty-seven; Lev Knipper (b. 1898), who wrote fourteen; Vassily Kalinnikov (1866-1901), who might have composed more than two had he not died at the age of thirty-five.

During the last fifty years Soviet composers have shown a sustained interest in the symphony. These include: Yury Shaporin, Vissarion Shebalin, Nikolai Peiko, Gavrriil Popov, Nikolai Rakov, Dmitri Kabalevsky, Aram Khachaturian, Shalva Mshvelidze, Andrei Balanchivadzè, Boris Lyatoshinsky, Otar Taktakishvili.

Among the later Scandinavian symphonists are: Vagn Holmboe, Niels Bentzon (Denmark); Dag Wirén, Hilding Rosenberg, Wilhelm Stenhammar (Sweden); Harald Saeverud (Norway).

The four symphonies of Albert Roussel have been significant additions to the rather meagre French list.

Soon after the turn of the present century, England produced several composers whose symphonies show power and originality. Edmund Rubbra, a pupil of Vaughan Williams and Holst, composed seven symphonies that contain some splendid movements. Michael Tippett has explored new forms of musical expression in his two symphonies, Rawsthorne two, influenced to some extent by Hindemith.

Sir William Walton has always been a slow, painstaking composer and although he began work on his *Symphony No. 1 in B-flat minor* in 1932, it was not until December 1934 that it was first performed in public, and then only three movements were played. The last movement was finished during the following year. When this symphony entered the stream of British music, some people saw in its tensions a reflection of troubled times and in its bitterness a prophesy of world tragedy.

Benjamin Britten, perhaps the most prolific British composer of this century, is more distinctly represented in works of other forms. His *Spring Symphony* is scored for a full choir, a chorus of boys and three vocal soloists in addition to a large orchestra. Britten's *Simple Symphony*, published in 1934, is written for string orchestra and based on material from works he had written between the ages of nine and twelve.

Other symphonies by twentieth century British composers that merit our attention are those by Malcolm Arnold, Benjamin Frankel, Peter Racine Fricker, Daniel Jones, Peter Maxwell Davies, C. Armstrong Gibbs, Alan Rawsthorne, Humphrey Searle, and William Wordsworth. Malcolm Williamson, Australian-born and a pupil of Boulez in Paris, has included a symphony among his writings.

Among the Australian composers who have composed symphonies are: Clifford Abbott, John Antill, Edgar Bainton (London-born), Arthur Benjamin, Clive Douglas, Edgar Ford, Felix Gethen, Raymond Hanson, Alfred Hill, Mirrie Hill, Robert Hughes, Dorian Le Gallienne, Douglas Lilburn, William Lovelock, James Penberthy, Horace Perkins, Larry Sitsky, Peter Tahourdin, Felix Werder, and Stanley Whitehouse.

While dealing with English-speaking countries, we can at this point consider the American composer and the symphony. Among those of the nineteenth century were: George Whitefield Chadwick, Mrs H. H. A. Beach, Edgar S. Kelley, Henry Hadley, Frederick Stock, and Edward B. Hill. We have already mentioned Charles Ives.

Edward Macdowell, born in New York City in 1861 has been called America's first major composer. Trained in Europe, a fellow pupil of Debussy, and encouraged by Raff and Liszt, he published a considerable number of compositions. Writing in an established romantic style, he did nothing to advance the symphony, but at least he turned the musical spotlight on his country and stimulated other American composers.

From about the nineteen-thirties, many composers of the United States have given attention to the symphony, among them: Roger Sessions, Aaron Copland, Harold Morris, Louis Gruenberg, Howard Hanson, Roy Harris, Randall Thompson, Quincy Porter, Gardner Read, Nicolai Berezowsky, Bernard Wagnener, Lazare Saminsky, John Powell, Samuel Barber, Ernst Bacon, Henry Cowell, George Antheil, Paul Creston, Wallingford Riegger, Peter Mennin, Don Gillis, the Austrian-born Ernst Toch, the Russian-born Nicolai Berezovsky, Vladimir Dukelsky, and Leonard Bernstein. And the list is still growing.

Concerto

Since film producers and record companies have borrowed the word as a label for their more tear-inducing products, it is not surprising that we so often hear the question, "What *is* a concerto?"

Music dictionaries tell us that a concerto is a composition for an instrumentalist and orchestra, and usually written in three movements, similar in form to those of a sonata or a symphony. In other words, it is a *concerted performance*. There are of course variations, e.g., more than one soloist performing with the orchestra, or a composition for less or more than three movements.

The word Concerto was first used by Ludovico Viadana when, in 1602-1603, he published a series of motets for voices and organ and called them *concerti ecclesiastici* (*concerti* being the Italian plural), or *concerti chiesa* (or *Church Concertos*). In time, other instruments were added to the organ, and in 1686 Guiseppe Torelli published a composition called *concerto da camera* (or *chamber concerto*).

In the late seventeenth and early eighteenth centuries, Italian composers, chief among them Corelli, Geminiani, and Vivaldi were writing *concerti grossi* (literally, *great concertos*), a kind of orchestral work in which there was interplay between the larger group of instruments (*ripieno*) and a smaller group (*concertino*). In this style there was contrast of tone and melodic treatment.

The concerto grosso reached its peak with Handel and Bach. The famous six *Brandenburg Concertos* of Bach, written between the years 1717 and 1781, are of the *concerto grosso* type. As a complete set, these are notable for their variety of instrumentation and tonal colour. Bach did, however, write other concertos for clavier and orchestra, and violin and orchestra, which were mostly for a single soloist. Exceptions are his *Double Concerto in D minor*, for two violins and orchestra and one for three claviers.

Haydn, closely identified with the foundation of Viennese classicism, began moulding the classical concerto as a work for solo instrument and orchestra, the form mounting to a climax with Mozart. This style of composition gave the soloist greater scope for independence and virtuosic display.

It was Mozart who finally established the construction of the classical concerto. Between the years 1773 and 1786 he composed twenty-three works for keyboard and orchestra, five concertos for violin, one concertone for two violins, one sinfonia concertante for violin and viola, one concerto for bassoon, one for oboe, one for flute, four concertos and one rondo for French horn, one for flute and harp, and one for clarinet.

By the time that Mozart was established in Vienna, the harpsichord was gradually stepping aside in favour of the pianoforte, which was capable of producing a more sustained singing quality of varied tone. This new tonal freedom and colour range opened up new possibilities, which Mozart lost no time in exploiting in his keyboard writing.

The normal plan of the three-movement classical concerto was quick-slow-quick; the first movement broad and emphatic, the second more lyrical, the third, with its rounding-off of responsibilities, gay, and fast in tempo.

While the classical concerto followed the same *sonata* (or *first movement*) *form* pattern as the sonata and the symphony, there was one important difference in the first movement. The concerto movement had two expositions, the first stated by the orchestra alone; the second, usually more florid than the first, played by the soloist and accompanied by the orchestra.

The first movement of a concerto adopted another distinguishing feature — the *Cadenza*. This became an ornamental passage, during which the orchestra remains silent while the soloist embarks on an elaborate commentary on what has gone before. This was either written in by the composer, or left to the performer's own discretion. In earlier concertos the cadenza came near the end of the first movement. In later years it was sometimes introduced sooner: for instance, in Mendelssohn's *Violin Concerto in E minor*, a short cadenza comes after the development, quite some time before the end of the movement. Cadenzas were often introduced in the other movements. In more recent times they became more a part of the movement. An unusual form of cadenza is the one introduced by Elgar in the last movement of his *Violin Concerto in B-flat*. In this, Elgar reviews the subject matter used in the first movement, with a soft accompaniment by strings.

With Mozart's signpost pointing the way, Beethoven advanced the scope of the concerto still further. He wrote five for piano and one for violin between the years 1795 and 1809, also a Triple Concerto for Piano, Violin, Cello and Orchestra in 1804.

As in the case of the piano sonata, the symphony, and the string quartet, Beethoven raised the concerto to a summit of greatness. The first two for piano, composed while he was still in his 'twenties, followed an established style. Programme annotations

Felix Mendelssohn (1809-1847). He enjoyed wide success in his lifetime, especially in England. The Overture to *A Midsummer Night's
Dream*, his masterpiece, was composed when he was seventeen.

usually mention that these lean on Mozart and Haydn, Clementi and Dussek, but on closer examination we see clearly the imprint of Beethoven's originality and musical independence.

Composed in 1800, the *Concerto No. 3 in C minor for Piano and Orchestra, Op. 37* represents a milestone in the scope of the concerto. Beethoven by now had travelled a great distance along the road he had mapped out for himself. In the concerto he was now giving greater prominence to the orchestra. When the *Concerto No. 4 in G major* was performed for the first time, with the composer taking the solo part, in 1808, the audience must have been puzzled at its opening bars. Instead of the conventional orchestral introduction, the piano enters at once with the principal theme. This was yet another of this composer's innovations. A year later the *Concerto No. 5 in E-flat major* appeared, to which someone, certainly not the composer, gave the title "Emperor."

Beethoven's *Violin Concerto in D major* was first played in 1806, and the *Triple Concerto in C major*, for pianoforte, violin and cello two years later.

With the full flowering of the Romantic era early in the nineteenth century, certain changes appeared in the concerto: one with a single movement, divided into sections; another of more than the customary three movements. Also, the placing of slow and quick movements varied.

Mendelssohn played the solo part in his *Concerto No. 1 in G minor* in 1831, when, according to the composer, "The audience went wild with delight." Time may have dimmed its brilliance, but it was a reflection of a romantic age. Mendelssohn was a pianist of outstanding ability, yet his compositions for piano, including his two solo piano concertos, and two for two pianos, do not share the importance of his larger works. His *Concerto in E minor for Violin and Orchestra* has remained a constant favourite with violinists and audiences since Ferdinand David gave it its first performance in 1845. In the 1960s the manuscript of *Concerto for Violin, Piano and String Orchestra in D minor*, written by Mendelssohn at the age of fourteen, was discovered, and given its first public performance by Eugene List and Carrol Glenn.

With Schumann and Chopin we move into the Romantic era. Both composers were born in 1810, one year after Mendelssohn. When Schumann, superb miniaturist and song-writer, was reaching towards musical expression, he wrote a Fantasia for piano and orchestra. Four years later, in 1845, he added an *Intermezzo* and an *Allegro*. In its completed form this became the *Concerto in A minor for Piano and Orchestra*. In this the soloist enjoys complete independence and follows a romantic pattern, with technical display kept within the bounds of poetic good taste, and the orchestra supporting gracefully.

Schumann's *Concerto in A minor for Cello and Orchestra* scales no great peaks, encompasses no dithyrambic curves, but moves nostalgically in a mood of autumnal reflection.

The manuscript of Schumann's *Concerto in D minor for Violin and Orchestra* bears the dates 21 September-3 October 1853, the year before his mental breakdown. Although Joseph Joachim played the concerto in private some few years later, he is said to have agreed with Clara Schumann, Brahms, and Dietrich that it should not be published. But for the composer's removal to a mental home, the work might have been revised.

The manuscript was acquired by the Berlin State Library under agreement that publication should be withheld until 1956, the centenary of the composer's death. In 1937, the violinists, Yelly d'Aranyi and her sister, Adile Fachire, great-nieces of Joachim, surprised the musical world with their statement that they had been exhorted by spirit messages to exhume the concerto and give it public performance. This d'Aranyi proceeded to do. It occasionally reappears in violinists' programmes.

When writing about Chopin's two concertos authors, while giving full praise to his solo piano music, point to his shortcomings as an orchestrator. He was not quite twenty when he completed these. He favoured the smaller forms of piano music, but as a concert pianist he realised that the public expected from him works on a larger scale.

In order of composition the *Concerto No. 1 in E minor* is actually the second of the two piano concertos. The *F minor* was written a year earlier, but as the *E minor* was the first published it became known as No. 1. Finding his romanticism too strong for the restrictions of the classic mould, he adorned the works with sections of pianistic brilliance, contrasted against flowing melodies of Lisztian lyricism.

Liszt, born a year later than Schumann and Chopin, composed two piano concertos, *No. 1 in E-flat* and *No. 2 in A major*. Both were revised by the composer several times. Although played without the usual between-movement breaks, the music falls into distinct sections that vary in mood, tempo, and style. But for the fact that Liszt gave no indication that these works contained any "plot," we might regard them as symphonic poems for piano and orchestra.

Brahms composed four concertos: *No. 1 in D minor* and *No. 2 in B-flat major for piano and orchestra; Concerto in D major for Violin and Orchestra; Double Concerto in A minor for Violin, Cello, and Orchestra.*

The *D minor Concerto* is an example of Brahm's rigid self-criticism. In 1853 he sketched it as a symphony, then later rearranged it as a sonata for two pianos. After further dissection and remoulding he turned it into a piano concerto. After its first performance, in 1859, with the composer as soloist and Joachim conducting, Brahms wrote to Clara Schumann, "It was a complete and brilliant failure. Hardly three people raised their hands to clap, and it was actually hissed. In spite of this, the concerto will please some day."

Whereas Chopin used the orchestra more or less as an accompaniment, Brahms treated it symphonically. Some biographers tell us that some of the writing of this concerto was coloured by Brahms's grief over Schumann's attempted suicide.

A period of twenty years separates the first piano concerto from the second. The latter was an immediate success. Here we realise Brahms's expressive control of the concerto form, the suppression of technical display for its own virtuosic sake, the balance between soloist and orchestra, the nobility of its structure, the song-like lyricism of its melodies.

In the violin concerto we again find these elements, and a perfect blending of the classical and the romantic. Brahms conducted the first performance in 1879, with Joachim as soloist. So technically difficult is the violin part, and so symphonically conceived the orchestral role, that this has been called not a concerto *for* the violin but *against* the violin.

The *Double Concerto* was Brahms's last composition calling for the use of the orchestra. In this he skilfully blended the two solo instruments so widely separated in their weight and tonal qualities.

Some time before the completion of the work, Brahms had quarrelled with his friend, Joseph Joachim. In 1887 he sent the manuscript of his double concerto as a peace offering. It helped to seal the rift between the two musicians and at its first performance in Cologne, Joachim played the violin part, with Robert Hausmann as cellist, and Brahms conducting.

In this work Brahms revived something of the *concerto grosso* style, scoring it as a profound dialogue between two solo voices of equal importance. Calling for complete technical assurance and unity of thought in performance, it restrains pyrotechnical posturing by self-conscious virtuosi.

The latter part of the nineteenth and the early part of the twentieth centuries witnessed an open season for concertos coloured by romantic influences. One that readily comes to mind is the *Concerto in A minor* (piano) by the Norwegian Grieg. The two piano concertos of the American MacDowell enjoy today less popularity than they did in the early 1900s.

Saint-Saëns's concertos total ten: five for piano, three for violin, and two for cello. Even if the cellist's repertoire were not so limited, *Dvořák's B minor Cello Concerto* would still rank as a great work. His *Violin Concerto in A minor*, though less imposing than the *B minor*, is written with a clear understanding of the instrument. His *Piano Concerto in G minor* has found comparatively little favour with present-day pianists.

Among the concertos written for violin are the technically-dazzling ones of Paganini. He wrote eight, the No. 1 (Op. 6) being the most frequently heard. The *D major* of Tchaikovsky has lost none of its audience appeal, yet in 1878 Leopold Auer, to whom it was dedicated, considered its difficulties insurmountable and refused to play it. Even when Adolf Brodsky performed it three years later, Tchaikovsky was to learn that "the première ended with a broadside of hisses, completely obliterating the polite applause coming from some friendly quarters."

The *Violin Concerto in D minor* by Sibelius was written in 1903 and revised two years

Peter Ilyich Tchaikovsky (1840-1893). One of the world's greatest composers, he expressed the sorrow of man, disillusioned and alone. Yet there is also much joy, hope, and beauty in his work.

later. When performed in Berlin, Richard Strauss conducted. With its tensions, lyric flow and brilliance, this carries some Tchaikovskyan overtones.

Like his violin concerto, Tchaikovsky's *Concerto No. 1 in B-flat minor* for piano, completed in 1875, got off to a bad start. Nicholas Rubinstein, director of the Moscow Conservatoire condemned it as "worthless and unplayable and so clumsy as to be beyond correction." Today it is probably the most frequently-performed of all piano concertos, overshadowing the *Piano Concerto No. 2 in G major*. This is surprising, for the latter has abundant throbbing melodies and plenty of Russian folkish atmosphere. The choreographer, George Balanchine, used the music for his ballet, *Ballet Imperial*.

Tchaikovsky's "*Third Piano Concerto*" was made up from movements of a discarded symphony. It is seldom played.

Even in these cynical times, some concertos, though heavily charged with sentiment, have remained in public favour.

Among such works are the *Violin Concerto No. 1* by Max Bruch, which is probably in every record collector's library, and the *Violin Concerto in A minor* by Glazunov, which is equally melodic in a sentimental style.

Standing apart from conventional patterns are the concertos for violin, for piano, and for cello by Delius, and the passionately moving Violin and Cello concertos of Elgar.

202

In the 1930s Ravel graced the repertoire with two concertos, the *G major* for piano, a work of exceptionally original character, and the *Piano Concerto in D major for Left Hand Alone*, written at the request of the German pianist, Paul Wittgenstein whose right arm had been amputated as a result of a wound sustained in the 1914-18 War.

A human interest story also colours the *Concerto for Violin and Orchestra* by Alban Berg. In 1934 the American violinist, Louis Krasner, asked Berg for a concerto. Berg, at best a slow composer, lingered over this work until, in the following year he was plunged into grief by the sudden death of Manon Gropius, the young daughter of Mahler's widow, and one of his circle of friends in Vienna. In a mood of sorrowing intensity, he completed the concerto within six weeks. A requiem for Manon Gropius, he dedicated the work "To the memory of an Angel." There is a spiritual quality in this beautiful work.

At first influenced by Richard Strauss, Chopin and Debussy, the Polish composer, Szymanowski, finally established an individual musical personality. His concertos, which merit closer attention than they appear to receive, are two for violin and orchestra and a work for piano and orchestra, called *Symphonie Concertante*. These combine both scholarly and poetic ingredients.

Much of the best music of the Swiss composer, Ernest Bloch, is written with a deep penetration into the Jewish character and with a racial accent. His works in the concerto form include *Concerto for Violin and Orchestra*, *Concerto Symphonique* (piano and orchestra), *Schelomo* (*Solomon*), a rhapsody for Cello and orchestra, *Suite* for Viola and Orchestra, and *Concerto Grosso* for piano and strings. These works carry much of Bloch's passionate rhetoric.

Bela Bartók died in 1945. Only now is the full significance of his writing being realised, if not fully even yet. Although much of his music is advanced in harmonic and rhythmic thinking, it is always linked with Magyar influences. His compositions include three piano concertos, a violin concerto, and one for viola. One of Bartók's last works, virtually a five-movement symphony, was given the title *Concerto for Orchestra* by the composer.

Unlike Bartók, who remained faithful to Hungarian influences, the Russian-born Stravinsky moved away from the Russian idiom, directing his music through a series of transmissions from the romantic to neo-classicism. There is a wide divergence of technical style and musical expression in his three piano concertos (the third unfinished) and his violin concerto.

Meanwhile performing musicians who were only too willing to introduce new works into their concert and recording programmes, continued to play safe by mixing them with established favourites. Violinists remained faithful to the concertos of the Polish Wieniawski and the Belgian Vieuxtemps, and occasionally sparing a thought for the German Spohr.

Pianists, too, found it profitable to please their audiences by giving yet another performance of the *Concerto No. 2 in C minor* by Rachmaninov. The story behind this work is well known, but it can be retold, if only for the benefit of filmgoers (or television viewers) who have heard its swooning melodies as an *obbligato* to the heroine's great sorrow.

Although Rachmaninov had been successful in London and in the United States, he returned to Russia deeply depressed, and succumbed to a state of pessimistic lethargy. He submitted to a course of auto-suggestion and hypnotism and in the autumn of 1900, at the end of his treatment, he found inspiration co-operating with his renewed ambition to work. His next work was the *C minor Concerto*, perhaps the best, certainly the most popular of his four for piano and orchestra.

Rimsky-Korsakov wrote only one piano concerto. Many people are surprised when they learn that he wrote any at all: in fact, the composer himself has said, "I cannot recall exactly when I conceived the thought of setting to work on the piano concerto." For all its colourful rhetoric and passages of showy brilliance, it is passed over by most recording artists.

For a time a pupil of Rimsky-Korsakov, Prokofiev was born only eighteen years after Rachmaninov but there is a wide difference between their musical styles. Prokofiev's early writing represented a reaction against the mysticism and the emotionalism of certain other Russian composers. He was called an iconoclast, his music described as acidic. Later he strove for a more melodic form of expression. He was an excellent pianist, but though the solo parts of his five piano concertos contain brilliant opportunities for the virtuoso, they clearly show his assured grip of orchestration. His two violin concertos are notable for their spontaneous lyricism.

Among the best known concertos by modern Soviet composers are those by Shostakovitch, Khachaturian, and Kabalevsky.

England has not been behind other countries in contributing to the concerto repertoire. If we start with Parry and Stanford, whose influence extended from the nineteenth to the early twentieth centuries, we find such names as Vaughan Williams, Bliss, Elgar, Howells, Moeran, Bax, Ireland, Walton, Rawsthorne, Tippett, Britten, Benjamin, Finzi, Gibbs, Somervell, Boughton, Rowley, Alwyn, Arnold, Maconchy, Easdale.

Australian and New Zealand composers in this field include Abbott, Antill, Arlen, Badger, Brier, Carr, Franchi, Gethen, Hanson, Hill, Hutchens, Hyde, Brewster Jones, Lovelock, Penberthy, Perkins, Sutherland, Tunley, Werder, Whitehouse.

To list all the concertos in the standard repertoire, and, in addition, those that appear from time to time in concert and radio programmes, and on records, would take full space in a Doomsday-size book. Among the composers of concertos for various instruments, ranging from harpsichord, string, woodwind, brass instruments, mandolin, harp, guitar, harmonium, etc., are Albinoni, C. P. E. Bach, J. C. Bach, J. S. Bach, Boieldieu, Britten, Castelnuovo-Tedesco, Cimarosa, Corelli, Couperin,

Dello Joio, Gabrieli, Geminiani, Handel, Hasse, Haydn, Krumpholz, de Lelande, Locatelli, Marcello, Mozart, Pergolesi, Quantz, Rameau, Rodrigo, Sammartini, Scarlatti, R. Strauss, Tartini, Torelli, Telemann, Vivaldi, and Weber.

Chamber Music

It would not be unusual to meet a music-lover who, while proclaiming a dislike for chamber music, will readily admit that he enjoys listening on the radio to the *Trout" Quintet*, the *"Archduke" Trio*, or "that little *Serenade* thing by Haydn." without realising that chamber music had entered his own living-room as a welcome friend.

This would suggest that the prejudice against chamber music is against the classification, rather than against the music itself. Just as a man might quote *Hamlet* in voicing his dislike of Shakespeare, so might the said music-lover pause in whistling one of the themes from Beethoven's *B-flat Trio*, to state with inverted pride that chamber works are beyond his musical understanding. Which, of course, is foolish.

To appreciate chamber music is to acknowledge the intimate qualities of its charm and to respect its purity of form and its interpretative demands that permit no soloistic attitudinising or technical slovenliness. It is not only one of the highest forms of musical expression; it is also the most unselfish in performance.

Chamber music, which has often been described as the music of friends, was originally, designed for domestic use, i.e., to be played in the home (therefore, *room music*), as distinct from music written for performance in a large public hall, a church, or a theatre.

In modern times the term chamber music has been applied to music composed for a small group of players, say, from three to eight or nine, each with a separate part. In chamber music each instrument must be treated independently, while all sounding agreeably together.

Before we mention certain exceptions to this classification, let us briefly consider some historical facts.

The chamber of music of the Renaissance era was primarily vocal, i.e., music written for a solo singer or a vocal ensemble, as distinct from a church choral group. The chief forms were the madrigal, the chanson, and the lied.

In the Baroque era, when violin playing had mounted to a higher level, and with the distinction more defined between the *sonata da camera* (chamber sonata) and the *sonata da chiesa* (church sonata), chamber music became predominantly instrumental. This took the form of solo sonatas, trio sonatas, and the concerto grosso, and brought about an idiomatic style of composition, particularly related to the string family. Later, other instruments were added.

Haydn has often been called "The Father of the String Quartet." As a form the string quartet existed before his time, but in establishing a new concept, a new texture, he extended its scope and brought a new unity and a new dignity to this kind of music which, previously, had side-tracked true sonata-form and which often had been merely a set of melodies for solo players accompanied by the other instruments.

Haydn indexed some of his string quartets as *divertimenti a quattro*. By a process of evolution his compositions for stringed instruments developed a unity that guided the quartet away from patterns that had been used by Sammartini, Tartini, Pugnani, and other Italian composers, patterns which had dated back to the the sixteenth century Nicola Vicentino.

In the eighteenth century the development of chamber music was to a great extent affected by the social environment in which it breathed, for until it became a part of public entertainment, it depended on the patronage of the aristocracy. Such music was written to be performed in the private music-rooms of royalty and the reception chambers of civic and religious dignitaries.

In the case of Haydn, we find that as early as 1755, when he was only twenty-three, he was invited by a Viennese nobleman, Count Fürnberg, to write for a quartet of strings. From 1761 to 1790 he was in the service of Prince Nicholas Esterhazy at Eidenstadt, during which period he composed orchestral and chamber music according to his patron's requirements, and with whatever instrumentalists were available to him. In this position as *Kapellmeister*, he was expected to produce at short notice any kind of composition.

Haydn is said to have written eighty-four string quartets and 125 other chamber works. His early quartets were produced in sets of six, these published against the Opus numbers 1, 2, 3, 9 and 17. The next set, Op. 70, written in 1772, show a stronger grasp of design and a new personality. In 1781 he brought out another set of quartets, Op. 33, dedicated to the Grand Duke of Russia; these are sometimes known as the "Russian" Quartets. The Quartets of the Op. 54, 55, and 64 were dedicated to Joseph Tost, a wealthy merchant who formerly had been a violinist.

The Opus numbers 71 to 77 contain some of this composer's finest music.

Having found a "father" in Haydn, the string quartet then passed into the care of Mozart who nourished it through a further period of development. This, too, applied to other kinds of his chamber works.

Mozart was born twenty-four years later than Haydn but developed musically at an earlier age. If, at first, Mozart learnt much of his craft from the older musician, Haydn was later to gain considerably in his chamber music from Mozart.

By the time he had reached the age of sixteen Mozart had written a *Quartet in C major, K. 80*. From October 1772 to March 1773 he composed his first set of six quartets, known as the *Milanese* quartets, and produced a further set of six towards the end of 1773, these known as the *Viennese* quartets.

His works that come under the heading of chamber music total more than seventy; these include twenty-five string quartets, six string quintets, a clarinet quintet, two

Three great soloists preparing for a recording of Beethoven's *Triple Concerto*. From left: Sviatoslav Richter (pianist), Msrislav Rostropovich (cellist) and David Oistrakh (violinist).

piano quartets, as well as trios, and works for other combinations. In the later of these he showed once again his genius for advancing the scope and beauty of forms already adopted by Haydn and other composers.

For a period of ten years Mozart wrote no more string quartets, then in 1783 he began a new set of six (Nos. 14 to 19), which he dedicated to Haydn. The following extracts are from a letter referring to these:

To my dear friend Haydn

A father who had decided to send out his sons into the great world, thought it his duty to entrust them to the protection and guidance of a man who was celebrated at the time and who, moreover, happened to be his best friend.

In like manner, I send my six sons to you. . . . These are, indeed, the fruit of a long and laborious study. During your last stay in this capital (Vienna) you expressed to me your approval of these compositions.

. . . Please then receive them kindly and be to them a father, guide and friend!

. . . I entreat you, however, to be indulgent to those faults which may have escaped a father's partial eye, and in spite of them, to continue your generous friendship towards one who so highly appreciates it.

Meanwhile I remain with all my heart, dearest friend, your most sincere friend.

Vienna, 1 September 1785   W. A. MOZART

The six *Haydn* quartets, which are among Mozart's most personal works in this form, were followed by the *Quartet in D major, K. 499*, dedicated to his friend and publisher, Hoffmeister, and then came the *Prussian* quartets, dedicated to Friedrich Wilhelm, King of Prussia.

The next important step in the progress of the string quartet was taken by Beethoven. It was a giant step. Beethoven regarded the string quartet as the purest musical form; his own, particularly the last quartets, are universally acknowledged as the greatest of their kind.

Beethoven composed the first of his sixteen string quartets, the six belonging to the Op. 18, between 1798 and 1800. In these we find, not a composer groping his way, but one certain of the direction he was taking, at the same time acknowledging his admiration for Haydn and Mozart. His earlier chamber music works include piano trios and string trios.

The three "Rasoumovsky" Quartets of the Op. 59, written in 1806, were commissioned by Count Rasoumovsky, the Russian ambassador in Vienna. Here we find the composer with his eyes fixed on more distant targets of expression. Two more quartets, Op. 74 (known as the "Harp" Quartet because of the harp-like *pizzicato* passages in the first movement), and Op. 95 were written in 1809 and 1810.

Other chamber works include the *Septet in E-flat major, Op. 20*, and the *Octet in E-flat major, Op. 103*, for wind instruments.

The "Late" quartets, composed between 1824 and 1826, bear the Opus numbers 127, 130, 131, 132, 133, and 135. These are landmarks in the history of all music.

A considerable quantity of chamber music in classic form was written by the contemporaries of Haydn, Mozart, and Beethoven, among them, Cannabich, Dittersdorf, K. Stamitz, and Hummel. With some exceptions, this music has drifted out of currency.

Schubert, the most romantic of the classic composers, wrote more than thirty chamber works, in which he moulded classic form to suit his own temperament. Many of these works were written for groups which met at his home, or at the homes of his friends. Of his sixteen string quartets, four were left unfinished.

Schubert's inexhaustible gift for melodic invention seldom deserted him and this endearing quality is to be found in his chamber works. The following works are in the standard repertoire of chamber music groups wherever such music is enjoyed:

Quintet in A major for Piano and Strings, which bears the nickname "The Trout." This comes from the song *Die Forelle*, which Schubert uses as the theme for a set of variations in the fourth movement of the Quartet.

Quartet in D minor (strings), known as "Death and the Maiden," so named because of the five variations which the composer built on his song of that title. (Schumann called this quartet the best consolation we have for its composer's early death.)

Quintet in C major, which calls for a second cello;

String Quartets in A minor; G minor; and *G major;*

Octet in F major for clarinet, horn, bassoon, and strings;

Trio in B-flat major;

Quartettsatz in A minor.

Mendelssohn brought his usual elegance of style and melodic flow to his chamber works, chief among them being the *Octet for Strings in E-flat major, Piano Trio in D minor, Piano Trio in C minor.*

In his compositions, Schumann passed through phases: 1840 was his song year, 1841 his symphony year, 1842 being fruitful in chamber music. Though he had written, somewhat tentatively, in this form as a young man, he was thirty-two when he composed his *Quintet in E-flat major for Piano and Strings*, a work of romantic beauty. Mendelssohn, who thought highly of this, played the piano part—at sight—at its first performance.

Other chamber works of Schumann are three string quartets, piano trios, an *Adagio and Allegro for Horn (or Cello)*, *Fantasiestücke*, originally written for clarinet and piano.

It is probable that the chamber music works of Brahms which he destroyed outnumber those published. We have his statement that he wrote twenty string quartets before he considered he had produced one worthy of publication.

His published works in this medium include: three string quartets, three piano quartets, two string quintets, one piano quintet, six piano trios (including one with clarinet and one with horn), two string sextets, one clarinet quintet, and seven duo sonatas (three for clarinet and one with violin and piano, two for cello and piano, and two for clarinet and piano).

In the intellectual and aesthetic enjoyment of these works we realise the truth of the statement that Brahms himself was his sternest critic.

While composers following on from Brahms composed in larger forms, e.g., symphonies, concertos, operas, most of them at some time gave attention to chamber music. The symphonist Bruckner wrote a single quartet for strings, the Czech composer Smetana two string quartets; Dvořák at least fourteen quartets, a piano quintet, trios, violin and piano sonatas; Janáček, a string quartet, said to have been inspired by Tolstoy's novel, *Kreutzer Sonata*; Martinů, six string quartets and other chamber music.

Of French chamber music, the most significant are the strings quartets of Debussy and Ravel, and two piano quartets of Fauré. The chief contributions to chamber music by the Swiss-born Bloch are four string quartets and a piano quintet.

From Russian composers came the *Sextet* (*Souvenir de Florence*) by Tchaikovsky, and the *String Quartet in D major*, which contains the well known *Andante Cantabile* which has been arranged for other combinations; also the two string quartets of Borodin.

Worthily representing Russia is Prokofiev, with two quartets for strings, a sonata for two violins, a sonata for solo violin and one for flute and piano. Prokofiev also wrote a quintet for oboe, clarinet, violin, viola, and double-bass for a one-act ballet, *The Trapeze*. Shostakovitch has composed imaginative chamber works, his *String Quartet No. 1 in C major* dating from 1938.

The Finnish Sibelius produced a fine string quartet in 1908, giving it the title *Voces Intimae*. Hugo Wolf, almost solely a song-writer, began work on a string quartet when he was only eighteen, but did not finish it until six years later.

Most music authorities agree that the greatest composer of string quartets in this century was the Hungarian Béla Bartók. His six quartets cover a period from 1908 to 1939; therefore they thread their way purposefully through almost the full extent of his composing life. Welding the Magyar idiom with classical traditions, they are musical structures of profundity and finely drawn texture.

Space does not allow us to consider in detail all the sonatas for string, piano, and wind combinations. These have come from Bach, Handel, Beethoven, Schubert, Schumann, Brahms, Fauré, Franck, Lalo, Grieg, Dohnanyi, Debussy, Ravel, Busoni, Respighi, Schoenberg, Berg, Pizetti, Malipiero, Rachmaninov, Stravinsky, Kodaly, Bartók, R. Strauss, Reger, Honegger, Martin, Hindemith, and numerous others.

On the American scene we find that Johann Peter was turning out chamber works in the late eighteenth century, his example followed by such composers as

Alfred Hill (1870-1960). Distinguished Australian composer, he wrote music in many forms, including seventeen string quartets. He was influenced by Maori legends.

Foote, Carpenter, Mason, Ives, Copland, Riegger, Harris, Porter, Schuman, Piston, Barber.

Among the numerous English composers in this medium can be mentioned Parry, Stanford, Mackenzie, Bridge, Howells, Ireland, Elgar, Delius, Bliss, Vaughan Williams, Hurlstone, Holst, Dale, Bowen, McEwen, Goossens, Holbrooke, Moeran, Tippett, Rubbra, Rawsthorne, Britten, Fricker, Finzi, Wordsworth, Berkeley, Frankel, Smalley, Mayer; three women composers, Elisabeth Lutyens, Elizabeth Maconchy, and Priaulx Rainier.

Chamber music has attracted a number of Australian and New Zealand composers, including Badger, Brier, Brumby, Burnard, Butterley, Carr, Crowe, Douglas, de Jersey, Elton, English, Freed, Gethen, Gifford, Hanson, Hill, Hobcroft, Holland, Hudson, Hutchens, Hyde, Jones, Kay, Le Gallienne, Lilburn, Loughlin, Lovelock, McLeod, Maconie, Meale, McKie, Overman, Penberthy, Perkins, Phillips, Pruden, Rea, Ritchie, Sitsky, Sculthorpe, Sell, Sutherland, Tahourdin, Tibbitts, Tremayne, Trumble, Tunley, Vick, and Werder.

Many of the "advanced" and *avant garde* composers have expressed themselves in works for various chamber groups. In addition to some names included in the foregoing, these may be added: Stockhausen, Kirchner, Webern, Boulez, Gerhard, Berio, Nono, Hába, Xenakis.

We have briefly, and all too incompletely, mentioned composers spread over four or five centuries who have given their time and skill to the writing of chamber music.

Many great composers have cut their teeth on a trio or a quartet and in most cases they have returned to this personal form of music at the full tide of their creative powers. Through the medium of three, four, or five instruments they have expressed a profound philosophy, where previously they had called upon a full orchestra.

Without spotlit soloists the performers of chamber music subordinate their own personalities to the entity of the ensemble. Selfish musicians have no place in this Olympian music. For one player in a quartet to stand out from the others with undue prominence (unless the composer has written such a passage) is as much an artistic incongruity as an ill-matched string of pearls.

Overture

During the seventeenth and eighteenth centuries composers wrote pieces of music to be played immediately before the performance of the main item on the programme in order to alert the audience and advise them that the time had arrived for them to give full attention to the stage or platform.

If audiences then were as inattentive to the introductory music as they often are today, the composers probably thought it a waste of time to devote much care to such compositions. The desired hush is not always obtained until the curtain has actually risen.

The first operatic composer to give a definite form to this type of work was Jean-Baptiste Lully (1632-1687), who created the "French," or "Lully" style of overture. This consisted of three movements, generally slow-quick-slow. Alessandro Scarlatti (1659-1725) modelled his "Italian" type of overtures on the quick-slow-quick plan.

While many composers wrote mere curtain-raisers, Handel (1685-1759) composed many overtures (sometimes called *sinfonias*) which were popular as independent pieces. According to the English historian of that time, Sir John Hawkins, Handel's overtures, "excellent as they were, were composed as fast as he could write, and the most elaborate of them seldom cost him more than a morning's labour." Handel, however, could work at high speed without sacrificing quality; many of these overtures have survived until today as works of polished workmanship and melodic invention.

Until the time of Gluck (1714-1787) overtures bore little association with the character of the opera itself. Gradually, composers came to introduce into the overture themes from the work. Wagner further extended his overtures to make them atmospheric preludes to the drama to follow, with the object of creating the right mood, and providing a summary to the whole dramatic-musical structure.

Beethoven wrote only one opera, *Fidelio*, first produced in 1805. So earnest was his desire that the overture should convey the right atmosphere that he wrote no less than four for it, these now known as the *Leonora*, or *Leonore Nos. 1, 2, and 3*, named after the principal female character in the opera. All were eventually superseded for this purpose by the *Fidelio Overture. The Leonora No. 3* is usually played during the interval between Scenes 1 and 2 of Act 2.

Overtures are also part of incidental music written for plays. We may mention as examples: *Egmont, Coriolanus, King Stephen, Ruins of Athens* (Beethoven); *A Midsummer Night's Dream* (Mendelssohn); *Preciosa* (Weber); *L'Arlésienne* (Bizet); *Pelléas et Mélisande, The Tempest* (Sibelius); *The Wasps* (Vaughan Williams).

Some overtures, like those of Suppé and Rossini, have survived the stage works for which they were written and are frequently played in our concert halls and on records.

There are, too, many concert overtures, independent of larger musical works, e.g., *Tragic* and *Academic* (Brahms); *Cockaigne* and *Froissart* (Elgar); *Portsmouth Point* (Walton); *Russian Easter Festival* (Rimsky-Korsakov); *Solemn Overture*, known as *1812*, and *Romeo and Juliet — Fantasy Overture* (Tchaikovsky).

Programme Music

The somewhat confusing term "Programme" Music generally refers to music that is linked with a non-musical subject. In other words, it is intended to describe an event or a series of events, tell a story, or paint a picture in sound. It could perhaps more appropriately be called "Illustrative" Music, but for the fact that a composer sometimes means only to create an impression, or evoke an atmosphere.

Programme Music, which can be imitative (the songs of birds, the tolling of bells, the crash of thunder), is distinct from "Absolute" Music, a term that might be applied to a Bach fugue, a Mozart symphony, or a Beethoven quartet.

Programme Music is not something new. The sixteenth century French composer, Clement Jannequin, wrote four long descriptive pieces, entitled *Le Chant des Oiseaux*, which imitated in words and notes various bird songs. In the eighteenth century the Italian Martini made the cuckoo's call the theme of a mass.

Certain early composers attempted imitative sounds in some of their serious compositions; for instance, John Blow (1648-1708), who introduced in his *Venus and Adonis* a musical figure intended to represent the baying of hounds. In his *Phoebus and Pan*, Bach, one of the most "absolute" of eighteenth-century composers, wrote a phrase to suggest the cry of a donkey, and Beethoven attempted realistic effects in one of his less respected works, *The Battle of Victoria*.

Beethoven's *Symphony No. 6 in F major* ("*Pastoral*") crosses the border of absolute symphony music into the realms of Programme Music. Its five movements carry the titles *Pleasant feelings on arriving in the country; Scene by the Brook; Merrymaking of country folk; Thunderstorm; Shepherd's Song and Grateful feelings after the storm*. This symphony paints a series of pictures in sound, though the composer described it as "an expression of feeling rather than mere painting."

213

Handel suggested the songs of the linnet and the thrush in his oratorio *Joshua*, and Haydn introduced discreet touches of "atmosphere" in his oratorios *The Creation* and *The Seasons*.

Respighi's orchestral suite *The Birds*, composed in 1927, is based on harpsichord pieces of the seventeenth and eighteenth centuries, one of them being Rameau's *La Poule* in which we hear the hen's strident notes. In the last movement of the suite Respighi uses a piece *Toccata with the Cuckoo Joke* by Bernardo Pasquini, the seventeenth century organist-composer.

There are, of course, numerous other examples of descriptive music that go back several hundred years.

Symphonic Poems, Incidental Music, and Film Music

Programme Music branched into an art form of its own when Franz Liszt (1811-1886) created the Symphonic Poem, both the form and the title, thereby laying a solid foundation in descriptive writing that followed no set laws. Between the years 1850 and 1860 he composed twelve works in this style. Among these may be mentioned *Mazeppa*, first written for piano and later orchestrated, inspired by Victor Hugo's verses, *Les Orientales*, and not, as might be supposed, by the more familiar Byron poem.

Discovered in the private chambers of the Lady Theresa by her husband the King of Poland, Mazeppa was tied to a fiery horse and driven off. The music takes up from the point where the dreadful ride begins, the galloping theme graphically depicting the onrush of the frenzied animal and its victim's agonised cries.

Liszt's *Orpheus* had its inspiration in the famous myth, symbolising the power of music. His *Totentanz* (*Dance of Death*) was written after Liszt had seen at Campo Santo the fresco, *The Triumph of Death*, attributed to Andrea Orcagna. The same composer's *Les Préludes* (after Lamartine's *Méditations Póetiques*), *Hamlet*, *Faust Symphony*, also some piano works are to a varying extent programmatic in character.

Influenced by Liszt's success with the symphonic poem, the French Saint-Saëns composed four of his own between the years 1871 and 1877: *Le Rouet d'Omphale*, *Phaeton*, *Danse Macabre* and *La Jeunesse d'Hercule*.

Today the fame of the French composer, Paul Dukas, almost solely rests on his symphonic scherzo, *L'Apprenti sorcier* (*The Sorcerer's Apprentice*), a vivid piece illustrating the Goethe ballad, *Der Zauberlehrling*, which derived from a dialogue contained in *The Lie-Fancier* of Lucien, the Greek satirist who lived in the second century A.D.

Much of Debussy's music, for both orchestra and piano, has pictorial or literary associations, but as leader of the so-called Impressionist Movement in music, Debussy sought to suggest, rather than to depict. Though such works could come within the range of programme music, we will consider them more closely in the chapter Impressionism.

214

César Franck, Belgian-born, but resident in Paris during most of his life, found the symphonic poem a rewarding medium for his imagination. *Les Djinns* is based on Hugo's verses about demons, *Les Eolides*, inspired by some lines of Leconte de L'isle, and *Le Chasseur Maudit* (*The Wild Huntsman*), which was based on a ballad by the poet Bürger, *Der Wilde Jäger*, of which Scott's *The Wild Huntsman* is an imitation.

The colourful *Symphonie Fantastique* of Berlioz contains many programmatic passages.

The symphonic poems, more often referred to as tone poems, of Sibelius contain some of his finest orchestral writing. Much of this was inspired by the *Kalevala*, the epic of Finnish mythology; indeed, all legends and superstitions of his country had appealed to him from his early days. Among the Sibelius works which derived from the *Kalevala* are: *Pohjola's Daughter*, which tells of a beautiful but heartless girl who taunts Vainamoinen into performing seemingly impossible tests; *Tapiola*, concerned with the kingdom of Tapio, the god of the Forest.

The *Lemminkainen Cycle* (Four Legends for Orchestra) are also based on episodes from the *Kalevala*. Of these *The Swan of Tuonela* is the best known.

En Saga is mentioned in lists of Sibelius's works as a tone poem, but the composer has left no hint as to its programme. Despite the attempts of imaginative annotators to make it so, *Valse Triste* is not in the true sense a tone poem. It was intended to accompany a scene in a play, *Kuolema* (*Death*), by Järnefelt, in which a woman on her sick-bed, instead of being allowed to pass away peacefully, is invited by Death to join him in a waltz, albeit a slow one.

Then there is *Finlandia*, usually referred to as a tone poem, composed to accompany an historical tableau. Contrary to popular belief, this does not make use of folk-song material. We have the composer's own words for this. "I have never used a theme that was not of my own invention. The material for *Finlandia* is entirely my own."

One of the most popular works in the category of programme music is the Moussorgsky composition, *Night on Bald* (*or Bare*) *Mountain*, which graphically depicts subterranean sounds, the celebration of a Black Mass, the Witches' Sabbath, and the evil spirits dispelling at daybreak.

Pictures at an Exhibition, a suite by Moussorgsky for piano, but orchestrated by several musicians, including Ravel, vividly suggests a series of pictures painted by Victor Hartmann.

Smetana's *The Moldau* (*Vltava*) is well known, more so than the other five symphonic poems by this composer. These come under the generic title *Ma Vlast* (*My Fatherland*), dedicated to Prague.

Among the most extended forms of programme music are the lavishly-scored symphonic poems by Richard Strauss: *Don Juan*, based on extracts from the dramatic poem by Lenau; *Tod und Verklärung* (*Death and Transfiguration*), to which Alexander Ritter appended a word picture after its completion; *Till Eulenspiegels Lustige*

Streiche (*Till Eulenspiegel's Merry Pranks*) : *Ein Heldenleben* (*A Hero's Life*) ; *Don Quixote*, styled "fantastic variations on a theme of knightly character"; and *Also Sprach Zarathustra* (*Thus Spake Zarathustra*).

In his symphonic poem *Stenka Razin* the Russian composer, Glazunov tells of the legendary figure of 17th century Russia who went from place to place, looting and killing until defeated by the Tsar's army. In this the composer sets out to describe the Volga, Stenka Razin, the man, the voice of the Princess, and the clash of arms.

Another Russian composer, Liadov, turned to programme music to illustrate the legend of *Kikimora*, a rather villainous type of goblin.

Of his Nightpiece for Orchestra, *Paris, the Song of a Great City*, Delius said, "This is a Nocturne, and describes my impression at night and early dawn in Paris, with its peculiar street cries, the Pan's flute of the goat-herd."

Some composers have left much to the listener's imagination, a case in point being Gershwin's orchestral work, *An American in Paris*. Of this, Gershwin has said, "The Rhapsody is programmatic only in a general impressionistic way, so that the individual listener can read into the music such as his imagination pictures for him."

As with the Delius work, Gershwin's introduces street noises.

Prokofiev's *Peter and the Wolf*, and Saint-Saëns's zoological fantasy *The Carnival of the Animals* are descriptive musical works that appeal to listeners of all ages.

There are many other works in the orchestral and the piano repertoire that could be brought within the category of programme music. It might not be out of place to mention briefly here another form of music that is often coloured by literary and other associations:

Incidental Music

From early times composers have written music to accompany plays. In many cases the music survived the plays. Incidental music goes back in one form or other to the earliest Greek and Roman drama. In Elizabethan times it played an important part, some of it commissioned from the most eminent composers. Samuel Pepys, in the page of his diary dated 27 February 1668, speaks of Dekker and Massinger's play, *The Virgin Martyr*, "Not that the play is worth much. But that which did please me beyond anything in the whole world was the wind-musique when the angel comes down; which is so sweet that it ravished me. I could not believe that ever any music hath that real command over the soul of a man as this did upon me; and it makes me resolve to practise wind-musique, and to make my wife do the like."

There is another quotation of some interest. It dates from 1605, when a theatrical company was addressed thus in an anonymous pamphlet entitled "Rapeis Ghost", "I pray you, quote Ratset, let me heare your musicke, for I have often gone to playes more for musicke's sake than for acting."

Some of the composers of incidental music that readily come to mind are: Purcell (*The Indian Queen, The Fairy Queen, King Arthur*, etc.); Beethoven (*Egmont*); Mendelssohn (*A Midsummer Night's Dream*); Grieg (*Peer Gynt*); Bizet (*L'Arlésienne*).

Film Music

Perhaps it would not be stretching the point too far to bring into our consideration of incidental music the musical scores composed for films.

During the last forty years film music has become an art, recognised by film producers, if not always by the audience.

As far back as 1924 the mercurial French composer Erik Satie composed the musical score for René Clair's early film, *Entr'acte Cinematographique*. Even before that, Saint-Saëns had written an original score for a full-length film, *L'Assassinat du Duc de Guise*.

Other eminent composers who have been commissioned to write music for films are: Prokofiev, Vaughan Williams, Honegger, Bliss, Walton, Milhaud, Auric, Korngold, Varèse, Alwyn, Arnold, Frankel, Rawsthorne, Grainer, Steiner, Britten, Bernstein, Copland, Thompson.

Variations

Composers from the fifteenth century, through the Haydn-Mozart-Beethoven period, and up to the present day, have found rewarding use for the Variation form.

Broadly speaking, variations can be paired under two main headings: (1) those in which the melodic theme is preserved throughout the composition; (2) those in which the variations become a series of independent studies based on the structure and harmonic framework, with the melodic outline subordinated to the overall plan.

By keen imagination, and skill in arranging the harmonic, rhythmical, and dynamic treatment of melodic material into various patterns, composers have built up long and vital works on a single theme, sometimes a slender theme. For instance, Beethoven in his *Diabelli Variations* wrote as many as thirty-three on a theme by the nineteenth century composer Antonia Diabelli, the theme itself being a naïve waltz tune of little importance in itself. Diabelli's childishly-simple theme, consisting of two sections, each of sixteen bars, was written in the key of C major. Apart from six variations, Beethoven retains this key throughout.

Other sets of variations of that period that come to mind are: Haydn's on the *Emperor's Hymn* that form the slow movement of his *String Quartet in C major, Op. 76, No. 3*, Mozart's set on the Air, *Ah! vous dirais-je, Maman*, which many will recognise as *Twinkle, Twinkle, Little Star*.

Many young piano students have met this musical form in a suite written for harpsichord by Handel, and later published for piano under the nickname *The Harmonious Blacksmith*. The nickname is not Handel's.

Symphonies written in the eighteenth century, as well as those up to modern times, sometimes contained themes treated in variation form, one notable example being the melody in the second movement of the *Symphony No. 94 in G major—"Surprise"* by Haydn.

The violinist's repertoire was enriched by the *Andante con variazioni* movement in Beethoven's *Sonata No. 9 in A*, known as the *Kreutzer* sonata. The colourful violinist-composer, Paganini, who was famous for his pyrotechnical display on his violin, found it necessary to create new material for virtuosic showmanship by taking a familiar melody and adorning it with variations. Among the tunes he adapted in this manner are: *God Save the King, Carnival of Venice*, and the popular Genoese air *Barucaba* with sixty variations in all keys.

Brahms was the complete master of the variation form and his works in this category include: Eleven Variations on an Original Theme; thirteen on a Hungarian Song; ten on a theme of Robert Schumann; twenty-five and a fugue on a theme of Handel; and fourteen on a theme by Paganini. The Handel set has been arranged for orchestra by Edmund Rubbra.

Brahms also made an important contribution to orchestral music with his *Variations on a Theme by Haydn* (originally for two-pianos). The theme which Haydn had borrowed from a suite was an old Austrian hymn, known as *St Anthony Chorale*.

Harpsichordists of today hold in great respect the thirty *Goldberg Variations*, written by Bach for his pupil, J. G. Goldberg. This work was written at the request of Count Kaiserling who wished them to be played to him every night as a solace for his insomnia.

The fourth movement of the *Piano Quintet in A major* of Schubert is a set of variations on his song, *Die Forelle*, hence the title *Trout Quintet*.

Moving into the Romantic period we find the Opus 1 of Schumann bearing the title *Theme and Variations on the name "Abegg."* Meta von Abegg was the name of a young lady whom Schumann met at a ball when he was twenty. Infatuated by her, he composed this work on a theme made up on the notes A-B flat-E-G-G.

The celebrated conductor, Hans Richter, who gave the first performance of Dvořák's *Symphonic Variations*, in 1877 described the work as a "brilliant addition to my programme." A few months before that, Tchaikovsky completed his *Variations on a Rococo Theme* for cello and orchestra.

César Franck's *Symphonic Variations* owe less to the variation form than the Fantasia. *Appalachia* by Delius is subtitled *Variations on an Old Slave Song*. In this work for orchestra and chorus, the composer has treated the slave song, *O Honey, I am Going Down the River in the Morning* to fifteen variations.

Another work of interest in this *genre* is *Variations on a Nursery Tune* by the Hungarian-born Dohnanyi. Written for piano and orchestra in a lavish manner, this takes as its theme *Ah! vous dirai-je, Mamam*, which Mozart had borrowed for the same purpose more than a century before.

Anton Dvořák (1841-1904). Leading Czech composer, he was influenced by Brahms but soon evolved his personal style full of melodic richness and rhythmic vitality.

Of considerable charm is a work by the nineteenth century Russian composer, Arensky, *Variations on a Theme by Tchaikovsky*. Originally written as the second movement of a quartet for violin, viola, and two 'cellos, and later scored for string orchestra, this takes for its theme the song *Legend* (*Christ Has a Garden*), the fifth of Tchaikovsky's *Sixteen Songs for Children*, from his Opus 54.

In the list of English compositions employing variations, Elgar's *Variations on an Original Theme* ("*Enigma*") must be given a place of high honour. When this work was performed for the first time in 1899, the conductor being Hans Richter, the score bore the dedication: "To my Friends Pictured Within." It was not until after the composer's death that the identity of his "subjects" was made public. The subtitle *Enigma* refers to a melody that underlies the work.

In 1945 Benjamin Britten was invited to write the score for a documentary film entitled "Instruments of the Orchestra." This score has since become widely known as *Variations and Fugue on a Theme of Purcell*, or as *Young Person's Guide to the Orchestra*. The ruling theme is a tune from Purcell's *Abdelazar, or the Moor's Revenge*. After the theme is stated by the full orchestra, it is taken up by each of the four orchestral families. To round it all off, the brass section plays Purcell's tune, while the other instruments carry on with Britten's fugue.

One of the most favoured compositions that falls within the scope we have been discussing is the *Rhapsody on a Theme of Paganini* by Rachmaninov, the theme being the same as the one Brahms used in his set for piano. Written for piano and orchestra, the Rachmaninov variations contain a blend of lyricism and brilliance.

Transcriptions, Arrangements, and Borrowed Tunes

Purists are inclined to condemn all transcriptions, perhaps overlooking the fact that even Bach transcribed some of his own works and those of other composers, including his contemporary Vivaldi, arranging them in a different form, or for different instrumental combinations. In no case was the original reduced in status.

Both words, "transcription" and "arrangement" have been used to describe this musical process, the dividing line being slender. These days we have come to regard an arrangement as implying the transference of a composition from one medium to another, a more literal reproduction of the original; a transcription, the transcribing of a work for a performing medium different from the original, or treating the original in a more elaborate style. A transcription, therefore, suggests a freer reworking of a musical composition.

Liszt's thirteen hundred works include numerous transcriptions, most of them for piano solo. As a lionised virtuoso, the greatest pianist of his time, he no doubt wished to increase his repertoire. So we find Liszt transcriptions for piano of the organ preludes and fugues, and other organ works, of Bach; the nine symphonies and the Septet of Beethoven; some works of Berlioz, including the *Symphonie Fantastique* and overtures; Weber's overtures; the Saint-Saëns *Danse Macabre*; more than forty arias and overtures from operas by Bellini, Donizetti, Auber, and Mozart; and numerous songs by Beethoven, Schubert, Schumann, and Weber. In the case of some operatic arias, and some trivial pieces, the transcriptions turned out to be improvements on the originals.

Beethoven and Brahms made arrangements of their own works, as did Ravel and many nineteenth and twentieth century composers. Ravel, one of the most fastidious composers of his time who aimed at perfection of detail in almost everything he wrote, composed *Ma mère l'oye* (*Mother Goose*) as a piano duet in 1908, later making an orchestral arrangement of it, in which form it was used as a ballet. *Alborada del Gracioso* and *Habanera* are two other works which Ravel transferred from their original piano creations to orchestral versions.

Busoni, the Italian pianist, composer, author, and editor, made some remarkable arrangements of Bach's organ works, as well as *The Art of Fugue*.

Moussorgsky's *Pictures at an Exhibition*, written for piano in 1874, was later orchestrated by several musicians; Ravel's superior version is the one we usually hear today, although it is still played by pianists in the original.

During recent times conductors have taken it upon themselves, with varying degrees of fidelity to the original, to make arrangements and transcriptions of standard works. A case in point is Leopold Stokowski's transcriptions for full orchestra of Bach's organ works.

Gounod added a melody of his own to the first prelude of Bach's *Well-tempered Clavier* and called it *Meditation*. Then someone else fitted words to this combination, since when it has been known as *Ave Maria* by Bach-Gounod.

Ballet has effectively brought music from another medium into the theatre; to quote some of the many examples: *La Boutique Fantasque* (Rossini-Respighi); *Les Patineurs* (Meyerbeer-Lambert); *The Good-Humoured Ladies* (Scarlatti-Tommasini); *The Gods Go A-Begging* (Handel-Beecham); *Graduation Ball* (Strauss-Dorati); *The Wise Virgins* (Bach-Britten). For the ballet *Les Sylphides* Chopin's piano music has been arranged and orchestrated by Glazounov, Stravinsky, and others. *Carnaval*, based on the piano suite of twenty-one pieces by Schumann, had for its orchestrators Arensky, Glazounov, Liadov, Rimsky-Korsakov, Tcherepnin, Wihtol and Vinkler. The music of Sir Arthur Sullivan, arranged and orchestrated by Charles Mackerras served for the ballet *Pineapple Poll*, first produced in London in 1951.

It would seem that arrangements and transcriptions, by whichever term they go under, are legitimate, provided that they are carried out in good taste and without distortion to the original. There is always a danger, however, that arrangers, striving for unusual and spectacular effects, may upset the balance and detail of a work as conceived by the composer, and thereby cause the original to lose its true character. The essential quality in carrying out alterations to the original, therefore, is a matter of artistic conscience.

There are many cases in music of different periods where a composer has borrowed, unconsciously or deliberately, a theme or a melody; that is, one not of his own creation. But, in many such cases, the treatment or expansion of that idea is different, and often quite legitimate. For instance, it will be found that there is a similarity between the march theme in *Marche Slave* by Tchaikovsky and the melody belonging to *Orientale*, one of the twenty-four works for violin and piano by César Cui in his *Kaleidoscope* collection. Both composers were Russian, and composers of that country often used a similar theme, probably with no intention of plagiarism. In this case, of course, the melody was actually a folk-song. Some musicologists have found a family likeness between Percy Grainger's *Country Gardens* and the old song, *The Vicar of Bray*. When someone pointed out to Brahms that a short passage in the first movement of his *Symphony No. 3 in F major* bore a resemblance to the sirens' chorus in *Tannhäuser*, he replied, "Any fool can see that." Perhaps Brahms intended the passage to be a tribute to the dying Wagner.

These, and many other similar examples, may be accepted without question, but in modern times arrangers of the Tin Pan Alley class have blatantly adapted a melody from a composition of a serious composer to a popular song, usually with flimsy, sometimes vulgar, lyrics.

Attempts have been made to defend the lifting of themes from concertos and symphonies on the premise that such "arrangements" tend to make the music of great composers more popular. (The use of the opening theme of Tchaikovsky's

Concerto No. 1 in B-flat minor for Piano and Orchestra to make a *Concerto for Two* is a typical example.) This is a false argument, for what the listener hears in a popularised and truncated version is far removed from the original; he is not forming a true assessment of the real work.

When the purist squirms on hearing a melody by a great composer, a folk-song, or a hymn turned into a popular song he may be little comforted by the fact that tune-borrowing has sometimes worked in reverse. Not only has the Salvation Army borrowed popular tunes for the vocal expression of their faith; their hymns have sometimes been based on tunes that had already been popularised in the music-halls and taverns. Also, the eighteenth century John Wesley who, in "taking the Gospel to the Masses," wrote some 6,500 hymns, was known to have borrowed "pop" tunes of his day. When someone accused him of this, he replied, "I see no reason why the Devil should have all the pretty tunes."

The purist is fully justified in gnashing his teeth in anger when he hears a well-known folk-song, or a melody from the work of a great and revered composer, used as a jingle for some radio or television "commercial" to extol the virtues of a cure for physical ailments or an article of intimate domestic use.

There are limits beyond which an honest arranger should not trespass.

Popular Music

So far we have spoken of serious, or so-called "classical" music, but it may not be out of place to refer, at least briefly, to the lighter forms, generally called "popular" music.

An English Dictionary will define the term "popular" in some such words as "of the people" (from the Latin *populus*, the people), or "pleasing to and suited to the understanding of ordinary people," which in a way does sound rather snobbish.

Music could very well do without snobs, a harsh word perhaps, but sometimes an appropriate one. We find musical snobbery at both ends of the line—with the pompous pedant and the myopic moron. We may find a person who will glibly talk about his physical complaints, describe in detail an operation, even admit there has been mental illness in the family, but refuse to own up that he enjoys popular music. He may make it known that he likes detective stories or Western films, but will frown snobbishly at the mention of Johann Strauss, stage musicals, and dance music.

There is the other person who considers that the works of such composers as Bach, Beethoven, and Mozart are solely for the highbrow.

Surely the chief function of music is to give pleasure!

Music, like language, is a living, moving thing. Let us attempt to trace the growth and spread of popular music in a few brief sentences, though the subject deserves a book to itself. Some of the notes that follow will repeat some facts that have already been discussed in more detail in specific chapters of this book.

In early times organised music belonged to the church; later it became the property of the privileged few. Noble families took the best composers and the most talented performers into their service, but such was the lowly status of the musician two or three centuries ago that they were treated as ill-paid lackeys. For instance, Mozart's life was a desperate struggle against poverty. He was buried in a pauper's grave.

In time music was used for the entertainment of "the people," and as the lines of communication between countries extended there was a greater interchange of musical ideas.

While the status of professional musicians advanced, amateur musicians found in music a satisfying means of self-expression, and that form of expression broadened in scope to embrace forms and styles more readily digested by the masses.

We have noted in a previous chapter that operas at first were performed privately; that the first "commercial" operatic venture took place early in the seventeenth century, this leading to the opening of opera houses for the general public in many cities.

While opera, the kind known as "Grand Opera" continued (as it has up to the present time), off-shoots from that serious form gave birth to lighter forms, e.g., the Zarzuela of Spain, a stage production, often topical and satirical, that blended music, songs, and spoken dialect.

In England *The Beggar's Opera* of 1728 gave an impetus to a stream of Ballad Operas that mixed spoken dialogue with existing music, often popular tunes of the day, set to new words. In the late nineteenth century the "Savoy" light operas of Gilbert and Sullivan provided genial fare of its own particular brand to countless theatregoers in English-speaking countries and in Europe.

It is a narrow line that divides Operetta from Musical Comedy, both blending music and the spoken word. When we think of operetta, such titles come to mind as *Die Fledermaus* and *The Gipsy Baron* (Johann Strauss, jr.), *La Vie Parisienne* and *La Belle Hélène* (Offenbach), *Véronique* (Messager), *The Merry Widow* and *The Count of Luxembourg* (Lehar), *The Student Prince* and *The Desert Song* (Romberg); *Merrie England* (German).

When *The Maid of the Mountains* was first performed in the nineteen-twenties, the composer Fraser-Simson saw it referred to as operetta, comic opera, and musical comedy. (He probably shrugged and said, "Take your pick.")

In the late nineteenth century and during the years that followed, fruitful seasons of Musical Comedy yielded such popular successes as *Floradora*, *The Geisha*, *The Belle of New York*, *The Arcadians*. Many works of this kind, while containing pleasant melodies that delighted millions of theatregoers, often were based on flimsy, unoriginal plots. Of recent years these have been replaced in popular favour by

"Musicals" which placed more emphasis on unity and theatrical realism. Titles that readily come to mind are: *Oklahoma, South Pacific, My Fair Lady, Brigadoon, Sound of Music, West Side Story.*

We have already mentioned that in early times instrumental music broke away from occasions associated with sacred worship into secular channels. In succeeding generations instrumental players were engaged to provide music for various public functions. Humble bands of players developed into small orchestra, these in time to symphony orchestras. Later, orchestras of the café type assumed increased numerical strength and more artistic responsibility, while "giving the public what it wants."

For many generations Band Music—that is music played by military bands, brass bands, and pipe bands on the march, in public parks, and in concert halls—has held its place in public favour. And with good reason. For instance, the Band has always been a part of British life. Developing from drum and fife groups, the bands of the British Army can be traced back to the late seventeenth century. Recently it was reported that there were about 2,500 brass bands in the British Isles, many of these supported by industrial firms. The Regimental Bands belonging to Royal houses have nobly upheld a tradition of their own. Pipe Bands have sent many a regiment into action with a firmer step. Even the humbler Percussion Band has helped to plant a stronger rhythmic sense in young people.

Every country has its own Band history. So far as America is concerned, one need only mention John Philip Sousa. Born in Washington in 1854, the son of a Portuguese father and a Bavarian mother, this famous bandmaster-composer toured the world in 1910-1911.

Jazz: The word Jazz has been subjected to as much careless mis-use as the word "classical." Jazz, that is, the real thing, is a specialised style in music, not merely a jumble of undisciplined sounds.

At the turn of the present century American popular music was still clinging to established European forms and conventions. Then a new stimulus arrived by way of the Negroes who injected into their music-making African chants and rhythms which were the bases of their spirituals and work songs.

One of the first widespread Negro influences was Ragtime, essentially a style of syncopated piano-playing that reached its peak about 1910. By the year 1920 jazz had become a dominating force in popular music, and New Orleans, one of the first cities to foster it, became more than just a point on the map.

In the early 'twenties America became caught up in a whirl of post-war gaiety. The hectic period would later be known as the Jazz Era. Soon jazz had begun its insistent migration across the world. While Negro musicians of America were recognised as the true experts in the jazz field, the idiom attracted white musicians, who found it stimulating and profitable to form bands to play in the negro style. Prominent among these white band-leaders was Paul Whiteman.

224

Paul Whiteman carried the title "King of Jazz" with pride and lucrative results. It is said that, in his heyday, he controlled eleven bands in New York City and seventeen in other parts of the U.S.A., as well as receiving royalties from more than forty bands who were featuring his copyright arrangements, many of these carried out by Ferde Grofé, his chief arranger.

Early in 1922 another name became associated with Whiteman and jazz. It was George Gershwin, already well known as a composer for Broadway shows. Further recognition came when Whiteman asked him to write a jazz concerto. Working against a dead-line, Gershwin completed a two-piano version of *Rhapsody in Blue*. Busy on other work at the time, and still unsure of his grip of orchestration, he asked that someone be brought in to score it. This responsibility was handed to Ferde Grofé. In February 1924 *Rhapsody in Blue* began its amazingly successful career.

Gershwin was not the first composer to attempt a bridging of the gap between jazz and "classical" music, but he was certainly one of the earliest to succeed in that field. "There has been so much talk," he said, "about the limitations of jazz which, they said, had to be in strict time; it had to cling to dance rhythms. I resolved to kill that misconception."

Some critics said that Gershwin had successfully arranged a true marriage between jazz and the classical idiom; others declared that it was an unholy alliance, while the purists denounced Gershwin's composition as being outside the periphery of True Jazz. Disagreeing with his critics that it was an isolated style, Gershwin replied, "Jazz is a word which has been used for at least five or six types of music."

While many self-appointed prophets were condemning jazz as vulgar, and others smugly foretelling its early death, some notable European composers attempted to weave the jazz idiom into their musical works. These included Debussy, Ravel, Stravinsky, and Milhaud, also the English Constant Lambert in his *Rio Grande*.

(Here one is reminded that several composers, including Debussy, Ravel, Liszt, Bizet, d'Indy, and Richard Strauss, befriended the much-maligned Saxophone, invented about the middle of the nineteenth century, and introduced it into the concert-hall.)

Before we leave George Gershwin, we should mention his *Porgy and Bess* which brought something daringly different to opera. That this work is truly a folk-opera has been a matter of much argument; whether or not, its originality and sincerity have stood up to the years. Based on the novel *Porgy* by Du Bose Heyward, it was first performed (in Boston) in 1935. The characters, credible human beings, are almost entirely Negro; the music, Gershwin's own, sounding so authentically Negro, that it is surprising that this rich score was written by a white American.

THE RECORD: As we have noted in its own chapter, the gramophone record has been one of the greatest forces of the twentieth century in bringing music to the masses. The record brought to millions of people the world over not only opera, choral, symphonic, chamber, and solo instrumental music, but every kind of light fare. Today its grip on the public's desire for entertainment is stronger than ever before, while competing with and aiding the ubiquitous transistor-radio which has played a vigorous part in spreading the cult of "pop" music.

RADIO: During the last half-century radio broadcasts have brought the best in all forms of music—serious, light, and "popular"—into the home, at the same time providing the performing artists with lucrative incomes. Listeners have come to realise that serious music, performed by the world's finest artists offers pleasure; that "classical" music can be enjoyed for itself. At the same time conservative music-lovers have found that, after all, there is something in less-serious kinds of music.

THE FILM: The film, too, has played an important part in making music popular. In the United States on 14 November 1940 *Fantasia* burst upon the film world with an impact of a bombshell. Produced by Walt Disney, it featured The Philadelphia Orchestra, numbering about 100 players, conducted by Leopold Stokowski. It was a spectacular break-through in sound-and-image technique that showed the "masses" what a symphony orchestra looked and sounded like. It proved that so-called "classical" music (works by Bach, Beethoven, Tchaikovsky, Stravinsky, Dukas, Moussorgsky, Ponchielli, and Schubert) could be enjoyed by those described by the dictionary as "ordinary people," at least people without previous musical knowledge.

Some critics quarrelled with Disney's visual interpretation of the music, the defence being that, at least, the film did bring fine music to the man in the street.

THE GUITAR: With a history that goes back several centuries, the guitar has met an upsurge of interest during the last twenty years or so. As well as being the means of reviving solo music of earlier times, and the art of Flamenco, it has been vigorously taken up by popular vocalists and small groups, thus providing an economical but effective type of accompaniment, helping a renewed interest in folk-song, and taking part in protest songs, popular ballads and the like.

It has also, it must be admitted, been to a great extent responsible for the hypnotic beat that drives along ephemeral "pop" explosions, the rhythm making up for a deficiency of original words and tunes.

The 1960s saw the long, sustained reign of The Beatles. This singing foursome, as well as performing in many parts of the world, bowing to hysterical audiences, appearing in films, and spending highly profitable hours in recording studios, managed to write some popular songs that had far more merit than many poured out by less-gifted pop groups.

NOW WHAT? In this technological age it is not surprising that electronics should have invaded the field of music. This new phase has ranged from the works of the German composer Stockhausen and other adventurous composers who have replaced conventional means of sound production with those artificially produced by revolutionary technical processes, to experiments brought into play by devices

226

intended to give music of the popular *genre* a new sound. Though many may be alarmed at such explorative tampering with sound, it must be admitted that the possibilities of electronically-produced music are immense.

In the late 1960s the Moog Synthesiser made its electronic bow to the record-buying public. A record entitled *Switched-on Bach*, being "Electronic Realisations" of that revered composer's preludes, fugues, inventions, and the like, became a best-seller. Johann Sebastian Bach achieved the distinction of being placed high in the popularity charts of the record industry.

The Moog Synthesiser has been used for mood music for movie films, in radio and television, also as incidental music to stage plays. Other famous composers have been invited to keep company with Bach in this new sound, and it is interesting to note that some music institutions have included the study of the Moog Synthesiser in their courses on electronic music.

Popular music today wears many faces and follows various courses. Between the verdant fields of classicism and the crazy pavements of Lower Tin Pan Alley lies a wide area of in-between music, all of which has a place in a heterogeneous community.

Never before has music — all kinds of music — been so popular. Never before has the world had greater need of its stimulation and comfort. As we said at the beginning of this book, we find the ultimate satisfaction in music, be it "classical" or "popular," when we have learnt how to reject the spurious and accept the genuine; when we have learned how to *listen*.

IMPRESSIONISM AND INTERPRETATION

10

AS a word, "Impressionism" came into use in France towards the end of the nineteenth century. As a cult it quickly spread to many parts of the world. In painting it began with such exponents as Monet, Renoir, Cézanne, and Degas; in poetry with Verlaine and Mallarmé; in music with Debussy, who became recognised as the leader of the Impressionist Movement in Music.

Impressionism came at a time when French music stood irresolute at the crossroads, its stream showing signs of eddying into a pool of stereotyped flippancy.

In much the same way as the painters of that time concentrated on the treatment of light and fleeting amorphism, disregarding graphic realism, and as the poets were concerning themselves with the sensuous *sound* of words, Debussy developed an absorbing interest in sounds *as* sounds. He aimed to suggest in tone mental images, emotion, and colour. In this way his musical textures became reflected fluid sound-shapes.

Departing from orthodox systems of harmonic procedure, Debussy experimented with the potent force of dissonance, chord progression, and overlaying harmonies to the point of his adventurous use of the whole-tone scale.

Debussy's harmonic palette was no less colourfully vivid than Wagner's, or that of the more advanced Russian composers, but it was the fusion of tone colours, harmonic subtlety, and sensuous "atmosphere" that gave his music a diaphanous

228

Howard Hanson (b. 1896). American composer, he served as the Director of the Eastman School of Music, Rochester, N.Y. His compositions include six symphonies.

quality. There was, however, wide contrast in his use of harmonic colour. To prove this point, one need only compare in his piano music the simplicity of his *Children's Corner*, or the earlier pieces (e.g. *Rêverie*, composed in 1890) with his *Estampes* and *Images*, composed between 1903 and 1907. To appreciate the amazingly varied range of tone-colour in Debussy's orchestral writing, we must also savour the harmonic and rhythmic structure of *Three Nocturnes for Orchestra*, *Images for Orchestra*, that masterpiece of tonal evocation, *La mer*, not forgetting the earlier *Prélude á l'après-midi d'un faune*.

In his last compositions, those written not long before his death in 1918, Debussy entered a new phase, often referred to as "neo-classic," when he returned to traditional form, while still pursuing new harmonic combinations.

Debussy's excursions into impressionism influenced numerous other composers, but few, if any, equalled him in the evocation of impressions and moods.

Some writers couple Ravel with Debussy, as if their styles were similar. This is not so. While developing his own plan of harmonic, melodic, and rhythmic expression, Ravel paid strict allegiance to classical form and precision of outline. His musical patterns and technique followed a different course from that taken by Debussy.

As we have said, impressionism spread to other countries, and many composers were described as impressionists when they were merely using non-traditional techniques.

Giacomo Meyerbeer (real name Jacob Liebmann Beer; 1791-1864). A German composer of popular operas. He was influenced by French, Italian, and German operatic styles.

Frederick Delius has been called, somewhat inaccurately, the "English Debussy." We could, however, strain a point and say that he brought impressionism to English music. Much of his music has a sensory, amorphous delicacy (he could also write vigorously), but his harmonies tend to reflect the romanticism of Grieg, rather than the illusive quality of Debussy. Perhaps we should regard Delius as a solitary figure on a hilltop, watching the sunset of Romanticism, and obviously sighing at the going-down of that luminous glow of a departing era.

Another English composer, Sir Arnold Bax (1883-1953), refuted the statement that he was an impressionist, preferring to regard himself as a "brazen romantic."

It also pleased certain writers to pin the "impressionist" tag on Ottorino Respighi (1879-1936), perhaps because he created such symphonic poems as *The Fountains of Rome*, in which he attempted musical impressions of moods inspired by the most beautiful fountains of the Roman capital. Each, according to the composer, was "contemplated at the hour in which its character is most in harmony with the surrounding landscape, or in which its beauty appears most impressive to the observer." In his *Pines of Rome* Respighi followed much the same pattern, causing surprise by introducing into the score the sound of a nightingale.

But these works are more pictorial than impressionistic in the Debussyian sense. Respighi had been a pupil of Rimsky-Korsakov from whom he no doubt gained much in brilliant orchestral technique, this applied to his quasi-impressionistic suggestion. Prunières, the musicologist, described Respighi's writing as "an able compromise

230

This photograph shows part of a full modern symphony orchestra in action. The remainder of the orchestra is shown overleaf.

Part of the Adelaide Symphony Orchestra during a
performance in the Adelaide Town Hall.

between the counterpoint of Richard Strauss, the harmony of Debussy, and the orchestration of Rimsky-Korsakov; the whole tinted with a little Italian melody."

Because some of it has a misty and exotic character, the music of Karol Szymanowski (1882-1937) has been labelled impressionistic. This Polish composer was influenced in turn by Franck, Scriabin, Strauss, and Debussy. There are some impressionist characteristics in some of his works; e.g., *Metopes* for piano, *Myths*, to which *The Fountain of Arethusa*, for violin and piano belongs.

It is arguable whether Szymanowski, Bax, Respighi, and some later composers mentioned in this context, share with Debussy the impressionism of the late nineteenth century.

INTERPRETATION

The word "interpretation" as applied to music explains itself, but it may be of some assistance, at least to the student, if we consider the term in some detail.

We can look at a picture, a statue, or a building and provided it obeys the laws of artistic discipline, find interest, pleasure, and satisfaction in what we see, but we need a performing artist to interpret for us a composer's musical work, which, until the performing artist breathes life into it, remains silent on ruled paper.

The printed words of a poem are, after all, a series of symbols, but those words come to life and convey their message when the reader's eye takes them in, or the ear hears them spoken. (This, of course, presupposes that the reader, the speaker, and the listener fully understand the words.) The printed page of music is also a series of symbols, but unless the reader has been trained to understand these symbols, the sheet of music, or the orchestral score, will be meaningless to him.

Let us assume that the printed page of music is in the hands of a trained musician. He accepts it as a guide, a blueprint, an instruction-chart, explaining the composer's intentions. This applies to both the solo performer and the conductor.

If the performer obeys all the written instructions; e.g., plays or sings the right note, sustains it for the right duration, causes it to sound loud or soft, phrases according to the composer's markings, pays due regard to accents and all the other directions, he will be doing technically what is expected of him. But he must do more than this. He must *interpret* the music according to the composer's individual style, respect the period in which the music was written, and conform to certain conventions. For instance, it might be artistically correct to slow down at the end of a composition by one of the "romantic" composers (e.g. Schumann or Liszt), but be out of place in a composition by a composer of the "classical" period (e.g. Bach or Handel) or, say, a motet from an earlier period. A piece of music by a composer of the "baroque" period might be played with a rigid rhythm and sound near to the composer's intentions; to play a Chopin waltz or mazurka, or a Debussy piece

William Schuman (b. 1910). An American composer who has used bitonal and jazz idioms. His opera *The Mighty Casey* is about baseball.

(shall we say *La fille aux cheveux de lin*) in strict time would be to rob it of its romantic quality.

In the case of some early music, composers set up few "signposts." Up to, say, the year 1800 the orchestra and its music were going through a stage of evolution, and composers were not always explicit in their directions as to tempo and other aspects of interpretation. In those times the performers were expected to "know."

Also many performances in those days were directed by the composers themselves.

The directions indicating tempo and dynamics which we find in modern publications of old scores have been added by editors and may or may not be strictly in accordance with the composers' ideas. During the last hundred years composers have set out considerably more detail in regard to such matters as, in orchestral works, the desired bowing for strings, the tongue-phrasing for wind instruments; in the case of singers and solo instrumentalists specific phrasing and dynamics.

TEMPO: Let us say that a conductor is preparing an orchestral work for rehearsal. He will at first establish in his mind the correct tempi for the various movements and sections of the work. There are usually such indications on the score as *allegro*, *allegretto, adagio*. He must interpret according to the character of the works, and the period in which it was written. The score may carry metronome markings, which indicate the number of beats to the minute; sometimes these vary from one edition to another.

232

Paul Hindemith (1895-1963). A highly original composer, he has had tremendous influence on twentieth century music. He was also a great teacher and theoretician.

An *allegro* of Haydn's day may be quite different from an *allegro* of a modern composer. A *presto* of Mozart might be little faster than an *allegro* of today. Perhaps the cultivation and worship of speed in modern times has led to a gradual quickening of pace in performing music. A record made by an artist at the beginning of this century may sound slow, even dragged, if compared with a recording of the same work made today.

We may compare three or four records of a work under different conductors and find the tempi different in every case. (The same of course applies to soloists.) Yet, if the variation is not unduly wide, and the performances are well controlled, it is possible that none of these will sound wrong. There are limits to the extent of this latitude. The rushed tempo of a Bach *Brandenburg Concerto* would offend the expert ear far more than the *personalised* tempo of a movement from a contemporary work.

The convincing, the "right" performance of a work, be it a Schubert song, a Chopin Polonaise, or a Beethoven symphony, will depend on not only tempo, but feeling. The difference in feeling or style may sometimes be made evident by playing two records of the same composition by two artists. The artists may be equally famous, but entirely different in their approach. Pianist A may sound convincing in a piece until compared with Pianist B. Also, pianist A may be a great exponent of Beethoven's music, but sound clinical and uninspired in that of Chopin. Pianist B may be a particularly impressive exponent of Chopin, but sound too capricious in Beethoven.

Peter Sculthorpe (b. 1929). One of the most interesting modern composers, he has experimented with new musical idioms, including electronic. His work has also been influenced by Oriental and pop music.

How does one differentiate between the definitive interpretation of a work and one out of keeping with the composer's style? The answer cannot be given in a few words. Artistic discrimination, the recognition of "rightness" can come only with training and experience.

The average music-lover will become accustomed to what he hears. In the case of a record which he can purchase and listen to frequently, that performance will assume a particular character for him. If it is a poor performance, and this can happen even on a record, the shortcomings, lack of knowledge or respect for the composer's intentions, or the personal eccentricities of the soloist or conductor will stamp that interpretation on the listener's mind. He will be prepared to accept it as definitive. Should he hear another artist or conductor performing the same work in the best possible way, he will be inclined to reject that interpretation as wrong. Once a style of performance has been planted in the average listener's mind, he will regard with suspicion any performance that is different, for it is true that a record collector will form a sentimental attachment to a recorded performance to which he has become accustomed. One cannot, therefore, stress too strongly the advantage of securing the best possible performances. This aspect is dealt with in more detail in the chapter devoted to the record.

One may ask what part imagination and inspiration play in interpreting a piece of music; in other words, just where do instinct and knowledge meet?

Inspiration, like imagination, can play a big part in the interpretation of a musical work, just as it can in the composing of it. But, just as a composer will not achieve much that is worthwhile by merely being inspired with good ideas, unless he has mastered the *craft* of composition, so will a performer fail to communicate the composer's message to an audience unless he has mastered *his* craft, that is, the technical aspects of his instrument, be it a piano, an organ, a voice, or a full orchestra. After that it becomes a matter of constant, probing study, allied to experience.

This does not mean that "correct" interpretations result in conventional performances; by no means. A true artist's personality will prevent that.

In his book, *Interpretation in Song* (first published in 1912), the eminent singer and teacher, Harry Plunket Greene has said, "Interpretation is essentially individual. If it became stereotyped there would be no scope for personality; imagination would count for nothing and originality would be a dead letter. The interpreter must start with four possessions: perfected technique, magnetism, sense of atmosphere, command of tone-colour."

New Works: The conductor of a new symphony, the performer of a new sonata, or what you will, has a big responsibility to the composer. The reputation of that work will to a great extent depend on how it is presented for the first time. Unless he is a friend of the composer and can work out details with him, he has nothing more to go on but the score. This then is where his skill, training, experience, and imagination must come forward. Unless he is familiar with the idiom, and has a true insight into the composer's intentions, the work in performance may fail to take wing, and so prove incomprehensible even to the most tolerant listeners.

Apart from such basic matters as tempo and dynamics, the conductor or performer, must pay particular attention to the quality of the sound of the work. The whole performance must be one of complete integration. It is likely then that communication between the performer and the audience will result.

MUSICAL
CRITICISM

11

BROADLY speaking, one could say that the function of a music critic is to inform the public, and keep the performer on his toes. It is the responsibility of the critic, with his training, experience, and balanced taste, to help the music-lover to form sound preferences, and at the same time to point out constructively to the artists where they are at fault.

There is, of course, always a danger to a composer, a conductor, or a performer if a music critic makes a wrong judgement, thereby possibly persuading other critics, as well as the public, to agree with him.

The written word often places an artist at a disadvantage. The critic can say what he thinks, but seldom has the artist "the right of appeal." Unless a performer gives an account of a work that is blatantly opposed to recognised standards, he is entitled to his own ideas of interpretation. In the case of a clash between a critic and a highly-qualified singer or musician, any difference between them must be a matter of personal opinion.

A critic's remarks should not be coloured by personal likes and prejudices, but based on the recognition of firmly-established artistic standards, and at all times they should be constructive and never spiteful.

In the case of instrumental music, the critic's ear plays an important part; one person may detect a violinist's occasional departures from accurate intonation, while

The final scene from Beethoven's *Fidelio*, the composer's only opera.
It took him many years to write, and he wrote fifteen versions of one
aria before he was satisfied.

another may not hear them. With singers, more than with other performers, the
artist's personality may act as a screen for certain shortcomings of intonation, voice
control, or interpretation. On the other hand, a singer who may create a favourable
impression by his records, or on radio, may irritate by mannerisms or an exaggerated
personal style in public.

One of the most difficult assignments a critic may be given is to express a guiding
opinion about a new composition, be it a piano sonata, a symphony, an opera, or any
other form of musical creation. Here, his personal likes and prejudices must be
subordinated to constructive judgement; has the composer "said" something really
worthwhile, and has he constructed the work on sound technical lines?

One may wonder if at times a critic's opinion is coloured by his digestion, or
general state of health; it is not uncommon to find that an expert critic has, on
reflection, reversed a decision. This proves that, no matter how well informed,

a critic is able to publish an opinion on a performance, or a composition, which he later feels invalid. It also proves that he has courage to come out in print and say so.

Byron has said, "A man must serve his time in every trade, save censure. Critics all are ready made."

The generous critic will approach an amateur performance, or a students' concert, with a different set of standards than those which he would apply to a recital by a celebrity artist. In the case of the former, he can be critical, provided his comments are constructive, and not likely to discourage a young, inexperienced performer not yet hardened to criticism in print.

If, on the other hand, an artist demanding high fees for a performance gives evidence of insufficient preparation, or carelessness, or displays a lack of respect for the tenets of interpretation appropriate to the composer, then the honest critic may feel it to be his professional duty to remark on such points, if only to make those who have heard the performance aware that the composer has received less than his due.

Some music criticisms are of passing interest only. Others remain in print to be read long after the event concerned. For instance, the writings on music by Eduard Hanslick, who was born in Prague in 1825 and became a leading figure in the musical life of Vienna, and was one of the most eminent of music critics of his time, and those by George Bernard Shaw, are still in print in book form.

Henry Pleasants tells us in the Preface to *Eduard Hanslick — Music Criticisms 1846-99* (Published by Penguin Books) that Hanslick's collected writings run to twelve volumes, including two volumes of autobiography. The following are extracts from some of his published criticisms: "Liszt belongs to those ingenious but barren temperaments who mistake desire for calling . . . There is no other work of Beethoven (*Missa Solemnis*) which crushes the unprepared listener with such gigantic strength, at the same time raising him up again, delighted, confused . . . I cannot doubt that for the *Mass in D*, as for the 9th Symphony, the time is approaching when shock and surprise will give way to understanding, admiration and love . . . In *Messiah* Handel erected a monument to himself, not only as a composer but also as a devout Christian well versed in the Bible."

Of Schubert's *Unfinished Symphony*, Hanslick wrote in 1865, after its first performance in Vienna, "This symphonic fragment may be counted among Schubert's most beautiful instrumental works, and I am especially happy to say so here because I have permitted myself more than once to speak warningly of our over-zealous worship and adoration of Schubert relics."

Brahms' *Symphony No. 1 in C minor* was first performed at Karlsruhe, Germany in November, 1876. Before that year had ended, Hanslick wrote, "Even the layman will immediately recognise it at once as one of the most individual and magnificent works of the symphonic repertoire. . . . The new symphony of Brahms is a possession of which the nation may be proud, an inexhaustible fountain of sincere pleasure and fruitful study."

Of Bruckner, he wrote, "The Philharmonic Orchestra devoted its entire concert to a new symphony by Bruckner. It is the 8th in the series and similar to its predecessors in form and mood. I found the newest one, as I have found the other Bruckner Symphonies, interesting in detail but strange as a whole and even repugnant. The programme seems to have been chosen only for the sake of a noisy minority. The test is easy: just give the Symphony in a special concert outside the subscription series. This would be helpful to all concerned, save probably the Philharmonic Orchestra."

Of the Symphonic Poem, *Tod und Verklärung* (*Death and Transfiguration*) by Richard Strauss, Hanslick wrote in 1893, "The composer of *Don Juan* again proved himself a brilliant virtuoso of the orchestra, lacking only musical ideas."

In 1899 he paid this tribute to Johann Strauss (II): "*The Blue Danube* not only enjoys unexampled popularity; it has also achieved a unique significance: that of a symbol for everything that is beautiful and gay in Vienna."

Hanslick did not by any means see eye to eye with Wagner; to quote extracts out of context from his copious writings on Wagner's music would do less than justice to both parties concerned.

Some forty or more years ago Constable and Company Limited of London first published in three volumes, *Music in London 1890-94*, comprising music criticisms that had been contributed to *The World* by George Bernard Shaw during the above years. In these Shaw revealed a penetrating insight into music, and the performance of it, his comments not always flattering.

· On 18 June 1890 he wrote of the Polish pianist, Ignace Jan Paderewski, who at that time was twenty-four years of age, "By the time I reached Paderewski's concert on Tuesday last week, his concerto was over, the audience in wild enthusiasm, and the pianoforte a wreck. Regarded as an immensely spirited young harmonious blacksmith, who puts a concerto on the piano as upon an anvil, and hammers it out with an exuberant enjoyment of the swing and strength of the proceeding, Paderewski is at least exhilarating; and his hammerplay is not without variety, some of it being feathery, if not delicate. . . ."

Speaking of opera on 12 November 1890, he said, "Is Gluck, the conqueror of Paris, at last going to conquer London? I hope so; for the man was a great master, one for whom we are hardly ready even yet."

Gluck died in 1787.

It would seem that in London in the 1890s concerts did not always begin on time, for on 4 March 1891 Shaw wrote, "On Wednesday afternoon last I went into St James's Hall at one minute before three o'clock to hear the Albéniz concert, intending to have the usual twenty minutes or so over the evening paper before business began. To my amazement Albéniz appeared at the stroke of three as if he had been sent up on the platform by electric wire from Greenwich . . . I shall henceforth regard Albéniz not only as one of the pleasantest, most musical, and most original of pianists, but as a man of superior character."

Early travellers were the first Europeans to be exposed to music of other lands, as in this scene of naval officers watching Fijian dancers.

Shaw does not say whether the rest of the audience was already seated.

We can now wonder if Shaw's judgement was at fault when he wrote on 14 October 1891, "Dvořák's *Requiem* bored Birmingham so desperately that it was unanimously voted a work of extraordinary depth and impressiveness, which verdict I record with a hollow laugh."

Mascagni's opera, *Cavalleria Rusticana*, was only eight months old when Shaw published this opinion on 28 October 1891: . . . "Mascagni has set *Cavalleria Rusticana* to expressive and vigorous music, which music he has adapted to the business of the stage with remarkable judgement and good sense."

In his book of memoirs, *Am I Too Loud* (Hamish Hamilton, London, 1962), Gerald Moore mentions an occasion when a critic "dismissed with opprobrium a violin and piano sonata by Eugene Goossens which he said in his notice he was hearing for the first time. He had overlooked the fact," Moore says, "that he had warmly praised the same work several months earlier. Both notices appeared in the *Observer*, Albert Sammons being the violinist on both occasions."

Composers' verdicts on the works of other composers have not always been in agreement with the universal approval subsequently accorded them.

Handel said of Gluck, "He has no more counterpoint than my cook."

240

After listening to a *Leonora* Overture of Beethoven, Haydn said, "I didn't understand a note," while Weber thought Beethoven "fit for the madhouse."

When Beethoven's *Symphony No. 1 in C major* was first performed in Vienna in 1800, one of the critics described it as "the confused explosions of the outrageous effrontery of a young man."

Concerning the *Concerto in D* for violin and orchestra: Beethoven composed this concerto for the celebrated violinist, Franz Clement, who gave the work its first performance in 1806. In keeping with the meretricious practice of the time, Clement interpolated between the first and the other two movements several of his own compositions which depended more on violinistic trickery than on musical quality, one of them being a sonata played on a single string, with the violin held upside down! This vaudevillian caper, together with the fact that Clement played the concerto without rehearsal, may have accounted for much of the indifference shown by the audience and critics.

"The work," one critic said, "contains many beautiful parts, but connoisseurs will notice that it lacks coherence and that the endless repetition of certain banal parts grows wearisome."

Later, this was to earn the title, "King of Violin Concertos."

That learned authorities did not agree about Beethoven's music can be seen from the following two published accounts. In 1854 Eduard Hanslick wrote, "The Ninth Symphony is one of those spiritual divides which lie between streams of opposite convictions: it can be seen from afar, but it can never be scaled."

In 1860 the violinist-composer, Louis Spohr, said, "I have never been able to relish the last works of Beethoven. Yes, I must even reckon the much admired Ninth Symphony among these, the first three movements of which seem to me, despite some solitary flashes of genius, worse than the other eight symphonies. The fourth movement is, in my opinion, so monstrous and tasteless, and in its grip of Schiller's Ode, so trivial, that I cannot understand how a genius like Beethoven could have written it."

Verdi spoke of the "sublime greatness" of the instrumental movements of the same work, but described the last (choral) movement as "terrible."

Tchaikovsky described the music of Brahms as, "Pedestal upon pedestal, while the statue is never forthcoming."

Hugo Wolf's opinion of Brahms' *Symphony No. 4* is summed up in these words: "Brahms' production has never been able to soar above the level of mediocrity, but the nothingness, hollowness and hypocrisy which dominate the E minor Symphony have never appeared so ominously in his works."

Brahms' judgment may have been at fault when he said, "In Bruckner we have to do with a fraud, who will be dead and forgotten in one or two years."

The *Symphony in D minor* of César Franck has survived the criticisms of its time. Gounod considered it an "Affirmation of impotence pushed to dogma," while the

Director of the Paris Conservatoire said, "This is no symphony. Who ever heard of a symphony employing an English horn?"

Of the *Symphony No. 2 in B minor* by Borodin, the Russian critic Ivanov declared, "There is heaviness in the lyric and tender passages. The massive forms are most tiresome."

When Tchaikovsky's Third Symphony appeared in 1875, the composer-critic, César Cui stated, "The symphony displays a degree of talent, but we have come to expect more from Tchaikovsky."

Another critic, Herman Laroche was more impressed, saying, "Beauty of form, nobility of style and originality all contribute to make this symphony one of the most remarkable musical works produced during the last ten years."

Rachmaninov was twenty-four when his *Symphony No. 1 in D minor* was first performed, with Alexander Glazunov conducting. Due to some extent to the conductor's uninspired direction, the performance was a failure. "How could a great musician like Glazunov conduct so badly?" Rachmaninov wrote to a friend. The critics made no effort to spare his feelings, César Cui going so far as to point to the composer's "morbid distortion of harmony and sickly addiction to sombre moods." After dealing with the work in painful detail, Cui concluded with this cruel thrust, "If there were a conservatory in Hell, and if one of its pupils were given the task of writing a symphony on the Seven Plagues of Egypt, and had written a work like Rachmaninov's, he would have received an enthusiastic response from the inhabitants of Hell."

Throughout most of his distinguished career, Prokofiev found carping critics snapping at his heels. One of his works was described as "Mendelssohn played on wrong notes," while another critic said that the finale of the Second Sonata "reminded one of a herd of mammoths charging across an Asiatic plateau," ending, "When a dinosaur's daughter graduated from the Conservatory of that epoch her repertory must have included Prokofiev."

When the *Symphony No. 7, The Leningrad* by Shostakovich was performed in 1941 the English critic, Ernest Newman, suggested that to find this on the musical map, "one should look along the seventieth degree of longitude and the last degree of platitude."

To retrace our steps to the end of the nineteenth century, we find the usually astute Krehbiel dismissing Debussy's opera *Pelléas et Mélisande* as "a flocculent web of hazy discord; novel, but is it Art?"

And so we could go on, but the examples given go towards proving a point — that critics, even the best of them, can sometimes be wrong. One may wonder how much a critic may lose in the enjoyment of music. As Jean de la Bruyère once said, "The pleasure of criticising robs us of the pleasure of being moved by some very fine things."

Nicolo Paganini, who in the early nineteenth century was regarded as the greatest violinist in history. His skill was so great that he became a legendary figure, and some people believed that the devil possessed him while he played.

THE
RECORD
12

History, Importance, and Care

IN the summer of 1877 Thomas Alva Edison put to use for the first time his invention, the "phonograph," a motorless machine which was turned by hand. On this a rotating cylinder had been covered by tin-foil. Setting a needle so that sound could be recorded as a series of indentations, Edison shouted into the mouthpiece, "Mary had a little lamb; its fleece was white as snow." Edison then adjusted the reproducer and heard, issuing from the machine, his own words, "Mary had a little lamb . . ." So the gramophone record was born.

Some historians would have us believe that man's attempts to record, and to reproduce, sound goes back to ancient times, but if we prefer to keep to facts we take the year 1680 as our starting point. At that time the English physicist, Robert Hooke, experimented with the production of sound by means of a toothed wheel revolving against a wooden or metal tongue.

About the middle of the nineteenth century a French typographer, Leon Scott, recorded sound waves, but did not actually reproduce them. Some fifty years later Faber of Vienna invented a hand-operated mechanism, controlled by a typewriter-like keyboard, and containing a rubber imitation of the human lips and tongue. And so, experiments in sound continued.

Then, in 1877, Edison proved that sound could not only be recorded, but reproduced. In the same year Charles Cros, a French poet and amateur scientist, deposited

244

with the Académie des Sciences a description of a machine to record and reproduce sound. This, however, was still a theory, while Edison's "phonograph" was a reality. Whereas Edison used a cylinder, Cros specified a disc.

(It is interesting to note that about this time Edison applied for a patent for the *electrical* reproduction of sound, which, however, did not come into force until years later.)

In 1885 Chichester A. Bell and Charles Sumner Tainter applied for a patent on a machine which substituted for tin-foil a cardboard cylinder covered with a mixture of stearine, soap, zinc and iron oxides, and a gouge-shaped sapphire cutter. They indicated separate machines for recording and for reproducing. In 1888 Edison produced the improved phonograph, which embodied certain principles similar to those of Bell and Tainter.

The next major development was introduced by Emile Berliner of Washington, who, having applied for a patent in September 1887, replaced the cylinder with a flat disc and changed the system of recording from the up and down ("hill and dale") method to a recording track of even depth, running from side to side.

Berliner improved on his original idea by etching on wax on a zinc record, thus making possible the multiple reproduction of discs. In 1897, using a clockwork motor, he produced the "Gramophone," this name being adopted to distinguish it from Edison's "Phonograph." The word found permanent use.

What had until this time been looked upon as an amusing toy was now being taken seriously. By the turn of the century several countries were marketing records, the flat disc then having a strong impact on the industry.

In 1902 Fred Gaisberg, who had joined Gramophone and Typewriter Limited, paid a visit to Milan where he signed up for ten recordings a little-known tenor named Enrico Caruso, then twenty-nine years of age. The fee of £100 decided on by Gaisberg was considered "exorbitant" by his superiors in London. From that date until his death in 1921 he was to earn almost £1 million in royalties from his records. Someone once said that while the gramophone record made Caruso famous, Caruso brought world-wide fame to the record.

By now the record was exerting an ever increasing influence on the musical world, and the labels during the next few years were graced by such famous names as Grieg, Massenet, Debussy; Sarasate, Joachim; Patti, Sembrich, Schumann-Heink, Melba, Homer, Crossley, Destinn, Farrar, Calvé, Gluck; Scotti, Plançon, de Reske, Chaliapin, Journet, Sammarco, McCormack, Dawson; Elman, Kubelik, Kreisler, Zimbalist; Pachmann, Paderewski, Rachmaninov, Cortot.

In 1905 attempts were made to record small orchestral accompaniments for singers to replace the tinny sound of the piano. The first symphony to be recorded complete is said to have been Beethoven's Fifth, played by the Berlin Philharmonic Orchestra in 1909. By 1917 the finest of the world's orchestras, choirs, and chamber music groups were being recorded.

Thomas Alva Edison, the American inventor of the phonograph. From the phonograph was developed the gramophone, which for the first time enabled countless people to enjoy fine music in their own homes. The original caption of this photograph reads: "Thomas A. Edison as he appeared after spending five days and nights perfecting the phonograph, his favourite of all his inventions."

Until 1925 records were made by *acoustic* means. Then electrical recording by microphone revolutionised the whole record industry. Another revolutionary innovation came in 1948 when the "long-playing" record, pressed on vinylite, appeared on the market. This presented several advantages over the former "standard" disc which was recorded at 78 revolutions per minute. One 12-in. "78" disc played for about four to four-and-a-half minutes, which meant that in the case of, say, a symphony, the records had to be changed or turned over every four minutes or so. The L.P. record, being recorded at the slower speed of 33 r.p.m. and having the grooves closer together, plays for upwards of twenty-five, even thirty, minutes per side. With the standard "78" disc there was a good deal of surface noise; with the microgroove record there is none. The later techniques of recording made it possible for us to hear qualities of sound which, before, had been lost to the ear.

The "78" discs had been sold in brown-paper envelopes. The L.P. records were

Above, at top: Double bass; *centre:* cello; *bottom left:* violin; *bottom right:* viola.

Below, at top: Double (or contra) bassoon; *on right:* bassoon, cor anglais (English horn), oboe, flute, and piccolo; *on left:* bass clarinet and clarinet.

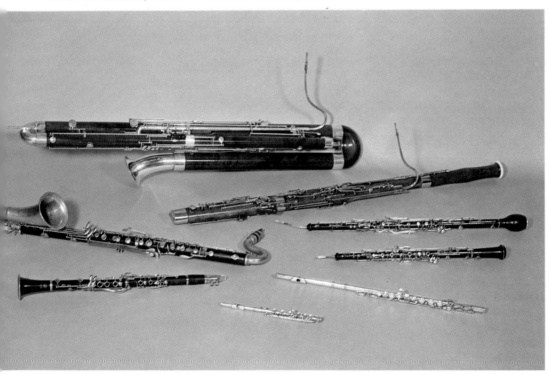

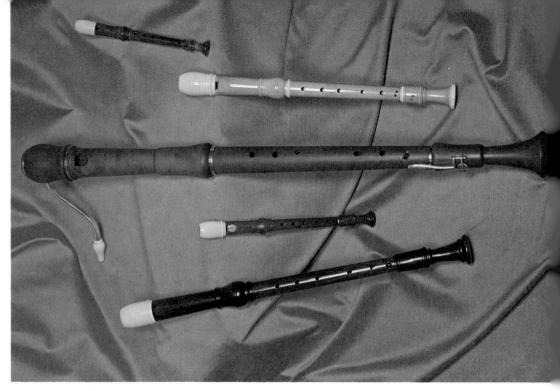

Above: Recorders. From top: Sopranino, treble, bass, descant. tenor.

Below, from left: Cornet, trumpet, with trombone and bass trombone above them; bass; French horn.

issued in attractive thin cardboard "sleeves," usually with information about the composer and the music printed on the back.

In addition to the 10 inch and 12 inch records, 7 inch discs, recorded at 45 or 33 r.p.m., permitted shorter works to be sold at a cheaper price.

Towards the end of the 1950s there was another major development in recorded music when the "stereophonic" record came on the market. As the word indicates, stereophonic (shortened to "stereo") means solid, or three-dimensional, sound. In other words, the stereo record reproduces with added width and depth, and with greater detail, than the "monaural" (pre-stereo) disc.

Our ears receive stereo sound in much the same way as the two pictures viewed through a stereoscope combine to produce a unified, solid, three-dimensional visual image in true perspective. In stereo sound our ears pick up separate left-hand and right-hand details of a performance, and the brain accepts a unified, spread sound.

Two further steps of importance in the record industry have been the stereophonically-recorded performance on tape, instead of disc, and the Cassette. Through the enterprise of the most skilful engineers available, the quality of recorded sound continues to advance.

Scope of the Record

With the aid of modern recording techniques, record companies have re-issued records made by the most famous singers and instrumentalists of yesterday; they have also helped to establish new artists within a shorter time than was possible formerly. More than ever before record companies are spreading the gospel of fine music, even to the point of bringing into people's homes in most parts of the world works that otherwise might have remained merely names in a musical dictionary.

So the record has been a publicity agent for both artist and composer. Earlier this century Sibelius was known outside of his own Finland by a couple of compositions of comparatively minor importance. Then the recording companies, enlisting the willing aid of the most suitable conductors, brought out "Society" albums that contained many of his major works. The music of Delius remained shamefully neglected until Beecham recorded it, so encouraging other conductors to take a chance by including one of his works in their concert programmes. Spurred on by these and similar ventures, some of the more dedicated recording companies helped to make the music of Hindemith, Bartók, Schoenberg, Webern and many contemporary composers better known, even if they could not always see the result as a money-making enterprise.

Complete operas, oratorios, symphonies, concertos, plays were constantly being replaced by even better performances. Record collectors were discovering new composers, new works, and it is true to say that the record was responsible for the revival of interest in the music of Vivaldi and other composers of the "Baroque" period.

The record catalogues of fifty years ago contained little of Wagner's works beyond

247

the familiar arias and overtures. In the late 1960s the complete "Ring" cycle was recorded complete on twenty-two double-sided records.

To say that the record has advanced musical taste and developed musical discrimination would be a masterpiece of understatement. The best records, with the best artists, have guided the otherwise musically untrained listener to differentiate between good, mediocre, and poor music; also to discriminate between good, mediocre, and poor performances.

There was a time when the average concertgoer accepted, as normal blemishes in this imperfect world, inferior performances; e.g., a violinist playing out of tune, a pianist's inexpert fingering or clumsy pedalling, a singer's poor breathing or phrasing. With the advance of recording techniques, the artist's work became more exposed; blemishes were more obvious, and defects when repeated on the record-player irritating. Critics and audiences demanded performances of more consistently high quality. The artists themselves heard their imperfections magnified by the immediacy and the stark clarity of the well produced record played on good equipment. Artists became more studious in their aim for perfection, and the music-lover benefited. The record we hear is often the synthesis of a number of "takes."

In 1908 the English journalist, Filson Young, wrote these words, "I fear that the gramophone, like the motorcar, has come to stay. I think that no one has done so much to make that deadly instrument popular as Melba has done. Therefore, she is the greatest sinner."

Melba's first record had been made in 1904. Between that date and 1926 she made more than 100 published recordings.

Peter Dawson, another Australian, also made his first record in 1904. He was to record 3,500 separate titles during his long singing career. To the Melbas, the Dawsons, the Carusos, and all who came after, we must forever be grateful for their faith in the future of the gramophone record.

Science and art have combined to bring to a state of near-perfection the record, and the means of reproducing it. It is, therefore, a source of sorrow to those who value these things that so many people remain insensitive to both the care of the record and the quality of the sounds produced.

Unless the reproducing equipment is capable of dealing faithfully with the finest details of the recording, the listener is not hearing the music as the composer and the recording musicians intended it should sound. (Similar comments equally apply to the radio set, many of which, through faulty construction, or inaccurate tuning, or both, reproduce music as attenuated, even distorted, sound.)

Care of the Record

Having introduced this gloomy note, it may not be out of place to add a few hints on the care of the record.

To avoid warping, keep it away from heat, even from direct sunlight.

Store all records firmly, but not tightly, in an upright position.

248

When it is not in use, replace the record in its transparent bag, then in its envelope, handling only the edges, or by an edge and the centre label. Even the natural oil from a washed finger will leave a clogging mark on the grooves.

Before playing the disc, clean it gently with the approved cloth or pad, or, better still, have a "dust-bug" attached to the tone-arm. These are obtainable at reliable record shops. Rubbing with a wrong material may do more harm than good.

If the stylus and the record are treated carefully, the stylus will last for a considerable time. If it is asked to track over a scratched surface, it could suffer immediate damage and spoil every other disc played by it. Most record dealers will examine the stylus point for you under a microscope.

Small particles of fluff have a habit of settling round the stylus point. It should be removed by a very soft artist's brush, *not with the finger.*

It is important that the turntable is level. A false level can cause the stylus to sweep across the record and spoil the whole surface; it can also track inaccurately and damage the grooves of the record. A small spirit gauge will check this.

It is good to always keep in mind: THE MICROGROOVE RECORD IS VERY EASILY DAMAGED. It will repay every care lavished on it.

Building the record collection: To the more adventurous traveller, it is surprising, and perhaps a little sad, that tourists visiting continental cities settle for roast beef or roast lamb, followed by apple-pie and custard, and leave untasted the indigenous foods of those parts of their travels. It is rather like going to Athens, spending most of the time in the general store, and neglecting to inspect the Parthenon.

Surely there is fascination in exploring new cities, tasting new dishes, and sampling new wines. And getting to know music that one has previously overlooked.

Record dealers will confirm that music-lovers generally are conservative, unadventurous, in their listening; that is, in their choice of records. They play safe with the familiar, standard works; they feel they have their feet on firm ground if they recognise a familiar title, and hear familiar melodies and harmonies. They know "what is going to happen."

Some people in recognising a familiar melody, or in literature a familiar quotation, perhaps gain a sense of secure superiority. They keep the unfamiliar at arm's length in case they make an erroneous judgement. The ears and minds of the conservative listener are so clogged with the conventional, the *recognisable*, that they are unreceptive to any musical work outside their limited orbit, no matter how rational it may be.

A couple of generations ago *The Stag at Bay* graced the walls of many parlours, the owners placing their copies in conspicuous positions because this was "a popular subject." It was a safe choice, its appearance confirming respectable conformity.

When choosing records for their home libraries, many music-lovers miss a great deal of enjoyable listening by not exploring a little off the beaten-track. By all means, let the *Pastoral Symphony*, the *Emperor Concerto* and the *Archduke Trio* take their honoured places in the collection. What a help musical nicknames are!

Ask each member of a group of people to name his or her favourite composer and you probably will get an eighty-five per cent vote for Beethoven. Beethoven sounds safe. He is usually referred to as one of the "great masters." And he's been dead long enough. This may not be a pose. Most people *think* they like Beethoven. Most people *do*.

The music-lover, if he is to get the fullest enjoyment from listening to music should not canonise a work merely because it is old or familiar, but rather because it has an enduring *rightness*. Nor should he favour a work just because it is new. Whatever the period of a musical work, it should say something, without reaching out a clutching hand for the support of clichés.

Record collectors should choose what they like, but a little more adventure in their listening, either by the record or by the radio, would not only widen their knowledge of music, but prove that even their favourite composers wrote other works apart from the hardy annuals.

MUSIC
IN
EDUCATION

13

THE following notes are intended chiefly for the schoolteacher without formal musical training who might be feeling his way in this most rewarding activity. The more advanced music scholar will probably know these things and will base his instruction and guidance on his own experience.

In the following comments the word "Education" is used in its widest sense, for the value of music appreciation as a part of everyone's general education cannot be too strongly stressed. What better place to begin than in the school classroom? With the young mind awakened to the sensuous beauty of ordered sound and to the stimulus of rhythm, a good start is made; what follows will be a deeper reaction to sound-values and a gradual assimilation of interesting facts.

It is important, however, that schoolchildren should not be *made* to listen; they should be *encouraged* to give full attention to what they hear and what they are told. What, in the control of disinterested teachers can be a bore, can, with the guidance of an imaginative one, become a recreational period of aural stimulation and factual interest.

Children should be encouraged to listen, then told how best to listen, then gradually trained to realise what is behind the sounds coming from the record player or from the piano. When hearing, say, a record of an orchestra, the child will at first accept it merely as *sound*, pleasant or otherwise, according to his individual taste, his home environment, his willingness and capacity to listen, and whether he is receptive to tonal quality and sound-patterns, or tone-deaf.

Later, if the child's interest has been caught and his appetite sufficiently sharpened, he will ask for more; that is, of course, if the person to whom his musical instruction has been entrusted treats music as something to be desired, and not just another curriculum chore; in short, if he waves a magic wand, instead of threatening with a rod. After he has learnt to enjoy the purely sensuous pleasure derived from musical sound, the young listener may develop a sense of enquiry, to know *Why* and *How*.

There must surely be cases where the teacher who accepts the responsibility of music appreciation merely as part of the burden that members of his profession must bear, will be only one step ahead of the brightest in his class. If the information he plans to impart has been obtained from a book (reliable or otherwise) just before the lesson, then that lesson will lose the ring of authority. It can even be misleading.

A teacher who possesses only a limited understanding of music can weary his young audience by thrusting at them uninteresting facts, or by playing unsuitable music too far beyond the easy understanding of those meeting serious music for the first time. Again, a teacher with a moderate understanding of serious music, may put his class on the wrong track by playing to them records which are his *personal* favourites, overlooking the fact that they may bore the young listeners and put them off music. By all means, let him play to them Bach, Beethoven, and Brahms, but let him make sure that the examples will be of the simplest, most readily digested, kinds; in short, music that will grip and hold the attention.

Schoolchildren, who are often victims of the ubiquitous transistor-radio, may at first be resistant to music appreciation classes and the playing of what they call classical music, often because they have the idea that music, other than pop tunes, is only for "squares." Therefore, they are unlikely to become converts to serious music if some ill-advised teacher insists that they listen, in the early stages, to a Bach fugue or a movement from a Mahler symphony just because it happens to be one of his own favourites, or because he knows that Bach and Mahler, like Shakespeare and Thackeray, are respected names.

A restless child's attention may be captured by a simple story about a composer whose music is to be played, some anecdote bearing on how the music came to be written. If the piece itself has a good story behind it, if, in fact, it *tells* a story, so much the better. The child will then "see" the purpose of the music through his ears.

The music lesson, then, should be conducted in a relaxed, pleasant atmosphere, and presented in an uncomplicated manner. Such classes, even if of short duration (they should never seem "too long"), will bring better results if they are regular. The pupils should come to regard them as part of their education, a pleasant part, and not merely a get-together when some teacher feels in the mood, or as an inside occupation on rainy days.

In time, some question may be asked, the convincing answer to which may be beyond the knowledge of a less than experienced teacher. Rather than give a wrong or evasive answer, it would be preferable for the teacher to delay the answer by saying

"I will find out for you." That will not only give the question importance, but will point to the teacher's honesty.

Getting the class to sing together is important; not only does it involve class-participation, but it helps to train the ear. The more the pupil is encouraged to *listen* to musical sounds, the quicker he will learn to create them in a pleasant and logical way.

Until a child learns to read music, that is, recognise music notation, the teacher can indicate on the blackboard a pattern of signs and symbols that bear a resemblance to the rise and fall of a melody. In more advanced stages of this kind of instruction, perhaps chalks of different colours may help. Likewise, the variation in the duration of notes can be suggested by the relative variation in the length of the chalk strokes, indicating notes.

By some such simple method as this, a phrase of a composition could be indicated in the following manner:

If the child's interest advances to the extent that he wishes to learn an instrument, this wish should be encouraged. The easiest instrument which a person (pupil or teacher) can learn to play with some degree of proficiency in a relatively short time is the recorder. Also, the recorder is an inexpensive instrument to purchase. (We will deal with this matter later.)

The (gramophone) record can be of immeasurable value in fostering a love, and an appreciation, of serious music and in broadening the child's musical horizon. Here, expert advice should be sought, both on the selection of records that will form the basis of a record library and suitable equipment on which to play the records. If inferior, both can create a false sense of tone-values.

THERE was a time when some educational authorities were slow in realising the need for the best quality musical aids in schools. Stereograms and records often were of inferior quality, purchased with an eye on the budget rather than on their true value as a teaching medium. Today, this situation has changed. Most schools have the best up to date equipment, which includes reproducing resources, records, cassettes, tape recordings, films. This matter is referred to also in the chapter on *The Record*.

253

Melody, Rhythm, and Harmony

After the teacher has encouraged his charges to recognise the rise and fall and the duration of notes that go to make up a melody, he can then go on to explain in more detail the components of a tune, as mentioned under *Melody* in the chapter *The Structure of Music*, which gives a simple analysis of the familiar tune *Drink to me only with thine eyes*. He can then point out where the introduction merely hints at what is to follow, and where the soloist takes up the melody itself.

Should the class be expected to sing a melody, it would be advisable to begin with a simple one that lies within a comfortable vocal range.

A starting point in the explanation of rhythm will be the beating of time and the class clapping to the rhythmic pattern. Percussion instruments can then be brought into use as an aid to defining the subtleties of rhythm.

Harmony can easily be explained if a piano is available. The teacher need not be a trained pianist in order to play a simple melodic phrase in single notes, this repeated with supporting notes, all played simultaneously; in other words, Chords. A richer harmony can be achieved if the teacher is able to add a bass line. The sonorous effect of harmonious chords can be brought into sharper focus if contrasting discords are played.

The Record in Class Work

It will, of course, be obvious to any teacher attempting to lead his class into an appreciation of serious music that the record, on which can be heard the world's greatest soloists, orchestras, choirs, etc., is one of the most valuable aids in this work.

The record has several advantages. It is always available. It can be played over and over again, where repetition, which is so important, is called for. It is likely that the student will concentrate better on a recorded performance than on one given by live musicians. In the latter case the performer's manipulation of the instrument, his appearance, or mannerisms may claim too much of the child's attention. Later, the presence of a live instrumental group will be a distinct advantage in letting the class see the instruments at close range; better still, if the players explain their instruments to the class.

Record shops have booklets, issued by record distributors, listing music under various categories, and grouped under composers. These, obtainable at no cost, can help both the teacher and student to become familiar with composers' names and their works.

It will soon be found that lessons in music appreciation will lead into kinds of, and styles in, music. Let us consider two examples: Following an explanation of the Waltz: its character and history, that it is in triple (3/4) time, with the accent on the first beat, examples can be played. The teacher can begin with a Viennese-type (e.g., Johann Strauss), making sure that it is performed in the true swooping, dipped

254

A pupil in the Yehudi Menuhin School for Young Musicians in England. The
aim of the school is to make music a part of life and not an isolated study, and
pupils practise their instruments in bedrooms, sitting rooms, and even before
the bathroom mirrors.

255

style; then a Chopin waltz, intended as a piano solo in the concert-hall. This could be followed by, say, the Tchaikovsky type, from "Swan Lake," "Sleeping Princess" or "Nutcracker"; lastly the ballroom type. The student will come to realise that music cast in the same time-mould, and under the same form-heading, can vary in character.

Likewise the March. Marches are usually in duple time, that is 2/4 time, but they vary in character to some extent, varying in colour and vigour, according to the writing and the performance. For instance, a march by Sousa, played by a brass band, will have a *colour* different from that of one of Elgar's *Pomp and Circumstance* marches, played by a full orchestra. The march that occurs in Kodály's *Háry János* Suite will sound different in character from the march in Act I of Tchaikovsky's *Nutcracker Suite*, and that different from the *Wedding March* from *A Midsummer Night's Dream* incidental music by Mendelssohn.

This can lead on to a simple explanation of other styles in music, even to *Colour* and *Moods*.

Colour can be demonstrated by playing a record of a familiar melody, first as a piano solo, then by a different instrument. If an orchestral version, or at least a version played by a group of instrumentalists is available, this can bring the demonstration a step further.

Having gone this far, the teacher may wish to say something about *Moods* in music. After playing a short excerpt from a work, he can invite his pupils to say what the mood of the music was. Taking such moods as joy, sorrow, exhilaration, humour, spiritual yearning (reverence), through to the grotesque, he can play appropriate examples and invite comments.

This, of course, presupposes that the teacher's own impressions of the mood of a piece of music are valid. If in doubt, the person posing this exercise for a class might ask for advice from a trained musician, a music therapist, or find out from reliable annotations. (Cover notes on records can sometimes assist here; at times they can be misleading, or too heavily clouded in academic or journalistic jargon. This is where the musician with a wide knowledge of all kinds of music can help.)

To aim too high too soon can have the wrong result, that of discouraging the pupil. But that applies to many aspects of teaching music appreciation.

Programme Music

Music that comes under this heading can be both interesting and instructive in class work. Although this is dealt with earlier, it may be appropriate at this point to explain the meaning of the term.

"Every composition may, theoretically, be described as either *Absolute Music* or *Programme Music*," says *Grove's Dictionary of Music and Musicians*, "since it will be set out to describe a series of events, or it will not."

Programme Music in its best form *suggests*. It can tell a story, or paint a picture in

Yehudi Menuhin, the famous violinist, explains a fine point in bowing to a pupil at his School for Young Musicians.

sound. We find it chiefly in orchestral music; sometimes in piano and instrumental pieces; only rarely in chamber music.

In the case of Absolute Music—for example a Bach fugue, a Mozart symphony, or a Beethoven quartet—it is sufficient to listen to the music for its own sake. Certain early composers, however, attempted imitative and descriptive sounds in some of their works, and Programme Music branched into an art form of its own when Franz Liszt invented the Symphonic Poem (or Tone Poem), thereby laying a solid foundation in descriptive writing for other composers of the Romantic period, and for those in the twentieth century.

In taking Programme Music as part of his instruction, the teacher will be advised to select for his class music that, so far as possible, lives up to the title and *sounds* like what it is meant to *suggest*. For instance, to play the first movement of the so-called *Moonlight Sonata* by Beethoven and expect the class to say that it represents moonlight is to invite disappointing answers. In fact, Beethoven did not give this

Nadia Boulanger, the octogenarian French teacher of composition, is one of the internationally famous figures who visit the Yehudi Menuhin School for Young Musicians and inspire the pupils with their own dedication to music.

sonata its nickname. (It is said to have come about from the fanciful idea of the German critic, Heinrich Rellstab (1799-1860), to whom the first movement suggested "moonlight on the Lake of Lucerne.")

Nor would *Clair de Lune* by Debussy suggest to the class moonlight, unless its title were announced before playing the piano piece; no doubt not even then.

The *Storm* section in the *Pastoral Symphony* by Beethoven does not indicate an actual storm by introducing realistic thunder effects (as a radio producer might do with "effects" records), but by *suggesting* the atmosphere of a storm by skilful use of ordinary orchestral instruments. (Beethoven described this symphony as "an expression of feeling rather than mere painting.")

Among the many examples of music that either tell a story, evoke an atmosphere, or paint a scene in sound, are the following:

    The Sorcerer's Apprentice (Dukas)
    Night on Bald Mountain (Moussorgsky)
    In the Hall of the Mountain King (from Grieg's "Peer Gynt" Suite No. 1)

258

Peter and the Wolf (*Prokofiev*)
The Carnival of the Animals (*Saint-Saëns*)
The Ride of the Valkyries (*Wagner*)
Pacific 231 (*Honegger*)
A Midsummer Night's Dream Overture (*Mendelssohn*), in which are suggested the
    fluttering of fairy wings, the impudence of Puck, the braying of Bottom, the
    hunting-horn of Theseus, the rustic dancing of clowns; even the merry
    winging of a woodland insect.
The Moldau (*Vltava*) (*Smetana*)
Parts of Nutcracker Suite (*Tchaikovsky*)
Scenes from Childhood, for piano (*Schumann*)

These should prepare the way for the more advanced symphonic poems of Liszt, Sibelius, and Richard Strauss, which, however, will be beyond the ready understanding of the younger school child.

The stories of ideas behind such music are often printed on the record covers; otherwise they can be found in appropriate books in public libraries, or in such books as *Making Friends With Orchestral Music* by James Glennon (Rigby Limited).

The process of teaching Programme Music can at times be reversed. It might be an idea to play to the class a short work and ask what it represents, or sounds like. For instance, *Steel Foundry* by Mossolov might be played and the question asked. The answers will surprise by their wide variety; perhaps no one will guess correctly. When they have been told the title and the record repeated, they will probably recognise the sounds as suggesting a large and busy machine factory.

All the music suggested in this chapter may not be available to the teacher; school libraries often are pitifully limited. It will therefore depend to a great extent on the generosity of the powers-that-be in the education departments, the willingness of friends to donate or lend the desired records, or on the use of records from the teacher's own library. (It goes without saying that if a record is borrowed, it should be given every care.)

Important in the selection of records is the principle that they should be appropriate to the subject to be discussed and within the mental and musical range of the pupils. Sometimes a piece of music of little musical importance in itself may be just the thing to underline the point to be made.

After the class has shown sufficient response to music appreciation sessions, records can be used to explain the instruments of the orchestra (see Chapter *The Orchestra* in this book). Records explaining and demonstrating all the instruments in turn have been issued by various companies. Also, records of *Peter and the Wolf* (Prokofiev), *Young Person's Guide to the Orchestra* (Britten) and *The Carnival of the Animals* (Saint-Saëns) can help along these lines.

A session to follow this may be one during which an orchestral excerpt is played through without comment, then repeated, the pupils being asked to name the

Claude Achille Debussy (1862-1918). Founder of musical impressionism inspired by the French impressionist painters and writers. His evocative music is unsurpassed for its tonal painting.

instruments as they take up their parts. Another method might be for the teacher to write the names of the instruments on the blackboard and point a stick to each instrument as it comes into focus.

As listening habits become more sensitive, the class can be asked to listen to two instruments playing at the same time, or to a record of a piano solo in which the left and the right hands have defined functions.

Young people should be encouraged to listen for and appreciate *beauty* of sound, if only as an antidote to the cacophony of today's mania for speed, noise, and the excesses of stridency emitted by untalented vocalists masquerading as pop-singers. Light music, even the "popular" kind, has its place in the enjoyment of sound, but there is a vast difference between the expert jazz combination, or a properly trained vocal group, and the cheap imitation that bears more resemblance to a wild night in Bedlam than it does to music.

Whatever course lessons in music appreciation take, whatever music is played, the class should always feel that music is for their pleasure, and not just a mental exercise, or a part of scholastic drudgery. They should feel that the learning about music and the appreciation of its make-up is no more arduous than learning to put a jig-saw puzzle together to form a picture, or to learn how to play an enjoyable

This unusual photograph by Camilla Jessel shows only a few
of the countless graceful positions of a harpist's fingers during
a performance.

game. Therefore, the approach of the teacher should be a human one, reflecting his own love of serious music, or, at worst, hiding any suggestion that it is a teaching burden. It is also important that during the playing of a record the teacher will remain as quiet as he wishes his charges to be, and not walk about, or do anything to distract the class's attention from the music.

A good tape-recorder can also aid a teacher in this work, but it must be capable of giving faithful reproduction by being coupled to a suitable amplifier.

The question of copyright must be considered. Record companies usually state that it is illegal to make copies from commercially produced records without permission from the makers. This is often granted when taped for educational purposes.

If a teacher is aware in advance of a broadcast of a suitable work on radio or television, and the broadcast time will fall within the young person's waking hours, he might ask the class to listen, or view, at home and give their impressions in a group discussion next day. This will not only promote anticipation and attention, but it can encourage healthy competition between the members of the class. Most

The illustrations on these two pages exemplify the span of music over the world and through the ages. At left is a nineteenth-century engraving of Indonesian musicians performing in the forest. At right is a Moog Synthesiser, the most sophisticated method of producing modern music.

parents will no doubt be prepared to forego their own listening or viewing in such a good cause.

Final points. When dealing with musical instruments, the teacher can with advantage display pictures of these; also he can encourage members of the class to collect illustrations, both for the school and their own collections.

When speaking of composers, the teacher should not worry his class with too many dates. If he wishes to fix the period of a composer's life, or the time of the first performance of one of his works, this might be done by coupling it with some historic or other event. If mentioning Beethoven, for instance, the student might be told that the year of his birth (1770) was the same as that when Captain Cook first sailed around the east coast of Australia.

Repetition. This is important. A child's attention or interest may not be caught at the first hearing of an unfamiliar work, or at the second, but after he has heard it several times, he may accept it as a friend. This applies equally to listeners of all ages.

What has been said in this chapter will be obvious to many, but, as we have already pointed out, these notes are intended chiefly for the schoolteacher without formal musical training who is likely to conduct music appreciation classes; also in the hope that they will stimulate further inquiry.

Perhaps there may come a time when a teacher will be asked by one of his pupils, "Which instrument shall I learn?" We ask that teacher's extended indulgence by offering some hints, elementary though they may be.

WHICH INSTRUMENT SHALL I LEARN?

The gramophone record has brought great music, performed by the greatest artists, into the home. Serious music can be heard more often and to better advantage these days than at any time in the world's history. It is easier for a person to be musical today than ever before.

If a child (or a person of any age, for that matter) listens attentively to the best records of serious music, or to the better programmes on radio, or attends concerts of high quality, there may come a time when he wishes to learn a musical instrument. Let us assume that he is young.

Would-be music students and their parents are often required to make a decision—which instrument will return the greatest reward for the effort of study? How long will tuition last? How much will it cost; the instrument, the tuition, the music albums, and other incidental expenses?

As a foundation to any music study, whether the young music-lover hopes to be an orchestral player, a concert soloist, a singer, a dance musician, or a pianist first and only, the piano is a safe bet. This, of course, presupposes that there is a piano in the home, or that one will be hired or bought. Usually, the purchase of other instruments cost less.

In the case of a child, whose temporary enthusiasm may be ahead of his natural musical ability or his capacity for sustained effort, it may be wise to hire, or purchase a moderately priced instrument until it is certain that the decision to be a musician is not just a passing fancy.

A word of caution may be added. If a student continues to play for any length of time on an inferior instrument his ears and mind could acquire false tonal values. If he is sensitive to tone quality he will be irritated and discouraged every time he takes up the instrument.

When it has become obvious that he has real talent, also a constant determination to study, no time should be lost in replacing the cheaper "experimental" instrument with one that will satisfy his ear and nourish his aesthetic appreciation. It is always wise to obtain the advice of someone who can assess accurately the quality of an instrument and ensure that it is not over-priced.

In selecting an instrument other than a piano, be it one of the string, woodwind, brass, or percussion families, it may be kept in mind that the player, when sufficiently advanced, may wish to become a member of an orchestra—school, amateur, or professional. Similarly, the study of brass, reed, and percussion instruments can also lead to a place in a brass or military band.

Some instruments demand more skill to play, therefore more practice. The violin, if for no other reason than that it requires an even keener ear than do the other members of the string family, is more difficult to master, because of the demands put upon it, than the viola; the cello more difficult than the string double bass.

A student may soon be able to play a flute with reasonable efficiency, but find the oboe and clarinet more demanding of his time and patience. The French horn, the trumpet, and the trombone, may call for more study than the tuba. This is a general statement; natural aptitude for a certain instrument may reverse these comparisons.

Naturally, every instrument, in spite of the good care it receives, will require "up-keep." The bows of stringed instruments will occasionally need rehairing, the strings replacement. Woodwind instruments require periodical replacement of reeds; the brass and percussion regular maintenance. Even a piano goes out of tune in time, a natural form of tonal indisposition too often neglected by the owner—to the discomfort, even torment, of sensitive neighbours.

If the cost of transport of an instrument from the home to the teacher's studio and back again, has to be considered, then the size of a harp, or that of a string bass may pose problems. It is obvious that the study of the organ requires regular availability of one on which to practise. These are some of the more practical considerations, but relatively minute when compared with the unceasing joy in having mastered a musical instrument.

The singer has the most precious instrument of all. It is also the most delicate. Bad teaching and bad playing will stand in the way of a person becoming a first-class instrumental musician, but it cannot do so much physical damage as the misuse of the vocal organs can. One wonders how many singers have been lost to the musical world through unqualified teachers and careless vocal students. The thought is a sad one.

Whatever the choice of instrument, the student, in addition to learning to play it, will need to know the theory of music, which will be part of his musical tuition. He will be on the way to becoming a better musician when he has absorbed something of the history, structure, and language of music.

ENCYCLOPAEDIA

OF

COMPOSERS

References to these and other composers are included in specific chapters
concerned with Symphony, Concerto, Opera, etc.

ADAM, Adolphe (1803-1856) France. In 1841, influenced by his teacher, Boïeldieu, began composing operas and operettas. Founded the Théâtre National in 1847, a venture which failed, plunging him into debt from which he did not free himself for five years. Principal works include thirty-nine operas, fourteen ballets (*Giselle* being the most famous), masses, motets, and songs.

ALBENIZ, Isaac (1860-1909) Spain. First appeared as pianist at age of four. After leaving Madrid Conservatoire, he supported himself by giving concerts in the U.S.A. and elsewhere. Became a pupil of Liszt, and studied composition with d'Indy, Dukas. A prolific composer, he added colourful compositions to the Spanish repertoire, including operas and orchestral pieces; 250 piano works, his masterwork being *Iberia*, a pastiche of Spanish scenes and moods.

ALBINONI, Tomaso (c. 1671-1750) Italy. A brilliant violinist and composer of forty-two operas and many works of *concerto grosso* type. Bach is said to have studied his music with interest.

ALBRECHTSBERGER, Johann Georg (1736-1809) Austria. Organist, teacher, and composer of sacred music. Beethoven was one of the many who studied counterpoint with him.

ALFANO, Franco (1876-1954) Italy. Completed Puccini's opera, *Turandot* from sketches left by the composer. His own works include the operas *Cirano di Bergerac* and *Resurrection*, symphonies, and chamber music.

ALLEGRI, Gregorio (1582-1652) Italy. His name is associated with a *Miserere* which Mozart, at the age of fourteen, is said to have copied down from memory after one hearing.

ALWYN, William (b. 1905) England. Composer of symphonies, concertos, *The Magic Island* (symphonic poem), and film music.

ANDRIESSEN, Hendrik (b. 1892) Holland.

Works include Roman Catholic church music, operas, symphonies, etc.

ANDRIESSEN, Juriaan (b. 1925) Holland. Pupil of his father, Hendrik. Works include orchestral and chamber music; also music for stage and radio.

ANERIO, Felice (c. 1560-1614) Italy. Upon the death of Palestrina, he was named *compositore* to the Papal Chapel. His compositions were chiefly for church use.

ANTILL, John (b. 1904) Australia. In 1934 joined the staff of the Australian Broadcasting Commission in Sydney; became their music editor in 1950. His ballet, *Corroboree* (1946), brought him world fame. Other works include operas, ballets, choral and orchestral works, songs, film and incidental music for plays.

ARENSKY, Anton Stepanovich (1861-1906) Russia. A pupil of Rimsky-Korsakov, but not part of his teacher's drive for "nationalism" in Russian music. Professor of harmony and counterpoint at Moscow Conservatoire. Died in Finland. Works include four operas, two symphonies, three suites for two pianos, two string quartets, a pianoforte trio, more than a hundred pieces for piano, and some songs.

ARNE, Michael (b. 1740 or 1741; d. 1786) England. Son of Dr Thomas A. Arne. A singer and composer, Michael Arne wrote much music for the stage, but for a time gave up all his time to chemistry, hoping to "discover" the philosopher's stone. Heavy financial losses forced him back to composing. Today, his best-known song is *The Lass with the delicate air*, often erroneously attributed to his father.

ARNE, Thomas Augustine (1710-1778) England. One of the most important English composers of his time. He was born in London, the son of an upholsterer. Rather than adopt law as a profession, as his father intended, he studied music in secret, and later obtained employment as a violinist in the band at Drury Lane Theatre. He composed music for masque, *Alfred*, of which the finale is now famous as *Rule, Britannia*. Numerous works include masques, operas, incidental music and songs for Shakespeare's plays; an oratorio, *Judith*; masses, organ concertos, sonatas for harpsichord, and many smaller works.

ARNELL, Richard (b. 1917) English. A pupil of John Ireland. Also conductor. Works include an opera *Moonflowers*; five symphonies; orchestral works, including *Lord Byron* (symphonic portrait); violin and piano concertos; chamber and ballet music; songs.

ARNOLD, Malcolm (b. 1921) England. Formerly principal trumpet with London Philharmonic Orchestra. Works include six symphonies; concertos for horn, piano, clarinet, oboe, and harmonica; *The Smoke*, *Tam O'Shanter*, *A Sussex*, and *Peterloo* overtures; other orchestral music, including ballets; chamber music; film music; *Song of Simeon* (Nativity cantata).

ATTERBERG, Kurt (b. 1887-1974) Sweden. Composer and conductor. Winner International Prize in Schubert centennial contest in 1928. Works include eight symphonies; *Aladdin, Fanal, Harvard Harpolekare, Stormen* (operas); concertos for cello, horn, piano, and violin; orchestral suites, and overtures; chamber music.

AUBER, Daniel François Esprit (1782-1871) France. Beginning as a composer at the age of eleven, Auber wrote mainly for the theatre and has been called the last of the true French *opera cómique* composers. His best-known operas are *Fra Diavolo* and *Masaniello*.

AURIC, Georges (b. 1899) France. Known internationally through his film music, Auric was the youngest member of *Le Groupe des Six* ("The Six"), which comprised also Durey, Honegger, Milhaud, Poulenc, and Tailleferre. Works include ballets and operas, many in a light style, also piano music.

BACH, Carl Philipp Emanuel (1714-1788) Germany. Second son of Johann Sebastian and Maria Barbara, he became court musician to Frederick the Great of Prussia, until appointed a director of music in Hamburg. A brilliant keyboard player, he published a comprehensive treatise on keyboard playing and is regarded as the father of modern pianoforte technique. A prolific composer, and a link between his father's style and that of Haydn, his works total about seven hundred, including sixteen symphonies, forty-one concertos for clavier, and 700 vocal and instrumental compositions.

BACH, Johann Christian (1735-1782) Germany. Youngest son of Johann Sebastian and Anna Magdalena. At the age of twenty he went to Italy, studied with Padre Martini, and after composing much church music, turned to opera. In 1762 he was invited to England and spent twenty fruitful years in London, becoming known as "the English Bach" and died in that city. He composed operas in the Italian style, forty-nine symphonies, orchestral music, and church music.

BACH, Johann Sebastian (1685-1750) Germany. Born at Eisenach, Thuringia, he came from a long line of musicians. Left an orphan at the age of ten, he lived with his eldest brother, Johann Christoph, at Ohrdruf. At fifteen he undertook to make his own living. In 1703 he became organist at Arnstadt. Four years later he became organist at Mülhausen and married his cousin, Maria Barbara Bach. In the following year he moved to Weimar, taking up the post of court organist and in 1714 was promoted to Konzertmeister. In 1723 he was given the post of cantor at the St Thomas Choir School in Leipzig.

In July 1720 his wife, Maria Barbara died, having borne him seven children, three dying in infancy and four surviving their parents. In December 1721 Anna Magdalena Wilcken (the name also given as Wölckner and Wülcke) became his wife and gave birth to thirteen children between the years 1723 and 1742.

Towards the end of his life Bach's eyesight failed; in 1749 he became totally blind. He died in Leipzig.

Bach's creative output was prodigious, but few of his works were published during his lifetime. It was Mendelssohn who rescued the manuscripts of many of his works after they had lain forgotten for a hundred years.

Among his principal works are choral, including five *Passions*, 200 sacred and secular cantatas, oratorios, *Mass in B minor*, motets, concertos, suites, chamber works, *The Art of Fugue*, *The Well-tempered Clavier* (forty-eight preludes and fugues), numerous solo works for organ, harpsichord, clavier, and other instruments, songs.

BADINGS, Henk (b. 1907) Dutch composer, born in Java. Works include symphonies, concertos, orchestral, and electronic music; also music for films.

BAINTON, Edgar Leslie (1880-1956) England. Studied at Royal College of Music, London under C. V. Stanford, Walford Davies, and others. Director New South Wales State Conservatorium 1934-1948. Works include

operas, a choral setting of Rossetti's *The Blessed Damozel*, three symphonies, orchestral and piano pieces.

BALAKIREV, Mily (1837-1910) Russia. Leader of "nationalist" group of composers, which included Borodin, Cui, Moussorgsky, and Rimsky-Korsakov. Poverty forced him to become a railway official. Further discouragements caused a nervous breakdown. In 1883 took a position as musical director at the Tsar's court. Principal works: two symphonies, symphonic poems *Thamar* and *Russia*; *Islamey* for piano (later orchestrated by Casella), piano pieces, songs, and folk-song arrangements.

BALFE, Michael William (1808-1870) Ireland. His family brought him to London while he was still a child. He later studied in Italy and Paris. Composed operas, the most successful being *The Bohemian Girl*.

BANKS, Don (Donald Oscar), (b. 1923) Australia. Settled in England in 1953. Pupil of Seiber and Dallapiccola. In 1959 awarded the Sir Arnold Bax Society's Medal for services as a Composer of the Commonwealth. His works include *Four Pieces*, *Divisions*, *Assemblies* for orchestra; concertos for horn and violin; *Five North Country Folk Songs* for soprano and string orchestra; chamber music; *Pezzo Dramatico*, and other works for piano.

BANTOCK, Granville (1868-1946) England. After studying for Indian Civil Service, made music his profession. In 1907 succeeded Elgar as professor of music at Birmingham University. Knighted in 1930. First conductor in England to perform Sibelius's music. Wrote vast amount of music in many forms; operas, orchestral and choral, song-cycles.

BARBER, Samuel (b. 1910) America. Played piano at six; at ten composed an opera to libretto supplied by family cook. Studied singing with his aunt, Louise Homer, and Emilio de Gogorza. Graduated Curtis Institute, Philadelphia, 1932. In 1928 won $1,200 Bearns Prize for violin sonata; in 1935 and 1936 awarded a Pulitzer Travelling Scholarship which allowed him to visit several countries. Met Toscanini, who gave several performances of his *Adagio for Strings*. His one-movement symphony was the first American work to be played at a Salzburg Festival. Received a Guggenheim Award in 1945.

His music covers several forms, much of it cast in traditional European idiom.

Principal works: opera, *Vanessa* and *A Hand at Bridge*, two symphonies, choral works, *Medea* ballet suite, concertos for various instruments, *Dover Beach* for solo voice and quartet, *Piano Sonata, Op. 26.*

BARNBY, Joseph (1838-1896) England. Organist, conductor, composer. Knighted 1892. Best-known today for his part-song, *Sweet and Low.* Other works include oratorio *Rebekah*, numerous services and anthems, 246 hymns.

BARRAUD, Henry (b. 1900) France. Critic and composer. Works include *Hommage à Rameau* and *Le Mystère des Saints Innocents* (for voices and orchestra); opera *Numantia*; ballet *The Astrologer in the Well*; string works; piano concerto, three symphonies.

BARTOK, Béla (1881-1945) Hungary. Now considered one of the outstanding composers of the twentieth century, Bartók suffered both neglect and bitter opposition during his lifetime. In 1898 he went to the Royal Academy in Budapest, where he came under the notice of Dohnanyi. After appearing as a brilliant pianist, applied himself to composition. Later he joined Kodály in collecting and editing authentic folk-song, proving that much in use, including Liszt's *Hungarian Rhapsodies*, were not genuine. When political tension in Europe increased, Bartók and his wife went to America, where the state of financial hardship he had known for so long continued. He died penniless in New York. Among his principal works are: *Bluebeard's Castle* (opera), *The miraculous Mandarin* (mime-play), *Concerto for Orchestra, Dance Suite* (orchestra), *Divertimento for Strings, Music for Strings, Percussion and Celeste*, concertos for violin, piano, and viola, six string quartets, Rhapsodies for violin and piano, sonatas and suites for piano, Hungarian and Rumanian folk dances, songs.

BATE, Stanley (1913-1959) England. Pupil of Vaughan Williams, Hindemith, and Boulanger. Lived in U.S.A. from 1942 to 1949. Works include three piano concertos, harpsichord concerto, *Perseus* and other ballets, piano works.

BAX, Arnold (1883-1953) England. London-born, but much of early life spent in Ireland, whose folk-lore influenced some of his music.

Visited Russia 1910. Knighted 1937; appointed Master of King's (later Queen's) Music 1942. He referred to himself as a "brazen romantic." His numerous works include: seven symphonies, violin concerto, cello concerto, symphonic poems, including *The Garden of Fand, Moy Mell, Tintagel, Mediterranean;* chamber music, piano pieces, some reflecting aspects of nature, with such titles as *November Woods, Hill Tune, Country Tune, Winter Waters.*

BEETHOVEN, Ludwig van (1770-1827) Germany. Destined to become one of the greatest composers of all time, Beethoven was born at Bonn, his mother, the daughter of the chief cook at Ehrenbreitstein; his father, a singer in the service of the Archbishop-Elector of Cologne, who later lost his employment owing to his irregular habits. By the time his father died in 1792, Ludwig had settled in Vienna where, after many disappointments, he won recognition as a pianist and teacher, in later years to receive the patronage of noble Viennese families. About the year 1798 he was increasingly troubled by violent noises in his ears; at the age of forty-five he was totally deaf, yet it was after that he composed some of his greatest works.

His brusque manner upset many; the composer Weber described him as "a square Cyclopean figure, attired in a shabby coat with torn sleeves." He never married, although several women, most from aristocratic families, were attracted to him.

He was slow and painstaking in all that he composed, and enriched every form of music that claimed his attention. He advanced the scope of the symphony, the concerto, the sonata, chamber music. By 1827, the year of his death, he had silenced the last of his critics. More than 20,000 people followed the hearse to his last resting-place in Währinger cemetery.

Among his principal works: nine symphonies, five piano concertos; one violin concerto, concerto for piano, violin, and cello; seventeen quartets, two quintets; thirty-two piano sonatas, ten sonatas for violin and piano; one opera, *Fidelio;* masses, motets, *Mount of Olives* for soloists, chorus, and orchestra; overtures, incidental music and other orchestral works; music for solo piano, violin, and instrumental groups; lieder; *Diabelli* and *Prometheus Variations* for piano.

BELLINI, Vincenzo (1801-1835) Italy. When only six composed a motet for solo voice. In spite of father's opposition, he early made music his profession and in 1825 wrote his first opera, *Adelson e Salvina*. Visited London; became idol of Paris; died, supposedly of cholera, in a French village. Two hundred prominent singers and instrumentalists took part in funeral mass held in Church of the Invalides, Paris.

Bellini was no operatic reformer, but the charm of his melodies is said to have influenced other composers, including Chopin, Liszt, and Tchaikovsky. Compositions almost solely opera, the best-known being: *La Sonnambula*, *Norma*, *I Puritani*, *Il Pirata*, *Beatrice di Tenda*.

BENEDICT, Julius (1804-1885). Although born in Germany, lived for over forty years in England where his reputation was exceptionally high. In 1850 accompanied Jenny Lind to the United States of America, where he directed most of her concerts. Returned to London 1852 and became conductor at Her Majesty's Theatre and Drury Lane. Knighted 1871. Compositions included five operas, the best known *The Lily of Killarney*; five oratorios and cantatas; two symphonies; two piano concertos.

BENJAMIN, Arthur (1893-1960) Australia. First a pianist, then successful composer, went to Royal College of Music, London, on an open scholarship at seventeen; served with Royal Fusiliers and Royal Air Force 1914 to 1918, shot down and taken prisoner. In 1919 became Professor of Piano Study at Sydney State Conservatorium; returned to London in 1922 to become member of teaching staff at the Royal College, numbering among his pupils Benjamin Britten, Muir Mathieson, and George Weldon. Moved to Vancouver in 1939; back in England seven years later. He died in London 1960.

Benjamin's *Jamaican Rumba* became immensely popular. In the first year of its life a Heifetz recording of it sold more than 250,000 copies, while in England broadcasts averaged five a week. Other works include *A Tale of Two Cities* (grand opera); *Prima Donna* (comic opera); *Spring* (choral); a symphony; piano concertos; ballet and film music; orchestral works; songs; piano pieces.

BENNETT, Richard Rodney (b. 1936) England. Studied for a time with Boulez in Paris. Has gained considerable prominence of recent years for his original style. Works include: operas (*The Mines of Sulphur* and *The Ledge*), a symphony, a cantata, a horn concerto, chamber music, orchestral pieces, piano works, film music. The world première of his opera *Victory*, based on the novel of Joseph Conrad, was given in London in April, 1970.

BENNETT, William Sterndale (1816-1875) English. At age of ten became a student at Royal Academy of Music, London. On advice of Mendelssohn, who remained his life-long friend, he went to Germany in 1836. He also met Schumann, who dedicated his *Etudes Symphoniques* to him. He later undertook a number of official appointments in England and received a knighthood in 1871. His numerous compositions include anthems and other choral works, orchestral and piano music, chamber music and songs.

BENTZON, Jorgen (b. 1897) Denmark. Pupil of Carl Nielsen and Karg-Elert. Composed much chamber music.

BENTZON, Niels Viggo (b. 1919) Denmark. Cousin of J. Bentzon. Works include five symphonies, orchestral and chamber music, ballet *The Courtesan*, sonatas, and piano pieces.

BEREZOVSKY, Nicolai (1900-1953) Russia. Moved to the United States 1922. Wrote concertos for oboe, clarinet, harp, violin, cello; *Gilgamesh* (for soloists, chorus, narrator and orchestra); four symphonies; chamber music, etc. Also conductor.

BERG, Alban (1885-1935). Born in Vienna, Berg worked and died there. As a boy he was stricken with bronchial asthma, which remained with him all his life. Schoenberg, recognising the young man's talent, taught him free of charge and this guidance lasted from 1904 to 1910. During the first World War he was attached to the Austrian War Ministry, having been rejected for active service.

Developing Schoenberg's methods, he adopted the twelve-tone technique about 1925, combining an atonal idiom with long-established structures. His opera, *Wozzeck* based on Georg Büchner's play, produced in Berlin in 1925, brought him added fame.

Principal works include, in addition to *Wozzeck*, a violin concerto, *Lyric Suite* for string quartet, other chamber works, orchestral pieces, songs.

BERGMAN, Erik (b. 1911) Finland. Studied in Helsinki and Berlin, served as choir director at the Vatican; later studied music of the East in Egypt and Turkey. In 1963 appointed Professor of Composition at Sibelius Academy, Helsinki. One of the pioneers of *avant garde* music in Finland.

BERIO, Luciano (b. 1925) Italy. Pupil of Ghedini and Dallapiccola. Works include those written in free style; chamber, orchestral, and electronic music. His opera, *Passaggio* (1963) is notable for its fine choral passages, and a kind of spoken chorus. In July 1970 his new work, entitled *Opera* had its première.

BERKELEY, Lennox (b. 1903) England. After leaving Oxford University, studied in Paris with Boulanger. Principal works: operas, *Nelson* and *A Dinner Engagement*; symphonies, concertos; *Serenade for Strings; Four Poems of St Teresa, Stabat Mater*, chamber music, film music.

BERLIOZ, Hector (1803-1869) France. The son of a country doctor, he attended medical school at nineteen, but soon abandoned those studies and, in defiance of his parents, devoted himself full time to music. He failed to distinguish himself at the Paris Conservatoire and was not proficient on any instrument, but became a revolutionary force in orchestration, on which he wrote an authoritative book. He became a successful conductor and a penetrating critic, and for a time found it necessary to fall back on journalism for a living.

When his music became recognised by such composers as Liszt, Schumann, Paganini, and Wagner, his fame grew. His works were conceived on massive lines. In 1827 his infatuation for the Irish actress, Harriet (or Henrietta) Smithson, inspired him to write his *Symphonie Fantastique*. They married, but separated nine years later. After the death of his first wife, he married Marie Recio, a singer. Of fiery temperament, he made many enemies, but lived to find his music widely appreciated.

Among his principal works are: *Symphonie Fantastique; Requiem, Te Deum, L'Enfance du Christ*, and *La Damnation de Faust* (oratorios); *Les Troyens* (operatic trilogy); symphonic version of *Roméo et Juliette*; operas; overtures;

Harold in Italy (orchestra and viola obbligato); songs with orchestra and with piano.

BERNERS, Lord (Gerald Hugh Tyrwhitt-Wilson) (1883-1950) England. In diplomatic service from 1909 to 1919, later became composer, painter, and author. His first musical studies were in Dresden and Vienna, later with Stravinsky and Casella. His works, some of them wittily ironic, include songs, piano pieces, and ballets, *The Triumph of Neptune*, and *The Wedding Bouquet*.

BERNSTEIN, Leonard (b. 1918) America. The eldest son of Jewish parents who had moved from Russia to the United States, he taught himself to play the piano at ten; later influenced by Copland and Piston, taking lessons in composition from the latter. From 1951 to 1955 was head of orchestral conducting department at Berkshire Music Centre and in 1957 appointed permanent conductor of New York Philharmonic Symphony Orchestra.

Bernstein has composed in many forms, his works including the symphonies *Jeremiah* and *The Age of Anxiety*; operas *West Side Story* and *Trouble in Tahiti*; operetta *Candide*; ballet *Fancy Free; Prelude, Fugue and Riffs* for large dance band; musical comedy *On the Town*; Song-cycle, *Five Kid Songs: I Hate Music*; chamber music, other songs.

BISHOP, Henry (1786-1855) England. Enjoyed considerable fame as composer and conductor; knighted in 1842. Edited some of Handel's works, including *Messiah*. Composed operas, including *Clari, or The Maid of Milan* (1823) which contains the famous song, *Home, Sweet Home*.

BIZET, Georges (1838-1875) France. Beginning music study at four, won an important prize at Paris Conservatoire at eleven, and at nineteen won the *Prix de Rome* for an operetta, *Doctor Miracle*. The first public performance of his *Symphony in C major* (completed at seventeen) was performed under Weingartner in 1935. As a pianist praised by Liszt, Berlioz, and Saint-Saëns; as composer held in high regard by opera singers and public. He married the daughter of his former teacher, Halévy. Died in Paris.

He was an experimenter in orchestral effects and wrote expertly for voice.

Principal works: operas *Carmen, The Pearl-fishers, The Fair Maid of Perth; L'Arlesienne*

Suites; *Patrie* (overtures), *Jeux D'Enfants*, for piano duet, which he later orchestrated.

BLACHER, Boris (1903-1975) Germany, but born in China of Russian parents. Succeeded Werner Egk as Director of the Hochschule für Musik, West Berlin. Evolved a system of "variable metres"; wrote numerous works in many forms, including operas, *Romeo and Juliet* and *Prussian Fairy Tale*; oratorio, *The Grand Inquisitor*; orchestral works, concertos.

BLISS, Arthur (1891-1975) England. Studied with Stanford, Vaughan Williams and Holst. In 1914 obtained a commission with Grenadier Guards; wounded on the Somme, 1916; gassed at Cambrai, 1918, and mentioned in despatches. Director of Music, B.B.C. 1941 to 1945. Knighted in 1950; appointed Master of the Queen's Music 1953. His earlier writing influenced by Ravel, Elgar, and Stravinsky; later adopted more advanced style.

Principal works: *A Colour Symphony*; *Checkmate* and *Miracle in the Gorbals* (ballets); *The Olympians* (opera); *Things to Come* (film); Music for Strings; piano concertos; piano sonata, clarinet quintet, and other chamber works; *Seven American Poems*; music for Royal occasions; songs. Also arranged *The Beggar's Opera* for its film version.

BLITZSTEIN, Marc (1905-1964) America. Pupil of Boulanger and Schoenberg. Some of his music expresses democratic ideas, for instance the operas, *No for an Answer* and *The Cradle Will Rock*. Other works *Regina* (opera), *Airborne Symphony*; concertos and piano solos. Adapted the Brecht-Weill *Threepenny Opera* in 1952.

BLOCH, Ernest (1880-1959) Switzerland. The son of a Jewish clock-dealer, studied in Brussels, Frankfurt and Munich. His efforts to earn a bare living took him to Monaco and Paris, then he returned to Geneva to take over the family business. In 1916 went to America to take up an appointment as director of Cleveland Institute of Music in New York. Lived quietly in Switzerland between 1930 and 1938, then made his home in the United States.

Bloch's most inspired works were written with a poignant racial accent. These include *Israel Symphony*, *Schelomo* (*Solomon*) for cello and orchestra. Other works: *Macbeth* (opera); *Voice in the Wilderness*; *Violin Concerto*; *Sacred Service*; *Scherzo Fantasque*; *Concerto Symphonique*;

rhapsody, *America*; four string quartets; *Suite Hebraique*; *Abodah* and *Baal Shem* for violin and piano.

BLOMDAHL, Karl-Birger (1916-1968) Sweden. Much of his music constructed on the twelve-tone system. Works include symphonies, concertos, chamber music, piano pieces, and opera, *Aniara*, set in a space-ship.

BLOW, John (b. 1648 or 1649; d. 1708) England. In 1668 became organist at Westminster Abbey, being succeeded in 1679 by Purcell. After death of Purcell in 1695 he resumed the position, holding it until 1708. Wrote many works, including English and Latin anthems, services, a masque, *Venus and Adonis*; odes; keyboard pieces and songs.

BOCCHERINI, Luigi (1743-1805) Italy. Considered the greatest instrumentalist of his time. As a boy found fame in Rome as a cellist and composer; in 1768 went to Paris, but soon left for Spain where he spent most of his life; he died in poverty in Madrid. The total number of his compositions is given as 467, including twenty symphonies, 125 string quintets, 102 string quartets, and other chamber works; four cello concertos, an opera, *Clementina*, church music.

BOELLMANN, Léon (1862-1897) France. A distinguished organist in Paris. Compositions of high quality for organ. Also wrote a symphony, *Variations Symphonique* for cello and orchestra, and chamber works.

BOIELDIEU, François Adrien (1775-1834) France. In his time one of foremost composers of *opéras-comiques*; today best remembered for *La Dame Blanche* and the overture to *Le Calife de Bagdad*.

BOITO, Arrigo (1842-1918) Italy. His fame as composer rests mainly on the opera *Mefistofele*. Also a talented poet; wrote librettos for Verdi's *Otello* and *Falstaff*, and Ponchielli's *La Gioconda*.

BONONCINI (or BUONONCINI), Giovanni (1670 or 1672-1747) Italy. Lived in Rome, Vienna, Berlin, also in London, where for a time his popularity rivalled that of Handel. Accused of claiming music by Lotti and others as his own. Works include operas, oratorios, masses, cantatas, and smaller compositions.

BORODIN, Alexander Porphyrevich (1833-1887) Russia. Said to have been the illegitimate son of a prince, he became a chemist by profession. Meeting Balakirev, he joined the "nationalist" group known as "The Five," the other members being Cui, Moussorgsky, Rimsky-Korsakov, and Balakirev. Composed only in spare time, or when sickness took him from his duties at the Academy of Medicine. Like that of Moussorgsky, much of his fine music was the victim of editing by others. Known today mainly for his opera *Prince Igor* (completed by Rimsky-Korsakov and Glazunov), which includes the well-known *Polovtsian Dances;* three symphonies (No. 3 completed by Glazunov); symphonic poem *In the Steppes of Central Asia;* two string quartets; songs.

BOUGHTON, Rutland (1878-1960) England. Wrote large-scale choral works and music-dramas, hoping to establish the British counterpart of Bayreuth at Glastonbury. His creative work considered uneven, his fame resting chiefly on the opera, *The Immortal Hour,* for which he wrote his own libretto.

BOULANGER, Lily (1893-1918) France. A sister of Nadia; first woman to win the *Prix de Rome.* Composed cantata, *Faust and Helen,* choral music with orchestra.

BOULANGER, Nadia (b. 1887) France. Teacher of many famous composers of several countries. Her own works include orchestral music and songs.

BOULEZ, Pierre (b. 1925) France. First works published in 1949. At first influenced by Debussy, Stravinsky, and his teacher, Messiaen, he had extended the *twelve-note* technique, and has guided many of the younger composers. Since 1960 has been recognised as a penetrating conductor of music by various composers.

BOWEN, York (1884-1961) England. Began career as a brilliant pianist. Composed three piano concertos, a symphony, many piano works in a Romantic style.

BOYCE, William (1710-1779) England. Master of the King's Band, organist to Chapel Royal, later at several churches; an authority on English church music. Compositions include; music for stage and for church, overtures, symphonies adapted from overtures of his early operas, songs.

BRAHMS, Johannes (1833-1897) Germany. Brahms began his musical career as a pianist. In 1852 he toured Germany with the Hungarian violinist, Reményi. A year later

he met Joachim, Schumann, and Liszt who helped him to become known as a composer. In 1863 he made Vienna his permanent home. A chill caught at Clara Schumann's funeral aggravated a liver condition from which he died in the following year.

As a composer Brahms stood as a link between the Classical and the Romantic periods in music, generally regarded as one of the greatest of his time.

Among his principal works are: four symphonies, two piano concertos, a violin concerto, and double concerto for violin and cello; *A German Requiem* and *Song of Destiny* (choral); *Alto Rhapsody* (contralto, male chorus and orchestra); *Liebeslieder Waltzer* (piano duet and vocal part); several sets of variations; chamber music; sonatas for piano, violin and piano, and cello and piano; *Hungarian Dances;* overtures; piano solos, including four *Ballades,* sixteen *Waltzes,* and thirty pieces grouped as *Rhapsodies, Fantasies, Intermezzi, Capricci,* five sets of *Clavierstücke;* lieder, and German folk-song arrangements.

BRIAN, Havergal (1876-1972) England. Has composed thirty-two symphonies, one entitled *Gothic* scored for 700 performers, including orchestra of 180 players, two brass bands, and more than 400 mixed voices. Completed in 1919, after seven years' work on it, this received its first performance in London in 1967. He has also written an opera, songs, and other miscellaneous works.

BRIDGE, Frank (1879-1941) England. Studied with Stanford, became viola player and conductor. Although he composed attractive orchestral works, is best known for his chamber music. The teacher of Benjamin Britten.

BRITTEN, Benjamin (1913-1976) Born in Suffolk, where he continued to live after spending from 1939 to 1942 in America. At five he could play the piano; later studied with Frank Bridge, John Ireland, and Arthur Benjamin. One of the most prolific composers of his generation. With Peter Pears and others formed the English Opera Group in 1946, and from 1948 has directed the Aldeburgh Festivals. Created a Companion of Honour 1953; awarded Order of Merit 1965. Created life-Peer (Lord Britten 1976).

Among his numerous works are: opera, *Peter Grimes, The Rape of Lucretia, Albert*

Herring, Billy Budd, A Midsummer Night's Dream. The Turn of the Screw, Gloriana; church parables, *Curlew River, The Burning Fiery Furnace, The Prodigal Son; Noye's Fludde* (musical mystery play); *Cantata Misericordium; The Prince of Pagodas* (ballet); *A ceremony of Carols, Hymn to St Cecilia, Hymn to the Virgin,* and other choral works; *A War Requiem; Spring Symphony, Simple Symphony, Symphony for Cello and Orchestra; Young Person's Guide to the Orchestra; Sinfonia da Requiem; Les Illuminations* (song cycle); piano concerto; chamber music; folk-song arrangements; songs; piano pieces; *Owen Wingrave* (TV Opera); *Death in Venice* (opera-cantata).

BRUCH, Max (1838-1920) Germany. After holding academic positions in Germany, spent three years from 1880 in England. His fame today rests chiefly on the first of three violin concertos and *Kol Nidrei.* Other works, operas, choral works, three symphonies.

BRUCKNER, Anton (1824-1896) Austria. After occupying several positions as organist, he settled in Vienna (1868), having been appointed professor of theory and organ at the Conservatoire. He became a disciple of Wagner, though he wrote no operas. Among his pupils were Artur Nikisch, Karl Muck, Frank Schalk, Gustav Mahler, and Bruno Walter. He was a devout Catholic; his music grew out of a fervent religious conviction and a simple faith that reflected joy in nature.

He allowed conductors and others to revise his works; in 1929 the International Bruckner Society was formed to publish the "original versions" of his symphonies. The musical world has taken a long time to make up its mind about his music.

Bruckner composed nine symphonies, four masses, choral works, including a *Te Deum;* motets; chamber music; organ works; songs.

BRUMBY, Colin (b. 1933) Australia. Studied Australia, London, and Spain. Works include orchestral, choral, organ, chamber, songs, some performed overseas. Also author of several books.

BULL, John (c. 1563-1628) England. Sang in Queen Elizabeth's Chapel Royal, became organist at Hereford Cathedral at twenty, subsequently holding positions of Gentleman of the Chapel Royal, Doctor of Music at Universities of Oxford and Cambridge, and Professor of Music at Gresham College,

London. In 1601 travelled in France, Belgium, and Germany; in 1617 became organist at cathedral in Antwerp, in which city he died. While less significant musically than those of his contemporaries, his compositions for virginals, viols, organ, and his church music have been well worth preserving.

BUONONCINI (see BONONCINI)

BURLEIGH, Henry Thacker (1866-1914) America. Negro singer and composer. Became famous for his arrangements of Negro spirituals.

BURNARD, David Alexander (1900-1971) Australia. Born in Adelaide, studied at Royal College of Music, London, with Vaughan Williams. Doctor of Music 1932. Senior Lecturer at N.S.W. State Conservatorium. Compositions include choral, orchestral, chamber music, performed in Australia and England.

BUSH, Alan Dudley (b. 1900) England. Studied with John Ireland; became pianist, conductor, teacher, writer. Works include operas, piano concerto, violin concerto; choral and piano music.

BUSONI, Ferruccio (1866-1924). Italian pianist who lived for most of his life in Germany. Compositions, distinguished by great technical skill and intellectual quality, include operas, concertos, piano music. Edited works by J. S. Bach and made many transcriptions of same.

BUTTERLEY, Nigel (b. 1935) Australia. Studied Sydney, Adelaide, and London. Compositions, which have been performed in Australia, Great Britain, and the United States, and revealing considerable originality, include liturgical, ballet, chamber, and film scores.

BUTTERWORTH, Arthur (b. 1923) England. Has written symphonic and chamber music.

BUTTERWORTH, George (1885-1916) England. His friendship with Vaughan Williams and Cecil Sharp stimulated his interest in English folk-song, these influencing his own work, e.g. *A Shropshire Lad, The Banks of Green Willow,* and *In the Highlands.*

BUXTEHUDE, Dietrich (1637-1707) Denmark. Organist and composer, who influenced Bach and Handel. His organ music is the most important of his compositions.

BYRD, William (1542 or 1543; d. 1623). Sometimes called the Father of British Music.

Together with Tallis granted from Queen Elizabeth monopoly of music-printing in England. Composed numerous church works, motets, madrigals, also many pieces for virginals and viols.

CACCINI, Guilio (Date of birth given as 1545, 1550 and 1558; died c. 1618) Italy. An important member of the Florentine "Camerata," whose *Euridice* (1600) was one of the earliest Italian operas. Wrote some charming songs, including *Amarilli*.

CADMAN, Charles Wakefield (1881-1946) America. A composer of facile talent, sometimes influenced by American Indian material. Such songs as *At Dawning* and *From the Land of Sky-Blue Water* became immensely popular. Also wrote *Pennsylvania Symphony;* cantatas, *The Father of Waters* and *The Far Horizon; Thunderbird* and other suites.

CAGE, John (b. 1912) America. A pupil of Schoenberg. Has written in an experimental style, including Concerto for *"prepared piano"* (his own invention). Other works include a ballet, *The Seasons*.

CARISSIMI, Giacomo (1605-1674) Italy. Helped to develop the early recitative, cantata and oratorio, influencing others, including A. Scarlatti.

CARPENTER, John Alden (1876-1951) America. His style derived much from the French. Works include *Adventures in a Perambulator* (suite); two symphonies; Violin concerto; *Sea Drift* (symphonic poem; choral works; songs).

CARTER, Elliott (b. 1908) America. Pupil of Piston and N. Boulanger. Works include a symphony; concerto for English Horn; a ballet *Minotaur*.

CASELLA, Alfredo (1883-1947) Italy. A pupil of Fauré in Paris, became pianist, conductor, and composer. Works include operas, symphonies, chamber music; an oratorio, piano music. Also orchestrated music of other composers.

CASTELNUOVO-TEDESCO, Mario (1895-1968) Italy. Pupil of Pizetti. His music, which includes an oratorio, two violin concertos, a guitar concerto, songs, and piano pieces, leans towards a lyrical style.

CATALANI, Alfredo (1854-1893) Italy. Composer of operas, e.g., *La Wally* and *Edmea*, successful in their time.

CAVALLI, Pietro (1602-1676) Italy. One of the most important of early Italian operas (he wrote more than thirty); he was the successor to Monteverdi over whom he made advances in melodic construction.

CHABRIER (Alexis), Emmanuel (1841-1894) France. Studied law and took a position in the Civil Service, his music a hobby until he was thirty-eight. His works, somewhat uneven in quality, are often brilliant in orchestration and wit. Now remembered for his opera *Le Roi malgré lui*, the orchestral rhapsody *España*, and *Bourrée fantasque*.

CHADWICK, George Whitefield (1854-1931) America. Studied with Reinecke (Leipzig) and Rheinberger (Munich), later working in cause of American music. Works include symphonies, string quartets, operas, and piano music.

CHAMINADE, Cécile (1860(?)-1944) French. Her piano pieces and songs, written in a conventional, melodic style, had a considerable vogue in drawing-rooms about the turn of the century. These, and her orchestral works, have lost favour in this sophisticated age.

CHARPENTIER, Gustave (1860-1956) France. Studied composition with Massenet. His fame today rests on his attractive opera, *Louise*. His orchestral *Impressions of Italy* was recast as a ballet about 1913.

CHARPENTIER, Marc-Antoine (1634-1704) France. Studied under Carissimi in Rome; later wrote incidental music for plays by Molière. Considered to be the rival of Lully. Composed some distinctive works, including operas (*Médée* his best known), numerous church works.

CHAUSSON, Ernest (1855-1899) France. Pupil of Massenet, later of Franck, whose disciple he became. His early death resulted from a bicycle accident. A talented composer of limited range, now best known for his *Symphony in B-flat*, *Poème* (violin and orchestra), a string quartet, and songs.

CHAVEZ, Carlos (b. 1899) Mexico. A collector of folk-song; many of his compositions carry a Mexican flavour, these comprising symphonies, ballet music, piano pieces.

CHERUBINI (Maria), Luigi (1760-1842) Italy. From 1788 lived in Paris, becoming an important figure in the history of French music. It is said that Beethoven admired his work. His compositions have been placed in

275

three periods: (1) masses and motets in a Palestrina style; (2) an operatic period, with *Médée, Lodoiska, Iphigenia in Aulis, Les Deux Journées, Faniska,* etc.; (3) sacred music, including two *Requiems.* Also wrote symphonic and chamber music.

CHOPIN, Frédéric François (1810-1849) Poland. Chopin lived for most of his life in Paris, apart from visits to England and Scotland. Though he never revisited his native country, he remained a Polish patriot. Before he had reached the age of nineteen he embarked on a career as a travelling virtuoso and found the houses of aristocratic families open to him. His playing, like his compositions, was distinguished by elegance, subtlety, strength, and passion. Notwithstanding his reputation as a virtuoso, he soon gave up playing before an audience; he once said to Liszt, "I prefer not to play in public. It unnerves me."

At nineteen he believed himself in love with Constantia Gladkowska, whom he had met at the Conservatoire. Any deep attachment was cut short when she announced her engagement to someone else. In the late 1830s consumption forced him into retirement. His liaison with the writer, George Sand (Aurore Dudevant), lasted for seven years. His health steadily deteriorated, but from those tortured years came some of his finest works. During a visit to Edinburgh he collapsed and was taken back to Paris where he died.

His piano music — he composed little else — contains an amazing range of melodic, rhythmic, harmonic, and dynamic expression and originality. He transferred such dance forms as the mazurka, the polonaise, and the waltz into the concert hall. Perhaps no other composer's piano music has been more harshly treated by drooling sentiment, or tastelessly subjected to "arrangements." For all that it retains its vitality and charm.

Principal works: two piano concertos; three cantatas; four ballades; four scherzi; twenty-five preludes; twenty-seven etudes; ten polonaises; nineteen nocturnes; fourteen waltzes; fifty-six mazurkas; *Barcarolle in F sharp; Fantasie in F minor.*

CIMAROSA, Domenico (1749-1801) Italy. Composed about sixty-five operas that were greatly admired in his day. Today, is chiefly known by *Il Matrimonio Segreto (The Secret Marriage).* Also composed church music.

CLARKE, Jeremiah (c. 1659-1707) England. Began career in the Chapel Royal under Dr John Blow. Composed music for church and stage, also *The Prince of Denmark's March,* which as *Trumpet Voluntary* was for a long time attributed to Purcell.

CLEMENTI, Muxio (1752-1832) Italy. Lived for most of his life in England, where he was renowned as pianist, composer, and teacher. Among his numerous pupils were J. B. Cramer and John Field. Said to have been the first composer to write for the piano in a pianistic, rather than a harpsichord, style. Became a member of a pianoforte manufacturing business. Compositions include: symphonies, chamber music, numerous piano works, including the book of studies, *Gradus ad Parnassum.*

CLIFFORD, Hubert (John) (1904-1950) Australia. On scholarship to Trinity College, London, went overseas in 1930; became music master at a boys' school, later head of Light Music Department of B.B.C. Compositions include a symphony, light orchestral pieces, and film scores.

CLUTSAM, George Howard (1866-1951) Australia. Settled in England in 1889, becoming widely known as pianist, critic, and composer of stage works. Adapted some of Schubert's music for operetta *Lilac Time.*

COATES, Eric (1886-1957) England. A composer of light, but well-constructed, orchestral works (e.g., *London Suite*), and songs (e.g., *Bird Songs at Eventide*), which have enjoyed continued popularity.

COLERIDGE-TAYLOR, Samuel (1875-1912) England. A British Negro composer, best known for his cantata-trilogy, *Hiawatha.* Wrote also orchestral works, a violin concerto chamber and piano music, and songs.

COOKE, Arnold (b. 1906) England. A pupil of Hindemith, he adopted his master's methods in his earlier works. Has written an opera, *Mary Barton,* concertos, chamber music, piano pieces, songs, three symphonies.

COPLAND, Aaron (b. 1900) America. One of America's most important composers, who has championed the music of his country, Copland is also a distinguished author, lecturer, pianist, and conductor. Among his many works are: ballets (*Rodeo* and *Appalachian*

Spring); opera (*The Tender Land*); three symphonies; chamber and piano music; film scores. He adopted a Latin-American idiom in his *El Salon México* for orchestra.

CORELLI, Arcangelò (1653-1713) Italy. The greatest violinist of his time, went to Paris in 1672, but meeting opposition from Lully and his supporters, embarked on further travel. Settled in Rome in 1685 and remained in the service of Cardinal Pietro Ottoboni. Is said to have left a valuable estate. Advanced the scope of violin technique and helped to crystallise the concerto grosso form. Left numerous works of concerto grosso type, instrumental suites, sonatas.

CORNELIUS Peter (1824-1874) Germany. Influenced by Liszt and Wagner, wrote *The Barber of Baghdad* and other operas, choral works, and songs.

CORNYSHE, William (c . 1465-1523) England. A composer, dramatist, and actor at the court of Henry VIII, wrote part-songs, sacred music, motets, and madrigals.

COUPERIN, François (1668-1733) France. Called "Couperin le Grand," became music-master to royalty and enjoyed the favour of Louis XIV. His publication *L'art de toucher le clavecin* influenced many, including J. S. Bach. Principal works: more than 200 harpsichord pieces; concertos; church and vocal music; works for organ and viols.

COWEN, Frederic (1852-1935) England. A musician from early childhood, held honoured place in English music. Wrote operas and operettas, six symphonies, chamber music, choral works, and about 300 songs.

CUI, César Antonovich (1835-1918) Russia. A military Lieutenant-General, became an authority on fortifications, music a spare-time occupation. A member of "The Five," a group of "nationalists" which included Balakirev, Borodin, Moussorgsky, and Rimsky-Korsakov. Although he composed some large-scale works, now best remembered for his miniatures, and *Kaleidoscope*, which includes *Orientale*.

CZERNY, Carl (1791-1857) Austria. Composed vast quantity of piano music, mostly studies. A pupil of Beethoven and teacher of many famous musicians.

DALE, Benjamin James (1885-1943) England. Frederick Corder, his teacher said, "Dale has written fewer and better works than any English composer of his generation." His works include choral, piano pieces, songs, and several compositions for viola.

DALLAPICCOLA, Luigi (1904-1975) Italy. Considered the leading Italian composer using the twelve-note technique, his music has influenced many younger musicians. Has written operas (*The Prisoner, Night Flight, Ulisse, Job*); and ballet, orchestral, choral, piano music. Was also a successful pianist and teacher.

DARGOMIZHSKY, Alexander (1813-1869) Russia. Followed Glinka in establishing a nationalist school of opera. His best known operas, written to texts of Pushkin, are *The Russalka, The Stone Guest*. Also composed some orchestral music and songs.

DAVIES, Peter Maxwell (b. 1934) England. His early interest in avant-garde music later changed to medieval forms. Works include *St Michael Sonata*, for seventeen wind instruments; orchestral and chamber works; settings of medieval carols; educational, choral, and piano music.

DAVIES (Henry), Walford (1869-1941) England. Organist, conductor, teacher, lecturer; as composer best known for his oratorio *Everyman*, church music, and *Solemn Melody*. Knighted 1922; Master of the King's Music, 1934.

DEBUSSY, Claude Achille (1862-1918) France. Studied piano for three years with Mme Manté de Fleurville, a former pupil of Chopin and the mother-in-law of the poet Verlaine. Entered Paris Conservatoire and in 1880 became private musician to Tchaikovsky's benefactress, Nadezhda von Meck, accompanying her on her travels. In 1899 he married Rosalie Texier; five years later transferred his affections to Emma Bardac and shortly after his divorce married her. In 1914 he was a semi-invalid and unfit for military service. Remaining in Paris, he died there in March 1918.

The most influential French composer of his time, he set up new harmonic structures and added a new dimension to pianism. He is generally regarded as the founder of the so-called "impressionistic" school.

Principal works: *Pelléas et Mélisande* (opera); *L'Enfant Prodigue* and *La Demoiselle Elue* (cantatas); *Le Martyre de St Sebastien* (incidental music); *Three Nocturnes for Orchestra; La*

277

Mer; Images for Orchestra; Prélude á l'après-midi d'un faune; Rhapsody for clarinet and orchestra; piano works, including two *Arabesques, Children's Corner, Estampes, Images,* twenty-four *Préludes, Suite Bergamasque, Suite pour le Piano,* and various single pieces; string quartet, violin and piano sonatas; songs, set to poems by Verlaine, Baudelaire, and other French poets.

DELIBES, Léo (Clément Philibert) (1836-1891) France. Studied composition with Adolphe Adam. Became one of the most successful composers of ballet music, although his opera *Lamké* still holds a place in opera repertoire. Best known works today: *Lakmé* (opera); *Coppélia, Sylvia, La Source* (ballets); *Le Roi s'amuse* (incidental music); masses; songs.

DELIUS, Frederick (1862-1934) England. A lonely figure in English music, he has been called "an intellectual solitary" and "a poetic recluse." It was once the custom to call Delius the English Debussy because he brought impressionism to English music. But, how *English* was Delius? He was born at Bradford, the son of a German family of Dutch extraction. After a period on an orange plantation in Florida, he studied at the Leipzig Conservatorium, took the Norwegian Grieg as his model, became an ardent lover of Scandinavia, and spent the greater part of his life in France, where he died.

Delius married Jelka Rosen, a Scandinavian artist, who remained his devoted companion. He spent his last years blind and paralysed. From 1928 Eric Fenby took down and wrote out the scores of many Delius scores.

Delius followed no "school." He wrote many of his works to evoke atmosphere, serenity, nature, although some of his compositions have a compelling vigour. His music reflected the dying rays of Romanticism; elusive, of amorphous delicacy.

Principal works: *A Village Romeo and Juliet, Irmelin, Koanga, Fennimore and Gerda* (operas); *Appalachia* (chorus and orchestra); orchestral works, including *Briggs Fair, On Hearing the First Cuckoo in Spring, Over the Hills and Far Away, In a Summer Garden, A Song Before Sunrise, Paris;* choral works, including *A Mass of Life, Sea Drift, Requiem, A Song of the High Hills;* incidental music to *Hassan;* a violin,

and a piano concerto; chamber music; songs written to English, Norwegian, Danish, French, and German texts.

DELLO JOIO, Norman (b. 1913) America. Pupil of Hindemith, Pulitzer Prize winner, has composed in established and modern styles. Among his works are: *The Trial at Rouen* (opera); *Joan of Arc Symphony; Fantasy and Variations* for piano and orchestra; a concerto for harmonica, piano works.

DIEREN, Bernard van (1884-1936) Holland. Educated with view to scientific career. Settled in London in 1909 and composed music of polyphonic and contrapuntal complexity, orchestral, piano, and for voice.

DITTERSDORF, Karl von (original name Ditters) (1739-1799) Austria. A friend of Gluck, Haydn, and Mozart, was a popular figure in German stage works and chamber music. Composed several symphonies.

DOHNÁNYI, Ernö (Ernst) von (1877-1960) Hungary. Resident in U.S.A. from 1948. Also pianist. Wrote in a more orthodox style than his contemporaries, Bartók and Kodály. Works include: symphonies, operas, string quartets, *Ruralia Hungarica* (suite), *Variations on a Nursery Tune;* songs.

DONIZETTI, Gaetano (1797-1848) Italy. Influenced by Rossini and Bellini, composed sixty-seven operas. He took a prominent part in the musical life of Paris, but a breakdown in health in 1845 forced him to give up composing, and for the rest of his life he lived in seclusion in the Pyrenees. His music, later anticipating Verdi, was notable for florid grace and sentimental lyricism.

Principal operas: *Lucia di Lammermoor, Don Pasquale, L'Elisir d'Amore, La Favorita, La Figlio del Regimento, Linda di Chamounix, Lucrezia Borgia,* and *Anna Bolena.*

DOUGLAS, Clive (1903-1977) Australia. Holds degree of Doctor of Music. Has conducted symphony orchestras for Australian Broadcasting Commission. Chief study teacher in composition, Melbourne University Conservatorium, 1959 to 1963. His works include operas, symphonies, choral, and orchestral music.

DOWLAND, John (1563-1626) England. One of the greatest of Elizabethan lutenists and composers of airs. From 1598 to 1606 held appointment as lutenist to King Christian IV of Denmark at a large salary. Composed numerous songs, many with lute accompaniment, also instrumental music.

DREYFUS, George (b. 1928) Germany. Settled in Australia in 1939, and became teacher of bassoon at Melbourne University Conservatorium. Has composed symphonies, an opera, *Garni Sands; From Within Looking Out* for soprano and instruments; ballet and chamber music; songs.

DRIGO, Riccardo (1846-1930) Italy. Conductor and composer. Best known today for his *Serenade* from his ballet *Harlequin's Millions*.

DRYSDALE, Learmont (1866-1909) Scotland. Composer of *Red Spider* (opera); *The Kelpie* and other cantatas; *The Spirit of the Glen*, *Thomas the Rhymer*, *Tam O'Shanter* and other orchestral works; songs, many of which influenced by his native country.

DUBENSKY, Arcady (1890-1966) Russia. Violinist and composer. Settled in the United States 1921. Works include: *Concerto for Trombone and orchestra*; *Concerti Grossi*; *Five Irish Pieces*; *Meditation for Harp and Strings*; several overtures; *Fantasia for Tuba and Orchestra*.

DUBOIS, Théodore (1837-1924) France. Composed operas, church music, orchestral music. Director Paris Conservatoire from 1896 to 1905.

DUFAY, Guillaume (c. 1400-1474). A Flemish singer-composer, who became one of the leaders of the first Netherlands polyphonic school and one of the greatest composers of the fifteenth century. Works include church music and songs.

DUKAS, Paul (1865-1935) France. Had this composer been less self-critical, his creative output might have been greater. Known today chiefly by his orchestral scherzo, *The Sorcerer's Apprentice; Adriadne and Bluebeard* (opera); *The Peri* (dance-poem); piano works, including a sonata.

DUNHILL, Thomas Frederick (1877-1946) England. A pupil of Stanford, became a composer, teacher, and lecturer. Wrote chamber music; a one-act opera, *The Enchanted Garden;* an operetta, *Tantivy Towers;* many songs.

DUNSTABLE, John (date of birth unknown, but thought to have been about 1370: died 1453) England. Also a mathematician and astrologer. One of the greatest composers of his time, works including sacred music, motets, and secular songs.

DUPARC, Henri (1848-1933) France. Pupil of César Franck. Sternly self-critical, he destroyed many of his works, his fame resting on sixteen songs, some of them the most beautiful of their era. Among the best-known are: *Chanson Triste, L'Invitation au Voyage, Phidylé, Elégie, Extase, Lamento, Soupir,* and *La Vague et la Cloche.*

DUSSEK, Jan Ladislav (1760, or 1761-1812) Bohemia (Czechoslovakia). Had instruction from C. P. E. Bach. Lived in various parts of Europe, also in London; died in France. Composed concertos, chamber music, and music for stage, also much piano music.

DVORAK, Antonin (1841-1904) Bohemia. Born about forty miles from Prague, the son of an innkeeper-butcher, Dvořák became the most universally recognised of his country's composers; influenced by Smetana. Between 1870 and 1874 he composed three operas, but it was the *Moravian Duets* that attracted the interest of Brahms who arranged for their publication. Brahms, Liszt, Joachim, Richter, and Bülow helped him to become known beyond his own country. He visited London nine times and Cambridge honoured him with the degree of Doctor of Music in 1891. He became professor of composition at the Prague Conservatorium and from 1892 to 1895 was director of the National Conservatorium in New York. After three years there he returned to become director of the Prague Conservatorium.

After discarding early influences of Liszt, Brahms, and Wagner, he developed a vital musical individuality and was recognised as a master of orchestration. He possessed a Schubertian gift for inventing expressive melodies. He withdrew some of his early symphonies, the others of recent years being re-numbered. The following list shows the numbering now accepted, together with the former numbers shown in brackets: No. 1 in C minor; No. 2 in B-flat major; No. 3 in E-flat major; No. 4 in D minor; No. 5 in F major (No. 3); No. 6 in D major (No. 1); No. 7 in D minor (No. 2); No. 8 in G major (No. 4); No. 9 in E minor (No. 5), known as "From the New World."

Among his many works: nine symphonies (as above); orchestral works, including

Slavonic Dances, Slavonic Rhapsodies, Scherzo Capriccio, Symphonic Variations, Serenade in E major, Carnival Overture; cello concerto; piano concerto; violin concerto; operas, including *Armida, Russalka, The Jacobin, Dimitrij; Stabat Mater* for soloists, chorus, and orchestra; chamber music; songs, including *Moravian Duets, Gypsy Songs, Biblical Songs.*

DYSON, George (1883-1964) England. Held such academic positions as director of music at Winchester College, and Royal College of Music, as well as lecturing and writing on musical subjects. His compositions include *The Canterbury Pilgrims* and other choral works, church music and chamber music. He was knighted in 1941.

EAGLES, Moneta (b. 1924) Australia. Graduated from Sydney Conservatorium of Music 1950, after winning scholarships awarded by Sir Eugene Goossens. Pianist and composer, having studied composition with Dr A. Burnard and in London with Matyas Seiber. Works include those for orchestra, choral groups, organ and piano; also songs and many compositions for documentary films. As Musical Director of the Commonwealth Film Unit, she represented Australia at the Edinburgh International Film Festival in 1960.

EGK, Werner (b. 1901) Germany. An imaginative composer, of whom Honegger said: "Egk's music is direct, frequently full of charm. It directly touches the listener." Composed operas, including *Peer Gynt* (after Ibsen), *The Government Inspector* (after Gogol); ballets, *Abraxas, Die Chinesische Nachtigall;* a violin concerto; suites on music by Rameau, Clementi and Kuhlau.

EICHEIM, Henry (1870-1942) America. Composed works in the Oriental idiom, sometimes employing Oriental instruments.

EINEM, Gottfried (von) (b. 1918) Austria. A pupil of Blacher. Began composing career with ballet music. Operas include *Danton's Tod* and *Der Prozess.* Has also written orchestral music, concertos, chamber music, revealing classical allegiance.

EISLER, Hanns (1898-1962) Germany. Pupil of Schoenberg. Lived in U.S.A. 1933-1948, then returned to East Germany. Composed an opera *Goliath*, orchestral, chamber, and film music, then political songs for the "masses."

ELGAR, Edward (1857-1934) England. Almost self-taught in composition, later called the greatest English composer since Purcell. The son of an organist who kept a music shop, he learned to play the organ, piano, violin, and bassoon. In 1882 he visited Leipzig, then returned home to succeed his father as organist at St George's Church, Worcester. In 1889 he married Caroline Alice Roberts. Until then he had composed mostly small pieces, then in 1900 he brought out his oratorio *The Dream of Gerontius.* Retiring to the Malvern Hills he produced many large-scale works, and became recognised in other countries.

In 1902 he was asked to write an ode for the Coronation of King Edward VII and two years later received a knighthood. He was appointed Master of the King's Music in 1924 and seven years later had a baronetcy conferred upon him.

Principal works: two symphonies; orchestral works, including tone-poem *Falstaff, Cockaigne Overture, Froissart Overture, Dream Children, Three Bavarian Dances, The Wand of Youth* suite, *"Enigma" Variations;* music for strings; violin concerto; cello concerto; oratorios, *The Dream of Gerontius, The Apostles, The Kingdom;* cantatas, *The Music Makers, Caractacus, King Olaf; Severn Suite* for brass band; song cycle, *Sea Pictures;* chamber music; songs; small pieces such as *Salut d'Amour. Land of Hope and Glory* is a vocal arrangement of the trio section of No. 1 of the five *Pomp and Circumstance* marches.

ELIZALDE, Federico (b. 1908) Spain. Born in the Philippines; studied with Bloch and Falla. Composed an opera *Paul Gauguin,* concertos.

ENESCO, Georges (1881-1955) Rumania. Violinist, pianist, conductor, and composer. Studied in Paris with Fauré and Massenet. Yehudi Menuhin was one of his pupils. Works include: three symphonies; two *Rumanian Rhapsodies;* piano sonatas; violin and piano pieces.

FALLA, Manuel de (1876-1946). Born in Cadiz, Falla began his musical career as a pianist. Won first prize in open competition for his lyrical opera *La Vida Breve;* spent seven years in Paris, where he enjoyed the friendship of Debussy and Ravel. Returning to Madrid, he produced some of his finest works, in which he aimed to free Spanish music from foreign, particularly French and Italian, influences. While he seldom used folk-tunes, his music has true Spanish colour and feeling.

Principal works: *La vida breve* and *El retable de Maeso Pedro* (operas); *El amor brujo*, and *El sombrero de tres picos* (ballets); *Noches en los jardines de España* (piano and orchestra); harpsichord concerto; *Homage pour le tombeau de Debussy* (guitar solo); seven *Canciones populares Españolas* (voice and piano); other songs, and piano pieces.

FARNABY, Giles (c. 1560-c. 1600) England. Little known of early life. Published madrigals, psalms, and some music for virginals.

FARQUHAR, David. Well known contemporary New Zealand composer. Studied in England at Cambridge with Benjamin Frankel. His First Symphony was first performed in New Zealand in 1960. Under a commission from the Arts Advisory Council composed the score for an opera, *A Unicorn for Christmas*, to a book by Ngaio Marsh.

FAURE, Gabriel (1845-1924) France. Before he was ten, Fauré went to Paris where he studied with Saint-Saëns and others. Held position as chief organist at St Sulpice, St Honoré, and The Madeleine. An excellent teacher, he numbered among his pupils Ravel, Boulanger, Enesco, Ducasse, and Schmitt. A perfectionist, his music is distinguished by impeccable taste and artistic restraint; his songs are among the most beautiful to come out of late-nineteenth century France.

Principal works: *Requiem*; *Ballade* for piano and orchestra; *Elegie* for cello; *Masques et Bergamasque*, and *Dolly* suites; chamber music; incidental music for Maeterlinck's *Pelléas et Mélisande*; *Pavane* for orchestra with optional chorus; two piano quartets and other chamber music; many songs, including *La Bonne Chanson*; *Penelope* (opera) and smaller pieces.

FAURE, Jean-Baptiste (1830-1914) France. A famous singer and minor composer of songs, including *Le Crucifix* and *Les Rameaux*, which are sometimes mistakenly attributed to Gabriel Fauré.

FENBY, Eric (b. 1906) England. Acted as amanuensis to the blind and paralysed Delius, scoring his later works from dictation. Composer of orchestral and other music.

FIBICH, Zdeněk (1850-1900) Czechoslovakia. Wrote more than 600 works in many forms,

but outside his country best known for *Poème*.

FIELD, John (1782-1837) Ireland. Pupil of Clementi in London; settled in Russia in 1803 and died in Moscow. Invented the *Nocturne* for piano, a form adopted by Chopin. Influenced other composers.

FINZI, Gerald (1901-1956) England. Apart from clarinet concerto, wrote mostly for voice, including many fine songs, some of which set to words of Shakespeare and Hardy.

FLOTOW, Friedrich von (1812-1883) Germany. Studied in Paris, where he became firmly associated with French music. Wrote operas in several languages, including *Martha* and *Alessandro Stradella*; also ballets, and chamber music.

FORD, Edgar (b. 1881) England. Settled in Australia from 1941, then holding such honours as D.Mus. Oxon, F.R.C.O., F.T.C.L., and M.R.S.T. His compositions contain a mixture of English Scholasticism, French Impressionism, and European Romantic elements; these include orchestral, choral works, also songs, many performed outside Australia.

FORD, Thomas (c. 1580-1648) England. An important member of the Elizabethan Lutenist and Ayre School, who followed Dowland. Composed airs, anthems, and some instrumental music.

FOSTER, Stephen Collins (1826-1864) America. Even without much musical training, became one of the most widely known song-writers. Because of intemperate habits, lived and died in poverty. His plantation songs have remained in record catalogues up to the present time.

FRANCAIX, Jean (b. 1912) France. A pupil of N. Boulanger and others. Has written in witty Gallic style and with much technical skill. Concertos, operas; ballet, orchestral, and piano music are among his works.

FRANCK, César (1822-1890) Belgium. Though Belgian by birth, he studied in Paris, and spent most of his life there, becoming a naturalised French citizen in 1873. He was a distinguished organist, and as a teacher gathered about him a devoted group which included d'Indy, Chausson, Pierné, Duparc, and Lekeu. Deeply religious, most of his music carries a spiritual yearning. His death was the result of a street accident.

Principal works; religious cantatas, including *The Beatitudes* and *The Redemption;* his one symphony (D minor); *Symphonic Variations* for piano and orchestra; *Psyche, Les Djinns,* and *Le Chasseur Maudit* (symphonic poems); piano quintet, string quartet, sonata for violin and piano, trio for piano, violin and cello; organ, and piano works, and songs.

FRANKEL, Benjamin (b. 1906) England. A versatile musician; pianist, violinist, orchestrator; composer in various styles, including orchestral, chamber, film music.

FRANCOEUR, François (1698-1787) France. A Parisian violinist in the King's band, composer of operas, ballets, instrumental works.

FRANZ, Robert, pen-name of Robert Franz Knauth (1815-1892). German composer, chiefly of songs which total more than 250.

FRESCOBALDI, Girolamo (1583-1643 or 1644) Italy. Called the first great virtuoso organist, he held positions in Italy and Antwerp, returning to become organist at St Peter's, Rome, where his first performance attracted an audience of 30,000 people. Wrote outstanding works for organ; also motets and madrigals, and pieces for harpsichord.

FRICKER, Peter Racine (b. 1920) England. Studied with Matyas Seiber. Has held teaching positions in London and Santa Barbara, California. In his compositions has at times used the twelve-note technique. Symphonies, concertos, chamber music, and piano pieces have been part of his creative output.

FUX, Johann Joseph (1660-1741) Austria. His compositions comprise operas and church music. His treatise *Gradus ad Parnassum,* formulating rules of counterpoint influenced many composers for a long time.

GABRIELI, Andrea (c. 1510-1586) Italy. Chief organist at St Mark's, Venice. Works include madrigals, motets, organ works.

GABRIELI, Giovanni (1557-1612) Italy. Nephew and pupil of Andrea Gabrieli whom he succeeded as organist at St Mark's, Venice. The teacher of Schütz. Adopted an emerging science of orchestration; wrote for brass choirs, organ; sacred music.

GADE, Niels (1817-1890) Denmark. Studied in Leipzig and became close friend of Mendelssohn and Schumann. Composed eight symphonies, choral music and orchestral music

which, popular in the nineteenth century, has long since fallen out of favour.

GALUPPI, Baldassare (c. 1706-1785) Italy. His many operas were popular in Italy and England, but today he is remembered by some instrumental pieces.

GARDINER, Henry Balfour (1877-1950) England. Composed operatic, choral, orchestral, and military band music. His *Shepherd Fennel's Dance* once enjoyed much popularity.

GEMINIANI, Francesco (1667-1762) Italy. A foremost representative of the Corelli school of violin playing. Died in Dublin. Composed music for violin, and for orchestra.

GERMAN, Edward, actual name Edward German Jones (1862-1936) England. Best known for his light operas, e.g., *Merrie England* and *Tom Jones.* Composed also two symphonies, *Welsh Rhapsody* for orchestra; *Nell Gwynn* and *Henry VIII* dances. Completed Sullivan's *The Emerald Isle.*

GERSHWIN, George (1898-1937) America. As a pianist, he began his career as a "song-plugger." At the age of twenty wrote the song *Swanee* which became a hit. In 1924 his *Rhapsody in Blue* brought him world fame. (This had been orchestrated by Ferde Grofé.) Studied orchestration. Wrote many successful musical shows. In 1931 *Of Thee I Sing* won for him a Pulitzer Prize. Most ambitious work *Porgy and Bess* first produced 1935. Died from a brain tumour, following an operation.

GETHEN, Felix (b. 1916) England. Lived in Australia since 1932, as member of staff of Australian Broadcasting Commission, lecturer, and composer. Works include orchestral, choral, and chamber music, some of which have been performed outside Australia.

GHEDINI, Giorgio Federico (1892-1965) Italy. Operas include *The Golden Flea, The Happy Hypocrite,* and *Billy Budd.* Also composed concertos, orchestral and church music.

GIBBONS, Orlando (1583-1625) England. Most famous of a family of musicians. Entered choir of King's College, Cambridge, at age of twelve; organist at Chapel Royal at twenty-one; organist at Westminster Abbey at forty. Wrote church music, secular vocal music, instrumental and chamber works.

GIORDANI, Giuseppe (c. 1744-1798) Italy. Composed operas, church and instrumental music, also the well-known song, *Caro mio ben.*

GIORDANO, Umberto (1867-1948) Italy.

Composer of operas, notably *André Chénier* and *Fedora*.

GIULIANI, Mauro (1780-c.1833) Italy. The foremost guitarist of his time. Settled in Vienna where he became acquainted with Haydn, Schubert, Hummel and others. Compositions for guitar total more than 300, some with full orchestra.

GLASS, Dudley (b.1899) Australia. Has spent most of his life in England. Works include light operas, songs. Also author, lecturer and music critic.

GLAZUNOV, Alexander (1865-1936) Russia. A pupil of Rimsky-Korsakov, he remained a conservative. Director St Petersburg (later Leningrad) Conservatoire. In 1928 went to Paris where he died. Works include: eight symphonies (his ninth remaining unfinished); ballets, including *The Seasons, Raymonda, Les ruses d'amour;* concertos for violin, and for piano; *Stenka Razin* (symphonic poem); songs, piano pieces.

GLIERE, Reinhold Moritzovich (1874-1956) Russia. Studied with Arensky, Taneiev, and Ippolitov-Ivanov; taught at Moscow Conservatoire. Today best known for *The Red Poppy* (ballet) and *Concerto for Soprano and Orchestra*. Also wrote operas, orchestral and chamber music, and songs.

GLINKA, Michail (1804-1857) Russia. The first Russian composer whose music earned recognition outside his country. Early in life took piano lessons from the Irish-born John Field. In 1856 went to Berlin where he became ill and died. He exerted a powerful influence on other Russian composers. Among his best known works: operas, *Russlan and Ludmilla* and *A Life for a Tsar;* orchestral music, *String Quartet in F;* piano pieces and songs.

GLUCK, Christoph Willibald (1714-1787) Germany. Spent some years in London and Paris and settled in Vienna where he died. A reformer of opera, stressed the theory that music, poetry, and dramatic action should combine to give opera reality. He composed more than forty-five stage works, his fame today resting on *Orfeo ed Euridice, Alceste, Iphigénie en Aulide, Iphigénie en Tauride,* and *Armide.*

GOEHR, Alexander (b.1932) England. A son of German-born conductor, Walter Goehr, studied in Paris with Messiaen. His music follows no "school." Works include: *The Deluge* and *Sutter's Gold* (cantatas), a symphony, violin concerto; *Arden Must Die* (opera), and *A Little Cantata of Proverbs,* after Blake. *La Belle Dame Sans Merci* (ballet).

GOLDMARK, Carl (1830-1915) Hungary. The son of a cantor in a Jewish synagogue, went to Vienna at fourteen and died there after a fruitful life as composer, teacher and critic. Best known works: *Rustic Wedding Symphony; The Queen of Sheba, The Winter's Tale, The Cricket on the Hearth* (operas), *Sakuntale Overture;* two violin concertos; chamber music; piano works, and songs.

GOLDMARK, Rubin (1872-1936) America. Nephew of Carl; pupil of Dvořák, and teacher of Gershwin. Composed orchestral, chamber, and piano music.

GOOSSENS, Eugene (1893-1962) England. Son and grandson of musicians. Conducted orchestras at Covent Garden, Rochester, Cincinnati; in 1947 appointed conductor Sydney Symphony Orchestra and Director New South Wales Conservatorium. Knighted 1955, returned to London 1956, died there. His compositions include: *Judith* and *Don Juan de Manara* (operas); *Apocalypse* (cantata); two symphonies; chamber music; piano pieces. Brother of Leon, Sidonie and Marie Goossens.

GOSSEC, François Joseph (1734-1829) Belgium. From 1751 lived in France, where he died. Furthered the symphony in France; wrote also operas and ballets; chamber music and small pieces of charm.

GOUNOD, Charles François (1818-1893) France. Studied at Paris Conservatoire; visited other countries, and in 1846 began two years' study in theology, intending to become a priest. An organist in Paris, also teacher and conductor, he became a force in French opera. Spent the years 1870 to 1875 in London, where he formed the Royal Choral Society.

Principal works: fourteen operas, *Faust* (1859) his most famous, also *Roméo et Juliette, Mireille;* nine masses; three symphonies; incidental music to plays; oratorio, *The Redemption.*

GRAINER, Ron (b.1926) Australia. Studied at Sydney. After spending much of his career in England moved to Portugal. Has written stage-musicals, music for films, and themes for successful TV shows.

GRAINGER, Percy Aldridge (christened George Percy) (1882-1961) Australia. Studied in Germany with Busoni; toured as pianist; ultimately became a naturalised citizen of the U.S.A. Friend of Grieg and Delius. Edited much folk-song material, and re-created many tunes of the British Isles. Composed choral works, many short orchestral pieces (e.g., *Country Gardens, Molly on the Shore, Shepherd's Hey*) which became immensely popular. Buried in Adelaide, Australia.

GRANADOS, Enrique (1867-1916) Spain. Important in efforts towards "nationalist" Spanish music. Drowned when the ship, *Sussex*, on which he was returning from New York, was torpedoed by a German submarine. Among his best known works: opera *Goyescas* (based on piano works of same name); chamber music; piano pieces; songs of considerable appeal.

GRE(T)CHANINOV, Alexander (1864-1956) Russia. A pupil of Rimsky-Korsakov, lived in France and in the U.S.A., wrote in a conservative style. Although his operas and symphonies were once popular, he is now best remembered for his songs.

GRETRY, André (1741-1813) Belgium. Settled in France in 1767, where he died. An important *Opéra-Comique* composer; wrote also orchestral music.

GRIEG, Edvard Hagerup (1843-1907) Norway. The most representative of Norwegian composers of the nineteenth century, Grieg was born at Bergen, studied in Leipzig and Copenhagen, and in 1867 settled in Christiania as teacher and conductor. In that year he married the singer, Nina Hagerup, who made many of his songs better known. Apart from visits to Italy, Germany, and England, he lived a secluded life near Bergen. He was essentially a miniaturist, helped to develop a national style, and influenced many other composers, including Delius.

Principal works: *Piano Concerto in A minor;* incidental music for *Peer Gynt, Sigurd Jorsalfar; Holberg Suite; Norwegian Dances* for orchestra; three sonatas for violin and piano; about 140 songs; many piano pieces.

GRIFFES, Charles Tomlinson (1884-1920) America. Studied with Humperdinck in Germany, influenced by French impressionism, and promised much for American music,

but died in poverty. Composed orchestral and piano music, and songs.

GRUENBERG, Louis (1884-1964) American composer of Russian birth. Pupil of Busoni in Vienna. Influenced by Negro music and jazz, composed *Emperor Jones*, after Eugene O'Neill, and other operas; *Daniel Jazz* and *Jazzberries* for piano; symphonic poems, and a violin concerto.

GUIDO D'AREZZO (c.990-c.1050) Italy. A monk who took the name of the town in which he lived. A famous teacher and innovator in musical theory and practice; said to have invented the musical staff.

GUILMANT, Felix Alexandre (1837-1911) France. A famous organist in Paris, he wrote numerous works for that instrument.

GUNG'L, Joseph (1810-1899) Hungary. Lived in Austria. Composed about 300 dances and marches.

GURNEY, Ivor (1890-1937) England. Composer of songs, many to his own poems, also orchestral and piano music.

GYROWETZ, Adalbert (1763-1850) Bohemia. A prolific composer, works including thirty operas, forty ballets, sixty symphonies, as well as masses, cantatas, songs. Died in Vienna.

HABA, Alois (1893-1974) Czechoslovakia. Studied at Prague Conservatory with Novák, then with Schreker in Vienna and Berlin. Adopted a musical expression based on East Moravian folk music, using quarter-tones and sixth-tones. Operas, orchestral and chamber music, piano solos are some of his works.

HAHN, Reynaldo (1875-1947) Born in Venezuela, but taken to Paris while a child. Massenet was one of his teachers. Wrote operas, operettas, orchestral and chamber music, but is now best known for his songs.

HALEVY, Jacques François (original surname Lévy) (1799-1862) France. A pupil of Cherubini at Paris Conservatoire, he also studied in Italy. He composed more than thirty operas, *La Juive* being the most famous. His daughter married his former pupil Bizet in 1869. A man of many interests, it was said that he could converse on a variety of subjects from morning till night without once mentioning music.

HALVORSEN, Johan August (1864-1935) Norway. Studied in Germany and Belgium. A noted violinist and conductor, he composed two symphonies, a violin concerto, stage music, and smaller works, some influenced by Grieg.

HAMILTON, Iain (b. 1922) Scotland. Works, which include symphonies, concertos, and a cantata *The Bermudas*, lean towards an involved style.

HANDEL, George Frederick (1685-1759) Germany. Born in Saxony, his name was Georg Friedrich Haendel, or Händel, but on being naturalised in England he adopted the English spelling. In face of parental discouragement, became proficient on the harpsichord and the organ; at twelve appointed organist in Halle, and six years later went to Hamburg as violinist in the opera house orchestra. His first opera, *Rinaldo*, was performed in Hamburg in 1705 and in the following year he went to Italy, where he composed several operas and oratorios, as well as instrumental music. First visited England in 1710. His first London opera, *Rinaldo*, was so successful that he decided to live in England, rather than in Hanover, where he had been *Kapellmeister* to the Elector.

In 1713 Queen Anne appointed him court musician. Despite his unrivalled reputation in England, he later reached a stage of near-bankruptcy after losing heavily on elaborate staging of his operas in London. Then, in 1741 his oratorio, *Messiah* (written within twenty-four days and first performed in Dublin) helped to turn poverty into riches. On his death he left a large fortune. About the middle of the eighteenth century he became partially blind and by 1753 was totally without sight. He died in London and was buried in Westminster Abbey. In addition to numerous other compositions, he wrote forty operas and seventeen oratorios.

Principal works: *Messiah, Saul, Judas Maccabaeus, Solomon, Samson, Belshazzar, Israel in Egypt, Joseph, Joshua, Jephitha* (oratorios); *Almira, Rinaldo, Berenice, Julius Caesar, Orlando, Xerxes, Alcino, Ariadne, Atalanta, Ezio, Ottone, Il Pastor Fido, Radamisto, Rodelinda, Rodrigo, Semele, Tolomeo* (operas); *Acis and Galatea*, and other masques; *Alexander's Feast* and other cantatas; anthems; eighteen còncerti grossi; many concertos for organ and other instruments; sonatas; orchestral works, including *Water Music* and *Fireworks Music*; harpsichord pieces.

HANSON, Howard (b. 1896) America. Studied in Rome; director of Eastman School of Music, Rochester. Works include six symphonies, piano concerto, opera, chamber music, songs.

HANSON, Raymond (Charles) (1913-1977) Australia. In 1948 became senior lecturer at the New South Wales Conservatorium in piano, composition, and aural training. Has composed more than a hundred works, including symphonies, concertos, sonatas, choral music; an oratorio, *The Immortal Hour;* operas, *The Golden Ring* and *The Lost Child;* chamber music; piano music.

HARRIS, Roy Ellsworth (b. 1898) America. Studied with Nadia Boulanger in Paris. Has held teaching positions. Works, leaning towards modern trends, but disciplined, include twelve symphonies, concertos, orchestral and chamber music.

HARRISON, Julius (1885-1963) England. Studied with Bantock. Works include orchestral music, a mass, many piano pieces and songs.

HART, Fritz Bennicke (1874-1949) England. Arrived in Australia in 1909, became director of Melbourne Conservatorium, and in 1931 took over the symphony orchestra in Honolulu. Works include operas, including *Land of Heart's Desire, Riders to the Sea, Deirdre of the Sorrows, Ruth, Pierrette;* orchestral, choral and piano music. Died in Honolulu.

HARTMANN, Karl Amadeus (1905-1963) Germany. A pupil of Webern, and cultivating an atonal style, he became one of the most important German composers of his generation. Wrote eight symphonies; an opera, *Simplicius Simplicimus*, two string quartets, and other works.

HARTY, Hamilton (1879-1941) Ireland. Pianist, conductor, and composer. Among his works: *Irish Symphony;* cantata, *The Mystic Trumpeter;* violin concerto; works for piano, and for cello. Arranged suites from Handel's *Water Music* and *Fireworks Music*. Knighted 1925.

HAYDN (Franz), Joseph (1732-1809) Austria. Son of Matthias Haydn, a wheelwright. At age of eight joined the choir of St Stephen Church in Vienna. Held several appointments, the most important that of *Kappell-meister* to Prince Nicholas Esterhazy, at Eisenstadt, from 1761 to 1790, then returned to Vienna. He fell in love with a daughter of a wig-maker named Keller. When she entered a convent he married the other daughter, who turned out to be something of a virago, and unappreciative of his great gifts.

He later became the idol of London which he visited in 1791 and 1794. On the latter occasion J. P. Salomon, an impresario, offered him £300 for six new symphonies, in addition to generous royalties. This led to his writing the twelve "London" Symphonies.

Haydn established a new concept of both the symphony and the string quartet, giving those forms a new unity and dignity, thus paving the way for Mozart.

Principal works: 104 symphonies; 84 string quartets; 125 other chamber works; oratorios, notably *The Creation* and *The Seasons;* early operas; concertos; sonatas; keyboard pieces; songs.

HEAD, Michael (1900-1976) England. A singer, pianist and composer. Best known for his songs.

HELLER, Stephen (1814-1888) Hungary. Studied in Vienna, and became a notable pianist. Compositions, mainly in a conventional, romantic style, consist chiefly of piano works.

HENZE, Hans Werner (b. 1926) Germany. Lived for some years in Italy. Highly talented composer whose works include operas *Boulevard Solitude, King Stag, The Prince of Homburg, The Bassarids; Ondine* and other ballets; an oratorio: *The Raft of the Frigate 'Medusa'*, and symphonies.

HERBERT, Victor (1859-1924) Ireland. Lived in New York from 1886. Successful cellist. Wrote operas and orchestral works, a cello concerto, but became best known for such successful operettas as *Naughty Marietta, Babes in Toyland*, and *Sweethearts*.

HEROLD, Louis (1791-1833) France. A leading figure in the *opéra-comique* style, now best-remembered for his *Zampa*.

HERRMANN, Bernard (1911-1976) America. Conductor of Columbia Broadcast Symphony Orchestra from 1940 to 1955, also other orchestras. Composer of opera *Wuthering Heights*; cantata *Moby Dick*; a string quartet; music for *Citizen Kane, Psycho, Fahrenheit 451*, and other films.

HESELTINE, Philip — see under WARLOCK.

HILL, Alfred (1870-1960) Australia. Lived in New Zealand at early age; studied in Leipzig for five years, and in early 1900s became one of the foundation members of New South Wales Conservatorium teaching staff and deputy conductor to its first director, Henri Verbrugghen. Visited the United States. A prolific composer, he wrote in many forms; operas, symphonies, chamber music, songs, some of his works influenced by Maori legends.

HILLER, Ferdinand (1811-1885) Germany. Studied with Hummel in Weimar; lived in Paris 1828-1835. Published operas, oratorios, orchestral and chamber music, and many pieces for piano.

HINDEMITH, Paul (1895-1963) Germany. A prominent viola player, became one of the most important composers of his time, influencing many others. Although he was not of Jewish origin, his music was banned in Germany as "degenerate." In 1940 moved to the United States; in 1953 settled in Switzerland, and died in Frankfurt.

Hindemith adopted the creed of *Gebrauchsmusik* ("utility music"), meant for social and educational purposes, also wrote works of advanced and intricate structure.

Principal works: operas, including *Mathis der Maler*, which he also arranged as a symphony, *Nobilissima Visione* and other ballets; oratorio *The Unending; Cardillac* (a musical psychodrama); orchestral works; *The Four Temperaments* for piano and strings; *Ludus Tonalis* for piano; chamber music; sonatas; piano works; songs; educational works; music for military band.

HODDINOTT, Alun (b. 1929) Wales. Choral works include *Job, Rebecca, Dives and Lazarus, Danegeld*. Has also written symphonies, concertos, chamber music.

HOLBROOKE, Joseph (sometimes Josef) 1878-1958) England. A prolific composer, wrote an operatic trilogy *The Cauldron of Anwyn*, and other stage works; symphonic poems; chamber music. Also conductor, pianist, and writer.

HOLLAND, Dulcie (b. 1913) Australia. Studied at Sydney Conservatorium with Frank Hutchens and Alfred Hill, and at Royal College of Music, London with John Ireland. Won Cobbett Prize for a chamber music work, also gained diplomas of D.S.C.M. and L.R.S.M. Has composed works for orchestra, chamber groups, choirs, solo instruments, many songs; scores for more than forty

Australian documentary films. Married to Alan Bellhouse, conductor and author of books on music.

HOLST, Gustav (1874-1934) England. A descendant of a Swedish family. A pupil of Stanford; held several academic appointments. In 1923 a fall from a platform at Reading resulted in a slight concussion that later caused physical discomfort when setting down his ideas on paper. Of an original mind, he successfully combined orchestral and vocal effects. Became interested in Hindu epics and, attracted by the hymns of the Rig Veda, he studied Sanscrit to enable him to make his own translations.

Principal works: *The Planets*, *A Somerset Rhapsody*, *Japanese Suite*, *Fugal Overture*, *Egdon Heath*, *Beni Mora* (all for orchestra); operas, including *The Perfect Fool*, *Savitri*, *At the Boar's Head*, *The Tale of the Wandering Scholar*; a double concerto for two violins and orchestra; choral works, including *The Hymn of Jesus*, *Choral Hymns from the Rig Veda*; suites for military bands; songs.

HOLST, Imogen (b. 1907) England. Daughter of Gustav Holst. Conductor, educationist and composer. Has composed an overture, songs, folk-song arrangements, including *Twenty Traditional British Folk Songs*.

HONEGGER, Arthur (1892-1955) France. Of Swiss parentage, he studied at the Paris Conservatoire with Widor and d'Indy, and lived most of his life in France. He became a member of *Le Groupe des Six* ("The Six"), which comprised Auric, Durey, Honegger, Milhaud, Poulenc, and Tailleferre. He composed in many forms, his music a blend of French and German qualities, romanticism and modern, and dissonant tendencies.

Principal works: five symphonies; stage works, including *Judith*, *Antigone*; *Le Roi David* (oratorio, or symphonic psalm); *Joan of Arc at the Stake*, for speakers, solo singers, chorus, and orchestra; *Christmas Cantata*; orchestral pieces, including *Pacific 231* and *Rugby*; film music, and piano pieces.

HOPKINS, Anthony (b. 1921) England. Works, mostly of light character, include operas *Lady Rohesia*, *The Man from Tuscany*, *Three's Company*; ballet and film music; music for voices and orchestra. Also pianist and witty speaker and broadcaster.

HOWELLS, Herbert (1892) England. Has composed choral music to religious texts; orchestral, chamber, and band music, and piano pieces. Some works show folk-song and Elizabethan influences.

HUGHES, Robert (b. 1912) Scotland. Lived in Australia from 1930. Works include orchestral; ballet music, some of which commissioned by English orchestras. Also editor and arranger.

HUMFREY, Pelham (name also spelt Humphrey and Humphrys) (1647-1674) England. Studied in France under Lully. Composed many fine anthems, church music, and songs.

HUMMEL, Johann Nepomuk (1778-1837) Germany. Son of Johann Julius. Pupil of Haydn and Mozart; teacher of Czerny and others. Compositions, which number more than 150, include concertos, church music, and many works for piano.

HUMPERDINCK, Engelbert (1854-1921) Germany. Was assistant to Wagner at Bayreuth. Famous now for his opera *Hansel and Gretel*; wrote others, also orchestral and choral music.

HURLSTONE, William Yeates (1876-1906) England. Enjoyed high reputation as pianist and composer, but died at age of twenty-nine. Works include orchestral, chamber, and piano music.

HUSA, Karel (b. 1921) Czechoslovakia. A pupil of Honegger and Nadia Boulanger, lived in Paris and later in the United States of America. Composed orchestral and chamber music.

HYDE, Miriam (b. 1913) Australia. Studied in Adelaide; later in London with Howard Hadley, Arthur Benjamin, R. O. Morris, and Gordon Jacob. Prominent as teacher, lecturer and examiner. Performed own works under several eminent conductors. Compositions written in several forms.

IBERT, Jacques (1890-1962) France. A skilful and often witty composer, essentially a miniaturist, although he did write operas. His music includes an orchestral suite, *Escales*, and *Divertissement*, both for orchestra; *Histoires* for piano, which includes the popular *Le Petit ane blanc*; music for the film *Don Quichotte*; *Concertino* for alto saxophone and other instruments.

INDY, Vincent d' (1851-1931) France. Christened Paul Marie Theodore Vincent, began career as pianist. Became a pupil and devoted disciple of César Franck. Strove to bring more dignity to French music and become one of the founders of *La Société Nationale*. His music, which combines skilful craftsmanship and sincerity, includes *Symphony on a French Mountain Air; Fervaal* and other operas; *Istra* (orchestral variations) a triple concerto; chamber music; piano works; songs.

IPPOLITOV-IVANOV, Mikhail (1859-1935) Russia. A pupil of Rimsky-Korsakov. An authority on Caucasian folk-music. Works include two symphonies; six operas; orchestral music, including *Caucasian Sketches;* vocal works with orchestra; chamber music; songs.

IRELAND, John (1879-1962) England. Pianist, organist, and composer, some of his works influenced by places, e.g., *Mai-Dun, The Forgotten Rite.* Other orchestral works include *A London Overture;* also wrote a cantata *These Things Shall Be;* a piano concerto; many piano pieces, and songs, and chamber music.

IVES, Charles (1874-1954) America. One of the most interesting, if unconventional, figures in American music of his time. In his youth he entered the Music Department at Yale, and there puzzled his teacher, Horatio Parker, by composing music of "eccentric" harmonic textures, basing it on a system of writing for two or more keys to be played simultaneously, and refusing to resolve his dissonances. Experimenting with tone and rhythmic complexities and abstract patterns, he anticipated Schoenberg and such composers in the use of polytonality and quarter-tones.

Naturally Ives' music brought him little financial gain. He therefore entered the business world as an insurance broker and in time became wealthy. Music had become a spare-time occupation, and he had reached the age of fifty-six before he withdrew from commercial life.

Most of Ive's music was composed before 1920; it was more than twenty years later that America realised his musical importance.

His works include five symphonies; *Three Places in New England*, for orchestra; piano music and songs.

JACOBS, Gordon (b. 1895) England. Pupil of Stanford. Works, mostly in conservative style, including symphonies, choral, ballet and chamber music. C.B.E., 1968.

JAMES, William G. (1892-1977) Australia. Toured as accompanist to several eminent singers. Pupil of Arthur de Greef in London. For some years Director of Music for the Australian Broadcasting Commission. Works include *The Golden Girl* (musical fantasy); ballet music; *Six Australian Bush Songs, Australian Christmas Carols*; orchestral suites; piano music.

JANACEK, Leoš (1854-1928) Czechoslovakia. Reduced Czech folk-songs to "speech rhythms." A composer of independent mind, his music waited for full recognition. Wrote eleven operas, including *From the House of the Dead, The Makropoulos Affair, Jenůfa, The Cunning Little Vixen;* choral, orchestral, and piano music; songs.

JARNEFELT, Armas (1869-1958) Finland, but became naturalised Swedish citizen in 1910. His sister married Sibelius. Works include choral and orchestral music, and songs of traditional melodic character.

JENSEN, Adolf (1837-1879) Germany. Became famous in his time for his many songs. Also composed choral, and piano music.

JOLIVET, André (1905-1974) France. Between 1920 and 1924 studied literature and art, then turned to music, and became a pupil of Varèse. In 1936, with Messiaen, Daniel-Lesur and Baudrier, founded the group *Jeune France*. Held important positions. In 1964 received an award for the living French composer most frequently performed in France. Works include orchestral; concertos; a comic opera *Dolores*; a ballet *Guignol et Pandore*.

JONES, Daniel (b. 1912) Wales. Composed symphonies, operas, choral music, chamber music.

JONGEN, Joseph (1873-1953) Belgium. One time Director of Brussels Conservatoire. Composed concertos, suites, chamber works, etc.

JONGEN, Léon (1885-1969) Belgium. Brother of Joseph Jongen. Succeeded brother as Director of Brussels Conservatoire in 1939. Works include symphonies, suites, concertos, piano pieces.

JOSQUIN DES PRES—Also known as Després (c. 1445-1521). A Flemish composer of great historical importance. A singer in the Papal

Chapel, Rome, 1486-1494. Composed much church music and secular songs.

JOUBERT, John (b. 1927) South Africa. Studied in London; appointed teacher at University College, Hull, 1950. Works include: choral music (*The Holy Mountain, Urbs Beata, Te Deum, Leaves of Life, Pro Pace*); operas (*Silas Marner* and *Antigone*); symphonies; a string quartet and other chamber works; orchestral pieces.

KABALEVSKY, Dmitri (b. 1904) Russia. Studied composition with Miaskovsky. His lyrical style owes something to Tchaikovsky, and to Soviet requirements. His operas include *The Taras Family, The Master of Clemency, Nikita Vershinin;* his choral works, the cantata *The Avengers;* his other works, symphonies, concertos, and songs.

KALINNIKOV, Vasily Sergeyevich (1866-1901) Russia. Wrote two symphonies, music for stage, and songs in an uncomplicated style.

KALKBRENNER, Friedrich Wilhelm Michael (b. 1785 or 1786; d. 1849) Germany. Lived in London and Paris, became famous as a pianist, and composed much music for piano, including three concertos.

KARG-ELERT, Sigfrid—real name Karg (1877-1933) Germany. Pianist, organist, composer. Best known for his organ works, although he wrote orchestral and chamber music, and songs.

KARLOWICZ, Mierczylaw (1876-1909) Poland. Studied conducting with Nikisch in Leipzig. Important composer, mostly of symphonic music; also a violin concerto and songs.

KHATCHATURIAN, Aram (1903-1978) Armenia. Studied with Gnessin and Miaskovsky and became one of the best known of Soviet composers. His works, sometimes influenced by Armenian folk idiom, include symphonies, concertos; ballets, *Gayaneh* (which includes the *Sabre Dance*) and *Spartacus; Masquerade* (incidental music), and smaller works.

KHRENNIKOV, Tikhon (b. 1913) Russia. A pupil of Shebalin, has written symphonies, piano concertos, and operas, including *Into the Storm, Frol Skobeyev,* and *The Mother.*

KILPINEN, Yrjö (1892-1959) Finland. This composer's reputation rests chiefly on his songs, although he has written piano music.

KODALY, Zoltán (1882-1967) Hungary. In 1900 Kodály entered the Budapest University for scientific training, but during the same period studied music, and in time became a national figure in Hungarian music. Joined with Bartók in collecting 4,000 Hungarian folk-songs. In 1910 he married Emma Sandor, also a composer. He was a man of great intellectual breadth and unaffected simplicity.

Principal works: *Háry János,* an opera from which he arranged an orchestral suite; orchestral works, including *Concerto for Orchestra, Dances of Galanta, Dances of Marosszek, The Peacock, Summer Evening; Psalmus Hungaricus* (for tenor, chorus and orchestra); choral works, including *Missa Brevis* and *Jesus and the Merchants;* string quartets; piano compositions; songs.

KORNGOLD, Eric(h) (1897-1957) Czechoslovakia. Naturalised American citizen from 1943. When only eleven years old, wrote a pantomime which was performed at the Hofoper in Vienna. Later composed operettas and operas, the most successful being *Die Tote Stadt;* also concertos and film music for Hollywood.

KOVEN, Reginald de (1859-1920) America. Composed stage works, including the operetta *Robin Hood;* ballet, and piano music; many songs, including *Oh, Promise Me,* which became very popular.

KREISLER, Fritz (1875-1962) Austria. Although one of the most famous violinists of his time, composed *Apple Blossoms* and *Sissy* (operettas); a string quartet; many violin solos; also "arranged" violin pieces by early composers, which later were found to be his own invention.

KRENEK, Ernest (b. 1900) Austria. Has lived in the United States since 1938. He won widespread fame for his jazz-inspired opera, *Jonny Spielt Auf.* Since then he has come to grips with "twelve-note" technique and other forms of expression, including electronic music.

KREUTZER, Rudolphe (1766-1831) France. Famous violinist, to whom Beethoven dedicated his *A major Sonata* (Op. 47). His compositions include thirty-nine operas and ballets, nineteen violin concertos; also a famous book of studies for violinists.

LALO (Victor Antoine) Edouard (1823-1892) France. Of Spanish descent, Lalo is remembered today for his opera, *Le Roi d'Ys,*

Symphonie Espagnole for violin and orchestra. Other works include ballet music, chamber music, and songs.

LAMBERT, Constant (1905-1951) England. Compositions include *The Rio Grande* for chorus, piano and orchestra, and influenced by jazz; ballets, e.g., *Horoscope*, *Pomona*; choral and film music, and songs. Successful as conductor and writer on music.

LANDINI (or Landino), Francesco (c. 1325-1397) Italy. As a child lost sight of both eyes from smallpox. Became a successful lutenist, organist, and composer of vocal music.

LANNER, Joseph (Franz Karl) (1801-1843) Austria. As violinist and composer of more than 200 waltzes, as well as other light music, enjoyed in his time a reputation equal to that of Johann Strauss the elder.

LASSUS, Orlande de—also known as Orlando di Lasso and Orlandus Lassus (c. 1530-1594) Belgium. Considered one of the greatest composers of the sixteenth century. His works for voice are said to number more than 2,000, written to Italian, French, Latin, and German texts.

LECLAIR, Jean-Marie (1697-1764) France. One of the greatest French violinists of his time. He was murdered near his home in Paris. Composed operas and ballets, but today he is known almost solely by his works for violin.

LECOCQ, Alexandre Charles (1832-1918) France. Composed many operettas that delighted the Parisians of his time, one to survive being *La Fille de Madame Angot*. His attempt at a more serious type of stage-work (*Plutus*) failed.

Le GALLIENNE, Dorian (1915-1963) Australia. Studied at Melbourne and London. Became music critic in Melbourne and wrote various musical works in accepted European forms, including orchestral, chamber, and vocal.

LEHAR, Franz (1870-1948) Hungary. A composer of immensely popular Viennese operettas, these including *The Merry Widow*, *The Count of Luxembourg*, *The Land of Smiles*.

LEHMANN, Liza (1862-1918) England. An English soprano and composer, best-known for her song-cycle *In a Persian Garden* (words from Fitzgerald's translation of Omar Khayyam), and ballads.

LEKEU, Guillaume (1870-1894) Belgium. A pupil of Franck and d'Indy, his early death ended a brilliant career. Compositions include a quartet for piano and strings, sonatas for violin and for cello; some orchestral music.

LEONCAVALLO, Ruggiero (1858-1919) Italy. Encouraged by Wagner, composed several operas, one being *La Bohème* which failed to stand up against the popularity of Puccini's version produced during the previous year. Fame rests on his one-act opera *I Pagliacci*, its first performance conducted by Toscanini in 1892.

LIADOV, Anatol (1855-1914) Russia. Pupil of Rimsky-Korsakov; collector of folk-songs; composer of symphonic poems, *The Enchanted Lake*, *Kikimora*, and *Baba Yaga*; also smaller works.

LIAPUNOV, Sergei (1859-1924) Russia. Pianist and composer in "nationalist" style. Works include two piano concertos; piano solos.

LIDHOLM, Ingar (b. 1921) Sweden. Pupil of Sieber. Wrote *Concerto for String Orchestra*, chamber music, piano music, his later works employing twelve-note method.

LIEBERMANN, Rolf (b. 1910) Switzerland. Works include operas, *Penelope*, *Leonora 40/45*, and *School for Wives*; concertos, and smaller works.

LIGETI, György (b. 1923) Hungary. In 1956 moved to Vienna. His compositions are frequently cast in an *avant garde* mould. Also teacher and author.

LILBURN, Douglas (b. 1915) One of New Zealand's best composers, studied with Vaughan Williams in England. Works include: symphonies, *Festival Overture, Diversions for String Orchestra*, and other orchestral compositions; chamber music and songs.

LINGER, Carl (1810-1862) Germany. Arrived South Australia 1849, settling in Adelaide where he taught, conducted orchestras and choirs. In 1859 won first prize with "Song of Australia" in national song contest. Married twice. Composed operas, masses, motets, orchestral works. Conducted first South Australian performance of *Messiah*. Died in Adelaide.

LISZT, Franz (1811-1886) Hungary. The greatest pianist the world had known and one of the most colourful musicians of the nineteenth century. His romantic alliance with the Countess d'Agoult lasted from 1833 to 1844, one of their children, Cosima, becoming Wagner's wife; from 1848 to 1861 he lived with the Princess Sayn-Wittgenstein. His virtuoso career ended in 1847; devoted the rest of his life to composition and to encouragement of young musicians, including Brahms, Schumann, Chopin, and Wagner. In 1865 took minor orders in the church and became known as Abbé Liszt. He died at Bayreuth.

A prolific composer of some 1300 original works and arrangements, his music reflects the lustre of gold and the false glitter of brass.

Principal works: numerous piano works, including *Sonata in B minor*, twelve *Etudes d'Execution Transcendante*, six *Paganini Etudes*, twenty *Hungarian Rhapsodies*, four *Mephisto* Waltzes, three *Liebestraum* (piano arrangements of songs), *Dante Sonata;* transcriptions of works by other composers; orchestral works, including such symphonic poems as *Mazeppa, Les Préludes*, and *Orpheus; Faust Symphony;* two piano concertos; choral music, including *Grand Mass* and *Via Crucis;* more than seventy songs.

LITOLFF, Henry Charles (1818-1891) England. As a child studied piano with Moscheles; lived in Paris; became music publisher and composer. Wrote more than a hundred works, but now known almost solely by his *Scherzo* from his fourth *Concerto Symphonique*.

LOCATELLI, Pietro (1693-1764) Italy. Violin pupil of Corelli; travelled widely, settling in Amsterdam. Helped in developing sonata form; composed chamber and violin works, also orchestral music of concerto grosso type.

LOCKE, Matthew (1630-1677) England. Works include operas, masques, church music, songs, and pieces for viol.

LOEFFLER, Charles Martin (1861-1935). An Alsatian-born violinist-composer who settled in the United States in 1881. His Russian-inspired *Memories of my Childhood* for orchestra won him a prize of $1000. Other works *A Pagan Poem* (orchestra and piano); cantatas, chamber works, songs.

LOEILLET, Jean-Baptiste (1653-1730) Belgium. Other dates are sometimes given, as the biographies of this family of Flemish musicians have become confused. A Belgian flautist and composer who spent much time in London. Wrote works for flute, recorder, and harpsichord.

LOEWE, Carl, or Karl: full name Johann Carl Gottfried (1796-1869) Germany. A prolific composer in many forms, now best known for his songs and ballad-settings. His songs, *Edward, The Erl-King*, and *Tom der Reimer* still find their way into recital programmes.

LORTZING, Gustav Albert (1801-1851) Germany. Enjoyed much success in his time as composer of operas and operettas. His *Tsar and Carpenter* is still performed in Germany.

LOVELOCK, William (b. 1899) England. After gaining many distinctions in London, went to Australia in 1956. Was director of Queensland Conservatorium of Music between 1957 and 1959. Has written symphonic works, concertos, and other music, as well as about twenty textbooks on various musical subjects.

LUIGINI, Alexandre Clément Léon Joseph (1850-1906) France. Violinist, conductor, and composer of choral music, a comic opera, and ballet music. His *Ballet Egyptien* is now his best known work.

LULLY, Jean-Baptiste (originally known as Giovanni Battista Lulli) (1632-1687) Italy. Of humble parentage, he taught himself to play the violin. While still a child, taken by the Chevalier de Guise to Paris where he became a scullion in the service of Mlle de Montpensier. He was about fifteen when his brilliant violin playing earned him the patronage of King Louis XIV, for whom he composed court ballets.

In 1664 Lully collaborated with Molière in a series of comedy-ballets, which eventually evolved into French opera, of which he is looked upon as the founder. He obtained a monopoly of opera production in France, accumulated a large fortune, and at his death left four houses, all situated in the most fashionable quarters of Paris. At the height of his fame he injured his foot with a long staff that he was using to beat time while conducting a *Te Deum*. From this developed an abscess, which caused his death.

In his operas, Lully developed the unaccompanied recitative, as suited to the French language. He created the French, or "Lully" style of overture; he wrote music of dainty charm, stately grandeur, broad humour, and religious fervour with equal facility.

Principal works: operas, including *Alceste, Amadis de Gaule, Armide et Renaud, Cadmus et*

Hermione, Persée; choral works, including *Dies Irae, Miserere;* incidental music for *L'Amour Médecin, Le Bourgeois Gentilhomme,* and *Monsieur de Pourceaugnac* by Molière; *Le Temple de la Paix* (ballet); church music; songs, *Au clair de la lune* being one of the best known today.

LUTOSLAWSKI, Witold (b. 1913) Poland. One of the most eminent of modern Polish composers. His works include: *Funeral Music* (dedicated to the memory of Bartók); orchestral works, including *Little Suite, Jeux Venitiens* (written for Venice Festival of 1951); *Silesian Triptych,* for voice and orchestra; choral music; songs.

LUTYENS, Elizabeth (b. 1906) England. Her many compositions include chamber music, e.g. six "Chamber Concertos" for various instrumental groups; choral music; concertos; film music; songs.

MacCUNN, Hamish (1868-1916) Scotland. A pupil of Parry. His works, some of strong national character, include several operas, cantatas, orchestral pieces, songs.

MacDOWELL, Edward (1861-1908) America. Studied in France and Germany. Settled in Boston and became recognised as the greatest creative musician the United States had produced. His compositions, leaning heavily on continental romanticism, include two piano concertos; piano suites, e.g., *Woodland Sketches* and *Fireside Tales.*

MacFARREN, George Alexander (1813-1887) England. Suffered at an early age from impaired eyesight, and ultimately went blind. Knighted 1883. Works include operas, church music, oratorios, orchestral works.

MACKENZIE, Alexander Campbell (1847-1935) Scotland. Knighted 1895. Composed numerous works in most forms. Also a successful conductor.

MACKERRAS, Charles (b. 1925) Australia. Resident in England since 1947. A successful conductor (Sadler's Wells, Hamburg State Opera, etc.); arranged Sullivan's music for ballet *Pineapple Poll.*

MACONCHY, Elizabeth (b. 1907) English, of Irish parents. Studied with Vaughan Williams. Has written orchestral and chamber music, operas, and songs.

MAHLER, Gustav (1860-1911) Bohemia. The son of a Jewish shopkeeper, Mahler studied at the Vienna Conservatoire. In 1878 he met Anton Bruckner, with whom he studied composition, and before he was twenty he had completed his first mature work, *Das Klagende Lied.* In order to support himself he conducted opera in German and Austrian towns, returning to Vienna in 1883. He held appointments as *Kapellmeister* at Prague and Leipzig; in 1892 conducted German opera in London. In 1897, due largely to Brahms's recommendation, he became director of the Hofoper (now the Staatsoper) in Vienna, a post he held until 1907.

In 1902 he married Alma Maria Schindler, a brilliant pianist. Mahler shunned the limelight, but at the age of fifty he found his fame had spread to many countries. Because of his precarious financial position, however, he found it necessary in 1910 to go to America again, where he became conductor of the New York Philharmonic Orchestra. In 1911 he went back to Vienna, his health impaired by overwork, and died there. He was buried at Grinzing.

Since Mahler's death opinions of his status as a composer have been divided, these ranging from probing criticism to hysterical adulation. His music is deeply personal, much of its structure dictated by the processes of a dynamic and original mind.

Principal works: nine symphonies, No. 10 unfinished; *Das Lied von der Erde* (for mezzo-soprano, tenor, and orchestra); *Das Klagende Lied* (cantata); song cycles, including *Kindertotenlieder, Des Knaben Wunderhorn, Lieder eines fahrenden Gesellen;* individual songs.

MALIPIERO, Gian Francesco (b. 1882) Italy. After writing operas, orchestral and chamber music in a classical-romantic style, turned to the twelve-note technique.

MALIPIERO, Riccardo (1914-1973) Italy. (Nephew of Gian Francesco Malipiero). Pianist, critic, composer. From 1945 adopted advanced techniques in composition.

MARCELLO, Benedetto (1686-1739) Italy. Held important government positions while studying music. His works include operas, oratorios, concertos. J. S. Bach edited one of his concertos for his own use.

MARTIN, Frank (1890-1974) Switzerland. His first works belong to German late-Romantic tradition. After 1920 he became influenced by French Impressionism; in 1930 adopted the twelve-note technique. Has lived in Holland for some years. Martin's works include:

Golgotha and *In terra pax* (oratorios), *Le Mystère de la Nativité* (Christmas oratorio), *Monsieur de Pourceaugnac* (opera); *Le vin herbé*, for voices and instruments; *Der Sturm*, an opera after Shakespeare; orchestral music; piano works.

MARTINU, Bohuslav (1890-1959) Czechoslovakia. Martinů was born in a church tower, his father, a cobbler and caretaker of the bells, being allowed to make it a home for his family.

At the Prague Conservatoire, which he entered in 1906 the young musician became an outstanding violinist. He spent from 1923 to 1940 in France, and the next four years in the United States. After Dvořák and Janáček, he became the most significant Czech composer, although his music had to wait for due recognition. While finding inspiration in folk music, he developed his own individuality in tune with modern trends.

In the 1920s he wrote the orchestral *Half-Time* and *La Bagarre*, and *Seven Czech Dances* for piano; in the 1930s the operas *Games about Mary*, *The Suburban Theatre*, and *Julietta*, also the *Double Concerto* for two string orchestras, piano, and drums. Six symphonies were completed between 1942 and 1955. Further works in several forms followed, his chamber music and violin concerto being of considerable importance.

MASCAGNI, Pietro (1863-1945) Italy. For some years he eked out a meagre living by conducting obscure opera companies. He was facing dire poverty when he won first prize with his one-act opera *Cavalleria Rusticana* in 1899. He continued to turn out operas, incidental music, film music, and choral works, none of which stirred more than a mild breeze on the musical scene. Among his other operas are: *L'Amico Fritz*, *Iris*, *La Maschere*, *Isabeau*, *Silvano*, and *Lodoletta*.

MASSENET, Jules (1842-1912) France. At the age of eleven he became a student at the Paris Conservatoire, later supporting himself by playing the drum in the orchestra of the Théâtre Lyrique. In 1866 he married one of his pupils, and in the following year, due to the influence of his former teacher, Ambroise Thomas, his first opera *La Grand'tante* was produced. From 1878 to 1896 he was professor of advanced composition at the Paris Conservatoire. He was held in high regard in Paris, his music marked by lyricism, flavoured by sentiment.

Principal works: twenty-seven operas, including *Le Cid*, *Werther*, *Thais*, *Manon*, *Hérodiade*, *Sapho*, *Don Quixotte*; orchestral suites, including *Scènes Pittoresques*, *Scènes Alsaciennes*, *Scènes Napolitaines*; incidental music for plays, including *Les Erinnyies* (of which *Elégie* is a part); *Cendrillon* and other ballets; a piano concerto, and about 200 songs.

MAW, Nicholas (b. 1935) England. A pupil of Berkeley. Works include *Eight Chinese Lyrics*; an opera. *One Man Show, Scenes and Arias* for three female singers and orchestra; *Nocturne* for voice and chamber orchestra; a string quartet; chamber music for oboe, clarinet, horn, bassoon and piano.

MAYER, John (b. 1929) India. Violinist, resident in England. Studied with Seiber. Has adapted Indian modes to Western musical form. Works include *Shanta Quintet* for sitar and strings.

MAYUZUMI, Toshiro (b. 1929) Japan. Has written electronic and concrete music, also a work for wind and percussion instruments and musical saw.

MEALE, Richard (b. 1932) Australia. Now referred to as one of Australia's most prominent *avant-garde* composers, he has discarded all that he had written before the age of twenty-eight. On a grant from the Ford Foundation, studied in the United States. Works include *Images* and *Nocturnes* for orchestra, chamber combinations.

MEDTNER, Nicolas (or Nicolai) (1879-1951) Russia. Toured Europe as pianist 1901-1902, settled in England in 1936. Works, in a traditional idiom, include many for piano, also chamber music, and songs.

MEHUL, Etienne Henri (1763-1817) France. The son of a cook, he became an important figure in French stage music. Operas include *Joseph*, *Ariodant*. Wrote also ballets and symphonies.

MENDELSSOHN, Felix (full name Jakob Ludwig Felix Mendelssohn-Bartholdy) (1809-1847) Germany. The son of a wealthy banker and surrounded by love and comfort, his musical career followed an even pattern of success. He dominated musical thinking in Germany and England and was honoured in many countries. By his twelfth year he had produced many compositions and at seventeen composed his Overture to *A Midsummer Night's Dream*. He was a brilliant pianist, yet his piano works, while faultless in style and workmanship, do not quite equal in importance his other major works.

In 1837 he married Cecile Jeanrenaud, daughter of a clergyman. He travelled often, and visited England several times, his oratorio, *Elijah*, having its first performance in Birmingham. He rescued the music of J. S. Bach from oblivion and brought it before the public. He died in Leipzig, his funeral service concluding with the final chorus of Bach's *St Matthew Passion* of which he had given the first public performance after it had lain forgotten for a hundred years.

Principal works: oratorios, including *Elijah* and *St Paul;* numerous choral works; five symphonies; two violin and two piano concertos; concerto for violin and piano; orchestral music, including an overture and twelve other pieces as incidental music to *A Midsummer Night's Dream; The Hebrides (Fingal's Cave), Ruy Blas,* and *Die Schöne Melusine* overtures; *Songs Without Words* and other piano pieces; organ works.

MENNIN, Peter (b. 1923) America. Works include six symphonies, orchestral, chamber, and piano music, some showing affinities with English music.

MENOTTI, Gian-Carlo (b. 1911) Italy. Now classed as an American composer, having lived in the United States since 1928. Studied in Milan and Philadelphia. In 1958 he founded the Festival of Two Worlds at Spoleto, Italy. He has written the libretti for his operas, which at times show influences of Puccini and later composers.

Principal works: operas, *Amelia Goes to the Ball, The Old Maid and the Thief, The Island God, The Medium, The Telephone, The Consul, Amahl and the Night Visitors, The Saint of Bleeker Street, Maria Golovin,* and the ballet-opera *The Unicorn, the Gorgon, and the Manticore;* ballets, *Errand into the Maze* and *Sebastian; Apocalypse* for orchestra; *Concerto in A minor* for piano and orchestra; *Concerto in F major* for violin and orchestra.

MERCADANTE, Giuseppe Saverio Raffaelle (1795-1870) Italy. Became blind in 1862, but continued to compose. Works include sixty operas; twenty masses; many motets and secular cantatas; instrumental pieces, and songs.

MESSAGER, André (1853-1929) France. Composer of French *opéra-comique* and English light opera. Among his works *Véronique* and *Monsieur Beaucaire;* ballets, including *The Two Pigeons*.

MESSIAEN, Olivier (b. 1908) France. One of the founders of *La Jeune France*, this French organist, composer, and writer has influenced many younger composers including Boulez. In 1942 he became professor of harmony at the Paris Conservatoire. His works, many of them of complex structure, include those with religious associations, e.g., *La nativité du Seigneur, L'Ascension, Trois petites liturgies de la Présence Divine*. Among his other works are *Turangalîla*, a symphony including piano and bells, influenced by Indian rhythms; *Visions of the Amen* for two pianos.

MEULEMANS, Arthur (b. 1884) Belgium. Has written fourteen symphonies; orchestral works including *Concerto for Orchestra, Evasions, Plinius Fontein;* three operas; incidental music for the theatre.

MEYERBEER, Giacomo (1791-1864) Germany. The eldest son of a wealthy Berlin banker, this composer was christened Jakob Liebmann Beer, but changed his name to Meyerbeer as a tribute to a relative named Meyer who left him a legacy. During a visit to Italy in 1815 he came under the influence of Rossini and other Italian composers. He lived in Paris from 1826 to 1842, went back to Germany as musical director to the King of Prussia, but returned to Paris where he died.

Meyerbeer's first operas were in German, some later ones in the Italian style, but he brought new ideas to French opera.

Principal works: operas, *L'Africaine, Dinorah, Robert le Diable, Les Huguenots, Le Prophète, Le Pardon de Pleormel;* some church music; orchestral marches; songs.

MIASKOVSKY, Nicolai Yakovlevich (1881-1950) Russia. Wrote twenty-seven symphonies, orchestral works, including a symphonic poem *Nevermore* (after Poe), a violin concerto, piano music and songs.

MIGOT, Georges Elbert (1891-1976) France. Distinct from "The Six" was called "The Group of One." Works include operas, sacred choral music, and many works for orchestra.

MILHAUD, Darius (1892-1974) France. A member of "The Six." A prolific composer, often engaging in polytonality. Wrote in many forms, works including *Le Carnaval d'Aix* for piano and orchestra; ballets, e.g., *La Creation du Monde* and *Le Boeuf sur le toit*; much chamber music, and many songs.

MOERAN, Ernest John (1894-1950) England. Influenced by John Ireland, and folk music, wrote orchestral, choral, and chamber music, piano works, and songs.

MOMPOU, Federico (b. 1893) Spain. A pianist, wrote much for that instrument, also songs, leaning towards a "national" idiom.

MONIUSZKO, Stanislaw (1820-1872) Poland. Although considered one of the most important Polish composers of his time, his music is not frequently heard outside his own country. *Halka* is one of his best known operas. Other works are for orchestra, choirs, and solo voice.

MONTEMEZZI, Italo (1875-1952) Italy. Abandoned a career in engineering for music. Best known for his opera, *L'Amore dei tre re*.

MONTEVERDI, Claudio (1567-1643) Italy. Held church and court appointments; at forty turned to opera and as a reformer, gave opera a greater dramatic expression and replaced flimsy accompaniments with a more vivid style of orchestration. His opera *Orfeo* (1607) became a landmark in operatic history, He became a priest in 1633.

Principal works: Many of his works have been lost, but his name has been kept alive by his operas *Orfeo, Arianna, L'Incoronazione di Poppea, Combattimento di Tancredi e Clorinda;* also some of his 250 madrigals, masses and other vocal music.

MONTGOMERY (Robert), Bruce (b. 1921) England. Composer of operas, choral music, songs, piano pieces, and film scores.

MOORE, Douglas (1893-1969) America. A pupil of N. Boulanger and Bloch. Works include operas, *The Devil and Daniel Webster, Giants in the Earth, Ballad of Baby Doe, The Wings of the Dove*; symphonies, including *A Symphony of Autumn; Puss in Boots*, a children's operetta; chamber music, and orchestral works.

MORLEY, Thomas (1557-1603) England. A prominent Elizabethan madrigal composer. Composed also church music, and songs. His setting of *It was a lover and his lass* and *O Mistress Mine* are among his best remembered songs.

MOSZKOWSKI, Moritz (1854-1925) Poland. A pianist-composer, trained in Germany, who wrote operas and other music. His *Spanish Dances* for piano duet once enjoyed wide popularity.

MOUSSORGSKY, Modeste Petrovich (1839-1881) Russia. Born into a family of wealthy landowners, Moussorgsky (or Mussorgsky) ended his life in poverty, having spent much of his life in squalid quarters, excessive drinking sapping his capacity for work. At eighteen he joined with Balakirev, Borodin, Cui, and Rimsky-Korsakov in a move to establish a truly "nationalist" school of music. He came to be recognised as one of the great names of nineteenth century Russian music.

Principal works: seven operas, including *Boris Godunov; Khovantschina, Sorotchinsky Fair* (both completed by others); *Night on a Bare Mountain* for orchestra; *Pictures at an Exhibition* (written for piano but orchestrated by Ravel and others); song cycle, *Songs and Dances of Death*.

MOZART, Wolfgang Amadeus (1756-1791) Austria. It is a matter for wonder that Mozart achieved so much within his short life. He was playing simple pieces on the clavier at three; a touring harpsichordist at six; an accomplished organist and violinist and recognised as a composer at nine.

He was born in Salzburg, his life a struggle against poverty. In 1782 he married Constanze Weber, a relation of the composer. During his composing career he elevated every musical form that occupied his attention, and pointed the way to those who followed him. His compositions were so numerous that Ludwig Koechel classified them and gave each a number, the total number in the catalogue standing at 626. He was given the poorest kind of funeral and as the few mourners reached the gate of the cemetery, a violent storm sent them running for shelter. Only the undertaker accompanied the hearse to the grave, now unknown.

Principal works: operas, including *Le Nozze di Figaro, Don Giovanni, Cosi Fan Tutti, Die Entführung aus dem Serail (Il Seragio), Die Zauberflöte, Idomeneo;* forty-one symphonies; orchestral works, including divertimenti, serenades (of which *Eine kleine Nachtmusik* is perhaps the best-known); cassations, marches, etc.; twenty-one piano concertos; six violin concertos; one clarinet concerto; *Sinfonia*

Concertante for violin, viola, and orchestra; *Concertone* for two violins, oboe, cello, and orchestra; chamber music, including twenty-four string quartets, six string quintets, clarinet quintet, oboe quintet; sonatas for piano; sonatas for violin and piano; sonatas for organ and orchestra; choral works, including *Requiem;* seventeen masses; motets; litanies; canons; organ works; arias for voice and orchestra; songs.

MURRILL, Herbert (1909-1952) England. Organist, director of music, B.B.C. (1950-1952); composer of two cello concertos; opera, *Man in Cage.*

MUSGRAVE, Thea (b. 1928) Scotland. Worked in Paris with N. Boulanger for four years. Compositions include orchestral, and piano music; *Cantata for a Summer's Day;* operas *The Decision* and *The Voice of Ariadne.*

NABOKOV, Nicholas (b. 1903) Russia. Has lived in Germany, France, and the U.S.A. Works include a piano concerto; works for orchestra (suites, etc.); opera, *The Death of Rasputin.*

NARDINI, Pietro (1722-1793) Italy. A noted violinist, pupil of Tartini. Wrote violin concertos, and chamber music.

NATHAN, Isaac (1790-1864) England. Sang at Covent Garden; composed songs to words written for him by his friend Byron. In 1841 settled in Australia and died there.

NEVIN, Ethelbert (1862-1901) America. Composer of sentimental ballads, including *The Rosary*, which is said to have sold more than six million copies within thirty years.

NICOLAI (Carl), Otto (1810-1849) Germany. At sixteen he ran away from an unhappy home, studied in Italy, and in 1837 went to Vienna where, later, he was to found the Vienna Philharmonic Orchestra. In 1847 became director of court opera in Berlin. Wrote operas, the best known today being *The Merry Wives of Windsor;* orchestral, and choral works.

NIELSEN, Carl (1865-1931) Denmark. Now spoken of as Denmark's greatest composer, Nielsen taught himself to play the violin when he was seven, received encouragement from Niels W. Gade, and in 1884 began studies at the Copenhagen Conservatoire. In time he became honoured by a grateful Danish public, but to most of the world outside his country he remained, until recent years, an obscure figure on the musical horizon.

Nielsen's sympathies were classical, the best of his works balanced in allegiance to traditional form, to melody, and to Danish folk-music, yet independent. His principal works include six symphonies; concertos for various instruments; operas, including *Masquerade, Saul and David*, and *Moderna ;* chamber music.

NIN, Joaquín (1879-1949) Cuba. Pianist and composer, has written music for stage and for solo instruments. Editor of old Spanish music.

NONO, Luigi (b. 1924) Italy. At first influenced by Webern and the twelve-note method, Nono has developed as an individualist, his music sometimes savagely percussive. Works include operas, orchestral, choral, other vocal; also music for various combinations.

NORDRAAK, Richard (1842-1866) Norway. During his short life he exerted considerable influence on other composers, including Grieg. Edited Norwegian folk-songs and composed orchestral music in a national style.

NOVACEK, Ottokar (1866-1900) Hungary. Violinist and composer, whose works include chamber music, violin pieces, and songs.

NOVAK, Vítězslav (1870-1949) Czechoslovakia. Studied composition with Dvořák at Prague Conservatoire where he was later director. Works include operas, choral music, symphonic poems, chamber music, piano pieces, folk-song arrangements.

NUSSIO, Otmar (b. 1902) Switzerland. Works include *Carnival à Montmartre, Ladinia Rustica, Soste Italiche*, and other orchestral suites; *Concerto Classico* for piano and strings; *Impromptu* for trumpet and orchestra; violin concerto.

OBRECHT (Hobrecht), Jacob (c. 1430-1505) Netherlands. One of the great musicians of the fifteenth century. In addition to his masses, motets, and secular songs, he contributed towards the form of Passion Music.

OCKEGHEM (Okeghem) Jean de (c. 1430-c. 1495) Netherlands. Another great fifteenth century musician; teacher of Josquin des Prés and many others; composer of masses, motets, and secular songs.

OFFENBACH, Jacques (1819-1880) Germany. Statements that his real name was Levy, Eberst, Eberscht, or Wiener lack confirmation. Born at Offenbach-am-Main, Germany, the son of a cantor in the Cologne synagogue, he was taken to Paris while young, where in time he became the most popular composer of operettas. Taking up the management of theatres, from small to large, he became over-lavish in his productions; in 1859 he faced bankruptcy, and when working on his *Orphée aux enfers* had to hide in small rooms to avoid his creditors.

After composing almost one hundred operettas which were successful, he found that his star was waning. To convince French audiences that he was more than a writer of frothy *opéras-comiques*, he began work on a serious opera, *Les Contes d'Hoffmann* but died before its completion. It was finished by Ernest Guiraud and first presented in February 1881, five months after his death.

Principal works: *Les Contes d'Hoffmann, Orphée aux enfers, La belle Hélène, La vie Parisienne, La fille du Tambour-Major, La Périchole, La Grande Duchesse de Gérostein, Madame Favart, Les Brigands, Geneviève de Brabant, Barbe-Bleu.*

ORFF, Carl (b. 1895) Germany. His work as conductor and editor of old music brought him in touch with various forms of art. His own music, strongly rhythmic and often percussive was said to have been a reaction against the operas of Strauss and Pfitzner and exaggerated forms of operatic expression.

Earned fame outside his own country with his scenic cantata *Carmina Burana*, based on texts dating back to the thirteenth century, discovered in an old monastery in the Bavarian Alps.

Other stage works, for which he wrote the libretti are *Der Mond, Die Kluge, Catulli Carmina;* incidental music for Sophocles' *Antigone*, and a new version of Monteverdi's *Orfeo*. After his *Carmina Burana* appeared in 1937, he "disowned" all previous work. Has also written music for children.

ORTHEL, Leon (b. 1905) Holland. Pianist and composer. Writing in a conservative style, has produced four symphonies, *Concertino alla Burla* for piano and orchestra; cello concerto; orchestral works, including ballet.

OTTERLOO, Willem van (1907-1978) Holland. Conductor of the Residenz Orchestra at the Hague; guest conductor in other cities. Composer of three symphonies; *Serenade*, and *Introduction and Allegro* for orchestra;

Symphonietta for Winds, Suite for Strings, and smaller works.

PACHELBEL, Johann (1653-1706) Germany. Organist and composer of organ music. Often called the "spiritual ancestor of J. S. Bach," having, with Buxtehude, paved the way for Bach's perfected development of the choral-prelude form.

PADEREWSKI, Ignaz Jan (1860-1941) Poland. One of the most famous pianists of his time; became the first Prime Minister of the newly created state of Poland in 1919. Composed two operas, *Manru* and *Sakuntala; Concerto in A minor* for piano and orchestra; orchestral music, including a symphony; songs; piano works, including the famous *Minuet in G*.

PAGANINI, Nicolò (b. 1782 or 1784; d. 1840) Italy. regarded in his time as the greatest violinist in history, he became a legendary figure with credence placed on the fiction that he was in league with the devil when he played. Superstition followed him to the grave; not until five years after his death was his body laid in consecrated ground. He wrote eight violin concertos, but only Op. 6 and Op. 7 were published. Others, found later, have been subjected to much editing. His twenty-four *Caprices* are still in the violinist's repertoire.

PAISIELLO, Giovanni (c. 1741-1816) Italy. Composed more than a hundred operas, also church music, orchestral works.

PALESTRINA, Giovanni Pierluigi da (c. 1525-1594) Italy. An historic figure in church music who took his name from the place of his birth, the town of Palestrina. In 1547 he married Lucrezia de Goris, a woman of considerable wealth. Eight months after her death in 1580 he married Virginia Dormuli, a wealthy widow. About that time he entered into partnership with a young man dealing in skins and furs, making large profits from his commercial transactions.

A perfectionist in musical matters, he brought to the highest point the beauties and the technical mastery of Italian polyphonic writing, and conferred a greater dignity on church music. He spent most of his musical life in the service of the church, in 1551 being summoned to the Vatican by the Pope.

Principal works: Although a definite estimate of the total number of his compositions cannot be given, he is known to have written about a hundred masses; 350 motets; thirty-five magnificats; sixty-four hymns; forty-two lamentations; ten litanies; 140 madrigals; also much secular music.

PALMGREN, Selim (1878-1951) Finland. A pianist and conductor, composed piano concertos, cantatas, operas, also many piano pieces of lyrical charm.

PANUFNIK, Andrzj (b. 1914) Poland. Went to England in 1954, where he became established as a conductor and composer. Among his works are symphonies, *Sinfonia Elegiaca, Sinfonia Rustica and Sinfonia Sacra; Tragic Overture; Concerto in Modo Antica;* Polish folk-song settings.

PARKER, Horatio (William) (1863-1919) America. Studied with Rheinberger in Germany. Wrote operas, oratorios, a symphony, an organ concerto, and smaller works.

PARRY (Charles), Hubert (Hastings) (1848-1918) England. For his distinguished service to music, he was knighted in 1898, and created a baronet in 1903. His many compositions include choral works, e.g. *Blest Pair of Sirens;* oratorios, *Job* and *Judith;* five symphonies; an opera; many songs, *Jerusalem* being one of the best known. Was director of Royal College of Music, London from 1894 to 1918; held other academic appointments, and wrote important literary works on music.

PEDRELL, Felipe (1841-1922) Spain. As a musicologist has held an important place in the history of Spanish music. Composed operas, church music, and orchestral works.

PENBERTHY, James (b. 1917) Australia. After gaining his Bachelor of Music distinction at Melbourne Conservatorium, studied in France, England, and Italy. A conductor, teacher, and critic. Compositions, which range from the romantic to *avant-garde,* include operas, piano concertos, orchestral music including ballets; chamber music.

PERGAMENT, Moses (b. 1893) Finland. Became a prominent figure in Swedish music. His works include concertos for piano, violin, and cello; *Jewish Songs* for soloists, chorus and orchestra; a setting for *Kol Nidrei* for cello and orchestra; *Rhapsody Ebraica;* music for ballet.

PERGOLESI, Giovanni Battista (1710-1736) Italy. Since his death the importance of this composer may have been exaggerated, but during his short life he was held in considerable esteem as a violinist, organist, and composer.

His *Stabat Mater,* and the opera, *La Serva Padrona,* are accepted as authentic, but he has been credited with many works which are thought to have been composed by others: for instance, the well known song, *Tre giorni son che Nina,* is probably the work of Legrenzio Ciampi.

PERI, Jacopo (1561-1633) Italy. A Florentine composer and dilettante and member of the artistic set called the *Camerati.* Is said to have composed the first real opera (*Euridice*) ever staged. Wrote in other forms as well. See under "Opera" in chapter headed *Kinds of Music* (vocal).

PERKINS, Horace (b. 1901) Australia. Music Supervisor for the Australian Broadcasting Commission, Adelaide, from 1945 to 1966. Works, some of which have been performed overseas, include three symphonies; two cantatas; violin and piano concertos; orchestral suites; songs.

PEROSI, Lorenzo (1872-1956) Italy. An Italian priest and composer; at one time director of the Sistine Chapel music in Rome. Composed many choral works in an old style.

PERSICHETTI, Vincent (b. 1915) America. Studied at Curtis Institute and with Roy Harris. Works include nine symphonies; concertos, orchestral music; violin and cello sonatas; chamber music; many pieces for piano.

PETRASSI, Goffredo (b. 1904) Italy. Works include operas; music for choir, and for orchestra; piano compositions; songs.

PFITZNER, Hans (1869-1949). German composer born in Moscow. His works, many in a conventional Romanantic style, enjoyed considerable popularity, which failed to spread far beyond his own country. Operas include *Palestrina, Christ-Elflein, Das Herz.* Also composed choral, orchestral, and chamber works, and songs.

PICCINNI (or PICCINI), Nicola (1728-1800) Italy. Considered in his time Gluck's greatest rival in Paris. Composed 200 works for the stage, including more than a hundred operas. Wrote also oratorios, and church music.

PICK-MANGIAGALLI, Ricardo (1882-1949) Bohemia. Became a naturalised Italian. Was director of the Milan Conservatoire. Composed operas; orchestral work, including ballets; piano pieces.

PIERNE (Henri Constant), Gabriel (1863-

1937) France. Succeeded César Franck as organist at St Clothilde, Paris; also a conductor. Wrote operas, ballets, and orchestral suites. Now remembered for such small works as *Entry of the Little Fauns*.

PIJPER, Willem (1894-1937) Holland. An influential composer, teacher, and writer. His works, some owing much to Debussy and Mahler, include symphonies; chamber music; piano works; arrangements of Dutch folksongs.

PILKINGTON, Francis (c. 1562-1638) England. A minor composer of madrigals, anthems, and pieces for lute. About 1612 he became a minor canon in the church.

PISTON, Walter (1894-1976) America. Of Italian descent. A pupil of N. Boulanger in Paris; later on the staff at Harvard University. Has written symphonies, a violin concerto, chamber music, his ballet, *The Incredible Flutist*, enjoying widespread popularity, and important books on harmony, counterpoint, and orchestration.

PIZZETTI, Ildebrando (1880-1968) Italy. A conservative but highly gifted composer in a lyric style. Works include operas, incidental music to plays, orchestral, choral, chamber music, and songs. Also a successful teacher and author of books on musical subjects.

PLANQUETTE, Robert (1848-1903) France. A successful composer of light operettas, including *Les Cloches de Corneville*, first performed in Paris. Others were specially written for London, e.g., *Paul Jones, Nell Gwynne*. It has been said that Planquette, in the 1880s, refused an offer of twelve thousand pounds from a publisher for the copyright of *Rip Van Winkle*.

PLESSIS, Hubert du (b. 1922) South Africa. Works include vocal works for soloists and chorus, and piano compositions. His *Sonata for Piano Duet, Op. 10* was selected for the World Music Festival at Stockholm in 1956.

PONCE, Manuel (1882-1948) Mexico. His music, in light melodic style, includes much for guitar. Has written orchestral and chamber works, also songs, including *Estrellita*.

PONCHIELLI, Amilcare (1834-1886) Italy. Beginning his musical career as a church organist, he later taught composition at the Milan Conservatoire, where Puccini was his favourite pupil. Wrote several operas, *La Gioconda* (1876) being the most successful. *Dance of the Hours* comes from this.

PORPORA, Niccola or Niccolò (1686-1767) Italy. A celebrated singing teacher and composer of operas and church music.

POULENC, Francis (1899-1963) France. A member of "The Six." Without much formal tuition in harmony and orchestration, Poulenc found himself at twenty famous as a composer. Received commissions, one from Diaghilev for music for the ballet *Les Biches*. Collaborated with Jean Cocteau. His music is clear-cut and often witty, his sacred music of deep sincerity.

Principal works: operas, including *Dialogues des Carmélites, Les Mamelles de Tirésias*; *Stabat Mater, Gloria, Quatre Motets pour un Temps de Penitence, Secheresses*, and other choral works; *Le Bal Masqué*, for solo voice and chamber orchestra; *Les Biches* (ballet); *Concert Champètre* for harpsichord, or piano, and orchestra; *Aubade* for piano and eighteen instruments; concertos for solo and two pianos, also for organ. He has also written incidental music for plays, film music, and many songs.

PRAETORIUS. The Latin name by which twenty or more sixteenth and seventeenth century German musicians named Schultz, or Schultze were known. Most were composers, particularly of church music. The best known was Michael Praetorius (1571-1621) who composed numerous works.

PROKOFIEV, Sergei (1891-1953) Russia. Having begun piano lessons at five, he composed his first piece at six and at eleven had completed an opera. He took lessons from Glière, Rimsky-Korsakov, Liadov and Taneiev. In 1914 he gained the highest award as a pianist, and for several years lived in London, Paris, Japan, and the United States. On his return to Russia in 1933 he was described as "The greatest single influence on Soviet music," but in the 1940s his compositions were criticised by the Central Committee of the Communist Party as "complex, marked by intellectuality, and formalist pervasions." In later years he adopted a more lyrical style of writing, became an honoured citizen of the U.S.S.R., and died in his native country. His death passed unnoticed because Stalin died on the same day.

Prokofiev's earlier works were a reaction

against the mysticism and emotionalism of certain Russian composers, but later he purged his writing of its former acidity and strove for more melodic expression.

Principal works: operas, including *The Love of the Three Oranges, The Flaming Angel, War and Peace* (after Tolstoy), *The Duenna* (based on Sheridan's play); cantata *Alexander Nevsky* (based on a film score); ballets, including *Romeo and Juliet, Chout, The Tale of the Stone Flower, Les Pas d'Acier, Cinderella;* seven symphonies; five piano concertos; two violin concertos; *Russian Overture, Winter Holiday,* for narrator and orchestra; *The Ugly Duckling* for voice and orchestra; *Lieutenant Kije* (incidental music); *Peter and the Wolf* (orchestral fairy tale); nine piano sonatas; chamber works; piano pieces; songs.

PUCCINI, Giacomo (1858-1924) Italy. A pupil of Ponchielli, he concentrated almost entirely on opera, *La Bohème* bringing him his first real success in 1896. His acute theatre sense and dramatic instinct led him to plots well suited to operatic treatment, these alternating between Italianate romanticism and stark melodrama. He had almost completed *Turandot* when a cancer of the throat caused his death. This last opera was finished by Alfano.

Principal works: *La Bohème, Tosca, Madama Butterfly, Manon Lescaut, La Fanciulla del West;* three one-act operas, *Il Tabarro, Suor Angelica,* and *Gianni Schicci;* and *Turandot,* completed by Alfano.

PUGNANI, Gaetano (1731-1798) Italy. One of the great violinists of his time and credited with carrying on the traditions of Corelli and Tartini. A prolific composer of chamber music and violin pieces. *Praeludium and Allegro* for violin, "arranged" by Kreisler was later found to be Kreisler's own composition.

PURCELL, Henry (c. 1659-1695) England. Perhaps the greatest English composer of his time, he succeeded his teacher, John Blow, as organist of Westminster Abbey, where he was buried. He composed works for church and state occasions, writing, as he said, "for God and King." His numerous works also embraced music for plays, and operas; his *Dido and Aeneas* (written for a Chelsea girls' school) is a landmark in early English opera. His greatness, and his advanced musical thinking influenced many who followed him.

Principal works: opera, *Dido and Aeneas;* incidental music for plays, including *The Indian Queen, The Fairy Queen, King Arthur, Don Quixote, Dioclesian;* numerous odes and sacred cantatas; works for keyboard, including organ, and instrumental groups; songs.

QUANTZ, Johann Joachim (1697-1773) Germany. The son of a blacksmith, Quantz became a celebrated flautist, taught Frederick the Great to play the flute, with whom he remained as court composer. He left almost 300 concertos for one or two flutes, numerous flute solos, as well as some vocal music.

QUILTER, Roger (1877-1953) England. Wrote many songs of light, graceful character, some to words of Shakespeare and Herrick. Larger works include an opera *Julia,* incidental music to the play *Where the Rainbow Ends,* and *Children's Overture,* based on nursery tunes.

QUINET, Fernand (b. 1898) Belgium. A cellist, conductor, and director of the Liège Conservatoire, has composed orchestral works, and songs.

RACHMANINOV (also spelt Rachmaninoff and Rakhmaninov), Sergei (1873-1943) Russia. A famous pianist, he studied piano with Liszt's favourite pupil, Siloti, and composition with Taneiev and Arensky. As a composer he wrote in several forms. In 1900 he returned to Russia from a visit to London in a depressed state of mind. His creative powers numbed, he submitted to a course of hypnotic suggestion from Dr Dahl. Later in that year he found a fresh ambition to work and completed his *Concerto in C minor,* the most popular of his four concertos for piano and orchestra. He found living under the new U.S.S.R. régime intolerable and settled in the United States where he died.

His music, much of it emotionally charged with a mixture of grandeur and sorrowful melodies, remained embedded in nineteenth century romanticism.

Principal works: three symphonies; four piano concertos; *Rhapsody on a Theme of Paganini* for piano and orchestra; *The Isle of the Dead* (symphonic poem); three operas, *Aleko, The Miserly Knight,* and *Francesca da Rimini; The Bells,* for chorus, soloists, and orchestra; chamber music, including *Trio Elegiaque,* and *Sonata in G minor* for cello and piano; many piano compositions, including twenty-four *Preludes*; suites for two pianos; songs.

RAFF, Joseph (or Josef) Joachim (1822-1882) Switzerland. Befriended by Liszt and Bülow, he lived in Germany. Although a prolific composer of symphonies, operas, and chamber music, is remembered today by such small pieces as *Cavatina*.

RAINIER, Priaulx (b. 1903) South Africa. This (woman) composer studied with N. Boulanger in Paris, later settling in England. Has composed works for orchestra, cello, piano, chamber groups, suites for wind instruments, and vocal music.

RAMEAU, Jean Philippe (1683-1764) France. Resisting his father's wish to study law, he mastered the organ, harpsichord and violin at an early age, and taught himself to compose. At the age of seventeen he became infatuated with a young widow, which resulted in his being sent by his father to Italy. He returned to France and in 1726 published his *Traité de l'harmonie*, a treatise that advanced revolutionary theories on harmony and chord progressions which had a powerful influence on other composers. He received many appointments as organist and after passing middle age wrote more than twenty operas and opera-ballets, as well as many other works.

In 1728 he married Marie Louise Mangot, a singer twenty-five years his junior. Contemporary writers described him as egotistical, churlish, and avaricious.

Principal works: operas, including *Castor et Pollux, Dardanus, Les Indes Galantes, Hippolyte et Aricie, Les Fétes d'Hébés, Platée*; ballets, including *Zais, Zephre*; cantatas, *Diane et Actéon, L'Impatience, Orphée*; chamber music; pieces for harpsichord.

RAMIREZ, Ariel (b. 1921) Argentine. Has carried out research into Argentinian music. Works include *Misa Criolla*, a Creole mass based on traditions of Latin-American folklore; also South American folk settings.

RANGSTROM, Türe (1884-1947) Sweden. Works include three operas, four symphonies; more than fifty songs.

RANKL, Karl (1898-1968) Austria. A resident in Britain from 1939, has been musical director at Covent Garden and Elizabethan Opera Company of Australia; has conducted elsewhere. Has composed the opera *Deirdre of the Sorrows*, several symphonies, and other works.

RAUTAVAARA, Einojuhani (b. 1928) Finland. Son of opera singer Eino Rautavaara, and nephew of singer Aulikki Rautavaara. Received his diploma in composition from Sibelius Academy in 1957. Continued studies in Vienna, in the United States with Copland and Sessions, in Switzerland, and in West Germany. Main works are four symphonies; an opera, *The Mine* (1961); three string quartets; two Rilke song-cycles, *Die Liebenden* and *Orpheus*; also choral and piano music. His *A Requiem in our time*, scored for a thirteen-part brass ensemble won first prize in the Thor Johnson Brass Composition Awards in 1953.

RAVEL, Maurice (1875-1937) France. Ravel was born in the Pyrénées, close to the border of Spain, his mother a Basque. Although his family took him to Paris at an early age, his pride in his Basque heritage never left him. This may account for the fact that much of his music was influenced by the Spanish idiom. In 1899 he entered the Paris Conservatoire as a pupil of Fauré and others. In 1901 he tried for the coveted *Prix de Rome*, to be awarded second place. When, after further attempts, he again applied in 1905, he was not allowed to enter the competition on the score that he was unlikely to bring credit on the Conservatoire. By the age of thirty he had written several works which, today, are considered some of his best.

In 1920 he refused the Légion d'Honneur; eight years later he accepted the degree of Doctor of Music conferred upon him by the University of Oxford. In 1928 he visited the United States. A motor accident in 1932 resulted in a serious illness. It was discovered that he had a tumour on the brain. In 1937 he entered a Paris nursing home for an operation on the brain. He suffered a relapse and died there.

Ravel's personality was one of extreme refinement. He was fastidious in everything that he undertook; his music is perfect in detail, his system of editing so precise as to leave no doubt concerning correct interpretation. He wrote with brilliance for the piano and used the orchestral palette with vital breadth.

Principal works: operas, *L'Enfant et les Sortilèges* and *L'Heure Espagnole*; *Concerto in*

G for piano and orchestra, *Concerto for Left Hand and Orchestra;* ballet *Daphnis et Chloé; Bolero* for solo dance; orchestral music, some of which were also written for piano, including *Ma mère L'Oye* (suite); *Rapsodie Espagnole, La Valse, Valses nobles et sentimentales, Pavane pour une Infante Défunte, Tombeau de Couperin;* chamber works, including *String Quartet in F, Trio in A minor, Introduction and Allegro* for harp, string quartet, flute, and clarinet; *Tzigane* for violin and piano; piano works, including *Jeux d'Eau, Gaspard de la Nuit, Miroirs, Sonaine, Piece en forme de Habanera* (originally a *vocalise*); songs, and song-cycles, including *Scheherazade, Cinq Melodies Populaires Grecques, Chants Hebraiques,* and a number of individual songs.

RAWSTHORNE, Alan (1905-1971) England. Influenced to some extent by Hindemith, he has developed a style in which compression and emotion are harnessed to discipline. He has written symphonies, various orchestral works, concertos for piano, violin, oboe, and clarinet; *Street Corner Overture;* ballet *Madame Chrysanthème; A Canticle of Man* (chamber cantata), *Practical Cats* for speaker and orchestra; chamber music, including *Quintet for Wind and Piano;* piano works.

READ, Gardner (b. 1913) America. Teacher, author and composer of symphonies; *The Temptation of St Anthony,* dance symphony; *The Golden Journey to Samarkand* for soloists, chorus and orchestra; *The Painted Desert* and other suites; music for strings, piano, cello, chamber groups.

REBIKOV, Vladimir (1866-1920) Russia. A composer of opera, orchestral, and piano works, some written in the whole-tone scale system.

REDMAN, Reginald (b. 1892) England. Organist, and formerly a music director with the B.B.C., has composed *Away on the Hills,* for strings; *From the Hills of a Dream,* for tenor, chorus and orchestra, as well as music for radio plays, and songs.

REGER, Max (1873-1916) Germany. A pianist, organist and conductor, Reger met much opposition in his earlier composing career for his "progressive" ideas, but ultimately became widely recognised. A prolific composer, his works include orchestral, chamber, organ, and piano works, also songs.

REIZENSTEIN, Frank (1911-1968) Germany.

A pianist-composer who studied with Hindemith and Vaughan Williams, settling in England in 1934. Works include *Voices of Night* (cantata): two piano and one cello concertos; *Danse Fantasque* for violin and orchestra; *Cirano di Bergerac Overture;* piano works.

RESPIGHI, Ottorino (1879-1936) Italy. A pupil of Rimsky-Korsakov, established himself as pianist, teacher, conductor, and composer. He was a vivid orchestrator. Among his best known works; *The Fountains of Rome, The Pines of Rome, Roman Festivals* (symphonic poems); *The Birds* (suite, based on seventeenth and eighteenth century music); *Rossiniana,* orchestrations of Rossini piano pieces; orchestrator of Rossini's music for the ballet *La Boutique Fantasque.*

REUBKE, Julius (1834-1858) Germany. A pianist-composer, son of Adolf Reubke, a famous organ-builder. He was a pupil of Liszt. Composed organ works and songs.

REVUELTAS, Silvestre (1899-1940) Mexico. Violinist, and composer of orchestral works, chamber music, and songs.

REYER, Ernest (real name Louis Ernest Etienne Rey) (1823-1909) France. Composed operas and other works, but best known outside France for his opera *Sigurd.*

REZNICEK, Emil von (1860-1945) Austria. Gave up study of law for music; held court positions; composed operas, one based on the legendary Till Eulenspiegel, his best-known being *Donna Diana.* Also wrote symphonies and church music.

RHEINBERGER, Josef (1839-1901) Germany. Organist, conductor, composer. Now best remembered by his works for organ.

RIEGGER, Wallingford (1885-1961) America. Came to be known as a radical, his music employing modern harmonic systems. Works include orchestral, *Music for Brass Choir, Study in Sonority* (for ten violins); concertos; chamber music.

RIESCO, Carlos (b. 1925) Chile. Pupil of N. Boulanger and Copland. Works include a violin concerto; orchestral music, some of which in Latin-American idiom.

RIMSKY-KORSAKOV, Nicholas (Nicolai) (1844-1908) Russia. He began to compose at age of nine, but soon after his twelfth birthday he entered the Naval College at St Petersburg and remained there for six years, with only Sundays and holidays free to him for musical studies. After resigning his commission in the navy, he joined with Cui, Balakirev, Borodin, and Moussorgsky in establishing a movement ("The Five") to rid Russian music of decaying traditions and outside influences. In 1871 he became professor of composition at the St Petersburg Conservatoire; among his pupils were Liadov, Ippolitov-Ivanov, Gretchaninov, Glazunov, Stravinsky, Respighi, and Prokofiev. He helped many Russian composers.

Principal works: operas include *Sadko, The Golden Cockerel* (also known as a ballet and an orchestral suite), *The Maid of Pskov* (or *Ivan the Terrible*), *May Night, The Snow Maiden, The Tsar's Bride, The Tale of Tsar Saltan, The Tale of the Invisible City of Kitezh, Christmas Eve*; symphonic suites, *Antar* and *Scheherazade*; *Russian Easter Festival Overture*; *Capriccio Espagnol* for orchestra; *Concerto in C-sharp minor*; songs and folk-song arrangements.

RIVIER, Jean (b. 1896) France. A skilful composer in a traditional style. Works include seven symphonies; concertos for various solo instruments; *Ouverture pour un Don Quixotte, Ouverture pour une Opérette Imaginaire*; *Burlesque* for violin and orchestra; works for chamber orchestra; songs.

ROCCA, Lodovico (b. 1895) Italy. Works include operas, including *The Dybbuk*; cantata *Ancient Inscriptions*; *Chiaroscuri* (Petite suite); *Biribu occhi di Rana* (for voice, piano, and strings).

RODRIGO, Joaquin (b. 1902) Spain. Although blind from age of three, went to Paris to study with Dukas. Especially successful in combining guitar and orchestra in his compositions.

ROGERS, Bernard (1893-1968) America. Studied with Bloch, Boulanger, and Bridge. Has composed several symphonies; *The Warrior, The Veil*, and *The Nightingale* (operas); *The Exodus* (cantata); *Elegy* (in memory of F. D. Roosevelt); *The Prophet Isaiah* (for solo voices; chorus and orchestra); orchestral suites; chamber music.

ROMBERG, Sigmund (1887-1951) Hungary. Became naturalised citizen of the United States. His most popular music such operettas as *The Desert Song, The Student Prince, New Moon*.

RONALD, Landon (real name Landon Ronald

Russell) (1873-1938) England. A pianist, accompanist to Melba, conductor, composer of many songs, e.g., *Down in the Forest* and *O Lovely Night*. Knighted in 1922.

ROSENBERG, Hilding (b. 1892) Sweden. One of most prolific of present-day Scandinavian composers, at one time influenced by Sibelius. Works include six symphonies, eight concertos for various instruments; operas, oratorios; orchestral music, including suites; chamber music; works for piano.

ROSSINI, Gioacchino (1792-1868) Italy. Between the years 1810 and 1829 he wrote thirty-eight operas. At the age of thirteen he sang in theatres and also played the horn in opera orchestras. At first lived on the edge of poverty, later becoming one of the most popular composers of *opera buffa*. For the last thirty-nine years of his life he lived as a *bon-vivant*, his only compositions during those years being little piano pieces which he wrote for private *musicales*. He lived much of his time in Paris, where he died.

Principal works: his thirty-eight operas include *Il Barbiere di Siviglia, L'Italiano in Algeri, Semiramide, L'assedio di Corinte, La Cenerentola, La Gazza Ladra, Guglielmo Tell, Mose in Egitto, Tancredi, Il Signor Bruschino, La Scala di Seta, La Cambiale di Matrimonio*. He also composed *Stabat Mater*; *Messe Solennelle*; songs, chamber music, and piano pieces.

ROUSSEL, Albert (1869-1937) France. Prepared himself for a naval career and made a special study of mathematics, then studied music, and became in 1896 a pupil of d'Indy. His music, while not always inspired, is fastidious in detail. Among his works are four symphonies; an opera-ballet, *Padmavati*, inspired by his visit to India; ballets, *Le Festin de l'araignee, Bacchus et Ariane*; *Concerto for piano and orchestra*; *Concertino for cello and orchestra*; *Aeneas*, for chorus and orchestra.

ROWLEY, Alec (1892-1958) England. A music-educationist. Compositions, usually in conservative style, include two piano concertos; *By the Deep Nine* (nautical fantasy); *The Boyhood of Christ* (suite for strings); various orchestral and piano music for teaching.

RUBBRA, Edmund (b. 1901) England. A pupil of Holst and Vaughan Williams; pianist, and lecturer. Compositions include ten symphonies; concertos for piano, and viola; two masses; *Te Deum* for soprano, chorus and orchestra; chamber music.

RUBINSTEIN, Anton (1829-1894) Russia. A famous pianist who composed symphonies, concertos, operas, and songs which have dropped out of favour, apart from such trifles as *Melody in F*. He was a brother of Nicholas (Nikolai): not related to Artur Rubinstein.

RUGGLES, Carl (1876-1971) America. An individualist, his music often favoured dissonance. Among his works are: *Men and Mountains*, a symphonic poem in three movements; *Sun Treader* for orchestra; *Portals* for strings.

SAEVERUD, Harald (b.1897) Norway. A composer of symphonies, ballet, and incidental music.

SAINT-SAENS (Charles) Camille (1835-1921) France. During his long and successful career he was held in high esteem as a brilliant pianist and organist, an erudite teacher, a scholarly author, a seasoned traveller, and a composer who wrote in almost every form. Halévy and Gounod were two of his teachers in music. He became organist at the Madeleine in Paris at the age of twenty-two. He championed progress in French music and he brought a new dignity to the French symphony. In 1893 the degree of Honorary Doctor of Music at Cambridge, England was conferred on him. His career was one of unbroken success.

Principal works: *Samson et Dalila* (opera); five piano concertos; three violin concertos; two cello concertos; five symphonies; four symphonic poems (*Le Rouet d'Omphale, Phaéton, Danse Macabre*, and *La Jeunesse d'Hercule*); *Le Carnaval des animaux* (zoological fantasy for two pianos and orchestra); *Suite Algérienne* (for orchestra); *Havanaise*, and *Introduction and Rondo Capriccioso* (for violin and orchestra); church music; chamber music; piano pieces; songs.

SALIERI, Antonio (1750-1825) Italy. In 1766 he went to Vienna, where he lived and died. His intrigue against Mozart has been exaggerated. Works were mainly operas.

SALLINEN, Aulis (b.1935) Finland. Studied at Sibelius Academy with Joonas Kokkonen. Appointed manager of the Finnish Radio Orchestra in 1960. From 1960 to 1968 was secretary to the Union of Finnish Composers. He has developed an individual style in his compositions; in one of these, *Mauermusik*,

quarter-tones for strings and woodwinds are used as a colouristic device.

SALZEDO, Carlos (1885-1961) France. Celebrated harpist who wrote works for that instrument. Took up residence in the United States. Works include *The Enchanted Isle*, *Préamble et Jeux* (orchestral), *Concerto for Harp and Seven Wind Instruments*; harp solos.

SAMMARTINI, Giovanni Battista (c.1693-1750) Italy. Known as "Sammartini of Milan" to distinguish him from his brother, Giuseppe. His style is said to have influenced Haydn. Some references give the number of his compositions as 2,800, although it has not always been easy to distinguish the work of the two brothers with certainty.

SARASATE, Pablo (actual surname Sarasate y Navascues) (1844-1908) Spain. One of the greatest violinists of his time. Composed many solo pieces for violin. Some of these, e.g., *Zigeunerweisen, Habanera, Caprice Basque*, and *Zapateado*, also several *Spanish Dances*, have remained in the repertoire of some violinists.

SATIE, Eric Alfred Leslie (1866-1925) France. The son of a music publisher in Paris and a British-born mother, Satie played piano accompaniments in cafés, later attending the Paris Conservatoire with disappointing results. He is said to have influenced many younger composers, including Debussy. Some of his musical compositions carry witty, sometimes absurd, titles. He wrote for orchestra, the theatre, ballet, and the piano.

SCARLATTI, Alessandro (1659-1725) Italy. An excellent harpsichordist and organist, and credited with having originated the Italian type of opera which became popular throughout Europe in the eighteenth century. He spent his late years in retirement, overshadowed by his son. His operas probably exceeded a hundred, but most of these were lost. His numerous compositions included oratorios, masses, cantatas, madrigals, chamber music, harpsichord pieces, arias, and songs.

SCARLATTI, Domenico (1685-1757) Italy. A son of Alessandro Scarlatti. In 1708 he met Handel, whose close friend he remained. In 1709 he entered the service of Marie Casimire, Queen of Poland, for whom he wrote several operas for her private theatre in

Rome. In 1729 he took a position as music-master at the Spanish court.

He was considered the greatest harpsichord player Italy had produced. Although he wrote many operas and some church music, he is best remembered for his harpsichord music, having composed more than five hundred works for that instrument. Many of these were published under the modest title *Exercises*, but have been listed as *sonatas*, although they do not follow the formal sonata pattern. He exercised considerable influence on keyboard music and technical aspects of keyboard playing.

Principal works: harpsichord music: *Stabat Mater* for ten voices and organ. (The ballet *The Good-Humoured Ladies* was based on movements from harpsichord sonatas of Scarlatti and orchestrated by Vincenzo Tommasini.)

SCHIBLER, Armin (b. 1920) Switzerland. An impressionable composer, writing in various styles, from Baroque and Romantic, to Modern. Among his works: *The Spanish Rose-Tree* and *Feet in the Fire* (operas); *Fantasie for Oboe, Harp and Small Orchestra*; *Fantasie for Viola and Small Orchestra*; *Prologue, Invocation and Danse* (horn and orchestra).

SCHMIDT, Franz (1874-1939) Austria. Organist, pianist, cellist, and composer. Composed symphonies, choral, and organ music in a traditional Austrian style.

SCHMITT, Florent (1870-1958) France. Pupil of Massenet, Fauré and Dubois. With a leaning towards French impressionism, he later wrote in various styles. Composed works for orchestra with solo parts for horn, saxophone, cello, piano, also a setting of Psalm 47 for soprano, chorus, organ and orchestra. Also writer on music.

SCHNABEL, Artur (1882-1951) Germany. Eminent pianist and teacher. Composed three symphonies and smaller works.

SCHOECK, Othmar (1886-1957) Switzerland. A pupil of Reger. Works, mainly in a German Romantic style, include *Penthesilea* (opera), *Concerto for Horn and Strings*, works for orchestra and chamber groups; songs.

SCHOENBERG, Arnold (1874-1951) Austria. One of the most influential musical thinkers of his time, he was self-taught in composition, but by the age of twenty he had produced several works and at twenty-five had com-pleted in three weeks his *Verklärte Nacht* (*Transfigured Night*), a string sextet version of a work that owed much to Wagner's influence. In 1901 he moved to Berlin, but three years later returned to Vienna. For a time he took up painting and exhibited his work in 1910. In 1933 he was driven from Germany by the Nazis, condemned by them as a Jew and as the composer of "decadent" music. He went to the United States, became professor of music at the University of California, Los Angeles, and died there.

Schoenberg's excursions into atonality and his adoption of the twelve-note method brought much abuse, but today many authorities are prepared to say that he will be universally remembered as one of the most revolutionary forces in the forward march of twentieth century music.

Principal works: *Verklärte Nacht* (later arranged for string orchestra); *Gurrelieder* for four solo singers, three male choirs, one mixed chorus, and large orchestra; *Pierrot Lunaire*, song cycle for voice and instruments; *Kammersymphonie*; *Five Pieces for Orchestra*; *Variations for Orchestra*; piano concerto; violin concerto; chamber works, including *Serenade for Seven Instruments and Bass Voice*; suites; quartets; operas, including *Erwartung* and *Die Glückliche Hand*; symphonic poem *Pelléas et Mélisande*; *Kol Nidrei* (Jewish Service) for reciter, chorus and orchestra; organ works, piano works; songs.

SCHREKER, Franz (1878-1934) Austria, born at Monaco. Studied in Vienna with Robert Fuchs; in 1920 appointed director of the Academy of Music in Berlin. Composed operas, works for orchestra and for solo instruments, and chamber music.

SCHUBERT, Franz (Peter) (1797-1828) Austria. When old enough, Schubert taught at the local school, but after two years of drudgery, decided to give all his time to composition. He was unsuccessful in obtaining appointments in music institutions, and at no time in his life did he hold a paid position, other than the short period that he spent as assistant schoolmaster, for which he received, in addition to his board and lodging, an annual salary of eight florins.

For some time Schubert lived with his friend Schober at a tavern frequented by musicians, but in August 1828 he took up residence in a house in a Vienna suburb, hoping that, being nearer the country, the air would relieve the attacks of giddiness that for some months had worried him. But his health deteriorated and, a victim of typhus, he died in November of that year. He was buried close to the grave of Beethoven, whose death had occurred during the previous year.

Schubert's compositions numbered close on a thousand, but from 1816 until he died in 1828, the total earnings from his music amounted to less than £600. Some of his larger works were bought by publishers for a few shillings, his songs for a few pence each. After his death a bundle of his manuscripts was sold for 8/6.

Schubert's works fall into many forms and include nine symphonies; ten overtures; many orchestral pieces; twenty-two string quartets; 452 dances for piano; forty-six *fantasies, impromptus, moments musicaux,* and other solo pieces; fifty-five piano duets; twenty-two piano sonatas; nine masses; 634 songs; also operas, choral works, etc., all written between 1810 and 1828.

Principal works: nine symphonies; *Rosa-munde* ballet music; chamber music (the *Piano Quintet in A,* known as *The Trout* being one of the best known); song cycles, including *Die Winterreise, Die Schöne Müllerin,* and *Schwanengesang;* some 600 individual songs, also works as mentioned above.

SCHUMAN, William (b. 1910) America. A pupil of Roy Harris, became head of the Juilliard School of Music, New York (1945 to 1961). His compositions, mostly in a modern mould, include *A Free Song* and *This is Our Time,* and other secular cantatas; nine symphonies; concertos; chamber music; a baseball-inspired opera, *The Mighty Casey; Judith,* a choreographic poem for piano and strings; *Newsell Suite.*

SCHUMANN, Robert (Alexander) (1810-1856) Germany. Schumann's arrival on the musical scene came at a time most suited to his imagination and temperament. It was a period when the Romantic movement was releasing literature and art from the tyranny of the pseudo-classical, and music was calling for composers to replace platitudinous formalism with more human and more personal concepts.

He studied at the Leipzig University, from which he matriculated in law. Meanwhile he had nourished his great interest in literature and music. In 1829 he met Friedrich Wieck, with whom he studied piano, and whose daughter he was to marry. Determined to become a great pianist, he invented a device for strengthening his fingers, which resulted in laming his hand. In losing another virtuoso, the world gained a composer. In 1834 he founded the publication *Die Neue Zeitschrift,* which he edited for ten years, its aim being to encourage promising composers and to throw a critical light on the spurious and the mediocre.

Schumann had met Clara Wieck when she was about nine; his affection grew into something deeper. In 1837 Friedrich Wieck opposed their marriage, partly because of the hopes he had for his daughter's career as a pianist, and because he could see little prospect for Robert as a successful son-in-law. After three years of separation, their marriage was sanctioned by court decree. Until then he had written little but piano music; in the first years of his married life he composed more than 130 songs, later branching into more extended forms.

In 1844 he suffered a nervous breakdown, and in 1854 he threw himself into the Rhine, but was rescued by boatmen. At his own request he was placed in a mental institution at Endenich, near Bonn, where he died two years later.

Schumann is sometimes referred to as the founder of the Romantic period in music. In his shorter works we find his finest writing.

Principal works: an opera *Genoveva;* a cantata *Paradise and the Peri;* incidental music to Byron's *Manfred;* four symphonies; *Concerto in A minor* for piano and orchestra; *Concerto in A minor* for cello and orchestra; *Concerto in D minor* for violin and orchestra; chamber music, including three string quartets, a piano quintet, and a piano trio; many piano works; song cycles, individual songs; a church *Requiem;* masses; part-songs; six fugues for organ on the name B.A.C.H.

SCHUTZ, Heinrich (1585-1672) Germany. Sometimes called the "Father of German music" and the composer of the first German opera, *Daphne,* or *Dafne.* Wrote four Passions, and an oratorio, orchestral music, madrigals, which were important in the development of German music.

SCOTT, Cyril (1879-1971) England. Composer, pianist, and poet; at the age of twelve went to Germany for music study. He took an advanced view of musical structures, producing operas, concertos, choral works, chamber music, piano pieces, and songs. He later became interested in occultism.

SCRIABIN, or SKRIABIN, Alexander (1872-1915) Russia. Studied composition with Taneiev, and became a touring pianist; from 1898 to 1904 was professor of piano at Moscow Conservatoire. Some of his earlier compositions were modelled on the style of Chopin, piano music being the greatest part of his creative output. He later adjusted his harmonic structure (inventing a so-called "mystic chord") more in keeping with his theosophical creed. Branching out into orchestral music, he wrote *The Divine Poem*, *The Poem of Ecstasy*, and *Prometheus, the Poem of Fire*.

SCULTHORPE, Peter (b. 1929) Australia. Studied in Melbourne, later in England, where his teachers were Rubbra and Wellesz. He has won several awards for composition and has received important commissions. In 1967 he took up a Harkness Fellowship at Yale University, New England. Among his compositions, some in an advanced style, are: *Sun Music* and *Irkanda* for orchestra; *Anniversary Music*, commissioned by the Australian Broadcasting Commission to mark the twentieth anniversary of the Youth Orchestral Concerts; *The Fifth Continent* for speaker and orchestra; chamber music, etc.

Works written during 1970 and early in 1971 include: *Music for Japan*, *Rain*, *Overture for a Happy Occasion* (for orchestra); *Love 200* (pop group and orchestra); *Dream* (for any large number of players); *The Stars Turn* (voice and piano); *Night* (piano), *Snow, Moon and Flowers* (piano); *Landscape* (for amplified piano); ballet-opera *Rites of Passage*.

SEARLE, Humphrey (b. 1915) England. Studied with Webern in Austria. His adoption of the twelve-note method has been flexible. Some of his works are: *The Shadow of Cain*, *The Canticle of the Rose* (choir); *Oxus* (Scena for voice and orchestra); *Gold Coast Customs* and *The River Run* for speakers and orchestra; five symphonies; opera *Hamlet*; piano con-

certos and sonatas; *Poem for Twenty-two Strings*; vocal music.

SEIBER, Mátyás (1905-1960) Hungary. Took up residence in England from 1935. While in his own country he studied with Kodály, later adopting the twelve-note method. His works include orchestral suites; a cantata, *Ulysses*; four string quartets, a violin concerto; piano works; film music.

SEROV, Alexander Nikolayevich (1820-1871) Russia. A composer and critic, who after visiting Germany in 1858 became a champion of Wagner, taking a hostile attitude towards the Russian "nationalist" school. Composed *The Power of Evil*, *Judith*, and other operas; a *Stabat Mater*; incidental music for *Nero*, and orchestral works.

SESSIONS, Roger (b. 1896) America. Graduated from Harvard University at eighteen; from 1925 to 1933 lived in Florence and Berlin, then returned to the United States to take up academic appointments. Compositions, in a logical, coherent style include *The Trial of Lucullis* and *Montezuma* (operas); *Turn O Libertad* (cantata); eight symphonies; masses; piano and violin concertos; orchestral and chamber works; songs; compositions for piano and organ.

SEVERAC, Déodat de (1873-1921) France. A pupil of d'Indy; influenced by Debussy, Franck and Albéniz. Composed two operas; works for orchestra, including ballet; chamber music; songs, and many piano pieces.

SGAMBATI, Giovanni (1843-1914) Italy. A pupil of Liszt, became an eminent pianist. Composed two symphonies, also works for piano and for violin.

SHAPERO, Harold (b. 1920) America. Studied with Piston, Hindemith, Křenek and others. Works include *Concerto for Orchestra*; *Symphony for Classical Orchestra*; *Serenade for Strings*; *The Travellers Overture*; *Nine-minute Overture*; piano pieces.

SHAPORIN, Yury (1887-1966) Russia. The opera *The Decembrists*, dealing with the unsuccessful uprising of December 1825, is one of his most notable works. Other works, *On the Field of Kulikovo* (cantata); a symphony; piano sonatas; songs.

SHARP, Cecil J. (1859-1924). A noted collector of English folk-songs and folk-dances. Visited Australia and in 1883, together with Immanuel G. Reimann, founded the Adelaide

College of Music which became the basis of the University Conservatorium, to be later known as the Elder Conservatorium of Music.

SHEBALIN, Vissarion (1902-1963) Russia. A pupil of Miaskovsky. Works include five symphonies; a violin concerto; opera, *The Taming of the Shrew*; Variations on a Russian Folk Song; piano sonatas; music for plays and films.

SHEPHERD, Arthur (b. 1880) America. Conductor, teacher, and composer. Works include two symphonies; *The Song of the Pilgrim* (cantata); *Fantasy for Piano and Orchestra*; *Fantasy on "Down East" Spirituals*; *Triptych for High Voice and Strings*; string quartets.

SHOSTAKOVICH, Dmitri (1906-1975) Russia. One of the most significant of Soviet composers. At nine he composed a *Theme with Variations*, and at thirteen took lessons in composition from Steinberg, Rimsky-Korsakov's son-in-law. To assist his parents financially, he played the piano in cinemas and wrote music for plays and films. In 1925 Nicolai Malko conducted the first performance of his *Symphony No. 1 in F minor*. From 1930 to 1932 he worked on his opera *Lady Macbeth of Mtsensk*, this stressing unsatisfactory aspects of the old régime. *Pravda*, the official organ of the Communist Party condemned it as "jittery, noisy and neurotic music."

Shostakovich continued to compose in many forms, all mirroring something of his complex personality which had to adjust itself to Soviet influences. One wonders how far bureaucratic control interfered with his artistic conscience in the earlier stages of his career.

Principal works: operas, *Lady Macbeth of Mtsensk*, *The Nose*; cantata, *Song of the Forests*; *The Execution of Stepan Razin* (for bass, chorus, and orchestra); fifteen symphonies; ballets, including *The Golden Age* and *The Limpid Stream*; piano concertos; violin concerto; church music; chamber music; piano works; songs.

SIBELIUS, Jean (1865-1957) Finland. Sibelius had reached the age of twenty before music claimed his attention; even then, while studying violin and theory, he enrolled at the Helsinki University in the faculty of law. Influenced by Järnefelt, whose sister he later married, and by Busoni, he decided on music as his true career and subsequently studied in Berlin and Vienna. In 1897 he received a grant from the Finnish Government which allowed him to give up teaching and concentrate on composition. In time he had graduated from the author of short pieces to one of the great symphonists of his time. Inspired by the *Kalevala*, the Finnish national epic, he composed tone poems based on age-old legends.

Sibelius followed no "schools." His symphonies are distinguished by organic unity and unforced transitions from the dramatic to the lyric. Though flexible, his allegiance remained true to classical traditions. His seventh symphony was completed in 1924, thirty-two years before his death, but he wrote no other. Perhaps he felt that he had expressed his last word in symphonic form.

Principal works: seven symphonies; tone poems, including *Pohjola's Daughter*, *Tapiola*, *Lemminkainen Cycle* (four "legends" for orchestra, of which *The Swan of Tuonela* is No. 2); *En Saga*, *The Oceanides*, and *Finlandia* (tone-poems); *Valse Triste* (from incidental music to play, *Kuolema*); *Karelia*, *Rakastava*, and *King Christian* suites; incidental music to *Pelléas et Mélisande*, *Belshazzar's Feast*, and *The Tempest*; *Hymn to the Earth* (chorus and orchestra); *The Song of Vaino* (chorus and orchestra); *Concerto in D minor* for violin and orchestra; string quartet entitled *Voces Intimae*; more than a hundred songs; piano solos.

SIEGMEISTER, Elie (b. 1909) America. His music was influenced by American life, sometimes using folk-tunes. Works include symphonies; operas, *Miranda and the Dark Young Man*, *The Mermaid of Lock Number Seven*, *Darling Corie* (operas); *Abraham Lincoln Walks at Midnight* (chorus and orchestra); *From my Window* (suite); *Concerto for Clarinet and Orchestra*; other orchestral pieces.

SINDING, Christian (1856-1941) Norway. Following a Romantic style, composed three symphonies; two violin, and one piano concerto. Best remembered for his *Rustle of Spring* for piano.

SINIGAGLIA, Leone (1868-1944) Italy. Had the friendship and advice of Dvořák and Goldmark in Vienna. Wrote for orchestra, solo instruments, but no opera.

SITSKY, Larry (b. 1934). Born in China of Russian parents, he studied in San Francisco with Busoni and Petri; has held teaching appointments in Australia. Works include *The Fall of the House of Usher* (opera); orchestral, choral, and chamber works; compositions for piano.

SIX, THE (Les Six). Name given to group of French composers: Auric, Durey, Honegger, Milhaud, Poulenc, and Tailleferre.

SKALKOTTAS, Nikos (1904-1949) Greece. A disciple of Schoenberg. Has written for orchestra, strings, cello, piano, etc., sometimes using Greek folk material.

SMETANA, Bedřich (1824-1884) Bohemia. Named the founder of the National School of modern Czech music. Appeared in public as pianist at age of six. At nineteen he moved to Prague with only twenty florins in his pocket. In 1859 he conducted the Philharmonic Society in Gothenburg, Sweden, having received assistance from Liszt. He became conductor of the Prague National Theatre and set about evolving a national school of opera.

The year 1866 saw the first production of his most famous folk-opera, *The Bartered Bride*, which at the time failed to arouse much enthusiasm. Other operas followed, also orchestral, choral, and piano works. An ardent patriot, he set out to glorify his homeland in a cycle of six symphonic poems under the group title *Ma Vlast (My Fatherland)*. These he dedicated to the city of Prague. In later life he became a victim to ceaseless head-noises which resulted in periods of sleeplessness and depression. In May 1884 he entered a mental home and died there.

Smetana was seldom attracted to abstract music when composing, most of his works, even his chamber music, being of the "programme" type. His love of the dance and folk idiom played a strong part in his writing.

Principal works: operas, *The Bartered Bride, Dalibor, The Kiss, The Devil's Wall, The Secret, Libusa;* orchestral works, including *Ma Vlast* (six symphonic poems, of which *Vltava* or *Moldau* is best known); two string quartets; songs; piano works.

SMYTH, Ethel (Mary) (1858-1944) England. Studied at Leipzig Conservatoire; had works performed in Germany and in England. Took prominent part in the cause of women's suffrage. Created Dame in 1922. Her works, leaning towards a German traditional style,

include operas, *The Wreckers, The Boatswain's Mate;* a mass; concertos; chamber music.

SOMERVELL, Arthur (1863-1937) England. Works for solo voice, chorus and orchestra include *Christmas, The Passion of Christ*, and *To the Vanguard; Symphony in D minor; Violin Concerto in G minor;* orchestral music; songs. Knighted 1929.

SOUSA, John Philip (1854-1933) America. Band-conductor and composer of many marches. Also wrote operettas.

SPOHR, Louis (1784-1859) Germany. In his time a famous violinist and prolific composer. Wrote seventeen violin concertos, also operas, orchestral, choral, and chamber music. As conductor, is said to have been one of the first to use a baton.

SPONTINI, Gaspar Luigi (1774-1851) Italy. The son of simple peasants, became a celebrated composer, chiefly opera, in his time. Now remembered almost solely for the opera, *La Vestale*.

STAINER, John (1840-1901) England. Organist, writer on music, holding academic positions. Composed church music of a conventional kind, his best known work being the oratorio *The Crucifixion* which is still often performed.

STAMITZ, Karl (Carl) (1745-1801) Bohemia. The son of a family of musicians, he composed many symphonies, concertos, and chamber music.

STANFORD, Charles Villiers (1852-1924) Ireland. One of the most distinguished British musicians of his time. He studied in Germany, became a noted teacher and conductor, and composed numerous works which included seven operas, *Shamus O'Brien, The Critic*, etc.; seven symphonies; church music, cantatas; songs. Knighted in 1901. The teacher of several famous British composers.

STANLEY, John (1713-1786) England. Though blind from early childhood had busy career as organist and composer. Wrote six concertos for organ or harpsichord, and strings; organ and vocal music.

STAROKADOMSKY, Mikhail (1901-1954) Russia. Studied with Miaskovsky. Wrote for orchestra, organ, chamber groups, and an opera.

STEFFANI, Agostino (1654-1728) Italy. Studied philosophy, mathematics, theology (was ordained a priest in 1680); musical director at Hanover; composed operas, church music, chamber music. Later became a diplomat.

STEVENS, Bernard (b. 1916) England. Works, mostly in lyrical style, include a symphony; violin concerto; piano, chamber and choral works.

STEVENS, James (b. 1923) England. Studied with Frankel, N. Boulanger, and Milhaud. Has lived much of his time on the Continent. Composer of symphonies, ballets, songs.

STILL, Robert (1910-1971) England. Works include a symphony, quintet for three flutes, violin, and cello, also other chamber music.

STILL, William Grant (b. 1895) America. Said to be the first Negro to write a symphony. Much of his music is influenced by Negro associations. Works include: *Afro-American Symphony*, other symphonies; orchestral music, including *Africa, Archaic Ritual, Dismal Swamp, Summerland; Troubled Island* (opera); *And They Lynched Him on a Tree* (narrator, contralto, double chorus, and orchestra); chamber music; songs.

STOCKHAUSEN, Karlheinz (b. 1928) Germany. In 1950 began studies with Frank Martin, later coming under the influence of Messiaen and Webern's twelve-note technique. In 1956 published the first electronic "score." Since then has experimented in electronic music, travelling widely. He has influenced many composers of various countries in the more advanced techniques of composition.

STOESSEL, Albert (1894-1943) America. Violinist, conductor and composer. Works include opera, *Garrick;* symphonic portrait, *Cyrano de Bergerac; Hispania Suite; Early Americana Suite;* violin sonatas, chamber music.

STRAUS, Oscar, spelt with one s (1870-1954) Austria. Wrote operettas, including *The Chocolate Soldier* and *The Waltz Dream;* also music for the film *La Ronde.*

STRAUSS — The Viennese Strauss "Dynasty" consisted of:

    I Johann Strauss (father, 1804-1849)
    II Johann Strauss (son, 1825-1899)
    III Josef Strauss (son, 1827-1870)
    IV Edouard Strauss (son, 1835-1916)
    V Johann Strauss (grandson, 1866-1939)

STRAUSS, Edouard. Composer of waltzes, dance music.

STRAUSS, Johann, the elder. Born in Vienna and died there. As a boy apprenticed to a bookbinder; in time joined an orchestra conducted by Joseph Lanner, but struck out on his own in 1825. He composed 250 light works, including 152 waltzes. In due course was overshadowed by his son, Johann.

STRAUSS, Johann, the younger. It was the wish of Johann Strauss senior that his sons should follow a profession other than music, but in time he realised that his son, Johann, more academically trained than he, was the more popular.

To Johann Strauss II and Josef Lanner belongs the credit of having created the Viennese Waltz. Strauss developed the form and in his later compositions extended both the introduction and the coda sections to symphonic proportions. He became known as "The Waltz King." He toured Austria, Germany, and Poland with his orchestra and undertook to direct summer concerts in St Petersburg. His compositions total 479, this number including sixteen operettas (*Die Fledermaus* and *Zigeunerbaron* being the most popular); 400 waltzes, including *An der Schoenen Blauen Donau (The Blue Danube)*; polkas; marches.

STRAUSS, Josef. Respecting his father's wishes, he became an architect, but studied the violin in secret, formed an orchestra of his own, and published 283 compositions. Also collaborated with his brother Johann in several works.

STRAUSS, Richard (1864-1949) Germany. No relation to the Viennese family mentioned above. Began to compose at the age of six and before his eleventh birthday he had two works published. Meanwhile he had studied the harp and had taken violin lessons from Bruno Walter. In 1885 Hans von Bülow helped him to secure the position of Assistant Musical Director at Meiningen, by which time several of his works had been performed in other countries, including America. In 1892 he travelled as conductor of several orchestras in Germany and paid his first visit to London. In 1894 he took over the direction of the Berlin Philharmonic Concerts and four years later succeeded Weingartner as conductor of the Berlin Royal Opera.

Now recognised as a penetrating conductor, he was invited by Wagner's widow to direct the first Bayreuth performance of *Tannhäuser*. In 1919 he became one of the directors of the State Opera in Vienna and, when not travelling, lived in a large house on land presented to him by the State.

Richard Strauss conceived his symphonic poems in terms of tonal splendour; in his operas and his lieder, as well as in his orchestral works, he aimed to translate literary concepts into a musical language.

Principal works: operas, including *Salome, Elektra, Ariadne auf Naxos, Der Rosenkavalier, Die Frau ohne Schatten, Arabella, Capriccio; Alpine Symphony;* symphonic poems, including, *Don Juan, Till Eulenspiegel's lustige Streiche; Tod und Verklärung, Also Sprach Zarathustra, Ein Heldenleben;* incidental music to Molière's *Le Bourgeois Gentilhomme; Dance Suite; Metamorphosen* for strings; *Symphony for Wind;* born concertos; many songs for voice and piano; *Four Last Songs* for voice and orchestra.

STRAVINSKY, Igor (1882-1971) Russia. By the time he had received a general education at the University, he was sufficiently advanced in music for Rimsky-Korsakov to take him as a pupil in orchestration. He abandoned law in 1906, and published a symphony, as well as other orchestral works and a song-cycle.

A new incentive came from his meeting with Diaghilev, the organiser of the *Ballets Russes.* After orchestrating some of Chopin's music for the ballet *Les Sylphides* he composed for Diaghilev *L'Oiseau de Feu* in 1910. *Petrouchka* followed a year later. Then came his most ambitious score, *Le Sacre du printemps.* His fame spread. He lived for a time in Paris until war interrupted his plans and in 1918 he was living in Switzerland, cut off from his financial resources in Russia. He subsequently settled in the United States. Few composers of our time have exercised more influence on the course of music.

Principal works: ballets, including *Les Noces, L'Oiseau de feu, Petrouchka, Le Sacre du Printemps, Pulcinella* (after Pergolesi), *Le Baiser de la fée* (after Tchaikovsky); operas and opera-oratorios, including *The Rake's Progress, Oedipus Rex, Le Rossignol* (part of which arranged as a symphonic poem); *L'Histoire du soldat* (for cast of three and instrumental group); *Symphony of Psalms* for choir and orchestra; orchestral works; *Concerto in D* for violin and orchestra; *Ebony Concerto* for clarinet and swing band; *Capriccio* for piano and orchestra; *Concerto for Piano and Orchestra; Burleske* for piano and orchestra; *Concerto for Piano and Wind Instruments; Requiem Canticles;* chamber music; piano works; songs.

STRINGFIELD, Lamar (1897-1959) America. Flautist, conductor and composer. Works include *From the Southern Mountains, Indian Legend, The Legend of John Henry, Negro Parade,* and other works for orchestra; *The Seventh Queue* (symphonic ballet); *Pastoral Scene* for flute and small orchestra.

SUK, Josef (1874-1935) Czechoslovakia. Member of the Bohemian String Quartet; son-in-law of Dvořák. Composed a symphony, symphonic poems; works for violin and for piano.

SULLIVAN, Arthur (1842-1900) England. The son of Thomas Sullivan of Irish birth. When only eight composed an anthem, *By the Waters of Babylon.* Sang in the Chapel Royal Choir; won a Mendelssohn scholarship. Later studied in Leipzig. In 1866 he was appointed professor of composition at the Royal Academy of Music. Aiming to be a serious composer, he wrote orchestral works, cantatas, and later an opera, *Ivanhoe;* also edited hymns, as well as composing several settings of his own, including *Onward Christian Soldiers.*

In 1871 he met W. S. Gilbert, with whom he collaborated on fourteen immensely successful operettas. He received a knighthood in 1863. He was buried in St Paul's Cathedral.

SUPPE, Franz von (1820-1895). Of Belgian descent, Suppé was born at Spalato (now Split) and christened Francesco Ermenegildo Ezechiele Suppé-Demelli. Composed many operettas, including *The Beautiful Galatea* and *Boccaccio;* also such popular overtures as *Poet and Peasant, Light Cavalry,* and *Morning, Noon and Night in Vienna.*

SUTERMEISTER, Heinrich (b. 1910) Switzerland. A pupil of Orff. Composed operas, including *Romeo und Julia, Die Zauberinsel;* cantatas; music for ballets; piano concertos.

SUTHERLAND, Margaret (b. 1897) Australia. In 1924 went to London, where she studied with Sir Arnold Bax, with further study in Vienna. Many of her works have been performed in and outside of Australia. These include *Concerto for Strings*; *Concerto Grosso*; *The Orange Tree* for voice, clarinet and piano; *The Child in the World*, for voice and string trio; orchestral pieces; chamber music; songs; and piano solos.

SVENDSEN, Johan (1840-1911) Norway. Trained in Germany and was associated with Liszt and Wagner. Travelled widely and lived in Paris for some time. Composed two symphonies, other orchestral works; cantatas; chamber music; pieces for solo instruments.

SWEELINCK, Jan Pieterszoon (1562-1621) Holland. A famous organist himself, he taught many other organist-composers. His works include those for organ and clavier, also choral works and psalms.

SZERVANSZKY, Endré (b. 1912) Poland. Teacher, critic, and composer. Works include a symphony; *Hungarian Soldier's Cantata*; concertos for flute and for clarinet; orchestral suites; *Oriental Tale* (ballet suite); Hungarian folk-song arrangements.

SZYMANOWSKI, Karol (1882-1937) Poland. Born in the Ukraine, he studied in Warsaw and Berlin and became one of the most respected Polish composers. His works include *Hagith* and *King Roger* (operas); symphonic poems, including *Penthesilea*; chamber music; many songs; two violin concertos; *Myths* for violin and piano, No. 1 being the well-known *Fountains of Arethusa*.

TAHOURDIN, Peter (b. 1928) England. Studied in London; took up residence in Adelaide, Australia in 1964. Has composed in several forms; a symphony; orchestral works, including *Diversions*, *The Swans*, *The Space Traveller*; chamber music. One of his special interests is electronic music, which he studied at the Toronto University in 1966, his electronic work, *Rondo*, being performed there in January 1967. *Riders in Paradise* is built around Elizabeth Barrett Browning's love sonnets.

TAILLEFERRE, Germaine (b. 1892) France. A pianist and composer, she became a member of "The Six." Her works include *Concertino for Harp and Orchestra*; orchestral music (ballets, etc.); a piano concerto; songs.

TALLIS, Thomas (c. 1505-1585) England. Joint organist with Byrd at the Chapel Royal; together these musicians held a State monopoly for music-printing in England. His works comprise masses, magnificats, and lamenta-

tions (in Latin); numerous motets; services in English; pieces for keyboard and for viols.

TANEIEV, Sergei (1856-1915) Russia. Pianist and composer. Studied harmony with Tchaikovsky. Was also an eminent teacher, numbering Rachmaninov among his pupils. Composed an opera, three symphonies, choral music, chamber music, piano works.

TANSMAN, Alexandre (b. 1897) Poland. Settled in Paris in 1921. At first influenced by Ravel and Stravinsky, wrote in an "advanced" style, symphonies, chamber music, ballets, and piano music.

TARTINI, Giuseppe (1692-1770) Italy. Founder of an important school of violin-playing and inventor of improvements in violin-making and technique. Works include many concertos, and sonatas, the *Devil's Trill* being one of his most famous.

TATE, Phyllis (b. 1911) England. Works include *Concerto for Saxophone and Strings*, *Occasional Overture*; an opera *The Lodger*; *Nocturne* for three voices and seven instruments; songs and folk-song arrangements.

TAVERNER, John (c. 1495-1545) England. Organist and composer. Took up an appointment at Cardinal College, Oxford. Becoming involved in religious controversies, was, in 1528, accused of heresy and imprisoned. For his duties at Oxford he received a salary of £10 per annum. Compositions include masses, Latin services, motets.

TAYLOR (Joseph), Deems (1885-1966) America. His operas include *The Dragon*, *Peter Ibbetson*, *The King's Henchman*. Wrote also *The Chambered Nautilus* (cantata), *The Highwayman* (cantata); *Through the Looking-Glass* and other suites; *Portrait of a Lady* (rhapsody for winds, piano, and strings); *The Siren Song*, and ballet music. Also noted critic and radio commentator. Gave the commentary for the Walt Disney film, *Fantasia*.

TCHAIKOVSKY, Peter Ilyich (1840-1893) Russia. His parents did little to encourage his early interest in music. The family moved to St Petersburg and arrangements were made for him to study for the legal profession. In 1859 he took employment as a clerk in the Ministry of Justice, but later entered the newly formed St Petersburg Conservatory. After graduation he taught harmony at Moscow Conservatory. He kept on composing, but recurring fits of depression caused him to doubt the merits of what he had written.

Although not attracted to the opposite sex, he married Antonia Ivanovna Milyukova. Within a few days both realised their mistake. A separation was agreed on and several weeks after the wedding, he left Moscow and travelled to Switzerland in a state of mental collapse. Relief from financial anxiety came when Nadezhda von Meck, a wealthy widow, gave him a yearly income of six thousand roubles, so that he could give his full time to composition. Her only stipulation was that he should make no attempt to meet her. By the time he had reached his fortieth birthday he had passed from obscurity to hard-earned recognition.

In 1893 he complained of indigestion, but refused to call in a doctor. When at last a physician was sent for, his trouble was diagnosed as cholera, the probable result of having drunk impure water. He died five days later.

Tchaikovsky's career was a mixture of success and failure. If his music is meant to please the ear and to stir the emotions, then we find the reason why today he is still one of the composers to whom public appreciation has remained steadfast.

Principal works: six symphonies; three piano concertos (No. 3 unfinished); one violin concerto; *Variations on a Rococo Theme* (for cello and orchestra); orchestral works, including *Capriccio Italien, Marche Slave, 1812 Overture, Hamlet Overture; Romeo and Juliet* (Overture-Fantasia); *Francesca da Rimini; Serenade in C;* ballets, including *Swan Lake, Nutcracker, Sleeping Princess;* ten operas, including *Eugene Onegin, The Queen of Spades, Mazeppa, Joan of Arc;* chamber music (*Quartet in D major* containing the *Andante Cantabile*, also transcribed for orchestra); choral works; piano pieces; songs.

TCHEREPNINE, Alexander (1897-1977) Russia. Pianist and composer; settled in Paris in 1921; later moved to the United States. Son of Nicolai Tcherepnine. Works include symphonies; piano concertos; *The Lost Flute* (narrator and orchestra); *Macbeth* (opera); *Stenka Razin* (ballet); *Romantic Overture; Sonata for Timpani and Orchestra;* piano works.

TCHEREPNINE, Nicolai (Nikolay) (1873-1945) Russia. Settled in Paris with his son,

Alexander, in 1921. Works include *Narcissus* and *Le Pavillon d'Armide* (ballets); *The Enchanted Kingdom* (symphonic sketch); piano concertos, etc.

TELEMANN, George Philipp (1681-1767) Germany. Almost self-taught in music, he played an important role in the evolution of music in Germany and in his time was considered the superior of J. S. Bach. He held several posts as *Kapellmeister*, and in 1721 took over the dual positions of cantor of the Johanneum and music director of the principal church in Hamburg. He travelled a good deal and while in Paris was influenced by French musical ideas. Telemann wrote fluently, often in the French and Italian styles.

Principal works: twelve complete sets of cantatas for every Sunday and holiday of the year; forty-four *Passions;* more than a hundred oratorios; forty operas; six hundred overtures in the French style; numerous instrumental and vocal works. He wrote the libretti for many of his operas and compiled his autobiography.

TEMPLETON, Alec (1909-1963) Wales. Blind from birth, became known as a pianist-entertainer in a humorous style. Composed *Concertino Lirico* (piano and orchestra); *Gothic Concerto* (piano and orchestra); *Rhapsodie Harmonique* (piano and orchestra); *The Pied Piper of Hamelin* (narrator and orchestra); *Suite for Strings;* also parodies on the classics, including *Bach Goes to Town.*

THOMAS (Charles Louis), Ambroise (1811-1896) France. Began career as pianist; for a time director of the Paris Conservatoire. Composed thirteen operas, including *Mignon, Raymond, Hamlet,* and *Le Caid;* ballets, church music.

THOMPSON, Randal (b. 1899) America. Pupil of Bloch. Also teacher. Works include symphonies; choral works (*The Last Words of David, Ode to the Virginian Voyage,* etc.); opera, *Solomon and Balkis; The Piper at the Gates of Dawn* for orchestra.

THOMPSON, Virgil (b. 1896) America. Studied with N. Boulanger in Paris. His many works include *Four Saints in Three Acts* and *The Mother of Us All* (operas); symphonies; *Arcadian Airs and Dances, Election Day, The Plough that Broke the Plains,* and other suites; *Bayou* and *Filling Station* and other ballets; concertos; incidental music; film music; songs in English and French. Also noted critic.

TIPPETT, Michael (b. 1905) England. In 1923 enrolled at the Royal College of Music, London, where he studied composition with R. O. Morris and Charles Wood, also conducting with Sir Adrian Boult and Sir Malcolm Sargent. He was for some time musical director at Morley College, Lambeth, but after the success of his oratorio *A Child of Our Time*, first presented in 1944, he gave up teaching and spent the next five years on his opera, *The Midsummer Marriage*, which was presented at Covent Garden in 1955. He has explored new forms of musical expression, and is also an authority on music of the Restoration period. Among his other works: two symphonies; *Crown of the Year, The Vision of Saint Augustine* (cantatas); motets, madrigals; chamber, piano, and organ works.

Principal works: choral, including *A Child of Our Time* and *Boyhood's End; The Midsummer Marriage* (opera); *The Vision of St Augustine* (cantata); two symphonies; *Concerto for Double String Orchestra; Fantasia Concertante on a theme of Corelli* (for strings); two piano concertos; *Fantasy Sonata* for piano; three string quartets. He was knighted in 1966.

TOCH, Ernst (1887-1964) Austria. In 1940 took up residence in the United States. Works include seven symphonies; *The Princess and the Pea* and three other operas; *Cantata of the Bitter Herbs, The Idle Stroller, Motley*, and *Little Theatre* suites; *Pinocchio, Circus*, and other overtures; *The Water* (cantata); *Allegro for Organ and Orchestra;* chamber music; film music.

TOMASI, Henri (1901-1971) France. A traditional composer, with a freedom of expression, who sometimes borrows from folk-lore. Compositions include concertos for flute, clarinet, horn, alto saxophone, trombone, trumpet, viola; suites, *Don Juan de Manara, Féerie Laotienne, Les Noces de Cendres*, etc.; operas, including *Sampiero Corso;* other works for orchestra; ballets.

TOMMASINI, Vincenzo (1878-1950) Italy. Composed operas, orchestral, chamber, and choral works, but best known outside his own country as the arranger of Scarlatti's music for the ballet *The Good-humoured Ladies*.

TORELLI, Giuseppe (c. 1658-c. 1708) Italy.

Violinist and composer who lived for some years in Germany. He is credited with having developed the Concerto Grosso. The last six numbers of his Op. 6 contain some of the earliest passages in orchestral music designed for solo performance. As this was new, he added a note to the scores: "If in any concerto you find the word 'solo' written, this must be played by one violin alone."

TOVEY, Donald Francis (1875-1940) England. In his time an eminent pianist, composer, conductor, and writer on music, who held the position of Reid Professor of Music at Edinburgh University. Composed much music, including an opera, *The Bride of Dionysus;* piano, and cello concertos; church music; chamber music. He was knighted in 1935.

TRANCHELL, Peter (b. 1922). English composer born in India. Has written an opera, *The Mayor of Casterbridge;* choral music, and songs.

TREHARNE, Bryceson (1879-1948) Wales. Received his musical education at Royal College of Music, London, under Stanford, Parry, Walford Davies and others and from 1901 spent ten years at the University of Adelaide, Australia. In 1916 he went to the United States; for several years was editor of the Boston Publishing Company. Died in the United States. His works include: operas; choral and orchestral compositions; piano pieces; more than 200 songs.

TURCHI, Guido (b. 1916) Italy. Works include *Five Comments on 'The Bacchae' of Euripides* for orchestra; *Invective* for choir and two pianos; chamber music.

TURINA, Joaquin (1882-1949) Spain. Studied with d'Indy in Paris. His works, in a clear, Spanish style, include *Procession del Rocio*, a brilliant orchestral study; *La Oracion del torero* for string quartet, and other chamber music; *Rapsodia Sinfonica* for piano and orchestra; orchestral music; piano pieces; songs; guitar solos.

TYE, Christopher (c. 1500-c. 1572) England. Appointed Magister Choristarum at Ely Cathedral about 1541 at a yearly salary of £10. Composed masses, services, motets, and anthems in Latin and English.

VACTOR, David van (b. 1900) America. Pupil of Dukas in Paris. A flautist, conductor, and composer. Works include symphonies; *Credo* (secular cantata); *Cantata for Three Treble Voices and Orchestra;* concertos for flute, violin, and viola; *Symphonic Suite; Three Dance Scenes; Variazioni Comedy Overture,* (Nos 1 and 2); *Passacaglia and Fugue for Orchestra,* ballet music, etc.

VARESE, Edgar (1885-1965) France. Studied with d'Indy and Roussel. Settled in the United States in 1915. Adopted a radical style, experimenting in tonal blocks. Works include: *Ameriques, Arcana, Hyperprism, Integrales* for orchestra; *Deserts* (with electronic tape-recordings); *Ionization* for thirty instruments of "percussion, friction and sibulation."

VAUGHAN WILLIAMS, Ralph (1872-1958) England. After study with Parry, Stanford, and Parratt in England, took his degree of Doctor of Music in 1901, then went to Berlin where he had lessons in composition from Max Bruch. In 1909 he visited Paris and had some instruction in orchestration from Ravel. He had reached the age of forty-two when war came in 1914, but he joined the army as an orderly, served in Macedonia during 1916 and 1917, and in the following year saw active service in France as a lieutenant in the artillery.

About 1901 he began an intensive study of English folk-song, an interest that remained with him and which flavoured many of his works. By 1920 he had produced an impressive number of compositions, had become a professor of composition at the Royal College of Music, and was the new conductor of the London Bach Choir. In 1919 he accepted an honorary doctorate in music at Oxford and in 1935 he received the Order of Merit from King George V.

During the early part of this century, Vaughan Williams did much to bring about a Renaissance in British music. He completed his ninth symphony at the age of eighty-five.

Principal works: nine symphonies; *Fantasia on a theme of Thomas Tallis; English Folk Songs Suite; Fantasia on Greensleeves; Flos Campi* (viola and orchestra); *The Lark Ascending* (violin and orchestra); concertos for piano, violin, oboe and tuba; *Concerto Grosso* for strings; *Wasps Overture; Partita for Double String Orchestra;* operas, including *Hugh the Drover, Pilgrim's Progress, Sir John in Love,* and *Riders to the Sea;* choral works, including *Dona Nobis Pacem, Magnificat, Hodie, Mass in G minor, Toward the Unknown Region, Sancta Civitas, Serenade to Music; Quartet in G minor* and other chamber works; *Job, a Masque for Dancing* (orchestra); song cycles, including *On Wenlock Edge, Songs of Travel, House of Life;* many other songs and hymns.

VERDI, Giuseppe (1813-1901) Italy. This outstanding figure in Italian opera was born into a poor family. He was sent to a neighbouring town where he obtained board and lodging for fourpence a day, taking music lessons from a grocer named Barezzi, whose daughter he married in 1836. At eighteen he applied for admission to the Conservatoire in Milan but failed to obtain this.

Later he received expert tuition and in time became recognised as the musical heir of Rossini and Donizetti. His first opera, *Oberto,* appeared in 1839 and, although selecting melodramatic, even tawdry, subjects, he found his operas gaining increasing popularity. In time he became a national figure and after writing nearly thirty operas, retired to live in seclusion. During the sixteen years that followed the production of *Aïda* in 1871 he composed little apart from his *Requiem* (1874), but at the age of seventy-four he wrote *Otello* and at eighty *Falstaff;* these are considered his greatest operas.

Principal works: *Nabucco, Ernani, Macbeth, Luisa Miller, Rigoletto, Il Trovatore, La Traviata, Les Vêpres Siciliennes, Simon Boccanegra, Un Ballo in Maschera, La Forza del Destino, Don Carlos, Aïda, Otello, Falstaff; Requiem* and other sacred music; a string quartet.

VERESS, Sándor (b. 1907) Hungary. Pianist, teacher and composer, also editor of Hungarian folk-music. Has written orchestral music, a violin concerto, piano music, etc.

VICTORIA, Tomas Luis de (name sometimes Italianised as Vittoria) (mid 16th century-1611) Spain. One of the greatest Spanish musicians of his time, studied in Rome, and ranked next to Palestrina in importance. Composed only church music.

VIERNE, Louis (1870-1937) France. Organist and composer; pupil of Franck and Widor. Became organist at Notre Dame, Paris. Composed orchestral music, a mass, some chamber music, but is best known for his organ works.

VIEUXTEMPS, Henri (1820-1881) Belgium. A celebrated violinist. Composed six concertos and other music for violin, also three cadenzas for Beethoven's violin concerto.

VILLA-LOBOS, Heitor (c. 1887-1959) South America. While still a child, was forced to earn his living by playing in cafés and theatres. About 1910 became interested in folk-lore and some years later ventured into the farthest reaches of the Amazon to study Indian and other folk-music at first hand. He derived inspiration from Brazil and Bach. This gave the general title *Bachianas Brasileiras* to a set of works, intended to fuse the Brazilian idiom with that of J. S. Bach. Carried out many experiments; e.g., his *New York Skyline* employed a theme that represented a skyline and was written to a geometrical pattern on graph paper.

Principal works: *Bachianas Brasileiras; Choros;* an opera, *Magdalena;* a cello concerto; compositions for guitar, voice, and piano.

VIOTTI, Giovanni Battista (Jean Baptiste) (c. 1753-1824) Italy. A famous violinist; pupil of Pugnani. He himself taught many famous violinists. Viotti composed about thirty violin concertos, other violin works, ten piano concertos; songs.

VITALI, Tommaso Antonio (mid 17th century-?) Italy. Details of birth and life obscure. Known to have been a violinist; remembered for his *Chaconne* for violin and keyboard accompaniment.

VIVALDI, Antonio (1678-1741) Italy. Now regarded as one of the great composers of his time, was in 1716 appointed *maestro dei concerti* at the *Ospedale della Pieta* in Venice, one of the four pious hospital foundations for foundling girls. Under Vivaldi's direction the girls' orchestra became the finest in Venice. For them he wrote numerous concertos in various styles and forms. He was also a priest and because of the colour of his hair became known as "the red priest." He died in obscure circumstances, and his music lost its former popularity soon after his death.

During the twentieth century there has been a revival of interest in his music, this to a great extent due to the gramophone record.

Principal works: more than 250 concertos, chiefly in the concerto grosso style, including *L'Estro Armonico*, a set of twelve concertos, dedicated to Ferdinando III, Grand Duke of Tuscany; oratorios; operas; church music.

VLAD, Roman (b. 1919) Rumania. Works

include *The Lady of the Camellias* (ballet); *Variazoni Concertante* for piano and orchestra; *Divertimento for Eleven Instruments*. Also critic.

VOGEL, Vladimir (b. 1896). Born Moscow, studied in Berlin with Busoni and settled in Switzerland in 1939. Has composed secular oratorios; orchestral, chamber, and piano works. Adopted twelve-note technique.

VUATAZ, Roger (b. 1898) Switzerland. Conductor, writer, composer. Works include *Jesus* (oratorio); church music; violin concerto; piano, and organ works.

WAGENAAR, Bernard (1894-1971) Holland. Settled in the United States in 1921. Violinist, teacher, and composer. Son of Johan Wagenaar. Works include four symphonies; *Pieces of Eight* (opera); *Triple Concerto* (flute, cello, and harp); orchestral works; songs, *Song of Mourning* (A reflection on Slain Dutch Patriots).

WAGENAAR, Johan (1862-1941) Holland. Was organist and director of The Hague Conservatoire. Wrote operas, cantatas, orchestral music, and songs.

WAGNER, Richard (1813-1883) Germany. Christened Wilhelm Richard, he dropped his first name at the age of twenty. At first he thought little about music, but decided to be a playwright. Influenced by Beethoven's symphonies, he applied himself to composition and in 1831 wrote a symphony. By the year 1834 he was conducting in small theatres, and, influenced by the singer, Minna Planer, whom he married in 1836, turned his talents to opera.

His first opera *Rienzi* freed him from financial strain. His next operas, *Der Fliegende Holländer* (1843) and *Tannhäuser* (1845) bewildered many operagoers. After *Lohengrin* (1850) he became convinced that new operatic forms must be created.

When political unrest touched Dresden, he made outspoken speeches and found it necessary to retreat to Switzerland. It was Liszt who assisted him in obtaining passports. He returned to Germany in 1861. In 1866 his first wife died; his next marriage was to Cosima, the illegitimate daughter of Franz Liszt and the Countess d'Agoult. By the end of 1882, in poor health, he sought peace in Venice, where he died.

Wagner reached his goal in his music-dramas. In 1873 the foundations of a "Wagner

Theatre," designed by the composer himself, were laid at Bayreuth. From that time to the present, with advice from Wagner's heirs, this Festival City has perpetuated the composer's genius in productions keeping strictly to tradition.

Principal works: *Die Feen, Rienzi, Der Fliegende Holländer, Tannhäuser, Lohengrin, Nibelungenring* (comprising *Das Rheingold, Die Walküre, Siegfried*, and *Gotterdämmerung*), *Tristan und Isolde, Die Meistersinger von Nürnberg, Parsifal;* orchestral works, including *Symphony in C major, Siegfried Idyll;* incidental music; *Wesendonck Lieder* and other songs; some small pieces of the *Albumblatt* kind.

WALDTEUFEL, Emil (1837-1915) France. Composer of popular waltzes and dance music.

WALLACE, William Vincent (1812-1865) Ireland. Arrived in Australia in 1835 where he made an impact during his short stay there. Composed in several forms, his opera *Maritana* having kept his name green.

WALTON, William (b. 1902) England. Apart from advice from Sir Hugh Allen during his Oxford days, was mainly self-taught in composition. He gained fame when his *Façade* music was first presented. From 1930 he continued to make outstanding contributions to British music. He was knighted in 1951 and went to live on the island of Ischia, Italy. His music displays in turn vigour, lyric romanticism, high tension, and Gallic gaiety.

Principal works: *Belshazzar's Feast* (oratorio); *Façade* (an entertainment set to poems by Edith Sitwell) and *Façade* Suite for orchestra; *Portsmouth Point* and *Crown Imperial* (marches); *Sinfonia Concertante; Symphony in B-flat major;* concertos for violin, viola, and cello; *Troilus and Cressida* (opera); *The Wise Virgins* (Bach's music arranged for ballet); Coronation "Te Deum" (chorus, organ, and orchestra); chamber music, piano music; music for films, including *Henry V, Richard III, Escape Me Never, The First of the Few*, and *The Next of Kin.*

WARD, Robert (b. 1917) America. Composer of operas, including *The Crucible* and *He who gets Slapped;* symphonies; choral works.

WARLOCK, Peter (assumed name used by Philip Heseltine) (1894-1930) England. Influenced by early English song and by Delius. Wrote orchestral works, e.g. *Capriol Suite;*

song cycle, *The Curlew;* songs; choral music; *Six English Tunes; Six Italian Dances; Serenade for Strings.*

WEBER, Carl Maria von (1786-1826) Germany. A member of an aristocratic family, Weber had excellent music training under Michael Haydn in Salzburg, Kalcher in Munich, and with the Abbé Vogler in Vienna. After experience as musical director at a Breslau theatre, he became court musician to the Prince Eugene of Württemburg, and in 1813 was asked to reorganise and direct the Prague Opera Company. He became the pioneer of romanticism in German opera. He wrote expressively for the voice and foreshadowed Wagner in the use of the *leitmotif.*

In 1824 London offered him £1,000 to direct two of his operas and to produce a new work. Against the doctor's orders he made the journey, and in 1826 he died at the house of Sir George Smart. He was buried in England but in 1844, mainly through the efforts of Wagner, his remains were transferred to Dresden.

Principal works: operas, including *Der Freischütz, Euryanthe, Oberon, Abu Hassan, Peter Schmoll und seine Nachbarn;* incidental music to plays, including *Preciosa, Turandot, König Yngurd;* two concertos and *Konzertstück* for piano and orchestra; two concertos and one concertino for clarinet and orchestra; a bassoon concerto; church music, including masses and cantatas; symphonies; overtures, and dances for orchestra; *Invitation to the Dance* for piano (later orchestrated by Berlioz and the word "Waltz" often being erroneously substituted for "Dance"); other piano works; songs.

WEBERN, Anton von (1883-1945) Austria. Studied at Vienna Conservatoire, and with Schoenberg from 1904 to 1910. His first published work was *Passacaglia for Orchestra,* Op. 1 in 1908. After adopting the twelve-note technique he developed his own particular style and experimented with contrapuntal patterns. He had a wide influence on younger composers. In 1945 he was accidentally shot dead in Mittersill. His works include symphonies, various orchestral works, cantatas, chamber music, and songs.

WEELKES, Thomas (date of birth uncertain; died about 1623) England. One of the great composers of the Elizabethan period. Adopted an original style in his madrigals; wrote church music and instrumental pieces.

WEILL, Kurt (1900-1950) Germany. Pupil of Humperdinck and others. After composing in several forms, moved to the United States in 1935 where he produced a series of musical works adapted to the American popular style. Married the actress-singer Lotte Lanya. Among his operas are *Mahagonny*, *The Protagonist*, *The Man Who Said Yes*, *A Kingdom for a Cow*, and *The Threepenny Opera*, a modern version of *The Beggar's Opera*; also a folk opera, *Down in the Valley*. Other works include *The New Orpheus* (cantata); *Concerto for Violin and Winds*; *The Seven Deadly Sins* for soprano, male chorus and orchestra.

WEINBERGER, Jaromir (1896-1967) Czechoslovakia. Studied in Berlin; took up residence in the United States in 1939. Among his works are *The Birds* (opera); *Spring Storms* (operetta); *Lincoln Symphony*; *Czech Rhapsody*; Variations and Fugue on *Under the Spreading Chestnut Tree*, *The Legend of Sleepy Hollow*, both for orchestra, but best known for his Czech opera, *Švanda the Bagpiper*.

WEINER, Léo (1885-1960) Hungary. Studied at the Landesakademie in Budapest and later joined its teaching staff. His works, following a German classical style, include divertimenti (some on Hungarian folk-dances); *Ballad for Clarinet and Orchestra*; *Variations on a Hungarian Folk Song* for orchestra; choral and chamber music; piano pieces.

WEINGARTNER (Paul) Felix (1863-1942) Austria. A noted conductor; also composer of opera, symphonies, and smaller works.

WEINZWEIG, John Jacob (b. 1913) Canada. Conductor, teacher, and composer. Adopted twelve-note technique. Works include tone poems, *The Enchanted Hill* and *Tale of Tuomotu*; *Wine of Peace* (soprano and orchestra); *Our Canada*, and *Red Ear of Corn* (suites); divertimenti for flute and for oboe; violin concerto.

WELLESZ, Egon (1885-1974) Austria. Studied with Schoenberg and others; took his Ph.D. in 1908; settled in England in 1939, and took up teaching appointment at Oxford in 1943. Edited the *New Oxford History of Music*. Lectured in the United States in 1956-1957. Has composed symphonies (No. 4 entitled *Sinfonia Austriaca*); cantata *The Leaden Echo and the Golden Echo* (soprano and four instruments);

church music; a violin concerto; songs, chamber music.

WERDER, Felix (b. 1922) Germany. To escape Nazi persecution left Germany in 1934, continued his studies in London, then settled in Australia in 1941. He has composed symphonies, operas, concertos for various instruments, orchestral works, and chamber music. Is music critic for *The Age* newspaper in Melbourne.

WERLE, Lars Johan (b. 1926) Sweden. Works include *The Dream about Thérèse*, an arena opera ("in the round"); orchestral and ballet music.

WHETTAM, Graham (b. 1927) England. Works include four symphonies; *Concerto scherzoso* for harmonica and orchestra; a viola concerto.

WHITE, Maude Valerie (1855-1937) England. Composer of songs, also some piano music.

WIDOR, Charles Marie (1845-1937) France. Famous organist; succeeded Franck as organ professor at the Paris Conservatoire. Composed operas and symphonies, but is now best known for his organ works.

WIECHOWICZ, Stanislaw (1893-1963) Poland. Composed choral works in a masterly style, also orchestral, piano works, and songs, some of his music connected with Polish folklore. Also critic and author of text-books.

WIENIAWSKI, Henri (Henryk) (1835-1880) Poland. One of the great violin virtuosos of his time. Toured widely. During a concert in Berlin he became ill and stopped in the middle of a concerto. Joachim, who was in the audience, went onto the platform, took up Wieniawski's violin, and finished the programme. Composed two violin concertos, and other pieces for that instrument.

WIHTOL, Joseph (1863-1948) Latvia. A pupil of Rimsky-Korsakov, became director of the Latvian National Opera. His works, often of romantic, melancholy character, include Latvian folk-song arrangements.

WILBYE, John (1574-1638) England. One of the great composers of madrigals of his time. He enjoyed the patronage of noble families. In addition to madrigals, composed some church music.

WILLAERT, Adrian (c. 1485-1652). Born in Flanders, he went to Italy and lived and died in Venice. One of the earliest composers to write madrigals. Also composed masses, motets, and secular vocal music.

WILLIAMS, Grace (1906-1977) Wales. Studied with Vaughan Williams in London and Egon Wellesz in Vienna. She has composed an opera, *The Parlour;* orchestral music, a trumpet concerto, *Sea Sketches* for strings; *Pentillion* (suite); *Fantasia on Welsh Nursery Tunes* for organ and orchestra.

WILLIAMSON, Malcolm (b. 1931) Australia. Studied at the Sydney Conservatorium with Dr Alex Burnard and Sir Eugene Goossens, and later with Boulez in Paris. Settled in England in 1953. Works include: operas, *Our Man in Havana, English Eccentrics, The Violin of Saint Jacques, Dunstan and the Devil, Julius Caesar Jones; Epitaph for Edith Sitwell,* and organ works; a symphony; church music; string quartet; piano music. In December 1969 his pantomime-opera *Lucky Peter's Journey* was given its first performance in London.

WIREN, Dag (b. 1905) Sweden. Studied in Paris. Reacted against the romanticism of Swedish "nationalist" composers, while carrying classical sympathies. Has composed symphonies; piano, violin, and cello concertos; *Concert Overture; Overture Joyeuse; Serenade for Strings;* chamber music; stage and film music.

WISHART, Peter (b. 1921) England. Pupil of N. Boulanger. Works include operas, *The Captive* and *Two in a Bush;* cantata, *Come, Holy Ghost;* a violin concerto; organ and piano music; song-cycles.

WOLF, Hugo (1860-1903) Austria. One of the greatest *lieder* composers. At fifteen he attended the Vienna Conservatoire but his lack of application to conventional training resulted in his dismissal at the end of his second year there. Most of his life was spent in poverty, perched on the brink of mental instability. As music critic for the Vienna *Salonblatt,* he championed Wagner and offended many by his bitter attacks on Brahms and other composers. In 1896 his opera *Der Corregidor* was performed—for one night. He died in a mental institution.

Wolf's songs are the perfect marriage between poem and music. He carried on the tradition of German *lieder,* but more than any other composer penetrated into the inner meaning of every word of the text. Not only

did he write with uncanny understanding for the voice, but he built the piano part logically, often from a single phrase. The title pages of many volumes carry the inscription, "Songs for voice and piano."

Principal works: Fifty-three song settings to poems by Mörike, forty-seven by Goethe, twenty by Eichendorff, thirty-four in the *Spanisches Liederbuch,* forty-four in the *Italienisches Liederbuch,* and many individual songs. Other works include the opera, *Der Corregidor; Italian Serenade* for small orchestra; *String Quartet in D minor.*

WOLF-FERRARI, Ermanno (1876-1948) Italy. The son of a German father and Italian mother, wrote music in several forms, but is best known for his operas, which include *Il Segreto di Susanna, I Gioielli della Madonna,* and *I Quatro Rustedhi,* the latter having the English title *School for Fathers.*

WOOD, Charles (1866-1926) Ireland. A professor of music at Cambridge, composed a passion, church music, cantatas, songs.

WOOD, Haydn (1882-1926) England. Composed some orchestral, piano, and chamber music, but became famous for his light ballads, e.g. *Roses of Picardy.*

WOOD, Ralph Walter (b. 1902) England. Works include a piano concerto; string quartets; *Concerto for Strings; Suite for Small Orchestra; Resurrection of Martyrs.*

WOOD, Thomas (1892-1950) England. Pupil of Stanford. Composed choral works, including a cantata, *Chanticleer.* Visited Australia and made known a local song, *Waltzing Matilda.*

WORDSWORTH, William (b. 1908) England. Works include symphonies; *Concerto in D minor* for piano and orchestra; *Hymn of Dedication* for chorus and orchestra; string quartets; songs.

WYK, Arnold van (b. 1916) South Africa. Went to London in 1938, studied there and for a time worked for the B.B.C. Returned to South Africa in 1946 and took up a university post there. Works include symphonies; *Kerskantate (Christmas Cantata);* song-cycle *Van Liefde en Verlatenheid* (Of Love and Forsakeness); chamber music; songs; *Night Music,* and other piano works.

XENAKIS (XENNAKIS), Iannis (Yannis) (b. 1922). Born in Rumania of Greek parentage, now included among the most interesting of present day Greek composers. He studied engineering in Athens, then joined the studio of Le Corbusier in Paris, working on architectural projects for twelve years. He later took music lessons from Honegger and Milhaud. Composes music according to mathematical formulas, with such titles as *Achorripsis*, *Pithoprakta*, *Diamorphoses*, and *Metastaseis*.

YON, Pietro (1886-1943) Italy. Settled in the United States in 1907. Works include *Concertino* for oboe and orchestra; *Concerto Gregoriano* for organ and orchestra; *The Triumph of Saint Patrick* (oratorio); masses, organ solos, songs.

YRADIER, Sebastían (1809-1865) Spain. Composer of popular songs, including *La Paloma* (*The Dove*). Bizet adapted one of his songs for his opera *Carmen*.

YSAYE, Eugène (1858-1931) Belgium. Celebrated violinist. Composed concertos and other works for violin.

ZAFRED, Mario (b. 1922) Italy. Composer of symphonies, concertos, choral music, piano music, songs.

ZANDONAI, Riccardo (1883-1944) Italy. A successful composer of operas early this century, his works subsequently dropping out of the repertoire of most companies. Among his operas are *Giulietta e Romeo*, *Francesca da Rimini*, and *I Cavalieri di Ekebu*.

ZELTER, Carl Friedrich (1758-1832) Germany. Teacher and friend of Mendelssohn; director of Berlin Singakademie. Composed sacred music and songs.

ZIMBALIST, Efrem (b. 1889). A celebrated violinist, pupil of Leopold Auer. Married soprano Alma Gluck. Became director of the Curtis Institute of Music, Philadelphia. Composed orchestral and violin works. Father of screen-actor, Efrem Zimbalist.

ZINGARELLI, Niccolò Antonio (1752-1837) Italy. Wrote many operas, mostly for La Scala theatre, also church music.

GLOSSARY

A short dictionary of some musical terms used in this book, or likely to be met in reading on musical subjects. These are in addition to (and including) those explained in detail in specific chapters. For instance, those terms referring to Pace, Degrees of Loudness and Softness, Force and Style (e.g., *Adagio, Piano, Forte, Agitato*) will be found in the Chapter *Dynamics and Related Musical Terms*; Concerto under its own section; Bach under Composers. See also Index.

ABSOLUTE MUSIC: Music that does not depend on anything outside itself; therefore, distinct from "programme" or illustrative music that tells a story, or depicts a scene.

ACCENT: An emphasis, most importantly one occurring at regular intervals of time to establish the rhythm.

ACCIDENTAL: A sharp, flat, or natural, independent of the time-signature, occurring temporarily during the course of a piece.

ACOUSTICS: The science of sound.

ALL', ALLA: In the style of, e.g., *Alla Marcia* indicates in the style of a march.

ANTHEM: A short, solemn vocal composition, usually with organ accompaniment.

ANTIPHON: Responses made by one part of the choir to another, or by the congregation to the priest.

ARABESQUE, ARABESK: Literally, after the manner of Arabian designs. Word has been borrowed from visual art (and ballet) and applied to a short piece in decorative style.

Debussy and Schumann are among the composers who wrote pieces to this title.

ARCO: Bow. Indicating that notes are to be played with the bow and not pizzicato.

ARIA: Air; song. Written for solo voice, with or without accompaniment; this usually consists of three sections, following such pattern as (a) a melody fully developed; (b) a contrasted melody; (c) repetition of first melody.

ARIETTA: A short air or aria, usually without a second section.

ARIOSO: A melodious piece in the style of an air, but less formal in construction.

ARPEGGIO: Harp-like. Notes of a chord played one after another.

ASSAI: Very: e.g., *Allegro assai*, very quick.

ATONAL: Music without a fixed key centre.

AVE MARIA: Latin, *Hail Mary*. The first words of a Roman Catholic prayer to the Virgin Mary. This has been set to music by many composers.

BAGATELLE: (French), *trifle*. A short piece, usually of light character. Beethoven wrote twenty-seven pieces under this title, *Für Elise* being one of the best known.

BALALAIKA: A Russian fretted instrument, the three strings of which are plucked. The body is of triangular shape, the size of the instrument varying considerably. It is used for solos and in groups.

BALLAD: The form, and meaning of the word have changed over the centuries. Originally from the Italian *ballata* (a dance), this was a song with dancing. It later became a song that told a story, or was of narrative character, the settings of Goethe's *The Erl King*, by Schubert and Loewe, being examples. Still later the word was applied to an English song of sentimental, "drawing-room" type.

BALLAD OPERA: A stage production with spoken dialogue and songs often based on popular tunes of the day. An early example was *The Beggar's Opera*.

BALLADE: Chopin first used this word for four piano works which, rather than taking on the character of a narrative, illustrated an idea. Other composers used the term later.

BAR-LINES: Vertical lines drawn across the staff to divide the music into equal portions. It has become the custom to use the word BAR for the space between two bar-lines.

BARCAROLLE: A boat-song of the type sung by Venetian gondoliers, or instrumental piece in the same 6/8 swaying time. Two famous examples are the *Barcarolle* from *The Tales of Hoffmann* and the *Barcarolle in F sharp minor* for piano by Chopin.

BAROQUE: An architectural term with various meanings (e.g., exuberant, twisting, extravagant) that has been applied to music written during the 17th and first half of the 18th Century.

BERCEUSE: Cradle song; lullaby.

BINARY: Two sections. (See chapter on Musical Form.)

BIS: Has two meanings, though related: (a) When written in music over a phrase or passage, it indicates that those notes are to be repeated; (b) Equivalent to *Encore*.

BITONALITY: The simultaneous use of two keys.

BRASS BAND: A combination of brass instruments, with or without percussion. Some woodwind instruments are sometimes included.

BRAVURA: A style of playing requiring technical brilliance in a performance of spirited display.

BRIO: Spirit, e.g., *con brio*, with spirit.

BURLETTA: A light operetta in the style of a farce.

BWV: Initials standing for *Bach Werke-Verzeichnis*, i.e., those placed with numbers from Schneider's thematic index of J. S. Bach's works.

CABALETTA: A short operatic song, resembling a *rondo* in form, the theme repeated with variations.

CACOPHONY: Harsh and discordant sounds.

CADENCE: A sequence of chords to form the close of a sentence, phrase, or part of a piece. See under "Cadence" in chapter headed *The Structure of Music*.

CADENZA: A florid passage of indefinite form, introduced by the composer for soloist during a movement (usually near the end), giving the executant opportunity for technical display.

CALANDO: Diminishing the tone, becoming softer and slower.

CAMERA: Chamber; small hall.

CANON: A contrapuntal composition in which the main melody is taken up by another voice or instrument, in imitation, at fixed intervals; a kind of "follow my leader" musical style. Examples: *Frère Jacques* and *Sumer is icumen in*.

322

CANTABILE: In a singing style.

CANTATA: See under "Cantata" in chapter headed *Kinds of Music* (*Vocal*).

CANTICLE: The name generally given to certain biblical hymns sung in different Christian churches, such as the *Benedictus*, the *Benedicite*, the *Magnificat*, and the *Nunc Dimittis*.

CANTILENA: The term is sometimes applied to the upper or solo part of a vocal work; more generally used to denote a flowing, song-like melodic line.

CANZONA, or CANZONE: (a) The name of a certain kind of early lyric poetry in the Italian style; (b) a song or air resembling a madrigal, but less strict.

CAPRICCIO; CAPRICE: A piece, usually of bright character, written in a capricious style, and not bound to any rigid form.

CARILLON: A set of bells, usually fixed in a tower, and so tuned and arranged that tunes can be played on them. (Sometimes mis-spelt *carrilion*.)

CAVATINA: A graceful melody, simpler than an aria, in that it contains one section, instead of the three of the Aria.

CHAMBER MUSIC: See under "Chamber Music" in chapter headed *Kinds of Music* (*Instrumental*).

CHAMBER OPERA: See under "Opera" in chapter headed *Kinds of Music* (*Vocal*).

CHIESA: Church.

CHITARRA: A guitar.

CHIUSO: Closed; stopped.

CHORAL: Referring to a choir or chorus.

CHORALE: A hymn tune to be sung in chorus for congregational use, dating back to the time of Martin Luther.

CHROMATIC: A scale, or passage, proceeding by semitones.

CLAVICHORD: A keyboard instrument, precursor of the pianoforte. See under "Keyboard forerunners of the Pianoforte" in chapter headed *Musical Instruments*.

CLAVIER: KLAVIER: See under "Keyboard forerunners of the Pianoforte" in chapter headed *Musical Instruments*.

CODA: A section added at the end of a piece of music to produce a more effective close.

CODETTA: A short coda, its purpose to round off a section, whereas a coda rounds off a movement.

COLORATURA: The ornamentation of vocal music with trills, runs, and the like. *Coloratura Soprano*, a singer whose voice and training are suited to this kind of music.

CON: With. Used in conjunction with another word, e.g., *con amore*, with affection, with ardent expression.

CONCERTO: See under "Concerto" in chapter headed *Kinds of Music* (*Instrumental*).

CONCERTANTE: A musical work in which each part is alternately principal and subordinate, as in a *duo concertante*.

CONCERTINO: A short concerto.

CONCERTSTUCK: A concert piece, less imposing than a concerto.

CONCERTO GROSSO: See under *Concerto*.

CONCORD: A combination of notes pleasing to the ear, as opposed to *discord*.

CONTINUO: A short form of the words *basso continuo*. An improvised part usually played by a harpsichord as a background to a choral or instrumental work of an earlier period. Given only a basic line of figures below the staff, the player had to work out for himself the appropriate harmonies.

COR: French word for Horn. The English Horn is also known as *Cor Anglais*.

CORO: Chorus.

COUNTERPOINT: Literally *point against point*. (Before the invention of notes, sounds were expressed on paper by points.) The art of combining notes against one another to form individual melodies of equal importance within strict limits.

COUNTER-TENOR VOICE: The highest male voice, sometimes called *alto*. Its *falsetto* quality was called on in music of Purcell and Handel, and with a revival of interest in the twentieth century.

CYCLIC(AL) FORM: A form in which a theme recurs throughout more than one movement of a sonata, a symphony, or a concerto.

DA: Italian for from, by, to, with, in.

DA CAPO: From the beginning. D.C. placed at the end of a movement indicates that the performer must return to the beginning.

DESCANT; DISCANT: A counterpoint, often extemporaneous, against a given subject or theme; an additional part.

DEVELOPMENT: The elaboration of original subjects or themes of a work by means of harmonic, melodic, and rhythmic treatment. See under chapter headed *Musical Form* and under "The Symphony" in chapter headed *Kinds of Music* (*Instrumental*).

DIAPASON: Original meaning, interval of the octave. The "basic" tone of an organ.

DIAPHONY: Mediaeval form of combining two "voices" or melodies.

DIATONIC: Proceeding naturally by tones, and semitones through major and minor keys, as distinct from *chromatic* and other scales.

DIDGERIDOO: A drone-pipe, made from bamboo or hollow sapling, used by Aborigines in the northern and certain parts of Australia. It is blown from one end. The usual length is about five feet, but for some ceremonial occasions the didgeridoo may be as long as ten to fifteen feet.

DISCANT: See Descant.

DISCORD: A dissonant combination of sounds, as opposed to a Concord.

DISSONANCE: A discord.

DIVERTIMENTO: A short composition, usually of light, pleasing style. A form used by Haydn and Mozart.

DOPPIO: Double.

DOPPIO MOVIMENTO: Twice as fast as the previous section.

DOUBLE-STOPPING: Fingering and bowing on two strings of an instrument at once.

DUO: Duet. Can mean two performers playing or singing together, or a work written for them.

DYNAMICS: Variation of tonal loudness and softness. See under chapter headed *Dynamics And Related Musical Terms*.

ECOSSAISE: A French word for Scottish, though it is disputed whether or not this lively dance is of Scottish origin. Beethoven and Schubert wrote in this style.

EIN; EINE: (German) One.

EISTEDDFOD: (Welsh) Originally an assembly of bards, first held in 1078. Now meaning a Welsh national music festival, the word being borrowed in other parts for music competitions. Plural is *Eisteddfodau*.

ELEGIE (French); ELEGY (English): A mournful or lamenting kind of music, usually for the dead.

EMBOUCHURE: A French word meaning the mouthpiece of a wind instrument; also used for position of lips on the mouthpiece.

ENHARMONIC: A word applied to a change in notation but not in sound; e.g., F natural and E sharp.

ETUDE: A French word for Study; usually a composition which exploits some particular technical difficulty.

EXPOSITION: The first part of a movement in "sonata-form," or the initial *exposition* of the subject of a fugue. See under "Sonata" in chapter headed *Kinds Of Music* (*Instrumental*).

FAGOTT (Ger.); FAGOTTO (Ital.): Bassoon See details under "Instruments of the modern Symphony Orchestra" in chapter headed *Musical Instruments*.

FANTASIE (Fr.); FANTASIA (Ital.); FANTASY OR FANCY (Eng.): A composition, often of a fanciful character, not conforming to regular forms; also a collection of tunes linked together.

FIORITURA: A florid ("flowering") passage decorated with ornaments.

FUGA (Ital.); FUGE (Ger.): Fugue.

FUGUE: From the Italian, meaning "flight." See chapter headed *Musical Form*.

FUNDAMENTAL: The root, or fundamental note of a chord or harmonic series. See under "Melody" in chapter headed *The Structure Of Music*.

FUNEBRE (Ital.) FUNEBRE (Fr.): Funereal, as *Marche Funèbre*, the third movement of Chopin's Sonata in B-flat minor.

FUOCO: Fire.

FURIANT: A lively Czech dance, often with changing rhythms. Dvořák used this for some movements in his works, although he did not always change the rhythm.

GALOP (Eng.); GALOPP (Ger.); GALOPPO (Ital.): A rapid dance, usually in 2/4 time.

GAMME: (Fr.) A scale.

GIGA (Ital.); GIGUE (Fr.); JIG (Eng.): A lively dance in 6/8 or 12/8 time. In early music it usually rounded off a suite.

GLISSANDO: A rapid, unbroken scale passage, obtained by sliding the finger along the strings of an instrument while bowing, or, on the piano, by quickly drawing the tip of the thumb over the white notes or black notes.

GLOCKENSPIEL: In German, literally "play of bells." See under "Instruments of the Modern Symphony Orchestra" in chapter headed *Musical Instruments*.

GOPAK: A Russian folk-dance in quick 2/4 time.

GREGORIAN CHANT: Ancient kind of Plainsong based on the tonality of Church

Modes, said to have been established by Pope Gregory in the 6th Century.

GRUPPETTO: A turn; a group of ornamental notes.

HALLING: A Norwegian solo dance for a man.

HARFE (Ger.): A harp.

HARMONY: The combination of musical sounds to form agreeable chords. See under "Melody" in the chapter headed *The Structure Of Music*.

HAUTBOY; (Fr. HAUTBOIS): An oboe.

HELDENTENOR: German for Heroic Tenor. The word is sometimes applied to the principal tenor, capable of singing dramatic (heroic) roles in Wagner.

HOMOPHONY: In unison; alike in pitch, as distinct from *contrapuntal* when different melodies are sounded simultaneously.

HOPAK: See Gopak.

HUMORESK (Ger.); HUMORESQUE (Fr.): A piece written in a capricious style. A term used by Schumann and Dvořák

HYDRAULIS: As the word suggests, a water-organ used in ancient times; the forerunner of the organ,

IDEE FIXE: A motto theme as used by Berlioz in his *Symphonie Fantastique*.

IDYLLE (Fr. and Ger.): A short pastoral poem, borrowed by Wagner (*Siegfried Idyll*) and other musical composers.

ILLUSTRATIVE MUSIC: See under "Programme Music" in chapter headed *Kinds Of Music (Instrumental)*.

IMPROMPTU: As the word means, improvised or without preparation, its use in music is usually applied to a short piece, the character of which suggests improvisation. Schubert and Chopin used this style.

IN: In, as *in tempo*, in time.

IN ALT: The notes that lie within the first octave above the treble staff.

INTERMEZZO: An interlude; intermediate, detached pieces placed between the acts or scenes of an opera. The word has also been used as a title.

INTERVAL: The vertical distance between two musical sounds.

INVENTION: (a) An old term for a species of exercise or short fantasia; (b) name given by J. S. Bach to a short keyboard work in two-part counterpoint.

ISTESSO TEMPO L': Literally, at the same tempo. Keeping the same speed, even though the beat may have changed.

JEUNE FRANCE, La: Young France. A group formed in 1936 by four French composers, Baudrier, Jolivet, Lesur, and Messiaen.

JIG: See *Gigue*.

JONGLEUR: A name given to wandering minstrels of medieval times. See under French Song in chapter headed *Kinds Of Music (Vocal)*.

K. and K.V. as applied to Mozart's works, see under *Köchel*.

KAMMER (Ger.): Chamber.

KAMMERMUSIK: Chamber music.

KAPELLE (Ger.): Chapel.

KAPELLMEISTER: Chapel master, or musical director. Originally used in association with a prince's private chapel. Later used for a conductor of an orchestra or a choir.

KEY: The group of notes on which a composition will in the main be based, thereby giving it a character. It can also mean the lever by which the sounds of a piano or organ are produced.

KEY SYSTEM: See under chapter headed *Structure Of Music*.

KLAVIER; CLAVIER: A keyboard instrument; e.g., harpsichord, piano.

KOCHEL (also spelt KOECHEL): The name of an Austrian musician and scholar who compiled a catalogue of Mozart's works, classifying them and giving each an index number. Therefore, "K.315" means Number 315 in the Köchel list. Sometimes this is written K.V., standing for Köchel Verzeichnis (Köchel list).

KOL NIDREI: A Hebrew prayer associated with the Day of Atonement. Max Bruch and others have used this as a title for works for cello and orchestra.

LANDLER: A slow, rustic kind of dance of waltz style, once popular in Austria and South Germany. Beethoven and Schubert wrote pieces in this style. The Ländler pattern is also present in movements of symphonies by Mahler and Bruckner.

LAY: A short, light song, or ballad.

LEDGER (LEGER) LINE: Short lines added for notes which go beyond the compass of the staff.

LEIT-MOTIF, or LEIT-MOTIVE: A leading motif, or theme; a theme used (e.g., by Wagner in his music-dramas) to identify a character, object, or situation and used recurrently.

LIBRETTO: The "book"; words or poem of an opera, oratorio, cantata, and the like.

LIED: (Ger.) Song; plural *Lieder*. See under "Song" in chapter headed *Kinds Of Music (Vocal)*.

LUNGA; LUNGO: Long.

MADRIGAL: A composition, contrapuntal in character, for several voices, sung in imitative manner, for secular use. Originating in Italy about the 16th Century, it migrated to England where it became immensely popular, some of the best examples being written by English composers.

MAGNIFICAT: The Song of the Virgin Mary, introduced into the evening (Vespers) service of the Roman Catholic and Anglican churches.

MAJOR: Greater, as opposed to Minor (less) as applied to scales. See under "Scales" in chapter headed *Musical Form*.

MANUAL: The keyboard of an organ played by the hands.

MARCIA (Ital.): March.

MELODY: A succession of single notes of .varying pitch and having a definite flow and shape. See under chapter headed *The Structure Of Music*.

MENO: Less.

MESSE: Mass.

META: Half.

MEZZO; MEZZA: Half in the sense that *mezzo-soprano* refers to the female whose voice-range is between soprano and contralto; also *mezzo-voce*, with moderate tone, or at half-voice.

MILITARY BAND: A combination of wood-wind and brass instruments, with percussion. A stringed double-bass is sometimes added, but not when the band is required to play on the march.

MINOR: As opposed to Major. See under "Scales" in chapter headed *Musical Form*.

MISSA (Latin): Mass.

MODULATION: The change of key or tonality by continuous, flowing succession of chords that sound agreeable to the ear.

MOLL: German for *minor*.

MONODY: Deriving from the Greek, when in Greek tragedy a poem was "sung" by a single actor; this has come to mean a melody sustained by a single voice, in contrast to an earlier *polyphonic* style, meaning the simultaneous sounding of different notes.

MOTET: A sacred composition, often in Latin, and sung in contrapuntal style; somewhat akin to the Anthem.

MOTIF; MOTIV; MOTIVE: A short melodic or rhythmical figure or leading idea.

MUSETTE: An early French type of bagpipe; also an air of pastoral character, over a drone bass.

MYSTERIES: Name given to sacred dramas in medieval times.

NOCTURNE: A night-piece, usually of romantic character. The term, in music, was first used by John Field, and later adopted by Chopin. Field wrote twenty and Chopin nineteen. The word has been used in a wider sense by other composers; for example, Debussy who wrote three under that title for orchestra.

NODE: The point at which the vibrations of a string or air-column meet.

NON: (Fr. and Ital.) Not.

NONET: A composition for nine voices or instruments.

NOTTURNO: A nocturne.

OBBLIGATO: Original meaning "indispensable," a part which cannot be omitted. In general terms, an accompaniment necessary for desired full effect. A case in point is the flute *obbligato* to the soprano voice in Bishop's song, *Lo Here the Gentle Lark*. (Incidentally, the word "here" in this title has sometimes been misspelt as "hear.")

ODE: A poem intended to be sung; in a musical setting it is often addressed to something or somebody. Two examples are Schiller's *Ode to Joy*, set to music by Beethoven in the fourth movement of his *Choral* Symphony, and *Ode for St Cecilia's Day* by Purcell.

OPER: German for opera.

OPUS (abbreviation, Op.): A work. A system of numbering compositions, supposedly in order of their composition; Opus 1 would mean the first work.

ORGEL (Ger.); ORGUE (Fr.): Organ.

OVERTONES: Harmonics; partials. See "Tone-Colour" in chapter headed *Pitch, Tone, and Tone-Colour*.

PARLANDO; PARLANTE: Speaking. This Italian word may be taken literally, or applied to a style of performance; a section (as in

326

opera) indicating speech or a near-approach to a speaking tone.

PARTIALS: Harmonics, or partial tones; notes of the harmonic series, the lowest ("fundamental") being the first partial.

PARTITA: Originally a collection of dance tunes, or an air with variations; a suite; Bach used the term in two senses, (a) as *suite* in his *Partitas for Clavier*, and (b) *Variations on Chorales*.

PASSACAGLIA: An old dance form; a composition in which a bass theme is frequently repeated. See also details in chapter headed *The Dance and Dance Forms*.

PASSEPIED: An old French dance akin to a quick minuet.

PASSION (PASSION MUSIC): A musical setting based on the biblical story of Christ's suffering and death.

PASTICHE (Fr.) PASTICCIO (Ital.): A medley; a composition consisting of music written by different composers; music written in the style of another composer.

PENTATONIC: (From the Greek word *pente*, five.) An ancient scale consisting of five notes.

PHILHARMONIC: (Derived from the Greek *love* and *harmony*, or, love of harmony.) When applied to an orchestra, it merely refers to a particular orchestra, but not the type, as would be the case with *symphony orchestra*.

PHRASE: A short musical sentence or group of notes forming a musical idea.

PIU: More; e.g., *più allegro*, more lively; *più lento*, more slowly.

PIZZICATO: Plucked, as in guitar playing. In string instruments the passage bearing this term (or *Pizz.*) is to be plucked with the fingers, instead of being played with the bow.

POCO: Little; not very.

POLACCA: A Polonaise; a Polish dance in 3/4 time.

POLYPHONY: Of "several voices." The simultaneous sounding of several lines of notes. The art of combining several melodies as in counterpoint.

POLYTONALITY: The simultaneous use of more than one key, as in some modern music. (*Bitonality* refers to the combination of two keys.)

PORTAMENTO: Gliding the finger from one note to another in bowed string instruments, or gliding the voice in a similar manner without break in the sound.

QUASI: As if; like to; in the manner of.

QUATRE (Fr.) QUATTRO (Ital.): Four.

QUATUOR (Fr.): Quartet.

QUINTOUR (Fr.): Quintet.

RAVVIVANDO: Reviving, quickening; returning to a previous faster tempo.

RECITANDO; RECITANTE: In a declamatory manner; in the style of a *recitative*. (See next entry.)

RECITATIVE: Musical declamation in free-style. A passage without a decided melody or rhythm.

REPRISE: The burden or chorus of a song. A repeat. The repetition of some theme or section. Term used in musical plays when a song (or theme song) returns.

REQUIEM: A Roman Catholic Mass for the dead.

RESOLUTION: The transition from a discord to a concord.

RICERCAR; RICERCARE: A term used in the 16th to 18th Centuries to denote a type of instrumental work written in learned or recherché counterpoint; sometimes in fugue or toccata style.

RIPIENO: As used in the *concerto grosso*, term referred to indicate the full body of players, as distinct from the solo group. Often used to denote additional parts intended to augment the effect of *tutti* in a chorus or orchestra.

RITENUTO: Held back; a dragging of the tempo; an immediate slowing down.

RITORNELLO (Ital.) RITOURNELLE (Fr.): A "returning" instrumental passage between the verses of a song, or as a postlude. Also an introduction, interlude, and postlude for orchestra to, between, or after the solo passages of a concerto.

ROCOCO: See under chapter headed *Periods in Music*.

RONDO: See under chapter headed *Musical Form*.

RUBATO: Robbed (robbed time). Playing a passage without giving the notes strict time values, so that some are "robbed" of their full value and others gain.

SACKBUT: An ancient name for the trombone.

SALTARELLA; SALTARELLO; SALTERELLO: An Italian dance in quick time. Mendelssohn used this dance form in the *finale* of his *Italian Symphony*.

SANGER (Ger.): A singer.

SAUTILLE (Fr.): A springing type of bowing.

SCENA (Ital.): Scene. Can mean a dramatic vocal concert piece in an operatic style.

SCHERZO: Jest or joke. A movement of light-hearted character.

SEGUE: Now follows; as follows. Instruction that the performer go on to the next section without a break.

SICILIANA (Ital.): A graceful Sicilian dance in 6/8 or 12/8 time.

SICILIENNE (Fr.): Siciliana.

SINGSPIEL: See German song and opera in chapter headed *Kinds Of Music (Vocal)*.

SONATA: See under "Sonata" in chapter headed *Kinds Of Music (Instrumental)*.

SONATINA: A short sonata.

SPICCATO: A springing bow. A clipped way of playing rapid detached notes on a stringed instrument.

STABAT MATER: Originally a poem in Latin associated with the Virgin Mary at the Cross. Now a hymn or cantata related to the Crucifixion.

STAFF; STAVE: The lines on which the notes of printed music are placed. See under "Staff" in chapter headed *Notation*.

SUBJECT: A leading theme. A group of notes forming the basis of a composition or movement, e.g., as used in connection with a fugue or a recurring element in a rondo.

SYNCOPATION: A displacement of accent to a beat not normally accented. The tying-over of a weak beat to the next strong beat.

TANTO: So much; as much; too much. Examples of use: *allegro ma non tanto*, quick but not too much.

TARANTELLA: See under the chapter headed *The Dance and Dance Forms*.

TE DEUM: A Latin hymn of praise and thanksgiving.

TEMA: A theme.

TERNARY: Three parts. TERNARY FORM: A composition in three sections. See under chapter headed *Musical Form*.

TESSITURA: The natural register of a voice or instrument. The general compass of a vocal part, excluding exceptional high or low notes.

THEME: A group of notes constituting a melody suitable for development.

TIME and TIME-SIGNATURE: See under chapter headed *Time, Time-signatures, and Accents*.

TOCCATA: A term generally applied to a brilliant composition designed to show the performer's speed and lightness of touch (*Toccare*).

TONALITY: Pertaining to the key or scale.

TRIAD: A chord consisting of a note, its third and its fifth above.

TRIO: (a) Three performers; (b) the second section of a minuet or march. (This was formerly played by three players, hence the term.)

TROPPO: Too much (e.g., *Allegro ma non troppo*, meaning quick but not too much.)

TROUVERE: Troubadour. See under French Song in chapter headed *Kinds of Music (Vocal)*.

TUTTI: All. All instruments playing together, especially used in a concerto where the *tutti* alternates with the solo parts. It can also mean in choral music the chorus as opposed to soloists, or the full chorus instead of a sectional chorus.

TWELVE-NOTE TECHNIQUE: See under chapter headed *Periods in Music (Modern)*.

UN; UNE (Fr.); UN; UNA (Ital.): One, a, an.

UND (Ger.): And.

UNISON: The sounding in identical pitch of the same note produced by two or more voices or instruments.

UNTER (Ger.): Under, below.

VARIATION: A new treatment of a theme. Details and examples under "Variations" in chapter headed *Kinds of Music (Instrumental)*.

VERISMO: Truth-like, realism. This term has come to be used in referring to "realistic" operas based on violent plots, certain operas of Mascagni and Puccini quoted as examples. See under "Opera" in chapter headed *Kinds Of Music (Vocal)*.

VIHUELA: See under chapter headed *Musical Instruments*.

VILLANELLA: An old Italian rustic song, or dance accompanied by singing. (Literal translation of Italian "a country girl.")

VIOL and related instruments described under "Early Instruments" in chapter headed *Musical Instruments*.

VOCALISE: (a) The practice of study of singing to vowels, usually A; a wordless composition for voice, either for study or as a concert item. Among examples of the latter may be mentioned *Vocalise* by Rachmaninov, *Bachianas Brasileiras, No. 5* (Villa-Lobos), and *Concerto for Coloratura and Orchestra* by Glière.

VIRGINAL(S): An earlier and smaller version

of the harpsichord contained in an oblong box. (For history and details see under *Early keyboard instruments*.)

VORSPIEL (Ger.): Prelude; an introduction.

WELL-TEMPERED: The tuning of a keyboard instrument to an equal "temperament," with equal semitones.

WELL-TEMPERED CLAVIER: Name given by J. S. Bach to his "Forty-eight Preludes and Fugues," it being his intention to test the system of equal temperament in tuning. "Clavier" meant any keyboard instrument.

WIEGENLIED (Ger.): Cradle-song; lullaby.

WOOD-WIND: Group name for musical instruments traditionally made of wood. These are itemised in chapter headed *Musical Instruments*.

XYLOPHONE: A percussion instrument. For details see chapter headed *Musical Instruments*.

ZAPATEADO: A Spanish dance in which the (solo) performer stamps out rhythmic patterns savagely with his heels.

ZIGEUNER: Gypsy.

ZINGARA: In a gypsy style.

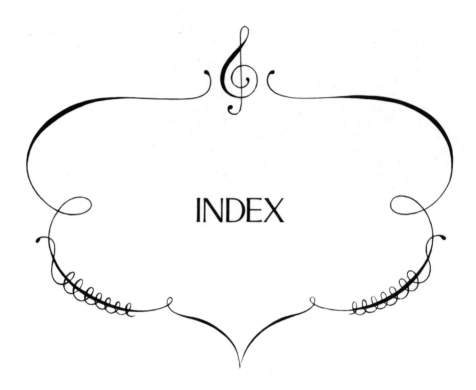

INDEX

Bach, Johann Christian,* 158, 204
Bach, Johann Sebastian,* 36, 157, 161, 163, 197, 200, 204, 210, 213, 218, 220, 227
Bach Werke Verzeichnis (BWV), 33
Bacon, Ernst, 183, 196
Badger, Harold, 204, 211
Badings, Henk, 48, 176
Bainton, Dr Edgar Leslie,* 182, 195
Balakirev, Mily,* 144, 178
Balanchine, George, 202
Baldasarino da Belgiojoso (Balthasar), 77
Balfe, Michael William,* 142
Ballad Opera, 142
Ballet, History, etc., 79
Ballet Arrangements, 221
Ballet Titles, 79-81
Bands, 224
Banks, Benjamin, 97
Bantock, Sir Granville,* 65, 162, 182
Bar; Bar Lines, 15
Barber, Samuel*, 63, 161, 183, 196, 211
Barbirolli, Sir John, 185
Baroque, 36, 51, 205
Barraud, Henry*, 165
Bartók, Béla*, 42, 162, 179, 203, 210
Basil, Colonel de (Ballets Russes), 79
Bate, Stanley*, 65
Baton, 114
Bax, Sir Arnold*, 65, 182, 193-194, 204, 230
Bayreuth,* 136
Beatles, The, 226
Beaumont, Geoffrey, 163
Beecham, Sir Thomas, 118, 123, 142, 155, 221, 247
Beethoven, Ludwig van,* 133-134, 161, 163, 167, 186, 189, 197, 199, 206-207, 210, 213, 217, 218, 220, 238, 241, 242, 249-250, 258
Bell, Chichester, A., 244
Bellini, Vincenzo,* 126
Benedict, Julius, 142
Benjamin, Arthur,* 143, 165, 195, 204
Bennett, Richard Rodney,* 65, 143
Bennett, William Sterndale,* 161
Benoît, Pierre, 175
Bentzon, Niels Viggo,* 195
Berezovsky, Nicolai,* 196
Berg, Alban,* 68, 138, 174, 203, 210
Bergsma, William, 161
Berio, Luciano,* 211
Berkeley, Lennox,* 65, 143, 163, 182, 211
Berlin Philharmonic Orchestra, 245
Berliner, Emile, 244

Berlioz, Hector,* 59, 128, 131, 155, 159, 161, 163, 164, 191, 215
Berners, Lord,* 182
Bernstein, Leonard, 63, 149, 161, 183, 196, 217
Berwald, Franz Adolf, 188
Billings, William, 62
Binery Form, 27
Bishop, Sir Henry,* 142
Bizet, Georges,* v, 132, 154, 164, 184, 191, 213, 217, 225
Blacher, Boris,* 67, 138
Blassis, Carlo,* 77
Bliss, Sir Arthur,* 65, 143, 182, 204, 211, 217
Blitzstein, Marc,* 63, 149
Bloch, Ernest,* 203, 210
Blomdahl, Karl-Birger,* 148
Blow, John,* 181, 213
Boehm, Theobald, 99
Boïeldieu, François Adrien, 204
Boito, Arrigo,* 128
Borodin, Alexander Porphyrevich,* 144, 145, 178, 192, 242
Borrowed Tunes, 220
Boughton, Rutland,* 143, 162, 182, 204
Boulez, Pierre,* 48, 59, 211
Bowen, York,* 211
Brahms, Johannes*, 159, 161, 163, 170, 186, 189-190, 200-201, 209-210, 213, 218, 220, 221, 238, 241
Breil, Joseph, 149
Bretón, Tomas, 147
Brewster Jones, 204
Brian, Havergal,* 65
Bridge, Frank,* 65, 160, 161, 182, 211
Brier, Percy, 204, 211
Britten, Benjamin,* 65, 123, 143, 160, 162, 195, 204, 211, 217, 219, 221
Broadwood and Sons, John, 89, 91
Brodsky, Adolf, 201
Bruch, Max,* 202
Bruckner, Anton,* 163, 191, 210, 239
Brumby, Colin,* 211
Bruyere, Jean de la, 242
Bülow, Hans von, 113, 122
Burleigh, Henry Thacker,* 183
Burnard, Dr David Alexander,* 211
Burney, Charles, 185
Bush, Alan Dudley,* 182
Busoni, Ferruccio,* 128, 210, 220
Butterley, Nigel,* 211
Butterworth, George,* 182
Buxterhude, Dietrich,* 161
Byrd, William,* 36, 64, 181

Haba, Alois,* 211
Hageman, Richard, 149
Hahn, Reynaldo,* 164
Halévy, Jacques François,* 131
Halvorsen, Johan August,* 55
Hamilton, Iain,* 15
Handel, George Frederick,* 141, 157-158, 161, 184, 196, 205, 212, 214, 217, 238, 241
Hanslick, Eduard, 238-239, 241
Hanson, Howard,* 63, 144, 161, 196
Hanson, Raymond,* 148, 195, 204, 211
Harmony, 23
Harris, Roy Ellsworth,* 63, 161, 196, 211
Harrison, Julius,* 65, 182
Hartmann, Karl Amadeus,* 67, 139
Harty, Sir Hamilton,* 182
Hauer, Josef Matthias, 47
Hawkins, Sir John, 212
Haydn (Franz), Joseph,* 158, 161, 163, 186, 188-189, 191, 197, 205, 205-206, 217, 218, 241
Haydn, Michael, 133
Head, Michael,* 65, 182
Henry, Pierre, 47-48
Henze, Hans Werner,* 67
Herbert, Victor,* 148
Hérold, Louis,* 131
Heseltine, Philip (see under Warlock)*
Hessler, Hans Leo, 167
Hill, Alfred,* 148, 195, 204, 211
Hill, Mirrie, 195
Hiller, Ferdinand,* 158, 161
Hiller, Johann Adam, 133, 167
Hindemith, Paul,* 42, 138, 174, 210
Hobcroft, Rex, 211
Hoddinott, Alun, 162
Hofmannstahl, Hugo von, 136
Holbrooke, Joseph,* 182, 211
Holland, Dulcie,* 211
Holst, Gustav,* 65, 143, 182, 185, 211
Holst, Imogen, 162
Homer, Sidney, 183
Homophony, 35
Honegger, Arthur,* 165, 210, 217, 259
Hooke, Robert, 244
Hopkins, Anthony,* 65
Hopkinson, Francis, 62, 182
Howells, Herbert,* 182, 204, 211
Hughes, Herbert,* 182
Hughes, Robert, 195
Hugo, John Adam, 149
Hummel, Johann Nepomuk, 209
Humperdinck, Engelbert,* 138
Hurlstone, William Yeates,* 182, 211

Hutchens, Frank, 204, 211
Hyde, Miriam,* 204, 211
Hydraulus (Water Organ), 92

Impressionism, 228
Incidental Music, 216
Indy, Vincent d',* 59, 159, 161, 164, 191, 225
Interpretation, 231
Interval, 26
Ippolitov-Ivanov, Mikhail,* 145, 178
Ireland, John,* 65, 182, 204, 211
Ives, Charles,* 47, 63, 161, 183, 193, 211

Jacobs, Gordon,* 162
Janáček, Leoš,* 53, 179, 210
Jannequin, Clement, 164, 213
Jaques-Dalcroze, Emile, 176
Järnefelt, Armas,* 179
Jazz, 224, 225
Jensen, Adolf,* 174
Joachim, Joseph, 200, 201, 245
Jolivet, André,* 132, 163, 165
Jones, Daniel,* 195
Jongleurs, 164
Josquin des Prés,* 36, 57, 163
Joubert, John, 66
Jullien, Louis Antoine, 115

Kabalevsky, Dmitri,* 51, 146, 178, 204
Kalevala, 214
Kalinnikov, Vasily Sergeyevich,* 178, 194
Karlowicz, Mierczylaw,* 178
Keiser, Reinhard,* 132, 158, 161
Khatchaturian, Aram,* 51, 204
Kilpinen, Yrjö,* 179
Klosé, Hyacinth, 100
Klotz, Egidi, 97
Knipper, Lev, 194
Köchel, Ludwig von, 33
Kodály, Zoltán,* 54, 163, 179, 210, 256
Korngold, Eric(h),* 68, 217
Koven, Reginald de,* 183
Kreisler, Fritz,* 245
Krenek, Ernst,* 65
Kreutzer, Rudolphe,*
Kuchka (The Five), 49, 144
Kuhnau, Joseph, 186

Lalo (Victor Antoine), Édouard,* 59, 132, 210

337

ACKNOWLEDGMENTS

The author wishes to express his sincere thanks to the following for their help in providing information and illustrations or for assisting in other ways: The Counsellor of the Royal Belgian Embassy, Canberra; The Information Officer of the Canadian High Commission, Canberra; The Royal Danish Embassy, Canberra; The Cultural Counsellor of the French Embassy, Canberra; Consulate-General of the Federal Republic of Germany, Melbourne; First Secretary, High Commission of India, Canberra; First Embassy Secretary for Press and Cultural Affairs, Netherlands Information Service, Sydney; First Secretary, New Zealand High Commission, Canberra; Dr S. Aronowsky, Music Librarian, South African Broadcasting Corporation, Johannesburg; Information Attaché, South African Embassy, Canberra; Information Officer, Information Service of South Africa, New York; Professor G. Gruber, Rhodes University, Grahamstown; The Director of the South African College of Music, Cape Town; Professor J. P. Malan, the University of Pretoria; The Cultural Affairs Officer, Embassy of the United States of America, Canberra; The First Secretary, Embassy of the U.S.S.R., Canberra; E.M.I. Records, London; Boosey & Hawkes Ltd., London and Sydney; Faber Music Limited; Novello and Company Limited; Schott & Co. Ltd., London (Music Publishers); the Australian Performing Rights Association. Special thanks are given to members of the South Australian Symphony Orchestra for their help in posing for photographs with relation to musical instruments, and for allowing their instruments to be photographed separately; to their Conductor, Professor Henry Krips; and to the Orchestral Manager and Music Supervisor of the Australian Broadcasting Commission (South Australia) for their help in arranging this photography.

The author and publisher wish to express their gratitude for permissions received to reproduce illustrations as listed below:—

COLOUR ILLUSTRATIONS: The Art Gallery of South Australia (*Broadwood piano*); Alan Foley Pty Ltd (*Sun Music Ballet*); Mr R. W. Maden, Washington, U.S.A. (*Salem Town Band*); The Aberdeen Art Gallery (*The Morse Family*); Holburne of Menstrie Museum, Bath, England (*Garton Orme at the Spinet*); South Australian Museum (*Primitive instruments*); Private collection (*Music box; Edison phonographs; guitars, accordions, banjos, bouzouki, concertinas, mandolins*); South Australian Symphony Orchestra (*Brass, woodwind, and string instruments; the full orchestra*); Mr M. McKelvey, Adelaide, S.A. (*Scottish dancers; bagpipers; Band of Central Command*); Miss Cecily Wood (*Recorders*).

BLACK AND WHITE ILLUSTRATIONS: Rijksmuseum, Amsterdam (*Lady with two children at a harpsichord: painting by Jan Miense Molenaar*); British Museum, London (*Page from Luttrell Psalter*); Metropolitan Museum of Art, New York (*The Guitarist: painting by Manet; Engraving of performance of opera Il Pomo d'Oro*); Michael Edgley International Pty Ltd (*photographs of the Red Army Choir singers and dancers; Mazoswsze Polish singers and dancers; Krasnayaskaya Folk Ensemble; Maurice Bejart 20th Century Ballet; Royal Winnipeg Ballet*); Hulton/Radio Times Photographic Library (*illustrations of J. S. Bach, L. van Beethoven, Johannes Brahms, Claude Debussy, Michail Glinka, Antonin Dvorak, C. von Gluck, Edvard*

Grieg, J-B. Lully, Gustav Mahler, Felix Mendelsohn, Giacomo Meyerbeer, C. Monteverdi, W. A. Mozart, G. Rossini, Robert Schumann, B. Smetana, R. Strauss, P. I. Tchaikovsky, R. Wagner, C. M. von Weber, Hugo Wolf, Franz Schubert); Camilla Jessel (Hands of a harpist; photographs taken in Yehudi Menuhin's School for Young Musicians); Mr Lawson Hanson, Adelaide (photo of young guitarists); Osterreichische Nationalbibliothek (performances of works by Haydn at Esterhaz and Vienna); Dr Fritz Reiner (photo of Bela Bartok); Mr John Ardoin (photo of Aaron Copland); Mr Peter Sculthorpe (photograph of himself); The South Australian Symphony Orchestra and the Australian Broacasting Commission (photographs of the Percussion Section of an orchestra and of the groups showing brass, woodwinds, and strings sections of an orchestra); Mr C. E. A. Foale, Adelaide (Indian musical instruments); The Boston Symphony Orchestra (photograph of the orchestra); Ernst Eulenburg Ltd (page from score of Brahms Symphony No. 1); State Library of South Australia (first music published in Australia, from "Lone Hand Magazine" of October 1907); Australian Opera Company (photographs of scenes from operas performed by the Company); United States of America Information Service, Washington (photographs of American composers and conductors); The London Symphony Orchestra (photographs of British composers and conductors); The London Electrotype Agency (photographs of British performances of opera); E.M.I. Records (photographs of Oistrakh, Rostropovich, and Richter); Oxford University Press (programme of Chopin recital in London); Miss Emma den Hollander, Adelaide (modern German harpsichord); Embassy of the U.S.S.R., Canberra (photograph of Bolshoi Ballet).